W9-AID-556

LAST LETTERS

HELMUTH JAMES VON MOLTKE (1907–1945) was born
into a well-known Prussian family at Kreisau, the Silesian
estate of his great-granduncle Helmuth von Moltke the Elder, a
decorated field marshal credited with defeating the French in
the Franco-Prussian War. The eldest of five siblings, Helmuth
James studied international law in Germany and Austria,
where he met Freya Deichmann. The couple was married in
1931; their sons, Helmuth Caspar and Konrad, were born in
1937 and 1941. With the outbreak of World War II, Helmuth
James was drafted into the Abwehr, the German military
intelligence service. Beginning in 1940, he convened what
would later be called the "Kreisau Circle": a group of dissidents
who met in small, separate groups but came together three
times at the Kreisau estate to discuss their opposition to
Nazism and their vision for a postwar democratic order—a
federated Europe. Von Moltke was arrested in January 1944 for
having warned an acquaintance of his imminent arrest. In the
wake of the assassination attempt on Hitler of July 20, 1944,
the Nazis discovered many members of the broader resistance,
including of the Kreisau Circle, and began to understand
Helmuth's role in that circle. He was charged with high
treason and was tried and executed in January 1945.

FREYA VON MOLTKE (1911–2010) was born Freya Deichmann into a banker's family in Cologne. She studied law at the
University of Bonn, then moved to Berlin after marrying

Helmuth von Moltke; she received her law degree at the University of Berlin in 1935. After the death of Helmuth's mother, Dorothy, in 1935, Freya moved to Kreisau to take charge of the estate, which Helmuth had just managed to save from insolvency a few years prior, while he remained in Berlin. His almost daily letters home from those years were published as *Letters to Freya*. During her husband's incarceration and trial, Freya traveled often to Berlin to be near Helmuth, provide him with what provisions she could, and write to him the letters that the prison priest Harald Poelchau smuggled in and out. After the war, she moved with her sons to South Africa, but, appalled by the apartheid system, returned to Germany in 1956, and then moved, in 1960, to Vermont to live with the historian and social philosopher Eugen Rosenstock-Huessy. After 1989, she became involved in efforts to establish Kreisau as a center for international youth exchange, serving as the honorary chair on the board of the Kreisau Foundation for Mutual Understanding in Europe, and in 2004 she helped to establish the Freya von Moltke Foundation for the New Kreisau. In 1999, she was awarded an honorary doctorate from Dartmouth College.

LAST LETTERS

The Prison Correspondence

SEPTEMBER 1944–JANUARY 1945

HELMUTH JAMES VON MOLTKE
and **FREYA VON MOLTKE**

Edited by
HELMUTH CASPAR VON MOLTKE,
DOROTHEA VON MOLTKE,
and **JOHANNES VON MOLTKE**

Translated from the German by
SHELLEY FRISCH

Afterword by
RACHEL SEIFFERT

NEW YORK REVIEW BOOKS

New York

THIS IS A NEW YORK REVIEW BOOK
PUBLISHED BY THE NEW YORK REVIEW OF BOOKS
435 Hudson Street, New York, NY 10014
www.nyrb.com

The translation of this work was supported by a grant from the Goethe-Institut.

Cover art: Karl Schmidt-Rottluff, *Kreisau, Blick vom Park mit dem Flüßchen Peile
auf die Költschenberge* (detail), c. 1942; © 2019 Artists Rights Society (ARS), New
York / VG Bild-Kunst, Bonn; photo: René Pech, Schlesisches Museum zu Görlitz.

Library of Congress Cataloging-in-Publication Data
Names: Moltke, Helmuth James, Graf von, 1907–1945. | Moltke, Helmuth Caspar
   von, 1937– editor | Moltke, Dorothea von, editor | Von Moltke, Johannes, 1966–
   editor | Frisch, Shelley Laura, translator | Moltke, Freya von. Correspondence.
   Selections. English.
Title: Last letters : the prison correspondence between Freya and Helmuth von
   Moltke, September 1944–January 1945 / by Helmuth James and Freya von Moltke ;
   edited by Helmuth Caspar von Moltke, Dorothea von Moltke, and Johannes von
   Moltke ; afterword by Rachel Seiffert ; translation by Shelley Frisch.
Description: New York : New York Review Books, [2019] | Series: New York Review
   books classics | Includes bibliographical references and index.
Identifiers: LCCN 2019012596 (print) | LCCN 2019020086 (ebook) | ISBN
   9781681373829 (epub) | ISBN 9781681373812 (alk. paper)
Subjects: LCSH: Moltke, Helmuth James, Graf von, 1907–1945—Correspondence. |
   Moltke, Freya von—Correspondence. | Anti-Nazi movement—Germany.
Classification: LCC DD247.M6 (ebook) | LCC DD247.M6 A413 2019 (print) |
   DDC 940.53/43092 [B]—dc23
LC record available at https://lccn.loc.gov/2019012596

ISBN 978-1-68137-381-2
Available as an electronic book; ISBN 978-1-68137-382-9

Printed in the United States of America on acid-free paper.
10 9 8 7 6 5 4 3 2 1

CONTENTS

EDITORS' INTRODUCTION

I.

> Sometimes I think about the fate of our long written conversations, and whether you and our sons will find them worth reading after ten, twenty, or more years. They originated in a situation that most likely has rarely been captured in writing, because normally the contact winds up being ruptured or monitored. When this time is over, when true peace has been restored, what will people say about these kinds of reflections? Will they be understood? Will it be believed that these were extreme situations that made people hysterical, will people be able to grasp the notion that a human being, this curious animal, can grow accustomed even to being executed?

HELMUTH James von Moltke wrote these words on January 2, 1945, three weeks before his execution for high treason by the Nazis. The "long written conversations" in this volume to which he refers had taken place over the course of the preceding three months in the form of near daily letters between himself and his wife, Freya, smuggled in and out of a Nazi prison at great risk by the prison chaplain. Thinking back over the exchange in the face of death and with war still raging about him in Berlin, Helmuth nevertheless manages to imagine a better future: a future for his wife and sons, a future after National Socialism, a future without war. To the degree that such a future is our present, the questions that Helmuth poses are for us to answer, and the present volume invites the reader to do just that.

These letters allow us to take part in the written conversations of Helmuth and Freya, suspended, as it were, between their married life prior to Helmuth's arrest and the certainty of his approaching trial and possible death, between hope and occasional despair, between love, faith, and cool rationality. Few accounts can match the immediacy of daily letters such as these and their power to capture how people think, feel, and act in the face of a murderous regime, how we as "curious animals" react, behave, and preserve our humanity in the face of the extreme terror that humans, too, are capable of.

When the Nazis seized power in Germany on January 30, 1933, Helmuth and Freya were two young, newly married law students pursuing their studies in Berlin.[1] Opposed to Adolf Hitler from the very start, the couple became actively involved in the resistance against the regime in 1940, when they jointly agreed to assume the risks and began to engage in conspiratorial activity, gathering like-minded friends and collaborators in a group that would become known as the Kreisau Circle. One of the most important resistance groups against the Nazi regime, the Kreisau Circle devised detailed political and economic plans for a democratic and European Germany after Hitler. Conscripted to work as a lawyer for the German Wehrmacht by day, Helmuth used his evenings, business trips abroad, and many a lunch hour conducting what he called "our internal war" against the dictatorship.

The letters that the couple exchanged during Helmuth's incarceration at Tegel prison span approximately four months, leading up to the day of his execution on January 23, 1945. Freya was at this point a thirty-three-year-old mother of two small sons living on the family's estate in the province of Silesia, some 250 miles from Berlin. Helmuth, aged thirty-seven, had been arrested unexpectedly by the Gestapo in January 1944 for having warned a colleague that the secret police had infiltrated meetings involving persons critical of the regime, including his colleague, who was tried and executed. But Helmuth avoided trial and instead was interned in a prison on the grounds of the Ravensbrück concentration camp, north of Berlin. During the months in which he was held here, Freya was able to see him several times near the prison under Gestapo supervision. The letters that the couple exchanged during those months were routinely censored by the Gestapo, and Freya and Helmuth consequently had to be careful in what they said and wrote to each other.

At this point, Helmuth's imprisonment, though it was trying and a cause for the couple's constant concern, was likely going to be temporary since the Gestapo had not discovered his clandestine work in the Kreisau Circle. The relative stability of his situation changed drastically after the failed attempt on Hitler's life by Claus Schenk Graf von Stauffenberg on July 20, 1944, which led the Nazis to redouble their terror and eradicate all pockets of resistance. In Ian Kershaw's words, the failed coup served as a "sharp accelerator," strengthening rather than undermining the regime's resolve.[2] Many of Helmuth's coconspirators—chief among them Peter Graf Yorck von Wartenburg, Helmuth's closest friend and ally in the group—had joined Stauffenberg's bomb plot following Helmuth's arrest and were now rounded up and executed. Helmuth, meanwhile, was moved from Ravensbrück to Berlin, to await trial in Tegel prison.

Freya's letter of September 29 marks the couple's first contact in the wake of Helmuth's transfer after the attempt on Hitler's life; it also represents their first uncensored communication since her husband's arrest. Thus begin the "long written conversations," which are now held at the German Literature Archive in Marbach. The fact that Freya and Helmuth were able to engage in this conversation at all is in itself something of a miracle. By all rights, they should not have been able to write to each other during the year of his incarceration—save for a few authorized, censored letters in Ravensbrück and then in Tegel prison. After the July assassination attempt, Helmuth was interrogated and placed under rigorous supervision, with contact between the couple strictly policed. By a stroke of incredible good fortune, Harald Poelchau was the prison chaplain at Tegel. Poelchau was a close friend of the Moltkes, a member of the Kreisau Circle who had also participated in the plenary meeting in Kreisau in the spring of 1942 but remained undetected. Thanks to Poelchau, they suddenly found themselves in a position to carry on this clandestine correspondence, in which they were able to talk freely, allowing us now to walk beside them through the remaining days of their life together. Poelchau smuggled every one of the more than 150 letters contained in this volume in and out past the guards on daily visits to Helmuth in prison, returning all correspondence to Freya after it had been read. She, in turn, hid the letters from the Gestapo in the beehives in Kreisau and safeguarded this treasure for the remainder of her life. Freya did not want these emotional letters in the public domain during her lifetime, but agreed to publication following her death in Norwich, Vermont, on January 1, 2010. They appeared in German in 2011 to great acclaim.

Two weeks after his transfer to Tegel, Helmuth was indicted, charged with treason, defeatism, and the attempt to overthrow the regime.[3] This development led the couple to expect the trial, verdict, and near certain execution within a matter of days, as the Gestapo typically sent prisoners to their execution on the day of the verdict. On Freya and Helmuth's wedding anniversary, October 18, however, they learned that the trial would not start before November at the earliest, and the tone of the correspondence shifts, as both once more begin to hope, to "turn toward . . . having a life together once again," and focus on honing Helmuth's defense.[4] November arrived with still no trial but permission for Freya to visit Helmuth in prison twice. There were to be five meetings in all during these months, always under supervision and generally obtained on Freya's pretense of having urgent questions to discuss regarding the management of the estate. The emotional intensity of the first November meeting subsequently plunged Helmuth into a severe depression that he had to surmount alone in his cell, albeit in conversation with Poelchau and, through the letters, with Freya. The next meeting in late November marked a high point of these four months as the couple were able to celebrate Communion together, with their friend Poelchau officiating in the office of the prison director. The year drew to a close on a quieter, more hopeful note—even as the two never for a moment forgot that Helmuth's death could come very suddenly. As Helmuth writes at the end of December: "For me, a strange year is coming to an end. I actually spent it among people who were being prepared for a violent death..."[5] On January 1, 1945, the trial date was finally set, putting the inevitable in motion. The couple saw each other once again before the proceedings on January 9 and 10, and then one last time when Helmuth's execution was delayed after the verdict.

Each of these letters is a farewell letter written in light of the constant threat of Helmuth's imminent execution, and each letter testifies anew to Helmuth and Freya's clear-eyed assessment of their situation. With every letter, they prepare themselves and each other for his execution and for her life without him. With extraordinary constancy, love, and faith they sustain each other through the correspondence while reminding each other over and over again of the inescapable conclusion toward which the passing days and weeks are heading. During that time, however, both on occasion also lose the remarkable inner peace that otherwise buoys them, and about this, too, each reports openly to the other. Helmuth's letter of November 14, 1944, and Freya's of January 13, 1945, provide especially vivid glimpses of the respective depths of their despair, from which they gradually emerge over the course of subsequent letters and with the help and reassurance of each other. And so this correspondence is also infused with the power of hope. As the trial is postponed several times, Helmuth plots different lines of defense in his cell. Freya undertakes various attempts to secure support from outside, stave off the execution, and obtain a pardon from high-ranking Nazi officials. Just as Freya reports about her efforts on his behalf, which take her on far-flung errands through war-torn Berlin (and occasionally back to Kreisau to look after their young sons and the estate), Helmuth keeps his wife abreast of his thoughts and dreams, his moods, and the details of prison life. Separated by the prison walls the couple draws intensely close during these months—"closer to you than ever," as Freya writes a few days before Christmas.[6]

Many passages are devoted to Psalms and Scripture, as they reassure each other of the strong faith that helps carry them through these months. Freya later wrote, "In all of this, we were supported by our faith, faith that came and went like the ebb and flow of the tide."[7]

Although brought up as Protestants, Freya and Helmuth gave priority to secular, social democratic ideas over religious questions. By the fall of 1944, this perspective had changed. Their confrontations with National Socialism made it increasingly clear to them and to many other members of the resistance that no matter how much the churches of both Protestant and Catholic denominations had adapted to the ruling ideology, they still offered places of orientation and refuge in a world that had lost all moral bonds. In crafting their plans for the reorganization of a future Germany, the members of the Kreisau Circle expected Christianity to have a significant role in that Germany and in Europe. While Helmuth had initially understood Immanuel Kant's categorical imperative to be an ethical guideline for the responsible statesman, the preamble to the Kreisau "Principles for the Reorganization," drafted in the fall of 1943, stated: "The government of the German Reich regards Christianity as the basis for the moral and religious renewal of our people, for overcoming hatred and lies, for the reconstruction of the European international community."

While the group also envisioned religious toleration as a cornerstone of any future German state, in hindsight the strong commitment to a Christian ethos inevitably raises questions about how the Kreisau Circle thought about justice for Jews in Germany after the Nazi atrocities.[8] Members of the circle had become aware of these atrocities early on, and many of them—including Helmuth and Poelchau, but also others such as the attorney Hans Lukaschek or Helmuth's colleague Paulus van Husen—worked actively to assist and protect Jews. When Peter Yorck faced trial and execution in the days following the failed assassination attempt, he explicitly stated that his actions had been driven by the Nazis' perversion of legal norms and by their treatment of the Jews. Whereas more conservative resistance groups could still harbor strong anti-Semitic resentments, the Kreisau Circle's foundation on Christian values led them to explicitly adopt a stance of "unconditional tolerance in questions of faith, race, and nationality."[9]

In his role as legal counsel for the German army, Helmuth had received and acted on information about deportations, mistreatment, and murders of Jews and prisoners of war. He wrestled with this knowledge, writing to Freya in 1941:

> May I know this and yet sit at my table in my heated flat and have tea? Don't I thereby become guilty too? What shall I say when I am asked: And what did you do during that time?...
>
> How can anyone know these things and still walk around free?... If only I could get rid of the terrible feeling that I have let myself be corrupted, that I do not react keenly enough to such things, that they torment me without producing a spontaneous reaction. I have mistrained myself, for in such things, too, I react with my head. I think about a possible reaction instead of acting.[10]

And yet, within the realm of his abilities to affect change, Helmuth did act on his knowledge throughout the entire Nazi period, seeing it as his duty to help save lives in the Jewish community. As an early student of Hitler's plans, he had counseled all persons with Jewish ancestry to abandon Germany, using his office to provide practical legal assistance in some cases. He presciently encouraged even those non-Jewish Germans married to partners with Jewish ancestry to flee a long way from the Third Reich, rightly telling a cousin of Freya's in such a marriage that neighboring Holland was not far enough. On his trips abroad, he helped to protect Jewish populations elsewhere, obtaining residence permits for Jews in Sweden and warning the Danish Jews of an impending raid and deportations by the occupying Germans.

Knowledge of these atrocities certainly played a role in the deliberations of the Kreisau Circle, especially when drafting the principles for the punishment of war crimes at their third meeting in Kreisau in June 1943. This said, the fact that the documents drafted by the various working groups in the Kreisau Circle nowhere explicitly mention the fate of the Jews under National Socialism remains an absence to contend with. The role of Jews and Judaism in any future Germany was similarly left open. Welcoming the contributions of the two Christian denominations, the "Principles for the Reorganization" of

Germany after the war left the legal position of other religious communities to be defined on the basis of a future dialogue.

If Christianity played a major role in the Kreisau Circle thanks to the participation of bishops and priests, Christian doctrine and faith also grew in importance for Helmuth over time. During his six months of confinement in Ravensbrück, he'd had ample time to read and to think after years of incessant work on his official and conspiratorial activities. He spent much of his time reading Luther and the Bible, and invited Freya to share in this experience. From then on, his Bible and hymnal were daily companions. In view of his ongoing dialogues with the prophets Isaiah and Jeremiah, the apostle Paul, the psalmist David, and the poets of the hymns, who all wrote under extreme circumstances, it is not surprising that their way of thinking and speaking rubbed off on Helmuth, as can be readily seen in several passages of the correspondence in this volume.

Freya experienced her closeness to God more directly in her daily life, in the experience of love; she felt "cradled" and secure. By the time Helmuth arrived at Tegel prison in the fall of 1944, they both considered themselves firmly rooted in their Christian faith. This gradual transformation from a fairly secular and liberal attitude to a Christian outlook on life later led Freya back to an intense confrontation with the notion of death: "You know, if you live in the face of death, you operate at a deeper and higher level at the same time; liberal ideas are no longer sufficient."[11] Even though doubts at times interfere, these letters are suffused with a shared faith; its teachings and its idioms often provide a language in which Helmuth and Freya offer comfort to each other.

For the rest of her long life, Freya never lost this faith that came to her so naturally. It kept her connected to Helmuth and formed one of the foundations of her bond with her later life partner, the Christian philosopher and former friend of Helmuth, Eugen Rosenstock-Huessy. Her encounter with Rosenstock-Huessy taught her to see Christianity and Judaism in a broad historical, social, and philosophical context. She devoted a great deal of time to considering questions of faith in the history of mankind. Christian ideas remained a source of important insights for her although she did not employ religious language to express them. Her connection to the church was loose, and it remained so.

In addition to the religious dimension and the language of the farewell letters, and despite the fact that they reflect the expectations of both Helmuth and Freya that the most likely outcome would be his violent death, the elegant prose of the correspondence often also reflects the authors' serenity and wit. Even as the war nears its end, a sense of peace radiates from Freya's descriptions of life continuing in the Kreisau Helmuth loved and of the beauty of autumnal Silesia, as well as from her depictions of birthday parties and Christmas festivities full of joyful children despite the shortage of gifts. Helmuth in turn describes his excursions to the prison's medical clinic, where he was able to enjoy some rare morsels of food and a sunlamp on his damaged sciatic nerve. Despite the doctor being a committed Nazi, the orderlies were all against the regime and took satisfaction from subverting the doctor's orders and helping the political prisoners.

Since Freya and Helmuth continued to expect that the trial would take place shortly, they were exposed to constant swings between hopes for Helmuth's life, realization of the hopelessness of their situation, and acceptance of God's will, whatever their fate might be. The tension between the struggle to survive and the readiness to die would at times become almost unbearable. "But if I think about your life and nurture my hopes," Freya wrote, "I can't help to prepare our hearts for death."[12] For Helmuth, the waves of his roiling inner sea rose higher and higher. Repeated deferral of his trial put him under immense stress, as it forced him to undertake intensive preparations time and time again—preparations not only for his confrontation with Roland Freisler, the capricious judge presiding over the People's Court, but also and above all for his own death. Every delay forced him to come back to terms with life. In his lonely cell, he had no choice but to withstand moments of terrible anguish and internal struggles, fighting to keep his faith until the moment he could once more stand on solid ground, until he could say of his own soul that it was "where I prefer to have it: way down deep, but on bedrock."[13]

These are love letters in extremis. They testify to the profound openness with which Helmuth and Freya confront their fears, declare their love, articulate their hopes, and find faith. Their import, however, far exceeds the singular couple who exchanges them. Written as bombs were falling on the German capital and the eastern front was nearing Kreisau during the final months of the war, these are farsighted historical documents of courage and resistance.

II.

At the beginning of this correspondence on September 29, 1944, the war had just entered its sixth year. Any sense that the Third Reich was nearing its end appeared only to reinforce the Nazis' iron grip on power. By the summer of that year, the Red Army had already advanced deep into Poland, handing the Germans their largest losses in military history. On the western front, the Allies had consolidated their gains in France and were advancing toward the Rhine, while the U.S. troops were pushing northward in Italy, having taken Rome in July. With an intensifying air war, many Allied military planners were convinced that the war would be over by Christmas. However, they did not reckon with the manic ideological rigidity of the Nazi terror, which kept soldiers fighting against all odds and ordinary citizens denouncing each other for the mere failure to believe in victory, which was labeled "defeatism" and could be punishable by death. "Anyone who speaks to me of peace without victory," Hitler proclaimed in these final months of the war, "will lose his head, no matter who he is or what his position."[14]

The brutal repression and surveillance by the Gestapo as well as the perversion of truth by blanket propaganda distortions confined any form of overt opposition within Germany to small groups of plotters, who were quickly eliminated once they appeared in public. Early left-wing dissenters had been interned in concentration camps, but occasional public opposition continued. The Rote Kapelle (Red Orchestra) was perhaps the best-known oppositional group: comprised largely of young men and women, the group posted calls for opposition in public spaces around Berlin. Other forms of resistance brought together students, such as Hans and Sophie Scholl of the Weisse Rose (White Rose). During the war, the group printed leaflets opposing the Nazis and distributed them both by mail and by scattering them at Munich University, where they were eventually caught. The Munich students were brought before Freisler at the People's Court in early 1943 to be tried and executed; Helmuth was able to ensure that some of the leaflets reached the Allies, who would later drop them over Germany from the air. But the Nazis' message was clear: Oppose us and you will forfeit your life. The same fate awaited anyone in the Nazis' camps and ghettos who attempted an insurrection. The brave attempts at Jewish resistance, most notably among these the uprising in the Warsaw Ghetto, were all met with brutal repressive force and murder.

Some members of the elites from the pre-Hitler days were galvanized into action as the deaths and atrocities of the war mounted. One group coalesced around the deposed mayor of Leipzig, Carl Friedrich Goerdeler, and the deposed general Ludwig Beck. However, they could not find influential serving generals to join them in an attempt on Hitler's life. Helmuth, some twenty years younger, believed that the generals had compromised themselves and that after the brutalities of the Nazis, any return to past structures was a betrayal of the victims. He and Peter Yorck decided that despite their youth and lack of positions of real power it was incumbent on them to bring elements of a functioning civil society together to discuss the structure of a forward-looking Germany after the Nazis had been eliminated, whether from within or without. To do this they recruited reliable participants from the civil service, theologians of the Catholic and the Protestant churches, and representatives of labor and the business world as well as academia and the legal profession, all united in the goal of devising common positions for a more peaceful and democratic future Germany. Members of the Kreisau Circle generally met in Berlin or Munich in small groups arranged as subcommittees dealing with defined topics. They formed working committees to look at questions of a constitution, economic policy and labor representation, education and religious freedom, and European integration. Helmuth reported about the work almost daily in his letters to Freya. When these were published in English and German in the 1980s, historians gained invaluable insight into the thinking within the resistance groups.[15] To achieve consensus and prepare a final draft, the group scheduled three plenary meetings, which for purposes of confidentiality were held in Helmuth's rural home in Kreisau, thus lending the group the later appellation Kreisau Circle. The work spanned from 1941 to 1943 and was completed in August 1943.[16]

In this work, which remarkably remained hidden from the Gestapo, Helmuth and his friends viewed with skepticism the efforts spearheaded by Beck and by Goerdeler, who had been designated as the future chancellor in the event that Stauffenberg's coup attempt succeeded. Both Beck and Goerdeler had been early sympathizers of the Nazis, but they had become disillusioned and turned to resistance when they realized the totalitarian threat to the state, the nation, and the law. While they consequently shared some of the Kreisauers' concerns, the group remained suspicious of Beck and Goerdeler's generally more conservative outlook. Even before the Nazis came to power, Helmuth frequently had to fight against German nationalist tendencies, sometimes within his own family; he assigned much of the blame for Hitler's seizure of power to the reactionary attitude of the traditional elite. He was unwilling to stand by and look on as these same groups returned to power following the catastrophe of the Hitler years. Guided by Helmuth and Peter Yorck, the Kreisau Circle, by contrast, wanted to see a Germany that would break radically with its top-heavy, authoritarian political tradition and work to overcome both political and economic inequalities.

Though the suspicion with which Helmuth and his friends regarded Beck and Goerdeler was evident at a January 1943 meeting between the two groups and in Helmuth's letters immediately afterward, in his correspondence with Freya from Tegel prison he exaggerates the differences. In retrospect his reference to the much older men as "excellencies" and his attempts to extricate himself from any association with what he now called the "Goerdeler mess" must also be seen in the context of his evolving defense strategy. It was an attempt to distance himself from the failed assassination attempt in whose wake the Kreisau Circle's activities had first come to light.

More complicated than the question of political differences, however, is the issue of Helmuth's opposition to the attempt on Hitler's life. In the short time he spent in the company of Stauffenberg in Berlin in late 1943, Helmuth came to respect the man greatly, even if the two did argue over major issues of substance. He continued for a long time to wrestle with the moral and political implications of an assassination attempt for a number of different reasons. First, he did not wish to see a future Germany born of an act of murder. The head of the Bavarian Jesuits, Father Augustin Rösch, who made the rejection of tyrannicide a precondition of his collaboration with Helmuth and his colleagues, would later report that Helmuth, in a face-to-face meeting dating all the way back to 1941, had spoken to him of the necessity of "taking the leadership out of Hitler's hands," but he also stressed the need to find "other means than murder."[17] Second, Helmuth thought that the use of violent means to stage a coup would lead to a repetition of the stab-in-the-back myth exploited endlessly by the Nazis during their rise to power in the 1920s—the legend that the German armies in World War I would have been victorious but for the so-called traitorous politicians who agreed to an armistice. Third, Helmuth held that no attempt at eliminating Hitler could have any prospect of success without the cooperation of the Wehrmacht—but he saw no grounds for trusting the army. Even Stauffenberg conceded that the generals had failed, drawing the conclusion for himself that it was now the colonels' turn.

In the winter of 1943–44, the assumptions of those involved in the resistance had undergone a shift. The Kreisau work on plans for a post-Hitler government had already been concluded, all the important documents written and hidden away. Stauffenberg had returned to Berlin following a war injury and subsequent convalescence, and Helmuth had been arrested. A number of the men who had been gathered around him and Peter Yorck welcomed Stauffenberg's desire to act and joined in planning the attempt on Hitler's life. Eight former participants in the Kreisau Circle's discussions were arrested in July and August after the plot's failure, and the Gestapo found ample clues leading back to Helmuth.

We will never know how Helmuth would have chosen to act had he not been taken into custody six months prior to the bomb plot. By the time he came to prepare his defense, the assassination attempt had already failed and all those directly involved had been executed. It is only natural that in building his defense he put as much distance as possible between himself and the failed assassination attempt of July 20th. Eugen Gerstenmaier, who had been actively involved in the bomb plot and who stood with Helmuth before Freisler's court in January 1945, would later say that, in view of the untold millions of dead still being claimed by the war, Helmuth likely would have stood by his friends and supported their attempt to remove the regime by force, had he not already been in custody. Similarly, the historian Peter Hoffmann considers the notion that Helmuth would not countenance any violent solution at any point a "legend," which becomes reinforced here by the tactical considerations prevailing in the letters from Tegel.[18]

Throughout their work, members of the Kreisau Circle tried to make contact with Allied governments via their friends whenever they were able to do so undetected on trips to neutral countries. However the Allied insistence on Germany's unconditional surrender imposed almost insurmountable obstacles on the conspirators' attempts to reach out across the borders of the Third Reich. And yet, some contacts did exist. Helmuth had studied for the bar in Britain where he had made many friends through the extensive network of his grandfather, a former chief justice of South Africa. Even before the onset of war, Helmuth had befriended the American journalist Dorothy Thompson, who would subsequently introduce him to an American mass audience as the pseudonymous addressee of her radio broadcasts entitled *Listen, Hans*. In fact, key individuals in the American government also knew of Helmuth and his work. Looking back, George F. Kennan, an American diplomat, ambassador, and strategic thinker of the Cold War period, considered him "to have been the greatest person, morally, and the largest and most enlightened in his concepts, that I met on either side of the battle lines in the Second World War." When Kennan first encountered him in 1940 while stationed in Berlin, with the United States still clinging to neutrality, Helmuth was a young international lawyer with legal qualifications in both Germany and England. In his recollection of the years immediately preceding the American entry into that war, Kennan noted that even then Helmuth had seen through the Hitler regime and anticipated the catastrophe that was bound to ensue. He had prepared himself and strove to prepare his people, Kennan wrote, "for the necessity of starting all over again, albeit in defeat and humiliation, to erect a new national edifice on a new and better moral foundation."[19] This work required bringing together trustworthy, representative figures of different political persuasions from various sectors of civil society. It was a hallmark of the Kreisau Circle that its members managed to think across the differences that separated various political groups, and thereby to project a just and democratic future for Germany and Europe. The surviving documents emphasize principles of subsidiarity, seeking to ground political decisions in local processes where possible and ensuring the representative and democratic nature of decision-making at all levels of government. In other words, at the height of the Nazis' totalitarian reign, the members of the Kreisau Circle jointly imagined and debated the principles of democratic government. This alone constituted a treasonous act in the eyes of the Nazis, who considered such projections seditious and defeatist. Helmuth consequently notes with some justification after the trial that "we're being hanged for having thought together."[20]

This statement, as devastating as it is pithy, requires some context and nuance. In his almost elated report on the trial in the letter of January 10, 1945, Helmuth notes that by being sentenced merely for thinking together, he and his coconspirators have been cleared of "any practical action." And yet, it would be misleading to conclude that either Helmuth himself or the Kreisau Circle as a whole performed no practical acts of resistance, or that they unequivocally opposed the more radical (though sometimes politically more conservative) paths taken by other plotters, including the groups around Stauffenberg and Goerdeler. As Hoffmann has pointed out, it is crucial to distinguish here between Helmuth's tactical considerations as a defendant and attorney before the Nazis' political judge on the one hand, and his actions and deeply held convictions on the other.[21]

For Helmuth had surely involved himself in "practical action" against the regime on multiple fronts prior to his incarceration in early 1944. In his position as a conscripted lawyer for the army, he worked relentlessly even if often unsuccessfully for the recognition of international law and the prevention of war crimes. He used his position to help protect hostages, prisoners of war, and civilians, and he actively assisted persecuted Jews to secure their emigration and escape from the Nazis' reach. The Gestapo never uncovered how much active resistance Helmuth had mounted against Nazi policies. They also knew only bits and pieces about his discussions with friends in Kreisau and about the group's wide-ranging plans for the future.

A lawyer by training, Helmuth spent countless hours in his Tegel cell drafting, revising, dismissing, and resuscitating potential lines of defense for the oft-delayed trial that finally took place on January 9 and 10, 1945. He tried to establish mitigating circumstances, considered whether the regime might use him for the war effort rather than execute him, and even involved Freya in a multifaceted attempt to secure clemency from high-ranking Nazi officials. Both Helmuth and Freya were granted face-to-face meetings with the general commanding the Gestapo, and Freya involved the judge, the state prosecutor, and senior officials of the Nazi government in seeking to save Helmuth's life. The Moltke family name in Germany granted them this access. For the Nazis the long-deceased nineteenth-century general Moltke was a Prussian hero and the estate inherited by Helmuth made him heir to that lineage. They recognized Helmuth as a committed opponent, but still wanted the respect of his family. Freya ventured into the lion's den with assurance, though always skeptical of her ability to succeed in saving Helmuth's life.

All these strands—Helmuth's family background, his various defense strategies, the work of the Kreisau Circle, acts of resistance, and the role of "thinking together"—came to a head in Helmuth's confrontation with Freisler in the People's Court. The trial had been delayed numerous times during the final months of 1944. When the five remaining members of the Kreisau Circle appeared before the court on January 9 and 10, 1945, Helmuth quickly realized that what ignited Freisler's indignation was not the Kreisauers' putative links to the failed assassination attempt but, above all, their deliberations and plans (though the Kreisau documents containing those plans remained undiscovered in the attic of the Kreisau Schloss), as well as the group's Christian character. Removed from the world of practical action by the twelve months of his imprisonment, Helmuth now stood before Freisler chiefly for his Christian, humanist beliefs. As he writes to Freya in the powerful letters reporting on his trial, he had succeeded in concentrating the duel between himself and Freisler around the one point where their fundamental incompatibility became crystal-clear—as Freisler himself pronounced, "There is only one way in which Christianity and we are alike: We demand the entire person!" For Helmuth there developed "a kind of dialogue—a spiritual one between Freisler and me [...] in which we came to know each other through and through."[22] This he saw as a triumph. The president of the People's Court had unwittingly revealed that he recognized the basic incompatibility of their two worldviews. In light of this dramatic confrontation, Helmuth and Freya confirmed to each other in the letters that Helmuth would be executed for the right reason. They remained steadfast in their belief that, in the end, the values of humanity for which they and their friends had risked everything would survive. As Helmuth puts it, the Nazis "have recognized that Kreisau would take an ax to the very root of National Socialism, and the result would go beyond a modification of the facade, as was the case with Goerdeler."[23] The Nazi henchmen might kill Helmuth, but as Freya writes at one point, "In the end, they can take nothing from you but your life!"[24]

III.

The incarcerated members of the Kreisau Circle who remained in the early fall of 1944 were split between two prisons. At Tegel, Helmuth, Father Alfred Delp, and Gerstenmaier had neighboring cells, while Theodor Haubach and Theodor Steltzer were imprisoned at the Lehrter Strasse Gestapo prison. They were joined in the trial by three members of the Bavarian resistance: Franz Reisert, Franz Sperr, and Joseph-Ernst Fürst Fugger von Glött. Through the assistance of Poelchau, the prison chaplain, and because of the daily joint outdoor walk, there were good lines of communication between the accused at Tegel, but everything proved more difficult for those kept at the Lehrter Strasse complex. Here, the prisoners' wives or other confidants had to convey clandestine messages to help coordinate strategy among the group's members—a very dangerous undertaking.

Imprisonment at Tegel—one of the prisons run by the civil authorities—was, despite everything, easier to endure and also more predictable in its routines than was detention at the Gestapo prisons on Lehrter Strasse or Prinz-Albrecht-Strasse, for example. The majority of the Tegel guards were well-inclined toward the political prisoners, and Freya and Helmuth were on very friendly terms with a few of them. Some even took the risk of relaying information and bringing in regular packages of food from prisoners' families during the weekly delivery of clean linens, in which small notes were very often to be found hidden as well. In exchange, these guards were given regular gifts of cigarettes or part of the prisoners' provisions. Thanks, in part, to their leniency, the prisoners at Tegel were able to write many private (uncensored) letters in their cells. Helmuth was brought in several times to the Gestapo offices for questioning. It was in the basement rooms of the complex at Prinz-Albrecht-Strasse that many detainees were tortured by the Gestapo. Helmuth later suspected that they had succeeded, on one occasion, in eliciting certain confessions from him by slipping a drug into his soup, confessions that he was sorely to regret later on. Although Helmuth was never tortured, it is probable that all other imprisoned members of the Kreisau Circle did in fact undergo torture.

At Tegel prison, Helmuth sat locked away in a seventy-square-foot cell on the fourth floor of Building I, a place reserved for those facing potential execution that was also known as the "house of the dead." Day and night, the lights burned overhead; day and night, the prisoners' hands and feet were kept shackled. Only at mealtimes were their handcuffs to be removed. Helmuth, beset by severe pain in his back, successfully negotiated that he should be left unshackled for a time in December and January. Following his trial and death sentence, however, the prison regulations were reapplied in all their severity, and he was once again handcuffed. The small cell grew cold during these winter months. Helmuth spent the bulk of his time seated atop his desk with a blanket wrapped around him, his feet resting on his chair, as he studied his Bible or his hymnal—he was no longer interested in reading anything else. He learned many verses by heart during those hours and even worked on committing entire passages to memory, now reciting them, now singing or whistling them to himself. Or he wrote letters in his tiny handwriting, often with bound hands. Once a day, the prisoners were let into the prison yard and allowed to march around in a circle for half an hour. In January 1945, however, they did not set foot outside once; it was too cold, and many of the prisoners had only thin, torn clothing.

Meanwhile, the end of the Third Reich was becoming apparent: the front was creeping closer, and those in power were increasingly on edge. Allied bombing runs, announced by the wail of air-raid sirens, picked up in both frequency and intensity over the course of Helmuth's detention at Tegel. While the guards were able to scurry down into the safety of the bunkers, the shackled prisoners had no choice but to endure the attacks in their cells, alone. Explosions rattled doors and windows, setting surrounding buildings ablaze. In the course of these few months, both the Tegel and the Lehrter Strasse prisons suffered partial bomb damage. As we learn from his letters, on each occasion, Helmuth was overcome by an intense fear of death.

What a different world it was for Freya, outside the prison walls. The same waves of air attacks that Helmuth suffered through in his cell were destroying houses and even entire city districts. The network of public roads and rails was extensively damaged and interrupted at many points; commuters and travelers frequently had no choice but to make long detours. Most mornings saw Freya leave from the apartment of Helmuth's cousin Carl Dietrich von Trotha, the Moltkes' own apartment in Berlin having been lost to bombs in 1943. She would set out for the various government offices to which Helmuth was constantly dispatching her on new missions. "Most of the time during those months," she remembered, "I was in Berlin always on the go or writing to Helmuth."[25] Wearing out and mending a pair of socks daily, she submitted petitions and attempted to obtain audiences with officials, and she worked her way to the Gestapo and the People's Court—"into the lion's mouth," as she put it; she traveled out to Helmuth's former office at the Armed Forces High Command (Oberkommando der Wehrmacht), to the prison at Tegel, and to meetings with friends, advisers, and others who could possibly be of assistance. As day turned to night, she would then regularly make a stop at the Poelchau family apartment to read Helmuth's letters and write her response; to share a meal with her friend Harald and his equally beloved wife, Dorothee; and on occasion to sleep there.

On the weekends, Freya would often make the trip back to Kreisau. At first, life in Kreisau went on quietly. She spent much of her time with her young sons, the seven-year-old Caspar and three-year-old Konrad, whom she entrusted to the care of her sister-in-law Asta and her housekeeper when she was away. She would also spend some of her time reviewing the state of the Kreisau agricultural operations, for which she now exercised joint responsibility alongside Adolf Zeumer, the manager of the estate. As noted, this estate had come down to Helmuth and Freya from Field Marshal von Moltke. During the Depression years, twenty-two-year-old Helmuth had rescued the deeply indebted property from its creditors, and the family had moved to the more modest but comfortable house formerly used by elderly members of the extended family, which was much easier to heat and maintain. Freya had been in charge of the farming already for all the war years. She spoke with the people from the village and those from the Schloss (manor house), where in the meantime many people in need had taken up residence—not only relatives but also Rosemarie Reichwein, the widow of the already executed Kreisau Circle member Adolf Reichwein, along with her four children and numerous refugees. The villagers were concerned about Helmuth and Freya's fate, and even those who were politically inclined toward National Socialism stuck by the family. Freya's weekend visits to Kreisau were invariably pleasant, satisfying days, but as long as she remained there she found it difficult to keep living in step with Helmuth as his death approached, and she was restless. For that reason, nothing could keep her at home for much longer than a few days. She would most often set off on Sunday evening, boarding the night train to Berlin so that she could be close to Helmuth once again come Monday morning. This pattern began to change only in January 1945, as the eastern front moved closer and closer; the urgent question then became whether her first concern should be Helmuth or their sons.

With the advent of the trial, Freya wanted to be close by in Berlin. After the trial, Helmuth was returned to Tegel prison, where he wrote his dramatic report, which relates in great detail the intemperate outbursts of the judge, the political nature of the charges against him, and the course of the proceedings. In addition, Freya and Helmuth were allowed one last face-to-face conversation; she made a further round of the city, knocking on every possible door. She went to the offices of the Gestapo and spoke with its chief, General Müller, who explained to her in a "friendly" way how it simply wasn't possible to remit Helmuth's sentence; her husband, now a convicted traitor, could not be spared the journey to Plötzensee prison, the site of the executions. Seeking to obtain a pardon she ventured on to the Ministry of Justice, where the relevant official at one point surprisingly remarked, "So then he'll die a martyr." Freya rejected this appellation, and she would continue to do so for the rest of her life. She feared that accepting it would only serve to put Helmuth on a pedestal, thereby creating a lofty, unreachable figure that instead of emboldening others to resistance would move them only to passive reverence.

Shortly before Helmuth's execution, Freya was obliged to make yet another trip back to Kreisau; the symptoms of social disintegration brought on by the looming loss of the war were already beginning to reach Silesia, and the front was now approaching Kreisau and her sons. It took a great deal of effort on her part, but she somehow succeeded in swimming upstream against the tide of refugees and reaching Kreisau, only to turn quickly around and come back with the families fleeing before the Soviet Red Army, arriving in Berlin late on the night of January 22, 1945. On January 23, 1945, the day of his death, Helmuth received Freya's report on her epic journey, and he also had the time to compose a letter himself, which she in turn received. Freya's letter of noon the same day never reached him. When Poelchau stopped by his cell once more, Helmuth had already been collected by the authorities. Poelchau immediately notified Peter Buchholz, the Catholic chaplain, who also served as a minister to the prisoners at Plötzensee. As Poelchau writes in his memoirs, Buchholz saw Helmuth and had the chance to give him his regards; afterward he was able to report back to Freya that "he took his final steps with complete calm, indeed with an inner cheerfulness, ready to die, finished with his farewell to the little boys he loved so much and to Freya."[26]

IV.

Unlike the correspondence from earlier years contained in *Letters to Freya*, these last letters form an intense, intimate, two-way conversation that preserves both voices, Helmuth's *and* Freya's. The reader comes to know Freya as an open, confident, and hopeful woman. Though she often speaks of her "complicated" husband and describes herself as "simple," she was a strong and, in her own way, complex figure. Possessing great insight and understanding, Freya had a talent for capturing difficult events and situations in a few telling words.

She knew herself, as distinct from her husband, to be "well suited to life." With the cheerful, buoyant character of her native Rhineland, Freya never lost her ability to laugh. Helmuth, by contrast, despite having a pronounced—though at times somewhat biting—sense of humor, had become a graver and more serious man, one whose keen sense of political realities led him early on to foresee his own violent death. By the same token, Freya would occasionally think ahead to a life in which she would no longer have Helmuth by her side, confident that he would "always remain inside me until I may die and find you again, one way or another." In other words, Freya, too, projected a future out of these four months of farewell, one in which "I'll grow old and I'll change," as she writes in her first letter to Helmuth in Tegel. [27]

She did grow old, treasuring not only the memory of Helmuth but also the "long written conversations" that they had been able to carry on during the last months of his life. Already in the correspondence itself, the couple discusses the importance of Freya holding on to the pain of the separation and living with Helmuth "inside" rather than alongside her. Half a year after Helmuth's death she would write to her mother: "I think it's fair to say that I'll never be truly alone again in my life, since I was able to part from Helmuth in such a beautiful manner."

Freya drew sustenance from this long parting, remaining true to herself and to Helmuth's memory for the decades of her life that followed—not only in the social work she performed in South Africa during the years after the war, in her writings and speeches on the resistance in postwar Germany and the United States, and in her political engagement, but also in the open house she led after settling in the small rural town of Norwich, Vermont, or in her frequent returns to Germany and Poland well into her old age. Wherever she was invited, she showed up as a passionate ambassador of resistance against injustice, oppression, and discrimination in all their forms. She was particularly eager to transmit the legacy of Helmuth, their shared life, and the work of the Kreisau Circle to younger generations, to render it meaningful for the future and not just as a relic of the past.

Freya survived her husband by sixty-five years. When she died on New Year's Day of 2010 in Norwich, news spread quickly in her native Germany. Three years earlier, the Federal Republic had commemorated the centennial of Helmuth's birth, honoring his memory as a key member in the German resistance. Obituaries also appeared in many other countries, particularly in Europe, but also in Russia and most of the English-speaking world. After Helmuth's death, Freya spent the many years of her remaining life standing for the principles that her husband and his friends had died for and speaking to audiences far and wide about their actions and the need to resist abusive regimes. Over the years, several biographies have been published of both Helmuth and Freya, and there now exists a substantial literature focusing on their resistance to the Nazis. Today, the Kreisau Circle and the work of its individual members are considered foundational for the self-conception of the Federal Republic of Germany.

Kreisau, her former home, has become Krzyzowa, a Polish village in the former Eastern bloc, now part of an expanded Europe. Already during the communist period, Freya returned several times to the houses and graves dear to the family and felt that Helmuth, as an opponent of the Nazis, had also been a friend of Poland and even a communist government of Poland might agree to a memorial stone in Helmuth's honor at Krzyzowa. While this was not granted prior to the fall of communism, 1989 brought democratic rule to both East Germany and Poland. The neighboring Polish and German governments wished to seal their new friendship and bury the enmity of the past with a Reconciliation Mass. They chose Krzyzowa as the place for this mass, which was celebrated by the prime ministers of West Germany and Poland on November 12, 1989, just three days after the fall of the wall in Berlin. The governments agreed to fund the restoration of the buildings on the former estate of the Moltkes, turning it into a site for youth exchange and conferences, which now brings people from all the nations of Europe together.

Since 1990, the Kreisau Foundation for Mutual Understanding in Europe has been the umbrella under which the former estate has once again come to life and found a new purpose. With facilities for meetings, seminars, and informal gatherings as well as accommodations for about 140 people, the foundation is one of the success stories of the new European focus on Silesia. About 5,000 young people from all over Europe—chiefly from Poland and Germany—meet with their peers from other countries there every year, bridging the divides of language, religion, and politics. They learn in multiday sessions about the Kreisau Circle's opposition not only to Nazi Germany but to communist dictatorships during the years of the Cold War. It is also the site of numerous meetings, seminars, and concerts for adults, making the estate a lively spot in southwestern Poland. For Freya, who worked closely with everyone connected to the project, this new incarnation of the former estate was the signal achievement of her old age and, traveling with a small backpack and one suitcase, she visited frequently well into her nineties. Built on the opposition to dictatorships, the foundation teaches young people to work together across national boundaries. With each encounter that it facilitates, the Moltkes' former home encourages visitors to work for a democratic Europe.

NOTES ON THE PRESENT EDITION

The present edition of letters is translated from the abridged version edited by Helmuth Caspar and Ulrike von Moltke, published by C. H. Beck in Germany in 2013. The unabridged version contained 172 letters. In preparing the German version of the abridged correspondence, the editors largely reduced repetitions in the discussion of possible legal defense strategies, shortened lengthy discussions of Bible passages, and excised digressions on family affairs. With one exception, the editors also decided to omit the handful of censored letters that the couple had to write to avoid suspicion of the parallel, secret correspondence. This permitted a greater narrative coherence and brought into focus the heartbeat of Helmuth and Freya's conversation, both of which we wished to preserve for the English reader as well. We have also introduced some minor additional modifications with a view to further enhancing the readability of the text. Thus, we have undertaken a handful of additional cuts to the text, largely in places where minor figures are mentioned who play no further role in the remainder of the correspondence. We have also omitted the abridged version's various ellipses that indicated where the editors had intervened in the original German text, and we have generally spelled out any abbreviations that the letter writers used, whether out of habit or to preserve space on the precious paper. Further we have clarified the identities of the many people referenced in the letters by adding missing first or last names in brackets at first mention in any given letter (with the exception of members of the immediate family, such as their sons, whom Helmuth and Freya mention only by first name, of course).

—HELMUTH CASPAR VON MOLTKE,
DOROTHEA VON MOLTKE, and JOHANNES VON MOLTKE
Norwich, Vermont, August 2018

NOTES

1. See Biographical Note.
2. Ian Kershaw, *The End: The Defiance and Destruction of Hitler's Germany, 1944–1945* (New York: Penguin, 2011), 52.
3. See Appendix: Additional Documents.
4. Freya to Helmuth James, October 20, 1944.
5. Helmuth James to Freya, December 28, 1944.
6. Freya to Helmuth James, December 15, 1944.
7. Helmuth James von Moltke, *Letters to Freya, 1939–1945*, edited and translated by Beate Ruhm von Oppen (New York: Knopf, 1990), 397.
8. See Ger van Roon, *Neuordnung im Widerstand: Der Kreisauer Kreis innerhalb der deutschen Widerstandsbewegung* (Munich: Oldenbourg R. Verlag GmbH, 1967), and Anna-Raphaela Schmitz, "Der Kreisauer Kreis und die nationalsozialistischen Gewaltverbrechen," master's the-

sis (Touro College, 2013).

9. "Memorandum bei Carlo Mierendorff, June 14, 1943," in van Roon, *Neuordnung im Widerstand*, 589.

10. Helmuth to Freya, October 21, 1941, in Moltke, *Letters to Freya*, 175.

11. Dorothee von Meding, *Courageous Hearts: Women and the Anti-Hitler Plot of 1944*, translated by Michael Balfour and Volker R. Berghahn (New York: Berghahn Books, 1997), 80.

12. Freya to Helmuth James, October 12, 1944.

13. Helmuth James to Freya, October 30–31, 1944.

14. See Kershaw, *The End*, 51.

15. Moltke, *Letters to Freya*.

16. Ger van Roon, *German Resistance to Hitler: Count von Moltke and the Kreisau Circle*, translated by Peter Ludlow (London: Van Nostrand Reinhold, 1971).

17. See Alfred Delp, *Gesammelte Schriften, Vol. 4: Im Gefängnis* (Frankfurt am Main: Joseph Knecht, 1984), 256.

18. Peter Hoffmann, "Moltke, Goerdeler und Stauffenberg: Fragen und Kontroversen," *Jahrbuch der deutschen Schillergesellschaft* 56 (2012): 473–503.

19. George F. Kennan, *Memoirs, 1925–1950* (New York: Pantheon Books, 1967), 121.

20. Helmuth James to Freya, January 10, 1945.

21. Hoffmann, "Moltke, Goerdeler und Stauffenberg," 476.

22. Helmuth James to Freya, January 10–11, 1945.

23. Helmuth James to Freya, January 21–22, 1945.

24. Freya to Helmuth James, November 17, 1944.

25. December 28, 1944, in Moltke, *Letters to Freya*, 396–97.

26. Harald Poelchau, *Their Final Hours: Recollections of a Prison Chaplain* (Monterey: Monterey Institute of International Studies, 1989).

27. Freya to Helmuth James, September 29, 1944.

ACKNOWLEDGMENTS

THE INTRODUCTIONS to the two German editions were co-authored by Ulrike von Moltke, whose influence remains in the present introduction as well. We want to take this opportunity to thank her for her sensitive and detailed work on these letters since Freya's death in 2010. With her eye for detail and her ear for nuance, she was an indispensable co-editor of the full German text of the letters and of the abridged version that serves as the basis for this translation. We have relied on her deep familiarity with the text for questions arising in the process of assembling the present edition as well. In more ways than we can reconstruct, the latter bears the marks of Ulrike's work even though she passed the baton to two of her children to join Helmuth Caspar von Moltke in the preparation of the English version. Konrad von Moltke, the second of the "little sons" in these letters, and brother and father to the editors of the present volume, did not live to see them published, but he would have taken enormous pleasure in their translations both into Polish and now into English. This work was done also in his memory.

This version would not exist without the patient and dedicated work of Shelley Frisch, who translated the letters from the German. We are extremely grateful to her for this work as well as for the collaborative and open-minded spirit in which she involved us in her process. As a result, we find that both Freya's and Helmuth's voices resonate in this translation into a language that was deeply familiar to both of them in their lifetimes.

Bringing the book to an English-language readership involved the support of publishers on both sides of the Atlantic. We want to thank

Jill Kneerim for helping us navigate the publishing terrain, as well as Susan Barba and Edwin Frank at New York Review Books for taking on this project. Karla Eoff's meticulous copyediting was a great help. We also wish to thank Keri von Moltke for steadfast support and advice. Back in Germany, we would like to thank the publisher of both the original and the abridged editions, C. H. Beck—and in particular Wolfgang Beck and Ulrich Nolte. Finally, we would like to extend our thanks to Agnieszka von Zanthier who was instrumental in bringing about a Polish edition of the letters during the time we were working on the present volume in a mutually reinforcing process from which we hope readers of both translations will now benefit.

TRANSLATOR'S NOTE

THIS EDITION draws on the abridged German volume of the letters. All passages from the Bible cite the King James Version, in accordance with the family's wishes. I have made minor adjustments to the punctuation when it obscured the meaning of the translated texts. In consultation with the editors, I opted to retain Helmuth's practice of referring to Caspar and Konrad as "the little sons" or "your little sons" (as opposed to "my" or "our" little sons) in many of the earlier letters, as it reflects his initial distance from them, even though this lack of specificity is more jarring in English than it is in German. "The friends," in reference to Harald and Dorothee Poelchau, serves as one of the many code names for people close to them, so as to limit the danger those people might face if the letters were confiscated; here, too, the deliberately distanced "the" has not been replaced by the otherwise more idiomatic "our." The footnotes throughout the volume have been reworked extensively to reflect the needs of an English-language readership and to update particulars. The book's annotated index of names was similarly adapted to serve the new readership.

As I worked through this correspondence, I found myself thinking back to Reiner Stach's three-volume biography of Franz Kafka, which I translated from the German not long before embarking on this project. Kafka's *The Trial* is, at its core, about an opaque, labyrinthine judicial system that requires Josef K. to try again and again—in vain—to make inroads with an array of bureaucrats to plead his case while facing topsy-turvy logic and unaccountable delays and hurdles at every turn. As I made my way through the correspondence of Helmuth James and Freya von Moltke, I was struck by how frequently this same illogic applied to their futile attempts to reframe the judicial charges against Helmuth, to lessen the harsh treatment he had to face on a daily basis, to reduce the ultimate verdict, and to delay its implementation. Had Helmuth and Freya been successful in postponing this fate by just a few months in the fateful year of 1945, he might well have survived. Helmuth James von Moltke died on January 23, 1945, which, a few short years later, would mark the date of my own birth.

We readers—and this translator—know the outcome of this heartrending correspondence from the start, yet we find ourselves hoping against hope for an ending other than the inevitable one.

—SHELLEY FRISCH
Princeton, September 2018

LAST LETTERS

Oh, my love, I will always, always see myself walking across the fields at your side. Where was my hand, where did it always want to go? How beautiful that was. But I don't want just to look toward the past; I want to love you, my love, I want to be able to keep on loving you always, even if I have to remain alone.

—FREYA VON MOLTKE
October 8–9, 1944

For Harald and Dorothee Poelchau

Berlin, 29 Sept 44

My Jäm, my love, my husband,[1] my dearest beloved, how wonderful that I'm able to write you a proper letter again.[2] How fulfilling it was for us to see each other.[3] How well everything is going, and how full of grace! It makes me so happy. My love, I think I know exactly what is going on inside you; even though I lag way behind you and will remain so, I still belong with you and that is how it will stay forever. I will have to go on living and that will be hard, but it will work out, because I will be able to go on loving you. I will love you in God and not disturb you on the paths you'll take, and I will love God more and better than I have before. But please, when you die, it must be in the certainty that apart from God I belong only to you. These fifteen years,[4] that was our life, my Jäm; what comes now will be a life for the little sons, for other people, for things—I don't yet know what, but my life, our life, my beloved Jäm, that is now coming to an end here. You always told me that you would die young. You promised me seven more years, but why talk about quantity. Quality is what counts. How good it is that I have experienced every minute with you consciously as a gift, that I fought for every one of them. Now I have the same treasures in me that you have enjoyed. We are really quite rich and we have, I'm convinced, enjoyed the greatest happiness this world has to offer. How good it is that you chose me after all,[5] how good that I wrested the little sons from you,[6] how much beauty and delight I will have to contemplate when you are no longer alive!

I'll grow old and I'll change, but you will always remain inside me until I may die and find you again, one way or another.—My love, how wonderful it was to really see you yesterday, for I saw right away what was going on inside of you, even before you discovered me, which happened quickly enough. You saw the same in me, and when we looked at each other, we knew everything. I keep reveling in it. It's part of the treasure trove! I think there's barely a chance that we'll get to see each other again, but it goes without saying that I'm doing everything I can to make it happen, though all paths seem to be totally blocked. They appear to be quite afraid of your group. It is so incredibly wonderful and delightful that this path leads so close to you.[7]

I've been speaking about myself the entire time now, and you still have such a hard road to go down, but since you've never liked living,[8] you really shouldn't find the prospect of your life coming to an end unpleasant. My love, you've always told me that the best way to die is the one you're now facing. I hope that's how it is, that you are not afraid, my love. I confidently believe that this is essentially the way it is, and that you'll find a way past the hurdles. I know that you're firmly in God's hands. And we have such good people who went before us: Mami, Carl Bernd, Granny, Daddy.[9] That's sure to be a welcome thought for you as well. My love, I don't have any notions about life after death. They'd be wrong anyway, but we had enough revealed to us and our feeling is strong and clear, so I believe, believe gratefully, and will go on seeing and believing more and more profoundly.

Your life seems beautiful and complete to me. You'll die for something worth dying for. It's uninteresting in the extreme that you might have gone on to become a "great" man. But it was important that the bomb didn't explode in front of your window back in January.[10] If you have to die now, I believe your death will have meaning. My Jäm, do you feel, as I do, how wonderfully in accord we are? Do you often feel, as I do, that we belong together so boundlessly, so suitably? At the same time, I'm not a spiritual person, but more like a growing plant in this world. This is far more my element than yours, but you must make sure I don't stay too plantlike, and I think you've already seen to that quite well!

You needn't worry about our lives—the little sons' and mine. I'm not at all afraid. We'll manage, with or without Kreisau, with or without money, with or without communism. The little sons will turn out just fine. I will tell Casparchen[11] that you died of an illness; I'll tell him more when he's older. I'll hang on to Kreisau[12] or the Berghaus[13] as long as I can, because it's everyone's home. But everything will turn out all right.

I'll probably go to Kreisau again tomorrow and when I return sometime next week, I'll bring you a warm suit. You think I know why I grabbed this other one again without thinking? I don't. On the way here I said to myself, "What a fool I am!" I'll try to bring a blanket too.

Well, my Jäm, now I'm going to Carl Dietrich [von Trotha]'s[14] to sleep. Here at the Poelchaus' home I've been able to write this letter in peace, gratitude, and tears—not bad tears, only good ones, my love. They're simply part of who I am. I have often let them flow quite freely when I'm with you. You know how I do that!

There's nothing else I need to tell you for now. I'm just as grateful as you. I've often written as much, and maybe I'll do it a few more times, and it will always stay that way. I am your P.[15]

---

1. Freya refers here and elsewhere to Helmuth as "Jäm," short for James, and as "mein Wirt," meaning "my host," a reference to Friedrich Schiller's play *Wilhelm Tell*, in which the husband and wife refer to each other respectively as "Ehewirt" and "Ehewirtin," or "marriage host." Helmuth, too, adopts this term to refer to himself as "Dein Ehewirt" ("your marriage host"), and occasionally refers to Freya as "meine Wirtin." 2. This was the first letter in nine months not subject to censorship by the Gestapo. 3. Freya and Helmuth happened to catch sight of each other across the Tegel prison yard on the previous day, when Freya was there for the first time. 4. Freya is referring to the fifteen years since they first met in Grundlsee; see Biographical Note. 5. Helmuth initially hesitated about whom to marry from among the young women in Eugenie Schwarzwald's circle. 6. During the first years of their marriage, Freya and Helmuth could not agree on whether they should have children in such times. In January 1937, Freya, having won the support of Helmuth's grandmother Jessie Rose Innes, decided the matter on her own,

and in November 1937, Helmuth Caspar was born. Helmuth and Freya were both in favor of having a second child, and in September 1941, Konrad was born. 7. The letters were written at the home of Harald Poelchau, the prison chaplain at Tegel prison who acted as postman for both Freya and Helmuth. 8. Helmuth had come to expect his premature death under the Nazi regime. 9. All predeceased family. Mami: Helmuth's mother, Dorothy von Moltke; Carl Bernd: Helmuth's brother, Carl Bernhard von Moltke; Granny: Helmuth's grandmother Jessie Rose Innes; Daddy: Helmuth's grandfather James Rose Innes. 10. On January 28, 1944, a bomb landed next to the Gestapo complex on Prinz-Albrecht-Strasse, near Helmuth's cell, but it failed to explode. 11. Their eldest son, Helmuth Caspar, is generally mentioned in the diminutive form abbreviated as "C.chen." As there is no diminutive form of the name in English, we have used the German diminutive "Casparchen." 12. The family estate. 13. The Schloss (manor house) was the home of the family until 1928, when they moved to the smaller Berghaus on the hill above the farm yard. During the war, many refugees from the bombing were housed there, including the Reichwein family. 14. Helmuth's cousin. 15. Freya signs almost all her letters with "P."; this letter stands "Pim," a nickname used only by the couple with each other.

HELMUTH JAMES TO FREYA, SEPTEMBER 30, 1944

30 Sept 44

My dear, we are now shackled day and night, which makes writing quite difficult, so if one feature or another in my handwriting strikes you as unfamiliar, this handicap is the cause. My love, I was so happy to see you for a few short seconds, since I knew nothing about you apart from what was in the little letter you sent me with my things in Drögen.[1] Other than that, the last news I got was from August 17.[2] I hope you will have seen that I'm well, surprisingly well under the circumstances; and you, my love, are a good part of the reason. Just think, since the time when everything has gotten worse, I haven't worried about you for a moment, not for an instant. I've felt so proud to have a wife I can trust to ride out the things in store for us. [Marginal note: handcuffs off] My love, I'm so certain of my cause, I'm so firmly anchored, that God willing, I will not for a moment lack the strength I'll need. I believe you can rely on that. It's also true, my love, that over these past weeks no earthly matters have been on my mind apart from you and the little sons, unless they concerned the fight for my life. I couldn't muster interest in anyone or anything. Even Asta [Wendland] [3] and Ulla [Oldenbourg] [4] and the others came to mind only in relation to you and the little sons, like so many bits of scenery. As you can see, I've spent this week quite close to the three of you, my love.

Since I don't know how much time I have left, I want to jot down a few other things. I can't sway your decision as to whether you stay in Kreisau, nor do I want to. I'm fine with whatever you decide, including, of course, your decision to stay. It would be wrong for someone uninformed about the factors in play to presume to judge the situation, especially if he cannot assess the extent to which pure sentiment is involved.

My case looks like this: It is well established that I knew quite a bit about Goerdeler and that I was determined to fight against his plans.[5] The issue is my failure to meet the obligation to notify the authorities, which can be regarded either as very serious, because I knew so much, or as very minor, because it is established that I did not approve of it, and, as long as I was free, I tried hard to fight these plans, but after my arrest I relied on Peter [Yorck][6] to continue fighting and to report them to the authorities as appropriate. So in my view, this case can be made.

The second issue is Kreisau[7]: *a.* Is it high treason? I counter this by pointing out that the Goerdeler case establishes that I was against any change in the form of government and all the plans were postwar plans. This issue might work out as well. *b.* Was it defeatism, based on an assumption that the war would be lost?[8] My argument: only prophylactically in the event of a catastrophe, until then: fight to the utmost, hence no defeatism. But some of those involved appear to have said that I was understood to be defeatist. In isolation, this issue could conceivably be handled as well. The difficulty is the constellation of the three issues, on top of which there is of course Kiep,[9] too, and furthermore the mere fact of my contact with Carlo [Mierendorff],[10] the bishops, and the Jesuits, as well as my visit to Rehrl,[11] the former governor of Salzburg, would appear to be regarded as just about all that is needed, once all these people—including Rösch and company—went over to Goerdeler following my arrest. I am thought to have brought them together, and Goerdeler put them to use. So this appraisal actually makes the case hopeless if it can't be thrown out. I see a glimmer of hope in only two fine lines of argument: *a*. the subjective one, determining that I did not want any of this to happen and that ultimately I was let down by Peter's failure to hold to this line during my imprisonment and don't want to pay the price for Peter's guilt now;[12] *b*. the objective one, with my overall attitude and past indicating that I am no reactionary and truly not part of the group of people involved in the events of July 20th. So it's worth thinking about whether you could talk over the matter with Dix,[13] and if Dix doesn't want to, with Sack, the defense lawyer who is said to be very good. You would just have to give some thought to explaining how you could have come to know all this; anyway, Dix can continue to represent the matter only if you two can see a way to do so without your being dragged into it as well. In any case, you should leave no stone unturned, because I don't think the matter can get any worse at this point.

I don't really know whether you ought to speak with those now in charge of me [marginal note: SS Major Neuhaus, Meinekestrasse] either, but I think it's basically harmless, provided that you get Lange's department on Prinz-Albrecht-Strasse, or Huppenkothen, to refer you there.[14] It might be best for you to say that I'm on doctor's orders to eat honey and plenty of sugar or else I'll suffer from fainting spells, and to ask whether you might be able to give me these things. I can get food only via the appropriate department,[15] and I'd need to take some with me when I'm there, because the prison doesn't allow it.— By and large I'm in favor of a visit to Neuhaus, because the personal impression this man gets of me could spell the difference between life and death, even if the bulk of the power lies with Freisler[16] and the chief Reich prosecutor.[17] One thing is certain in any case: I get along better with Neuhaus than with Lange and company. He runs the church department, and is thus a raging heathen, but he's educated.

Chief Reich prosecutor and Freisler: You need to talk this over with Dix. The question is whether we should try to enlist Carl Viggo [von Moltke]'s[18] help. Do discuss this with Dix, at any rate. Maybe Steengracht[19] can also be swayed into joining this game somehow or other. But don't waste your energy on getting me additional comforts now; that can only be the grounds for your visit to Neuhaus, yet any serious actions have to be directed at the ultimate verdict.

Don't think that I am clinging to these possibilities with any sort of hope. I'm writing about it so extensively because I think everything possible ought to be done, even if we don't think it will help. After all, you can never know. But don't pin your hopes on it. Please let me know if you have understood my line of defense or need any elaborations.

As for things I'll be needing, they include a winter suit in exchange for the one you just brought me, a winter coat, and a hat. It's very cold here. I would also like to have a blanket and a pair of cuff links sewn with mother-of-pearl buttons or fabric, none of my decent ones, as well as a necktie and shoe-cleaning kit. I'd also like a couple of envelopes. Maybe I can write you more than one letter after all.—Finally, a fountain pen would be very nice, since mine got lost when I was brought here. In the five days between my first interrogation in Ravensbrück and when I was issued prison fatigues, had my books confiscated, etc., I already pictured what lay ahead, so I memorized a series of passages from the Bible, and recited them to myself every day in the mornings and afternoons, while continuing to discover new things in them. I'm sending you a list so you'll know what I'm working on. I also whistle hymns all the time.—The guards here in the prison are very friendly and willing to do anything possible, but they are of course unable to go against the regulation that we remain shackled at all times.

My dear, those are all the practical things I have to report. Most of all, I want to repeat that if nothing inside me changes, my mental state appears to be quite safe and sound, and whether I'm shackled or not, have bedbugs or not, sit in a cold and dark cell, can't read and write, hear nothing from you and wind up getting shouted at, beheaded, or hanged, one thing will remain as is: I know exactly where I am firmly anchored: above and beside me. Over the course of these past few weeks, I've come to find anything else—or so I think and hope—utterly unimportant. On this issue, have a look at the end of the first passage from the Epistle to the Romans on my slip of paper. Nor do I think that I'm somehow overstating things here; on the contrary, I feel quite balanced, and find that this balance has now grown quite naturally rather than being artificially cultivated. If this weren't the case, I'd be much more worried about you, my love. But where in all this is the first and most natural thought of a devoted husband and father, to speak in the style of an obituary? It is simply not there; instead, every thought of the three of you lends me support and strength, and for this I cannot thank the Lord enough, and you through Him.—My love, I think everything's been said, even though nothing has yet been said. Needless to say, I was happy about the things you sent; that is like a warm ray of sunshine. All of them are really useful and actually necessary, because there's not enough food here, to say nothing of the days I'm interrogated, when I sometimes get no food at all. I smuggled a can of sardines from Ravensbrück, which I kept as my reserve fund, and I still have it. Maybe Neuhaus will arrange for you to be able to leave a few cans at the Meinekestrasse offices and I can then take them with me in my bag. Fat and sugar are sorely lacking. The midday mush is tolerable and not repellent; the bread is always dry and acceptable. You just can't let yourself get sick. Obviously there is nothing fresh, and no protein. That's why sugar is in such demand and, to some extent, even necessary, because a good deal can actually depend on whether you have a full stomach at the trial or you're hungry and shaky.—I'm curious how the village takes the news about my arrest. Make it clear that I have no direct connection to July 20th, and was only dragged into it by friends. My love, you can be absolutely certain of one thing: If the Lord wishes to preserve me, He will preserve me, no matter how hopeless the situation might appear; if He wishes to call me to Him, it will ultimately come to pass, regardless of whether it happens along the elaborate path by way of Herr Freisler or in a direct manner. All of you are in His hands just as surely as I am, and we will want to take what we have learned from this time into a more distant future or a different existence.—Just let everyone help you in everything, and don't hold back. We can fall back on a treasure trove of love and friendship, and that's what we should be doing. Just don't accept all kinds of advice from everyone; instead, rely on one person for certain questions, and on another for different ones, and don't be sparing with money or other resources. In this case, failing to do everything would mean tempting God, not relying on Him.

I figure that the time frame will be as follows: By the middle of next week at the earliest, the Security Service's final report will be filed. From that point on it generally takes three weeks until the trial. They could also hold it up by bringing me in for additional questioning, or the three-week period could also be prolonged as a result of the large number of cases on the docket. It is also possible, though, that I have now risen to a level of relative prominence and will therefore move up in line, but that can't make much difference. Originally I was supposed to appear in the first civilian trial, with Goerdeler–

Tegel prison: View from a cell in 1944

Hassell. The fact that I was taken off that slate and won't be part of the trade union trial[20] either—which they told me next—is an indication of a slight improvement in my status. Last week I made a very risky statement,[21] which, in turn, could either improve or worsen things. With so much material from the interrogations, combined with the possibility that Neuhaus takes an interest in me, all of that can take a good deal longer and drag on for months, and to a certain extent, the later my case is heard, the more promising the outlook. That, in any event, is how I judge the situation.

How nice that you have such a source of support in little Konrad. I hope that continues to be the case. Say hello to them all for me, my love—and what should I say about you. Nothing at all. J.

Another two clothes hangers, please. One trouser hanger, one pair of shoe trees, shoe-cleaning kit, one pillowcase, one towel, salt.

Incidentally, I said that Peter and I had a very clear agreement that Goerdeler's undertaking had to be prevented by all available means, and if there was no way around it, it would have to be reported to the authorities.

1. Security policy academy in Drögen, their meeting place during Helmuth's incarceration at the Ravensbrück concentration camp. 2. On August 19, 1944, Helmuth's status as a privileged *Schutzhäftling*, a prisoner in "protective custody," was revoked, after which he was no longer entitled to write or receive letters. 3. Helmuth's sister, Asta Maria Wendland. 4. Ulla Oldenbourg, a friend whose prayers Helmuth valued highly. 5. Carl Friedrich Goerdeler was the prospective head of the government if the plot to kill Hitler had succeeded. 6. Peter Graf Yorck von Wartenburg, with whom Helmuth created the Kreisau Circle. 7. He is referring to the Kreisau Circle discussions that took place in Kreisau and Berlin and the plans for a new Germany. This is the first of numerous mentions of the place with different connotations. 8. The National Socialists regarded a lack of faith in a final victory as a serious offense. 9. Helmuth was first taken into "protective custody" on January 19, 1944, in connection with Otto Carl Kiep's arrest; see Editors' Introduction. 10. Carlo Mierendorff, a leading Social Democrat and Nazi opponent who died in a 1943 air raid. 11. Franz Rehrl, an Austrian politician who had been considered for a role in government in the event of a successful coup. 12. Peter Yorck, in close collaboration with Count Claus Schenk Graf von Stauffen-

berg, decided to join the attempt to assassinate Hitler on July 20, 1944. At this point, Helmuth was already incarcerated at Ravensbrück; see Editors' Introduction. 13. The attorney Rudolf Dix. 14. Herbert Lange and Walter Huppenkothen, Gestapo officers, had overseen Helmuth's interrogations in Drögen. In the letters, the government agency is generally designated as "Prinz-Albrecht-Str.," the Gestapo headquarters. 15. That is, the Gestapo, whose offices in this case were at Meinekestrasse 10. It soon proved possible for food supplies to be brought directly to Helmuth at Tegel prison. 16. The president of the People's Court, Roland Freisler. 17. Ernst Lautz. 18. Helmuth's uncle Carl Viggo von Moltke. Though pro-Nazi he helped his nephew during this period in every way. 19. Gustav Adolf Steengracht von Moyland, the secretary of state in the Foreign Office. 20. Goerdeler was sentenced on September 8, 1944, but not executed until February 2, 1945. Ulrich von Hassell was also sentenced on September 8, 1944, and executed the very same day. The Social Democrats Adolf Reichwein, Julius Leber, and Hermann Maass were sentenced and executed on October 20, 1944. 21. The reference is probably to an interrogation that took place in the last week of September; see the following letter of October 1, 1944.

HELMUTH JAMES TO FREYA, OCTOBER 1, 1944

Berlin, 1 Oct 1944

My dear love, my Pim, my little one, your letter[1] strengthened and delighted me beyond compare. If you say you're like a plant, I have to bow down humbly before this plant, which has never strayed or erred when it mattered. I had no doubt that you would find what is right, but it gives me strength to know it for a fact.—Yes, my love, our life is at an end. Not until this year did I learn to be fully grateful for this life. How was it possible for me not to have known it always? Mami and you have guided me from the womb to my grave, and I haven't known a single cold, loveless hour in my entire life. I'm joined to you, my love, by a bond that is so much firmer, deeper, and more enduring than I ever dreamed possible. Now I know it. And you, too, know what a gift of grace this is, my love. I can only wish for you that in the span of time that may still be granted to you, you don't lose hold of this feeling of our belonging together. It is a gift from our

Father, and may He keep it forever unaltered within you. I hope and believe, my love, that the little sons, our little sons, will thrive under your care. They should be a real comfort to you, but you know full well that the true bringer of comfort lives above us and that He can provide the only true and enduring comfort.—I've already told you that I'm not worried about your, and the little sons', mental and physical well-being. I hope that you will remain close to Lionel [Curtis] and Julian [Frisby] and Nan [Petronella van Heerden][2] so that they, too, may benefit from Mami's cultural heritage. But there is one thing you must know, my love: All decisions are now yours alone, and you mustn't feel bound in any way by wishes I might express; that would be utterly wrong.

We both knew that this price might have to be paid. I don't find it so easy to pay, because it is being demanded in apparent relation to a matter I can only disapprove of. After two nights of suffering this disjointedness within me, I said some things at night on the following day, when I was taken in at 10, that would have been better left unsaid, better for myself and for others. I was able to defend matters relating to Kreisau only by abandoning my positions as to what I knew about Goerdeler's machinations, and I did so far too thoroughly, which will likely result in the official verdict being built on what I said. I want you to know that, because this matter could come up later at some point and not be understood.[3] I made a mistake, without a doubt, not in bad faith but rather in my reduced powers of resistance.—It certainly did nothing to alter the outcome for me, as they kept talking about the "Kreisau Circle" and the "Moltke Group," which made it clear what was going to become of me. It's just that I would rather go to my death if the formal reason reflected my own thoughts.

I have no fear of death and I believe that I will be holding on to all of you in some form or another, and I have a creaturely fear of dying, and it pains me that I will not see you and the little sons again with these eyes of mine. I feel that I have had so much in this life that I have no right to make any more demands, but I don't feel as though I'm the harvest calling for the reaper. I believe that I have described my inner state as well as I can. I would probably gain control over this creaturely fear and the pain of parting if I were to resign myself to this fate. But I feel obliged to fight against it, and to do so, I have to sustain my will to live, no matter what the adverse consequences. I hope to be able to clarify all this by the time I am killed.

My love, these past eight months have not been a loss for us. The two of us have likely become somewhat different people. I have reaped a bountiful harvest, I have discovered my bond with you in the deepest depths and on the highest heights, I have also loved our little sons more dearly than ever before, I have learned to give thanks and have learned to say, "Thy will be done." The Lord is calling home a different man from the one He put to the test on January 19.[4] I hope, no, I believe that He will forgive my many trespasses and that, in Him, I shall find you again, along with those who have gone before us. And in my best moments, I'm sometimes able to be glad that I can take this step so deliberately.

So, my love, that is enough talk about death. I can see your future life very clearly before me. For a long time I've been asking the Lord daily to comfort you if He should call me to Him, so that you may remain a whole person. And never have I felt His affirming answer to my prayer with such confidence. Any details are so unimportant by comparison. Just as my last request will be to ask for His mercy, my next-to-last will be for you, and I'm certain He will grant what I ask.

I'll stop here, my love. I don't know whether I'll be able to write you again. I regard every letter I now write as the last one, and you won't find much that is new in them. I'll give back the old letters of yours that I still have, and will keep only your birthday letter[5] and Casparchen's first letter to me with the five little flowers. Those will be my last provisions. The verse in Mami's eulogy applies to both of us: "For whether we live, we live unto the Lord; and whether we die, we die unto the Lord: whether we live therefore, or die, we are the Lord's."[6] J.

1. The letter of September 29, 1944. 2. Lionel Curtis, Julian Frisby, and Anna Petronella van Heerden were close friends of the Moltkes in Great Britain

and South Africa. 3. Helmuth had adamantly distanced himself from the stance and political viewpoints of Goerdeler, so he could not disavow his knowledge of Goerdeler in the interrogations. 4. On January 19, 1944, Helmuth was arrested. 5. Freya's birthday letter, dated March 8, 1944, is published in German in Helmuth James von Moltke, *Im Land der Gottlosen*: *Tagebuch und Briefe aus der Haft 1944/45*, edited by Günter Brakelmann (Munich: C. H. Beck, 2009). 6. Romans 14:8.

FREYA TO HELMUTH JAMES, OCTOBER 4, 1944

Wednesday evening

My dear, my Jäm, I have already shed many happy and sad tears over your farewell letter. I've already read the letter often, and the tears came again and again. I have taken every word and brought it deep within me, and from there the words keep rising back up. Every word is a testament to us and forms a part of our life, every word comes from you and forms a part of me. My dear, what happiness! I actually have nothing to add to the words you write; I understand them all and find that I'm suffused with them. I also understand your thoughts on death, and am grateful from the bottom of my soul that all that had been weighing on you so heavily on Monday has been lifted from you. How it must have tormented you. Yes, I, too, have learned to give thanks, and I, too, have learned to say, "Thy will be done." That is the very thing. It began to grow within me quite some time ago. I know that it had already filled me back when we buried Hans-Adolf [von Moltke] at the church in Bresa.[1] You sat next to me, and I was grateful, yet prepared to take the cross upon myself if it came to that. It has continued to grow, and now all my pleas dissolve into "Thy will be done"—though not my plea that God may help you, guide you, and strengthen you. Oh, my Jäm, I am such a novice in matters of prayer, yet hope to lend help to you with this prayer. But if I pray for you to remain on this earth—which means everything to me, my so beloved heart—my words keep turning into "Thy will be done." I took all that with me yesterday as I left here to go home, commending it to God from the bottom of my heart, then I fell asleep and woke up knowing that it was right to fight for your life even if it was to no avail, to leave nothing undone, to do everything in my power. I just feel as though I'm bungling everything I undertake, but I know what you mean, and I'll try not to hope while continuing to act. But when it comes right down to it, my beloved, the two of us are calm and strong and united, and so I can say: I am doing well. I am so grateful that I can live so close by, because I am always near you. That's why I'm so happy to be in Berlin, not because of the physical proximity, but rather because I am alone so often here—even in the city—and then I am always close to you. In Kreisau I get far too little peace and quiet from others or from myself, and here I'm always running around, yet I'm constantly at your side, because no one is disturbing me. Even so, I would like to spend these weeks with you in great intimacy and closeness so that they knit us together even more closely and strengthen our bond. My Jäm, pray for me that I never have to lose this feeling. Then I won't be alone and solitary, though I'll surely always love solitude so that I can feel you. I may not know everything, but I do know quite firmly that we are together in God's hands, and that everything will grow properly for us out of that certainty.—Yesterday I was thinking about Communion; I didn't know whether I would be able to take it, but now I think I can. I have read the passages and will do it. I don't yet know when and how, but I wanted to tell you that.

My love, you write that I shouldn't go by your wishes. It will be hard to get it right, but what's certain is that your spirit will have to stay alive in all that I decide, because your spirit belongs to me, because it is a part of me. For me and for our little sons. I will always be guided by your thoughts. I will gauge my decisions by your wishes, but I will grow old and will change, and your wishes may be expressed in different ways within me, which is why I have to carry you within me and live with you, but that can work only with God's help and His will. My Jäm, I know that, and I also know that He is my comforter. It makes me very happy that Mami's epitaph unites us so beautifully. The fact that it can bring us together so wonderfully, if you have to depart from your life, is a great source of happiness.

Tomorrow I'll go to see Neuhaus. Steengracht wanted a letter that I wrote although I didn't think it was a well-written one. I also have to discuss something else with Harald [Poelchau] and I'd like to know your response.[2] I get the feeling that I'm ruining everything for us. My dear, I have to stop now. My dear, my dear love. I think of you full of tender love. I am and will forever remain your P.

1. Hans-Adolf von Moltke, who died while he was the German ambassador in Spain, was buried after a state ceremony in Breslau on March 31, 1943, in Gross-Bresa (now called Brzezina) in Silesia. 2. The subject was apparently Freya's plan to go to the chief of the Gestapo, Heinrich Müller; see Freya's letter of October 8–9, 1944.

HELMUTH JAMES TO FREYA, OCTOBER 6, 1944

Tegel, 6 Oct 1944

My dear, I keep reading your letters with great happiness, during the day and at night when I'm awake. After all, we go to bed at 6 and are out of bed again at 7, because they handcuff us at 6 and remove the handcuffs at 7, so there are always periods when we're awake during the night. Since we sleep only with the lights on, these can be very valuable hours. You needn't worry about the handcuffs. People get totally used to them and become quite adroit with the handcuffs on. We simply reserve any activities that require free hands for the hour (or hour and a half) that we're unshackled: mornings, lunchtime, and evenings: 7–8:30, 11:30–1, 4–5:30. Also, the guards are very friendly, and if we have a plausible reason—such as needing to mop up—they don't handcuff us between noon and the evening, since they find the process troublesome and distasteful.

My love, when I think about the situation carefully, I find that the past few months, and particularly this last week, have actually been the time of our most intimate togetherness. You have been inside me more than ever before, and you have also known more about me than ever before, so your old complaint about this point doesn't apply to this moment. In any case, that is an odd and very gratifying outcome of this misfortune. And then, we are even more strongly connected on high than ever before. So let us hope that any blows that may come our way similarly carry blessings within them.

What a blessing Poelchau is for us. We cannot thank him enough. I hope you know that he is always bringing me supplies, and that you'll compensate him for it. I have no qualms about accepting everything, because it pleases me, and because I think that it may help me to tolerate being shouted at without losing my composure. My diet of honey rolls, bacon, eggs, and sugar is a boon and is certainly doing its part to keep me cheerful. I eat mountains of these treasures, my love, only in the hope that you can replenish them, and in the expectation that this will take just a few more days anyway.

I was also happy about the coat and other clothing,[1] but even more about the feeling that you and I were under the same roof, only 100 meters apart. I find your presence in Berlin so pleasing that you might say I actually feel at home. Just stay, if you can.

Until I see you again, my dear beloved heart, God willing, in this world, or else in the hereafter. Stay whole and unbowed, even when I'm no longer here. I ask the Lord to preserve your feeling that I'm with you and supporting you, no, not your feeling, your certainty. Take pleasure in your little sons, keep them safe, and be a blessing for them and others. Send them all my regards. They are all in my heart, especially the poor Sister.[2] May the Lord protect all of you. J.—Do you like the picture of little Casparchen with the currant smudge?[3]

1. Clothing was exchanged in one of two prison areas: either the "waiting room" (see Freya's letter of October 11, 1944) or "downstairs" (see Helmuth's letter of October 12, 1944). 2. Ida Hübner, the district nurse in Kreisau village and a confidante, from an order based in Frankenstein in Silesia. 3. Helmuth had enclosed a photograph of Caspar that had been among his possessions.

HELMUTH JAMES TO FREYA, OCTOBER 8, 1944

Tegel, 8 Oct 44

My dear, it's Sunday at noon. How are things at home? Did your little sons come visit you in bed? At any rate, that's where I looked for you all at 6:30 this morning when the wake-up bell rang.— Everything you wrote greatly interested me, of course. Now it's of the utmost importance for me to figure out my own line of defense. I've made a brief outline and would welcome an opinion from someone versed in criminal law. But apart from the criminal-law angle, I'd also welcome tactical advice: When can one speak? Can one present an uninterrupted narrative, or is it best just to stick to answering questions? How are new facts accepted? Can one present requests for evidence to be admitted, provided that the witnesses in question are being held in local prisons and can be brought in within thirty minutes or an hour? Or is one limited to what was discussed in the preliminary proceedings? Which of the official public defenders are good and which would advocate on behalf of the accused? Of course that's important only if choosing one's own legal counsel isn't permitted.— What is the current definition of high treason and of defeatism? As regards the latter, what is the role of subversive intent? In both cases, what is the role of subjective elements if they are more favorable to the defendant than the objective facts? Or does the question of intentionality come into play only if the objective facts of the case aren't sufficient?—As you see, a big array of questions. You'll also see that I'm devoting serious thought to the legal side of my case, although I know full well that in the end, all this has nothing to do with jurisprudence. But especially if I'm assigned an apathetic public defender, it's important for me to know at least something about the standard procedures or the prevailing categories at the People's Court.[1]

I assume, my dear, that you will come again tomorrow. Some 75 percent of our people were taken away last night;[2] I don't know who yet, because the damage from the bombings has so far kept us from having our walk today. But I do get the feeling that they've left only about twenty men here, those who are next in line for their hearings, and that the rest were transferred to a camp. Of course I much prefer to stay here, but this does seem to indicate that things will now go quickly. Neuhaus didn't have me brought in, which doesn't necessarily mean anything, though; he might have wanted to limit his interrogation of me to clearing up some matters without asking me about issues that have any direct bearing on my case.

My love, just to make sure I always keep you up to date, in case I suddenly get called up, I wanted to tell you that I have now memorized the 32nd and the 111th Psalms, as well as the beginning of Jeremiah 3, the rest of John 14 and 1 John 19 through to the end. The last of these has really helped me, as you surely know. I'm going to keep on memorizing, because I assume that once I'm sentenced and have to wait it out, I'm unlikely to have anything with me, so I want to be as fully equipped as possible.—Incidentally, Psalm 118 (especially verses 17 and 18)[3] has been helpful to me.

Here's one more thing that might help you as you think things over, though perhaps only in a negative way, since I find that positive thoughts about immortality are not possible. Herr Kant[4] has helped me grasp with absolute certainty that all thinking in this world occurs within the concepts of time and space, and that neither of these can apply to any kind of otherworldly existence. At death, we step outside the coordinate system of time and space, so—to put it in mundane terms—we might arrive on the other side "simultaneously" even if you live another sixty years, and I would not have to wait for you in spite of it all. You can find hints of this insight in many biblical passages, for example, Psalm 90:4 and John 1:15. And in one passage Christ says [marginal note: John 8:58] that he has seen Abraham or David. This implies that a mind that can think only in terms of space and time simply cannot envision the hereafter.

So, my love, enough for today; it's the afternoon, and it is an odd feeling to see the evening approaching, an evening when the messenger may come with the indictment, and to say to oneself: Tomorrow at this time I may already be dead. People really ought to say that to themselves always, but they don't unless they're forced to, as I am now. Farewell, my love, may God watch over you and your little sons and us. J.

1. The Volksgerichtshof, often abbreviated as VGH in the original German. 2. Sixty-one of the eighty prisoners were transported back to the Lehrter Strasse Gestapo prison; they had been brought to Tegel from this prison because of damage from bombs. 3. Psalm 118:17–18: "I shall not die, but live, and declare the works of the Lord. The Lord hath chastened me sore: but he hath not given me over unto death." 4. During his imprisonment at the Ravensbrück concentration camp, Helmuth had spent a good deal of time studying Immanuel Kant's *Critique of Pure Reason*.

FREYA TO HELMUTH JAMES, OCTOBER 8–9, 1944

Kreisau, Sunday

My dear love, here I am, sitting at my desk in Kreisau, where since yesterday my eyes have been looking over so much that's very dear and familiar to you, and thought only about how glad I would be to have you see it. Yesterday was a mild, gently hued autumn day. After lunch I made the rounds with Zeumer,[1] but as I spoke to him about you and had to describe the gravity of the situation, too many tears ran for me to be able to enjoy it properly amid all that splendor of home, which belongs to you so much, and thus belongs to us. We weren't in Wierischau,[2] but we went everywhere else. We were threshing wet beet seed and digging up potatoes, but we also went out to Kreisau, where no work was going on. The sun was shining and Kreisau lay sweetly and cozily in the valley, the Great Owl mountain appeared far away and high up and the Zobten peak[3] so soft, the foliage on the shrubs beginning to change color. When we were up there, Casparchen was with us, sitting on my lap, but I could think only of you, full of love and longing, and it all hurt. At the same time I felt as though I had to soak it all up inside me, all that beauty, so that I could describe its sweet charms to you even if it causes you pain; that way you'll be able to feel how beautiful it was. Oh, my love, I will always, always see myself walking across the fields at your side. Where was my hand, where did it always want to go? How beautiful that was. But I don't want just to look toward the past; I want to love you, my love, I want to be able to keep on loving you always, even if I have to remain alone.—While I was on the train, I was unsettled by the news that Friday's air raid happened quite close to you. That must have been quite an ordeal at the very least, or wasn't it? Later I found two nice pieces of news for you in the mail. Mother Rademacher had news from Susi [Rademacher], by way of Sweden. She saw Willo [von Moltke] in the capital[4] during the summer. She says he's working in the South, and wants to stay there, and that he looked "quite well" and "seemed to be quite content with his architectural work." It's so nice to have a sign of life at long last. The other news came from Jowo [von Moltke]. It would interest you to know that Curtis had been informed about your whereabouts.[5] What might be going on inside you, my dear! How might you be doing, my beloved Jäm. I want to be near you, it's what I plead for, and indeed am.—Monday evening: I'm now at Poelchau's, at the desk I love so much. Here I have such peace and quiet for writing. Yes, what Poelchau is doing for us goes beyond any possibility to thank him adequately. I hope he senses that and finds it fulfilling. And I accept everything he offers, because I sometimes get the feeling when I'm here that I've spoken to you in person—that's how much detail he provides, and besides that, the two of them[6] surround me with love, friendship, and caring, and I'd like to sit here forever. Everything you're eating, my love, comes from Kreisau, of course, except for the rolls. I recently brought along a great many things, and did so today as well, not just for you. I let them freely dispose of them as they see fit, but everything you have gotten so far was grown in Kreisau. It comes with the Poelchaus' love as well as mine, and for the eggs, Frau Rose's too; as she said with deep feeling yesterday, "At least this way he'll get something too." And Sister Ida [Hübner] said, "Give our best regards to the count," then voiced her dismay about your situation, as you were the person they had all invariably turned to. The mood around here, my love, is unmistakable.—My love, I now have your little letter of the 6th in my hands once again, and it fills me with happiness. I got it as soon as I arrived here from the 7:30 train and was once again given such a warm welcome. Yes, I am very close to you, and that is why I find even this time to be lovely in many ways, lovelier than ever before. I'm so intensely close to you. Yes, I know quite a lot about you as well, but looking back I have no complaints that things were different before. My Jäm, I often didn't know what you were *thinking*, but I was always very close to you, much closer, I think, than you knew. I do know quite a bit about you and always did, which is why I've totally forgotten that I ever had a complaint, because thinking isn't the least bit interesting compared with the feeling of closeness that arose within me so clearly in July 1929,[7] a feeling that has continued and will endure. How wonderful it is that you like my presence here, as I do. Yesterday I felt within me all this impatience to be back here, and I'm so happy to be sitting here, close to you. On Thursday I can bring your warm suit and other things of that sort and be filled with happiness, just like you, at the thought of our closeness. If things should go badly, my love, I will certainly fight for the possibility of seeing you again, even though I don't have much hope for that either.

Tomorrow I will take up the various trails here once again and will report back to you. I spoke with Müller[8] for half an hour on Friday. He is really somebody, no doubt about it. He promised me he'd speak to you again, but there's no question that he wants to have you killed. He doesn't take you altogether seriously, and thinks you should have kept out of it, since you're a philosopher and your place is among books. He figures you're not a man of action. The trial is still ahead for you to mount your defense, he pointed out, but he would meet with you again if I'd like. They've been so loyal, he said— whereas you!!! With me he was polite, friendly in fact, and sincere to a degree, very thorough and not impatient. He was certainly not displeased with me. He came running after me and said that when everything was over, I should come by to see him again and he would give me a detailed explanation of the circumstances so I'd see that they hadn't done you an injustice!!! At one point I said that as your wife, I think very highly of you, and he replied that I should certainly hold to that view, but I mustn't resent their need to prosecute you. That's how it went. I hope it didn't ruin anything! He encouraged me to write a letter to Himmler and another to Hitler. Should I? I'll write up a draft, and tomorrow I'm also going to see Dix.

Last night I spoke with Ulla [Oldenbourg]⁹ about whether it might be possible to continue being supported by you, not losing you, yet not disturbing you on the new paths that you will be taking, far from mine. This has been preying on my mind, but in a hopeful way.

Yes, I find the little picture of Casparchen beautiful, but don't you want to hold on to it, my dear? Oh, how I hate to stop writing. I hope I'll be able to continue. It brings me so much happiness.

I feel close to you, my Jäm, in love. I plead for you in burning love and in pleading I feel very close to you. I'll write more tomorrow. I am your P.

1. Adolf Zeumer, the manager of the Kreisau estate's agricultural operations. 2. The Kreisau estate had land in the villages of Wierischau, Kreisau, and Gräditz. 3. Great Owl and Zobten are mountains in the vicinity of Kreisau. 4. Washington, D.C.: Helmuth's brother Wilhelm Viggo von Moltke had been working in the United States as an architect since 1940 and later served in the US Army. Freya here disguises the country she is referring to. 5. Lionel Curtis was close to the British government and they would have been aware of the threat to Helmuth's life. 6. Harald and Dorothee Poelchau. 7. Helmuth and Freya first met in Grundlsee, Austria, in July 1929, when she was eighteen years old; see Biographical Note. 8. Heinrich Müller, the chief of the Gestapo. 9. Freya and Helmuth were impressed by Ulla Oldenbourg's ability to provide emotional support and shape events by means of vigorous prayer. She was a follower of the Christian Science movement, which originated in America and sees the principle of the universe in God and in the spiritual realm. It teaches that devotion to the divine origin can heal or surmount diseases, sins, and death.

HELMUTH JAMES TO FREYA, OCTOBER 10, 1944

Tegel, 10 Oct 1944

My dear, yesterday the food supplies you sent arrived and were tremendously welcome, because I'd just eaten up the last bacon in the morning and I was almost out of sugar. My dear, I'm going overboard with the food, because, first of all, it's cold; second, because food adds such pleasant diversity to the day; and third, because when it's morning, I expect that I'll be dead within thirty-six hours, and when it's the evening, I put my death within twenty-four hours. These short-term extensions of life stifle all my normal urges to be thrifty. It is bound to happen soon; I'm not nervous in the least about whether it will happen.

My love, as much as I try to stop myself, my mind keeps dwelling on your future life. And maybe I can say something about it without causing any harm. The time now won't be so bad for you, the time right after my death will also be all right, but after a while, your daily routine will set in, and that will be the worst moment. But you have to go through this low point and bear the pain. Don't try to skip past this part by overloading yourself with activities or else you won't reap the fruits of your tears, and you will constrict that little place inside you where I want to go on dwelling. Pain expands that little space. My love, I was shying away from writing this to you because it smacks of possessiveness from beyond the grave and because it is a cruel piece of advice, easy for me to dispense, hard for you to follow. But in the end I thought about all the unpleasant advice I've given you in my life, so I can't now omit this bit of advice.—I found a very beautiful song in Poelchau's hymnal: no. 296, "What mean ye, to weep."

My love, I have nothing to say. Everything is good as it is. I have firm and confident trust in the Lord that He will continue to guide me and you and us in a way that is good for us. I ask that He may rescue me from this plight in this temporal realm as well, but I feel absolutely certain that nothing and no one can do me harm and that your pain—should you have to bear it—will also make its meaning and its fruits manifest.

Farewell, my dearly beloved heart; may He shelter and safeguard you and your little sons. J.

FREYA TO HELMUTH JAMES, OCTOBER 11, 1944

Wednesday

My dear, I'm just returning from my visit to you, after eating in town. I sat in the waiting room and sent all my thoughts of love up to you. I felt you thinking of me and I joined with you and was truly happy to feel that again, so fully and warmly and strongly. Then the friendly guard came with your things. The vest was still warm from you and although it didn't exactly bring a kiss, there was a bit of one there. I took it all and went on my way in the knowledge that you were going with me. My Jäm, you've written me many beautiful things since then. I am happy about so much. Before I come to the practical part, I have to talk it all out with you. I was happiest of all with what you wrote about my life without you. I'd wanted to write about that in the last letter, but didn't, for the sake of our friends' sleep.[1] Actually I'd just spoken about it with Ulla [Oldenbourg], and she told me she still has as strong, powerful, and loving a bond with her husband as ever and continues to feel supported and guided by him, and keeps feeling his nearness and his life. But it's no easy matter to retain all this truly alive in herself, to care for and watch over and continue to want that bond, and that requires time, solitude, leisure, inner balance, and serenity, and I can't allow the busyness of everyday life to atrophy our most delicate organs, the ones that allow us even now to intuit our way out of this existence. But maybe that's where you'll be, my beloved, my eternal soul mate, and if I don't want to lose you, I have to take care of these organs, overcome my penchant for pointless busyness, and struggle to preserve my contact with God. That, my love, is what I'd wanted to write to you the day before yesterday, and then yesterday your beautiful description of the pain I am feeling about you arrived, and it said exactly what I wanted to be told. Why is that a cruel piece of advice? I've known for quite a long time that the pain I will feel about you will be my most precious possession if you should be taken from me, and that is when I will pray to God to let me make the most of it, to live within it. I understand quite well what you write to me, and it makes me feel happy and validated, and

I am grateful for your words, as they show me once again that we are of one mind. (Have you given me a lot of unpleasant advice in our lives? I've been thinking about it and haven't discovered any instance of it, apart, perhaps, from your saying that I need to be prepared for you to die an early death.) But now I have to add that I am not convinced that I will be up to this task. I do see that this is where the continuation and culmination of our marriage must lie, and I picture the task before me, but I'm weak, worldly, earthbound, eager, and capable, and I spread myself thin among 1,000 things, you know all that full well, my dearest, I'll have quite a lot to do and work on, my daily routine will be immense, and in the evenings I'll wearily sink into bed. Oh, my Jäm, I certainly see that it shouldn't be this way. I'll need God's help in this, my Jäm, and you need to pray to Him on my behalf. I don't know whether you'll actually find a way to be with me, my dear; if God requires us to be separated, I will feel and discern it, but I think I shouldn't dare to draw you into my daily life. Oh, my Jäm, now we're approaching questions that we are barred from judging and understanding here on earth. I've said what I wanted to say about this. You can think it over, and you will now realize that I know the path I will be traveling. What you write about being lifted out of space and time is also quite lovely. I had never thought it through to its logical consequences, and it is comforting, very much so. Thank God that the relativity and inessentiality of time can be sensed even here on earth, and that props me up when I contemplate the fifty to sixty long years—no, of course short years—ahead of me. My Jäm, all this might be demanded of us so that we truly learn to overcome materialism, so that we recognize once again that the spirit lies within us, so that we know that we are God's children. While in the throes of tormenting thoughts, I can find this conviction enveloping me with a feeling of true happiness. Then everything within me dissolves, and I feel and know then that I have the prospect of seeing within me not my self but God's creature, and so of escaping the terrible grip of pharisaism, complacency, and ambition. Oh, that comprises everything. My Jäm, all that pertains to me, yet it also pertains to us. Still, I need to turn to other subjects in this letter so that I won't have to give our good man[2] three sheets of paper. I'm so terribly presumptuous. I take everything he offers me, and he offers me so very much. I have no choice! What good fortune that you're still here; every day I consider (and fear) that you might be taken away and we have nothing but thoughts and prayers to rely on. Taken away, that is, to a similar place, as I was told yesterday that I could come by again next Tuesday to inquire about your indictment, which would not be issued prior to that day. I don't get the impression that the man is lying to me; his way of discussing what was on the agenda for each individual day of this week strongly indicated that it was true. But I think your time will come next week. It's also unclear how things will proceed from here. Sometimes it really takes only twenty-four hours until the trial, but at times things get drawn out. It took Romai [Reichwein]'s[3] husband fourteen days. But it will be his turn this week. I went to see Dix *yesterday*, to ask what you wanted to know, but I didn't have your very concrete questions yet. So I'll go again tomorrow. I just asked general questions about the nature of the trials and about Freisler. That's what I'll tell you about first. Yes, it is a proper trial, and in Dix's view, in contrast to Poelchau's, the verdict will be decided only on the basis of the proceedings. The proceedings start with the brief formal statement of charges, then there's a *very thorough interrogation* of the accused. Dix emphasized that Freisler is an outstanding "examiner" who asks *very thorough and varied* questions. He allows the accused to speak, but he's so temperamental that he often interrupts. When that is over, the charges are brought forward, along with the oral defense, followed by the defendant's closing statement, where he can provide a comprehensive account of his case. On the subject of Freisler, Dix said he considers him the smartest man in the entire regime, a real crackerjack and a brilliant interrogator. He is said to be like a boa constrictor with its prey, crushing any defendant who isn't intellectually up to par. A trial presided over by Freisler could at times be breathtakingly fascinating. He's reputed to be quite educated and highly knowledgeable. So he's a worthy match,[4] something I hadn't known at all. I thought all he did was shout. Dix has the same basic view about him as we do, but it seems to me that one ought to be well informed about his stature. I personally still have a need to tell you not to put up with anything. If he shouts, shout back! I think it's important for you to emerge from this process standing tall. Being daring will get you further with him. I also feel that you have to defend yourself to the utmost, but you shouldn't be evasive, and you won't need to. Above all, you can't let them drag you through the mud! At the very least, these men have to realize that they are dealing with an intellectual force that they can't touch, no matter what they try. I can't tell how Dix knows that you have "excellent deportment," but he did bring it up. The SS men bring it up as well, as Peter [Yorck] is still very much on everyone's mind. You truly do have this kind of deportment, coming from deep within you, and I have no doubt that you'll have it on the day of your trial too. But I think it's important for the others to sense it. The idea that you should be subjected to all that shouting is deeply repugnant to me. That all sounds easy to say and is in fact quite difficult, but destiny can also demand something from you. You are quite a special person, so you'll manage. Whether this will or will not entail death is a different question. You can be quite bold—indeed, you have to be—for you are in God's hands.

Once more, in closing: I'm happy you know how great my pain will be when I have to go on living without you. I'm full of the most profound gratitude for the contents of these weeks. Yes, we have been given a great gift, so rich and marvelous, and it is such great fortune that we have been given it together. May God grant us the strength to keep on saying, "Thy will be done." I'm sending you a tender embrace, my beloved Jäm, because I love you through and through, and your body too, your hands, your head, your face. Haven't I often, when we were in bed together, taken a long and intensive look at your face, a long, long look, while you were reading! In these moments, I often found myself thinking about how I ought to absorb your image into me forever! With all my love, I am your P.

1. Harald and Dorothee Poelchau, whom Freya generally refers to as "the friends." 2. Harald Poelchau. 3. Rosemarie Reichwein, the wife of Kreisau Circle member Adolf Reichwein. 4. Freya uses the English word here.

HELMUTH JAMES TO HIS SONS, CASPAR AND KONRAD, OCTOBER 11, 1944

Tegel, 11 Oct 1944

Dear Caspar, dear Konrad,

Since I will probably no longer be alive in just a few days, and since I will therefore not be able to stand by you and help you in your lives, while I still have time, I want at the very least to write you a letter. I really don't know you, little Konrad, because the last time I saw you in good health, you were still a baby, and now you're already a little person.

I want to begin with the most important thing of all. Make sure always and unwaveringly to love each other and Reyali.[1] I know that it will be that way, but I have to make a point of saying it. You see, I got so much love and warmth from my mother that a person could draw on and be warmed by it his entire life. Reyali will give this to you as well. But you also have to bear in mind that I spent the second part of my life surrounded by Reyali's love and that she will now be without her husband. Never forget that, because I'm asking you to show her enough love to keep her from feeling so acutely that I'm no longer there. You two will have to love her for me as well.

I won't be able to stand by you and help you in your lives, the way I would have wished, nor can I give you any general advice, because we all have to learn and gather experience for ourselves. We are always learning, and I learned many of the things that are most important to me during the months I was in prison. This knowledge isn't something-thing I can transfer to you: See whether you wind up learning and experiencing the same things. I just want to tell you that I will die in the certainty that I will come to God through Jesus Christ and that the four of us, Reyali, the two of you, and I, will always be united in His love; no one can know how, so it's impossible to inquire into it either. I'm not saying this to make you believe it: One can't just be told these things by someone else, you either know it or you don't; knowing it is a gift of grace. I'm telling you this so that you know at least one important part of me, and above all, so that you have respect for this faith, even if you don't share it. You have to respect every faith held by your fellow man, for that is the most important point in every person.

I want to tell you one more thing: You'll surely learn on your own where my father came from. But it's not as self-evident that you will know what kind of mother I had, and what kind of people her parents were. Still, it's something you should know, because it is a great part of your inheritance, maybe even greater than that of your father. Take in everything you learn about them, and see to it that you also visit the land of your grandmother at some point.[2] To me it's like a second home.

The issue that will result in my being killed will go down in history, and no one knows in what form. But I want to say the following to you: Throughout my life, even back in school, I have always fought against a spirit of narrow-mindedness and violence, of arrogance and lack of respect for others, of intolerance and an absolute and merciless stringency, which is inherent in the Germans and has found expression in the National Socialist state. I have also done what I could to see to it that this spirit and its terrible consequences, such as an excess of nationalism, racial persecution, lack of faith, and materialism, could be overcome. In this sense, then, my being put to death is justifiable from the National Socialist standpoint. But I never wanted or encouraged acts of violence like those of July 20th; quite the contrary. I fought the preparations being made for them, because I disapproved of such measures for many reasons and above all because I believed that this was not the way to eliminate the fundamental spiritual evil. In that sense my being put to death is unjustifiable. No one can say today how all this will look from a later perspective, nor can we tell whether my part in these events will be recognizable as something special. But you should simply know that I must not be lumped together with the men associated with the July 20th plot.

My dear little sons, whom I will never see again with these eyes, I can only pray that you thrive, bringing happiness to yourselves and to Reyali, and that the Lord may bless and protect you. I hope that you will grow up in accordance with your baptismal verses.

Caspar: "I will bless thee and thou shalt be a blessing."[3]

Konrad: "Watch ye, stand fast in the faith, quit you like men, be strong."

And that each of you will fulfill his part of the other's baptismal verse.

Yours from the bottom of my heart,
Helmuth

1. The children called their mother "Reyali," a diminutive of "Reia," short for Freya. 2. South Africa. After the war, Freya moved to Cape Town with the boys for nine years. 3. See Helmuth's second letter of November 1, 1944, note 3.

HELMUTH JAMES TO FREYA, OCTOBER 12, 1944

Tegel, 12 Oct 1944

My dear, yesterday was a day of intense ordeals. I hope that is behind me now; in any case, I got up in good spirits after a very bad night and felt safe and comforted once more. But I very much hope for a chance to unburden myself a bit today so I can be sure to make a clean sweep of things. The saddest part was that all this put a damper on my pleasure from your visit downstairs, but the visit was still an uplifting ray of sunshine.

Now to the main issue. I have the feeling that haste is called for, so I hope you've sent the letter to Himmler (not Hitler). But the meeting that Müller wants to grant me is equally important. The only chance I have—tiny as it is—lies in the interplay of these factors.

I would go to see Müller as soon as possible after the verdict and apart from getting a briefing, try above all to come away with a reasonable arrangement for yourself, as you're sure to have a much harder time of it than Marion [Yorck] if you're ostracized.—I enclose a letter to our sons. I'll leave it to you to decide whether you want to give it to them sometime later on.

My dear love, today I am back to feeling warm and safe with Him and with you. Yesterday I did not feel that way. I don't know how this change is possible, but looking up from that hell, I see what a heaven I live in, and once again I am full of gratitude. But at the worst moment yesterday, this thought started running through my head: "All right then, let's get to it! I'll be that much steadier when this is behind me." Let's hope that's right. It also made me realize that somewhere there was a shore to be reached. There will be only another two or three hours in my life when I have to be absolutely certain, and if I get these ordeals behind me, it will be better than beginning to entertain doubts during that time. My love, pray for me during those hours. I'm not afraid, but the human heart is weak.

Another thing: You need to tell everyone that I carry them with me in my heart. You know that. They've all become extras beside the three of you, not because I care for them less but because I care for all of you more. How nice that you had such nice days in Kreisau. Sometimes I get wistful when I think about that, but mostly I'm just happy and grateful to guard these images inside me.—The news from Willo [von Moltke] made me happy. He will likely find his way back into the family fold as well.

My dear, dear love, what a rich life lies behind us, what a rich life lies ahead for you. I can only hope and believe that you will be able to summon enough strength from our fifteen years and from these weeks to begin this third chapter of your life without breach, that you will have an ample reserve of strength. May the Lord give you the fortitude you need.

I'm always writing as though I were already dead. Since yesterday I've had the feeling that my case is imminent, although I had that same feeling several times in Ravensbrück as well. But in any case we have to concentrate all our energy on my meeting with Müller. That's what we have to pray for at this point, my love.

May God watch over you, my love.

J.

HELMUTH JAMES TO FREYA, OCTOBER 12, 1944
[ADDENDUM TO FREYA'S LETTER OF OCTOBER 11, 1944]

Last night I suddenly had a nasty sore throat and cured it in twenty minutes with your honey.

My dear, I've gotten through yesterday's suffering, I'm just still exhausted from it. At the trial, I'll do everything in my power, but Müller is even more important. Most important of all to me is to hear how Dix evaluates my arguments regarding an obligation to inform the authorities: what the police knew and how Freisler incorporates new facts that haven't been touched on in the preliminary proceedings, whether he permits them or seeks to dismiss them out of hand.

Your letter is beautiful, my love, do save your letters from this time too, for you will find many things in them that time will seek to wrest from you.

Psalm 139.[1] My thanks to Poelchau! Yours always. J.

1. About the omnipresence of God: "O Lord, thou hast searched me, and known me..."

FREYA TO HELMUTH JAMES, OCTOBER 12, 1944

Thursday

My dear, whenever I look up at the night sky now, I almost always discover our friendly little dolphin constellation up there.[1] It lit up the beginning of our love so beautifully! My Jäm, what was tormenting you so terribly, my poor one, I still find traces of it in your letter, my love. Wasn't Poelchau able to help you? Maybe he did help you. Even so, one is always utterly alone in a hell of that kind. My poor one. Must this suffering add to your other troubles!? Yesterday I wrote only of your death and today I thought constantly about your life. The whole day! But if I think about your life and nurture my hopes, I can't help to prepare our hearts for death. One day is this way and the next day is that. Oh, how hard it is to live our fate as it should be lived, and it has to be lived fully, my beloved Jäm. So it goes, back and forth, but so far I—who still have it so much easier—have succeeded, again and again, in dissolving all my fear and worries, all the back-and-forths, into a readiness to embrace what God sends our way. My Jäm, may God send you His sturdy and consoling strength and help. He will surely do this, my dear, and after the hells you've been through, you will feel it far more strongly. I also wanted to tell you that countless people are keeping you in their thoughts, with love, love, love, and friendship. That surely strengthens us without our being aware of it. Ulla [Oldenbourg] goes to great pains to help you, constantly. And so do all the others. They will stand by me as well if you have to leave me. But this I know: I have to be and stay alone in order to keep you. I know this full well. I know my way.— Marion [Yorck] wants you to know: Peter [Yorck] disapproved of what you disapprove of, just like you. He was drawn in.[2] She wants you to be certain of that.

Now I need to write you the passages of the book of Wisdom 3:1–6: "But the souls of the righteous are in the hand of God, and there shall no torment touch them. In the sight of the unwise they seemed to die: and their departure is taken for misery, And their going from us to be utter destruction: but they are in peace. For though they be punished in the sight of men, yet is their hope full of immortality. And have been a little chastised, they shall be greatly rewarded: for God proved them, and found them worthy for himself. As gold in the furnace he tried them, and received them as a burnt offering." And then there's Wisdom 4:7–14: "But though the righteous be prevented with death, yet shall he be in rest." I love you so much, my Jäm, you know that. I am, and will remain, your P.

1. A small summer constellation in the Milky Way. 2. That is, into Stauffenberg's plans, which led to the attempt on Hitler's life on July 20, 1944.

HELMUTH JAMES TO FREYA, OCTOBER 13, 1944

Tegel, 13 Oct 44

Yes, my love, it is hard to hold on to pain in the right way, so that it remains but doesn't become a fetish. It's like the task of keeping a fire at a constantly moderate flame. I'm familiar with it only from Mami's death. This pain has never left me, as you may have noticed in my chronicle of my childhood for the little sons.[1] Granny and Carl Bernd [von Moltke][2] are still too close to me; I can't pass any judgments there.

Poelchau has called my attention to a very beautiful stanza (4) from Hartmann's hymn[3] "Now the Crucible Is Breaking":

> Sorrows gather home the senses,
> Lest, seduced by earth's pretenses,
> They should after idols stroll,
> Like an angel-guard, repelling
> Evil from the inmost dwelling,
> Bringing order to the soul.[4]

J.

1. In a letter he had written to his sons after his initial incarceration in early 1944: see Günter Brakelmann, *Helmuth James von Moltke: Eine Biographie* (Munich: C. H. Beck Verlag, 2007), 365. 2. Helmuth's brother Carl Bernhard had been killed in action on December 30, 1941. 3. Karl Friedrich Hartmann (1743–1815), a pastor and hymnodist from Württemberg; "Now the Crucible Is Breaking" is generally regarded as the "song of suffering." 4. This translation is from *The Breaking Crucible: And Other Translations of German Hymns*, translated by James W. Alexander (South Yarra, Australia: Leopold Classic Library, 2015), 4.

FREYA TO HELMUTH JAMES, OCTOBER 13, 1944

Friday evening

My dearest. It is so comforting to know that you are thinking over my path in life and seeing it before you. But, my Jäm, I continue to hope, and consider your rescue possible, even though the paths that our love and our life and our union have taken in these weeks, paths along which God has made them travel, prepare us well for our parting. Still, we have to fight, and how I want to!

My dear, do you realize that I spend practically every evening at the friends' house, sitting, writing, talking, and feeling very much at home and with you. Often I don't leave until 10:30, though sometimes a bit earlier, but I'm reluctant to go. They are so naturally full of affection and friendship to me. They are so good to me.

Another thing: Your letter to our sons is quite beautiful. I will try to take good care of it, because they absolutely must get it. For the time being I'll love it all by myself. It says everything it needs to say. May God make them into people who will understand it! I know that in them another era is growing up, yet even so, reverence is truly the crux of all upbringing and must remain so if human beings are to remain human.

It's 10. Time to be considerate. Good night, my dear love. May you sleep in peace, without any bites or sore throat. My love is great and fulfills me completely. I am and will remain your P.

HELMUTH JAMES TO FREYA, OCTOBER 14, 1944

Tegel, 14 Oct 44

My dear, did you see that in the evening I added something at the end of your next-to-last letter, probably the one on the 11th, including my comment that I am now past everything? Don't be worried; with His help, I will cope with it if it should come back.

I've thought of a new argument for Steengracht; maybe you can talk to him again. I wonder whether he'll use it now, though he really would have to. This is what you can tell him: that for years before the war, I was treated by the *Round Table* circle[1] and by Milner's Kindergarten[2] as a kind of Continental European member, and whenever I was over there in England, there would always be meetings between these men and me; as far as you knew, the subject of these meetings, in which senior officials from the Colonial Office sometimes took part, was how Continental Europe, and Germany in particular, could be enabled to contribute in some manner to the Empire and Commonwealth, above all to its African colonies. The whole thing was planned for the long term, less as an issue of the day than as a planning task. The aim, as you understood it, was to create an outlet for Germany's overabundance of spirit and drive to get things accomplished, not just a commercial outlet but also an administrative and, *à la longue*, a political one, to provide the Empire and its dominions with a contribution of Europeans ample enough to make it possible for them to resist the pressure coming from the Americans and colored peoples.[3] As far as you knew, this was the basis, and you should say that the reason you didn't speak of it was that you were sure I didn't want that; given the current situation, and especially after your conversations with Müller, you decided to volunteer this information. Tell them I was quite certain *a.* that no other Continental European had enjoyed a similar level of trust in these issues, and *b.* that this trust had not been affected by the war. Say that I owed this special status not to myself but to my mother, who, you might say, was the only sister in Milner's Kindergarten, and I was accepted as her son, or was adopted. This status is therefore also attached to my person. You'll ask them to consider whether these facts might warrant *a.* having me interrogated on this complex of issues by a specialist in foreign policy, and *b.* even in the event of a death sentence, keeping me alive, simply not carrying out the sentence right away and deliberating, once things are calmer, whether I might be put to better use than being hanged. Add that as a matter of fact, a legally valid death sentence, even if not carried out, would be quite a formidable punishment for me and would affect me most directly, whereas a death sentence that was carried out immediately under these particular circumstances might affect all of Germany. You could also hint that this matter could be of interest to the Foreign Security Service. Recently I was interrogated about *The Round Table* without any advance notice, although only cursorily and only about names. This story is by and large correct. The problem is that there were also postwar plans, but I'll have to deal with this problem if I'm questioned about it; it needn't affect you.

But it strikes me as important to give Steengracht departmental jurisdiction and to find an argument for my uniqueness, and I think this story has both. He needs to start by asking that if at all possible a Foreign Office official be present when I am questioned about these matters and that the results of this questioning be made available to him, and that I not be executed until he has assessed the situation. You just need to make it clear that these were nothing but unilateral British measures, not negotiations, and that I acted as an adviser to the British, not as a spokesman for Germans. Tell them you were informed only about the basic outlines and knew next to nothing about these matters. Think about whether this might work; maybe you should talk it over with Dieter [von Mirbach],[4] whom Steengracht can consult; he could handle things in a purely businesslike manner.

My love, everything you write about your future is very clear to me. It is a daunting task, my love, but I think you'll be up to it. And another thing: Because we have been in close contact, some things will be more difficult for you than if, say, you had been locked up and unable to do anything.[5] It could easily happen that subsequent information makes you think everything could have gone differently if only... Don't allow room for such thoughts; they are wrong and could be a terrible burden on you. Whatever He sends our way is right, and it is not ours to decide whether He chooses this or that path. Don't agonize over this, but if you do find yourself agonizing, go straight to Poelchau and get his help.—To some extent, you will be maintaining the spiritual legacy of those of us who die. Try to make it fruitful, and don't be too modest about it; you owe that to everyone. As for who should help you with this: That depends on who survives; I do ask, though, that if at all possible you bring in the people who, I hope, have now become Jowo [von Moltke]'s friends;[6] keep Konrad [von Preysing][7] in mind as well. I've already told Poelchau that if it's feasible, I think it would also be right to hold a memorial service if you and Kreisau still exist.

My dear love, what a time this is! What fruit will it bear? Will we have gained something that will make it easier for those who come after us, our own little sons above all, to gain insight, to plumb new depths and scale new heights? Or is each and every individual such an autonomous idea of God's that he does, suffers, accomplishes, sows, reaps everything solely for himself? It is a matter of indifference, of course, yet this question does weigh on my mind. But one thing will remain for the little sons: You will carry these weeks within you, as a wellspring and as a host of angels watching over you, as something you can draw on, and the little sons are sure to sense and experience this

[The letter breaks off here.]

1. Refers to *The Round Table: A Quarterly Review of the Politics of the British Empire*, co-founded in 1910 by Lionel Curtis. 2. A group of young people who had studied in Oxford and worked in South Africa under Governor Lord Alfred Milner after the Boer War ended in 1902. Curtis belonged to this group as well. 3. This line of thinking shows how, in his attempts to find a defense strategy with any hope of success before the People's Court, Helmuth tried occasionally to think in terms of the fascist ideology by which he would be judged. In this case, thinking out loud for Freya's benefit, he strategically adopts a colonialist position, ostensibly in line with Germany's own expansionist policies at the time. On the other hand, the supposition that Germany would have cooperated with the British Empire through some kind of "contribution" to its colonial enterprise would have been anathema to Nazi policy, particularly at this late stage of the war. 4. Dietrich von Mirbach, a relative who worked under Steengracht in the Foreign Office. 5. Many of the wives wound up being held in *Sippenhaft*, a kind of guilt by family association, in Moabit prison in Berlin. 6. People in the Norwegian resistance who were affiliated with the Protestant church. Joachim Wolfgang von Moltke had been transferred to the armed forces staff in Oslo by the arrangement of Helmuth. 7. Count Konrad von Preysing, the Catholic bishop of Berlin.

HELMUTH JAMES TO FREYA, OCTOBER 17, 1944

Tegel, 17 Oct 44

My dear, tomorrow is the 18th,[1] and I'll probably live to see it, come what may. My dear love, what a happy day for us, a happiness, a grace that nothing can destroy. I know for certain that it will remain with me, for if the Lord should call me away, it will be one of the few treasures I'll be able to take with me. When we must part, may this grace remain with you as well, seeing as how all this will be far more difficult for you.—The day after tomorrow, my dear, will mark nine months of my imprisonment, and that means you will have carried your worries and fear for me as long as you carried your little sons. If I must die, then I hope that through these nine months I'll be reborn to you and can stay with you as your exclusive possession—on this earth—that no one else can claim. During this time, you've had to endure far more than I have, my love, and you have surely earned having your third son given to you.—My love, there's one more thing that I want to say to you: You have accomplished something truly great in the years since 1933: You have always been prepared to sacrifice your husband. Never have you stood in his way out of concern for yourself, never have you flinched when something unpleasant needed to be done. No one will ever thank you for this, but you should know that through all these years, it has filled your husband with pride and joy. In this you stand totally alone among all the women involved, because all the others spent many years on the sunny side of politics.[2]—Recently it has all been coming back to me powerfully, every time I've thought about the many things for which I owe you my gratitude, how very much you have done and had to bear without knowing it. I know that it has ultimately enriched you as well, that you have also been sustained by the fact that the two of us have never wavered in our stance, that we never experienced any rupture.[3] Still, it is nevertheless a real achievement on your part, one that is sure to have bolstered your strength to meet the challenges now facing you.

My dear, on Saturday I was given an arrest warrant,[4] which indicates that I will be going on trial along with Haubach, Steltzer, Gerstenmaier, Reisert, Sperr, and Fugger. I'm no. 1, and so it follows that this is an attack against Kreisau.[5] The addition of the three Bavarians,[6] whom I barely know, in connection with the fact that there are explicit statements to the effect that we were planning a violent overthrow, if need be with an act of violence against the

Führer, makes me assume that the Gestapo has something specific from the Bavarian side. I don't know what, but given the impossible conditions for mounting a defense before the People's Court, even errors and mix-ups will be difficult to refute. At any rate, it seems clear that I am to be convicted because of Kreisau, not because of Goerdeler. Don't let this message weigh down your efforts, for ultimately I have to act on the assumption that I will be able to refute this allegation, which goes way too far.

My love, I cannot imagine that I'll have any more opportunities to write to you, so I'm sending back your birthday letter and Casparchen's first letter. I don't want the executioners to ridicule them. Maybe they wouldn't, but I don't want to give them the chance.

So until we meet again, my dearest love, my Pim, my tender, friendly, dearest wife. Until we meet again, here or there. Let us pray to the Lord that He may save me by a miracle, let us believe that He wants this and therefore can make it come about, but let us bow to His will if He has decided otherwise, and let us hold to our conviction that He has decided this for the sake of our salvation, even if we don't understand. I'll be leaving you in severe distress on the exterior, my love, but, I believe, with great inner strength and freedom. And so I needn't worry about you and the little sons. He will watch over all of you and hold his hand over you. My love, I need to remind you once again that this verse unites us: "For whether we live, we live unto the Lord, and whether we die, we die unto the Lord: whether we live therefore, or die, we are the Lord's."[7]

J.

1. Their thirteenth wedding anniversary. 2. This is an exaggeration. Many of their friends stood in opposition to National Socialism from the outset, just like Helmuth and Freya, though some had cooperated with the regime in earlier years. 3. Freya and Helmuth had opposed the Nazis from the beginning; see the Editors' Introduction. 4. See Appendix: Additional Documents. 5. Kreisau used here to mean the opposition meetings held there in 1942 and 1943. 6. Franz Reisert, Franz Sperr, and Joseph-Ernst Fürst Fugger von Glött, who were part of a Catholic Bavarian resistance group. 7. Romans 14:8.

HELMUTH JAMES TO HIS SONS, CASPAR AND KONRAD, OCTOBER 17, 1944

Tegel, 17 Oct 44

Dear Caspar, dear Konrad,

I have one more thing I need to say to you, because no else can tell you this. Ever since National Socialism came to power I have tried to ease things for its victims and to pave the way for change. My conscience drove me to do this, and this is, after all, a duty for a man. This is why I've had to make material sacrifices and expose myself to personal dangers from 1933 onward. Throughout all these years, Freya has never tried to hold me back or even pressure me not to do what I thought was necessary, even though she was the one who suffered the most from the material sacrifices and has had to live with the constant worry that I might be arrested, locked up, or killed. She has taken everything upon herself willingly; she has always been prepared to sacrifice me if necessary. And I'm telling you that this is far more than I have done. Even running known risks is nothing compared with a willingness to let the person to whose life you have bound your own run risks that cannot be foreseen. And it is also far more than what a soldier's wife takes upon herself, because she, of course, has no choice in the matter; but I did have a choice, and one word from Freya would have held me back from much of what I undertook.

So, my dears, I want you to know what a brave mother you have. Love her, love one another, and may you thrive in body, heart, and soul.

Your Helmuth

FREYA TO HELMUTH JAMES, OCTOBER 17–18, 1944

Tuesday afternoon

My Jäm, it's not so urgent after all. This morning I was expecting it[1] and was distressed when I received the two old letters with your nice new one, but as it turns out, we still have some time after all, and the arrest warrant seems to be a mere formality. I've known since last week, and said as much, that you are on a list with these others and in that order. There was a folder on Schulze's desk,[2] where I was able to study all of you. On the bottom it said "high treason and betrayal." I don't know whether we can necessarily draw the conclusions that you're drawing from this. In any case, Schulze said today that the agenda indicates that your trial could not take place before November;[3] every slot is taken for this week, and from the end of the week until November 3, the court would not be convening.

You wrote a lovely letter to me, my dearest; and it didn't give me any delusions of grandeur, although you regard my accomplishment as greater than it is. I achieve my true accomplishments unwittingly, and that is how I recognize the extent to which I belong not to myself but to God. (You wrote your letter this morning, this morning, just now, you thought about and wrote this. That's how close we are, my husband!) The idea of the third son is also lovely, even though the sons don't belong to us, yet we likely do belong to each other. But maybe I can carry you within me, somewhat longer at any rate, my love. I always want to carry you within me and never give birth to you, my love, and I can do that too. In these nine months, I've sometimes been so worried and anxious about you, though not always. Occasionally things have been calm for long periods of time, and I've been carefree, even though I was never free, but don't overestimate that. Yes, I've always found that I would have to be prepared to sacrifice you, because a human life doesn't acquire its true value until one is prepared to stake that life on something. Only in the past ten years have we learned that. I have always understood your putting your life on the line. That's the way it has to be, and the consequences must also be accepted. Maybe we have to do this. But the other women see it the same way; Marion [Yorck], in any case, is just as aware of this.

I agreed with and approved of everything else you wrote. You could have held on to the letters. I'll write you a new, more encoded one, and give you back the one from Casparchen. I don't think the executioners will be ridiculing them. Why should they be stored away? They're yours, not mine, and they should be with you, but I can also understand your wanting to die free of things, then you can tear them up in the end.

Wednesday afternoon: You see, the letter stayed where it was, and meanwhile a day went by that was happy for me. I visited you,[3] I thought of you. You were with me, warm and sheltered in me; I wasn't alone at all. I was doing well. My love! I'm sending you a tender embrace. P.

1. The imminent trial. 2. Kurt Schulze, the prosecutor assigned to Helmuth's case. 3. Freya was in the prison to exchange Helmuth's clothing, but she did not see him.

FREYA TO HELMUTH JAMES, OCTOBER 19, 1944

Thursday afternoon
My dear love, I just read your letters again and enjoyed them. I left most of them in Kreisau, but now I have new ones again. Do you sometimes think of Peter [Yorck]? Is he on your mind? Is he one of the people making your departure easier? How do you feel about him? That interests me. I'm so fond of him and am also quite attached to the women in his life.[1] I really love him, the way I love my brothers and yours, and he was very close to me in the past few months with his unceasing helpfulness and friendship. He really loved you!—I'm reading various passages in the New Testament, mostly the passages on your note; I read those again and again.[2] I stand before these inexhaustible sources of help and comfort with amazement and delight and gratitude, and still have everything ahead of me. Muto was telling me about one passage, and I must pass it along to you. Do you know it? 2 Cor. 6:3–10.[3] It's beautiful, isn't it. But you can't get so caught up in Paul that you forget the Gospels. Yesterday I read the Sermon on the Mount, but it has to be read again and again and again. It takes a while to unearth its treasures. I'm also reading and

rereading Psalm 139. I like it so much. I read it and think about you and hope that it will always help you when your peace of mind is threatened. I am so sure, my love, that God will not abandon you.

Hans [Deichmann][4] is about to call, he wants to come by and get me, and we'll eat sandwiches here. I'll have to stop when he calls, make tea, and pick him up at the commuter train. I wonder what happened the other day when you were gone! Will I hear about it tonight? When I'm cradled in my joy, I often get frightened and wonder what I'll find when I've gone up the stairs and pressed the button. How nice it is that Hans hasn't called yet. It's so nice to write along with you. I see my beloved head and my beloved hands in front of me. I kiss them and love them and am with you with all my feelings and thoughts. May God watch over you, my beloved husband. I am and will remain your P.

1. Marion Yorck and her sister-in-law, Irene Yorck, known as Muto, both of whom participated in the Kreisau Circle discussions. 2. See Helmuth's letter of September 30, 1944. 3. 2 Corinthians 6:9–10: "as unknown, and yet well known; as dying, and, behold, we live; as chastened, and not killed; As sorrowful, yet always rejoicing; as poor, yet making many rich; as having nothing, and yet possessing all things." 4. Freya's brother, Hans Deichmann.

HELMUTH JAMES TO FREYA, OCTOBER 19, 1944

Berlin, 19 Oct 44

The things you brought yesterday were delightful. But don't take any more chocolate away from your little sons for the sake of your gluttonous husband.

On the 17th I spent about forty-five minutes with Müller.[1] He was very friendly in his comportment and well briefed, and he had a very good though not entirely fair opinion of me. The essence was: "You are an opponent of National Socialism. At the very least, you have shielded traitors by not providing evidence, and you lied to us, not formally but in substance; even if I take a very lenient view of your own part in this, you have permitted, or weren't able to prevent getting caught up in, the net of the sly old foxes[2] and thus did their bidding."—He also assured me that he had no reason to sling mud at me, and this is why he told you that you could raise the little sons to have respect for their father. So the overall thrust of the discussion revolved around imminent killing, which was only to be expected. At two points, however, there were hints that the verdict wasn't set in stone yet. I've forgotten the first one. The second one came at the end, as we were saying goodbye, when he remarked, "Perhaps we can discuss this issue after the verdict, but for now you need to head to the People's Court." This may have been meant to guard against suicidal tendencies. That is possible. Still, maybe there is something to it. If I consider this comment along with another one, "The anger about your conduct has dissipated, but we have to act according to sober political considerations, and they necessitate your conviction for high treason," it seems to me that there's a very small window of opportunity, but one that requires two things: *1.* that the trial goes reasonably well and that from their point of view the impression they have of me isn't utterly catastrophic, and *2.* that there is a straightforward political interest in sparing me for now. The first assumes that Freisler is dealt with, and the second, that Steengracht comes through. I would strongly urge that dealing with Freisler is mainly entrusted to Carl Viggo [von Moltke]. He's better in this case. The only way forward I see is for them to want me to be kept alive for a future purpose; a petition for clemency necessarily leads to carrying out the sentence. The arguments—he surely didn't want it, he got entangled in all this against his own will—can only serve to bring the trial to a tolerable end, one that you might give a grade of D+, so to speak, with this "plus" making it possible to justify a deferral by citing the interests of the state. I didn't get the impression that Müller despised me or has his mind set 100 percent. My dear, the whole thing is quite complicated, just like everything your husband does, and I hope that as you ponder it, it will get somewhat simpler.

Goodbye, my love, may the Lord watch over you. J.

1. It must be emphasized how extraordinary it would have been for the chief of the Gestapo to meet with a prisoner destined for execution before the trial. 2. Members of the Goerdeler and Beck group; see Editors' Introduction.

HELMUTH JAMES TO FREYA, OCTOBER 20, 1944

Tegel, 20 Oct 44

My dear, hold on to the letter from Casparchen. It is such a lovely letter, I carry it in my heart, and maybe it will bring you and him joy later on. It was hanging on the closet of my cell[1] all these months and was the most colorful thing in the cell. It caught my eye a hundred times a day, and reminded me of the golden heart that, God willing, is blossoming under your care. I can't put the letter on the wall here; it's just lying in my folder, and I'm worried it'll get lost.

I have a need to use these days to the fullest, to spend every hour working on us and on making ourselves ready. But after the strain of the past three weeks things eased up when the announcement came that there is time until November 3, and it's no longer going at full blast. The result is that I'm interested in all kinds of things that had already disappeared from view, such as the fields in Kreisau, the development of your fruit trees, the plantings in the wooded areas between the fields, and so on. I'm quite amused at myself. But now, when I wake up at night, I suddenly think of the blooming fruit trees in the garden; only five or six days ago, I always turned to passages from the Bible or hymnal verses at times like these. Just goes to show how weak the flesh is under normal circumstances. I'm sending you a few hymnal verses that have delighted me. And I embrace you, my love; may the Lord watch over us. J.

1. In the Ravensbrück concentration camp. The letter survived and was donated to the Ravensbrück prison museum.

FREYA TO HELMUTH JAMES, OCTOBER 20, 1944

Friday evening

My dear, I'm already at the friends' house, my dear love. I wanted to get your little letter first. I understand so well what you write: my experience resembles yours. This respite has also made my gaze turn toward us having a life together once again, and the fact and the outcome of the Müller conversation reinforced that tendency in me even more, but today was Reichwein's trial,[1] and even though I have yet to learn the outcome, it was definitely decided by 12, when I spoke with the attorney in the superior court to give him something from Romai [Reichwein]. Romai has Reichwein's two best friends with her, so she's not alone. But today the whole thing kept me from feeling any false optimism. My Jäm, I certainly understand the approaches you've written me about. I will speak to Carl Viggo [von Moltke] again and deal with Steengracht next week. He can be told quite a bit, because he'd like to help and is very distressed about this matter. He's quite serious about it. Last night I spent some time feeling proud that

Harald and Dorothee Poelchau, 1927; Freya wrote and received letters at the Poelchaus' apartment in Berlin

you really got to Müller, and that clouded my vision and made everything seem too rosy.—My Jäm, it seems that Hans [Deichmann] will
even come with me and go from Kreisau to Upper Silesia on Sunday
at noon. That is lovely and delightful. As you can imagine, he asked
me to send you greetings from him. My Jäm, when should I celebrate
Casparchen's birthday,[2] next Sunday? It has to be planned lovingly,
since he's already looking forward to it so much and wants to invite
a good many children. Then I want to know if I may, or should, move
into your room if you have to leave me. That is a childish and perhaps
pointless question, but it does me good to discuss it with you. Otherwise Casparchen needs to move in, if you'd rather I stay in Mami's
room. I don't really know what I want. I'd like to live near you.

My Jäm, my love, the friends have to go to bed again. But it's so
enchanting to answer such a fresh little letter. I am and will remain
yours. P.

1. The trial of their friend Adolf Reichwein at the People's Court. He was
executed the same day. 2. Caspar's birthday was November 2, which fell on a
Thursday that year.

HELMUTH JAMES TO FREYA, OCTOBER 21, 1944

21 Oct 44

How do I feel about Peter [Yorck]?[1] Somewhat ashamed, because I
feel as though I love him less than he does me. I had great regard for
him, I was close friends with him, he was as dear to me as my brothers and your brothers, yet I've always felt that we're not on an entirely
equal footing, that he has given me more than he received from me,
that he has been more generous to me than I was to him. That has
always weighed me down a bit. If you see what I mean.—During the
period after July 20th, his participation also created a distance between
him and me. I was unhappy about it right from the first day, but I
wasn't able to do anything about it. Here in Tegel it has finally become
better and I am probably past that altogether. The criticism of him

that I feel regarding this situation—I've been told that he wanted to become Goerdeler's undersecretary—is still there, because to me it's incomprehensible how he could bring himself to do it, but this criticism is aimed lower and doesn't strain my relationship with him any more than if I sometimes don't agree with what you do.

No, oddly enough, I'm not focusing at all on those I hope to meet "over there." During the past eight days I have developed an oddly strong will to live. I suddenly have the feeling that I'm not finished here, that I have something left to do. Everything is different from when I came here. I'm not concentrating on externals here; instead, I try to polish myself on the inside. That has no effect whatever on my readiness to be done away with, but if I said "a beautiful life is coming to an end" two weeks ago, I'm now saying, more than anything, "a life whose mission was not completely fulfilled is coming to an end." Odd, isn't it? It's not a strain on me at all, and it shouldn't put a strain on you either, because we aren't the ones to decide whether it was or wasn't fulfilled. I just get the feeling that someone within me is saying: You haven't achieved fulfillment yet. Well, we'll wait and see.

Now to Carl Viggo [von Moltke]. He must, of course, insist to Freisler that it could never have been my intention to use force, because I am generally against violence. He needs to stress that. He can also put it like this: There is certainly a lack of criminal intent on my part, even though this is difficult for me to prove as a consequence of some unfortunate entanglements. So he has to aim primarily for a prison sentence as a maximum.—He can also say that I was interested in conflicts of ideas, not in power struggles. Maybe also this: I always stayed out of politics. I always withdrew from things I was interested in, such as work camps,[2] sheltering people in the village, etc., as soon as they hit the choppy waters of politics. If in this case I evidently didn't pay enough attention to the boundary between intellectual principles and politics, it must be acknowledged that I was actually incarcerated during the pivotal half year, yet evidently my friends did not get caught up in politics until that time.

I would celebrate little Casparchen's birthday on the 29th. The following Sunday is too risky.—As for the question of whether Casparchen or you ought to sleep in my spot, my love: This is one of those questions about which a dead man can't venture an opinion. You should do whatever your heart tells you.

What you tell me about Steengracht makes me very happy. I'd actually expected it.—Maybe you could cautiously broach the question of who will actually be going to the trial, and point out that Müller's underlings clearly hated me, so a fair judgment could hardly be expected from them. Maybe Kaltenbrunner[3] has an adjutant whom Steengracht knows and can send, maybe even someone who could be persuaded to oppose Müller's people, at least to some extent. In any case, this point is quite important, because if Lange, etc., see that someone else is there, they will report more objectively. In any case ask Steengracht to make the significance of this question quite clear. A man who is working directly under Kaltenbrunner is, however, more important than one from my office.[4]—Also, Steengracht could think over whether and how he might involve Bürkner. Most likely Bürkner is largely dependent on him for news, and I wouldn't discount the possibility that he does something under pressure from Steengracht and offers a positive assessment at least of my work. That, in turn, can make matters easier for Steengracht and Kaltenbrunner.

How feeble all these machinations are! Ultimately it's just futile. We have to bear that in mind throughout. Only an act of God can help here. But we have to spin these thin strands of spiderwebs, none of which does any good.

---

1. See Freya's letter of October 19, 1944. 2. See Biographical Note. 3. Ernst Kaltenbrunner, the head of the Reich Main Security Office and the Gestapo. 4. Helmuth was thinking of officials from his former office at the Armed Forces High Command, of which Leopold Bürkner was the head.

HELMUTH JAMES TO FREYA, OCTOBER 24, 1944

Tegel, 24 Oct 44

My dear, Müller told me I could submit a written defense. He said he would pass it on to the People's Court. I didn't want to do that at first, but I've now started working on it after all.

My love, I hope you arrived safe and sound, in time for breakfast, as it must be just about 8 o'clock there. I hope everything was all right at home, the little sons healthy and everybody loving. Tell me, did you get to extract the honey a second time? And how much honey did you harvest this year altogether? Whereas the dead were once given honey as food for the journey, I can make do with knowing about your harvest.

I'm doing disconcertingly well. Somehow I'm not happy about that, and I wish I were in a slightly more subdued mood. But you can't force the issue, and so I have to leave it to Him to know what this burst of good cheer might signify. When I think it over with my limited mortal power of understanding, I tell myself: This is bound to bring on a new low, and I'd really dislike that during the trial; I am well aware that these are very self-absorbed thoughts.—It's odd, though, how you can get used to violent death around you. I've been experiencing that for more than 9 months now, because people were constantly being murdered, sometimes quite summarily. At first it sickened me each time someone made his exit, but I started to take it quite calmly, and the news about Reichwein saddened me but didn't upset me in the least. I hope that doesn't mean I'm getting habituated, but rather that I'm gaining insight, though I don't know, and it might be both. Only when my time has come, and the habituating factor is thus eliminated, will I know whether it was or wasn't a matter of insight. For so many insights, there is a physical and a spiritual interpretation. The physical one is front and center, and should not be disparaged; but I'm striving for the spiritual one, and over and over again I feel unsure about whether I've really grasped this latter dimension. The sad thing is that these kinds of intellectual gifts and insights can't be lastingly secured, but instead have to be regained on a daily basis; and if that process comes easily for once, it's a clear sign that one has strayed from the path, even if that happens in the best of faith; maybe it is obtained only with the brain and not with the spirit, maybe one has fled from spirit to ethos. The deepest distrust you can have of yourself is, as a rule, still too lenient toward oneself. Regarding this intrinsically hopeless dilemma cheerfully is something that ultimately only the Holy Spirit can bestow on a person, or else the flesh in its need for comfort.—So I'm full of skepticism and misgivings about my own good mood, which unfortunately fails to put a damper on my mood.

My dear, whatever pain you may be feeling about your husband, make sure to help the other women. You and Marion [Yorck] will have to accomplish something in this regard, because first, the two of you have been aware of the human dimensions, and second, you are, I believe, the most grounded, and third, on the whole, you have options to fall back on, materially and otherwise. I know, of course, that you'll do this anyway, but I wanted you to know how agreeable it would be to me. Don't let them all drift apart; instead, try to ensure that they retain the feeling of mutual support and a common cultural heritage.

I embrace you, my love.

J.

FREYA TO HELMUTH JAMES, OCTOBER 24–26, 1944

Tuesday evening

My dear, I was very sad not to be able to write you a peaceful letter this morning. Writing to you after these two days in Kreisau and getting the letter to you quickly was very important to me. But I did it badly, and it can be made up for, can't it?! I am well aware of the preciousness of each and every day and of each and every letter that I can still write, my dear love. In the past week I have focused far more on your life than on your death. What is prompting this? I don't know. Most of all, I don't want to let too much hope cut into what may be the last days we have together on earth, and yet I'm too inclined to keep spinning the thin strands and to keep up hope. It is an odd life, hovering between life and death, and therefore so intense at times. There are hours, moments of unbelievable intensity, and then many hours go by that are still close to you, but they move along calmly, hours in these days that may be the most precious for me. My love, none of this is easy to live well and in the right way, and yet it's so astonishing that in many respects I find it a source of great happiness. You do understand that, don't you?—Today I got right down to typing in the morning, and when I was finished with that and had gone to see Carl Dietrich [von Trotha], Romai [Reichwein] called, and I had to—and wanted to—meet with her before she goes to Kreisau tomorrow. Three hours between sentencing and death.[1] Everything is very inhumane toward the wives. Nothing can be known until it is received in writing. But don't think that this impresses me personally, or Romai. It just rebounds on the Nazis themselves. At any rate, this pace is still the norm (though not always). Then the wives receive a kind of pension upon filing an application, it seems, and, evidently, the return of their personal effects as a routine matter. I don't care the least bit about all that, in my heart of hearts, you know that, I'm writing this only for you to be able to picture it. The children shouldn't notice anything, etc. Now I want to tell you about Kreisau. I came home with Hans [Deichmann], well and in good time, and went to bed. When I fall into my bed, you know what I'm thinking. I think with gratitude about the way it went, and [am] certain that I will continue to think along these lines, and when everything overwhelms me, as it does from time to time (but this time that wasn't the case), I've thus far always been able to think of a way out. I took another look at the sweetly sleeping little sons. Casparchen looked delicate, Konrad big and stocky, and both quite to my liking. Sunday morning was spent lounging around, but first the two boys came. They're both so tender and dear. "Where were you?" Konrad said again, and Casparchen said, of course, that he was fine, and had apparently forgotten his obviously nasty boils altogether. Konrad gets in and out of my bed, needing to look out the window for the train, get books, etc., but keeps coming back. We had a lovely breakfast with Hans. Before we ate, I covered up the bees and hid the letters in the hives for the time being. I also stopped by Zeumer and Sister Ida [Hübner]. At 4 the nicely spiffed-up sons—in their white silk shirts—and I went to Aunt Leno [Hülsen]'s for high tea. It was her birthday. I reassured them all with a good mood and normal behavior. I am in fact calm, and I am doing well, but they're worried about us. Carl Viggo [von Moltke] will come as soon as I call him. He would like to help you, and he's quite willing, but he's not all worked up like Maack.[2] He has a very good picture of you, in any case, regarding his assessment of your position in this matter. I didn't come back until noon, on my bike, and right after eating I spent two hours going over the fields with Zeumer, I was in the Schloss and wherever else I wanted to get to, had a relaxed snack with Asta [Wendland], did my packing, and at 7:30 traveled by way of Breslau, where I met up with Muto [Yorck] and Marion [Yorck] before I boarded the train from Breslau and managed to get a lovely corner seat. That was the course of events in Kreisau, and you know what I've been doing here since then.—My dear, I'm full of love, my beloved, I hope you feel it and it warms you. I see you, my darling, sitting atop your table wrapped in your blanket, as Poelchau recently told me. Yesterday the prospect of your death grabbed hold of my thoughts again. It is absolutely crucial that we not lose sight of it. Our skill lies in being able to see that and still not to despair, but rather to feel gratitude and a strong love. Death lies ahead for you, and for me, a life alone in which our love must remain alive. We have to embrace both death and life, compose ourselves, and stay close together, my dear love: how difficult that is, yet how full of the most beautiful consolations. I love you very much, my heart. I embrace you, and I am and will stay, stay, stay yours, your wife, your P., and no one else's "your."

1. Beginning in September 1943, the clemency proceedings were sped up considerably. "The haste with which the 'clemency proceedings' were curtailed...creates the impression that the Reich Ministry of Justice had

worked itself up into a bloodlust." Victor von Gostomski and Walter Loch, *Der Tod von Plötzensee: Erinnerungen, Ereignisse, Dokumente 1942–1945* (Meitingen/Freising: Kyrios-Verlag, 1969), 25. 2. Freya had to console the attorney Maack about Helmuth's situation.

HELMUTH JAMES TO FREYA, OCTOBER 26, 1944

26 Oct 44

My love, there's nothing new, I slept poorly, for after the first time I woke up, I didn't fall asleep again but instead worked on my defense, which was also quite useful. The more I think it over, the more important it seems to me not to excuse anything, not to tone things down, but rather to mount a very aggressive defense. Then there will be a tough battle, but the way I see it, that will be the only chance to achieve something, not only for me but above all for the others involved: Husen, Carl Dietrich [von Trotha], Einsiedel, etc. I'll try that, in any case.

My dear love, I have no more time to write something tender because I have to try to get as far as possible with the written defense. But you know everything. Bon voyage, my dear, give Casparchen—and everyone else—a warm embrace from me. May God watch over you.

HELMUTH JAMES TO FREYA, OCTOBER 26, 1944

Tegel, 26 Oct 44

My dear, everything that came was splendid, as always, and received with gratitude. Today I'll give you a letter to Casparchen, but it has to arrive with the postal service, it seems to me, and 4 other letters,[1] which you should or shouldn't hand over after my death, as you see fit.

My love, since yesterday my death has become closer and more real, and I am very happy about it. I'm in good spirits even so, or for that very reason, and nonetheless determined to fight for my life. But there is no doubt whatsoever that only a miracle of God can save me. Today, when I was half asleep, I had an odd idea, half idea, half dream. I went to Plötzensee for my execution, and the executioner said, "How am I supposed to execute just the left one without the right one; that won't work." And when they looked at me, you had grown onto my right side, like a Siamese twin, making an execution impossible. It was very beautiful, and then I was fully awake.

I've been wanting to describe the details of my daily routine to you. The times of day are guesswork, because I don't have a watch: The first time I wake up is at about 1 o'clock at night and then I read hymns aloud, mostly some particular group, one after the other, until I feel sleepy again. Then I wake up once and for all at about 5:30 and reflect, think about you, the little sons, and I enjoy that until 6:30. Then, when the others are waking up, I read the hymns in the "morning" section. Then I get up and do what I can, pour myself some water, do 100 squats, and things of that nature. At about 7:10 I'm unlocked, which is to say unchained, and wash and clean up and eat breakfast. That takes me to 8 or 8:30, depending on what I have planned. Then I write to you or do something else until 9:15, when I'm shackled again. After that I walk back and forth until 9:30 and recite Psalms to myself. Then we go out and are back in at 10:10. I spend the whole morning, from 10–11:45, reciting Bible passages, to which I've now added Psalms 111, 118, and 139, and I recite Romans 8. In the mornings the newspaper is delivered,[2] and if I read it, I won't finish my reciting. At 11:45 our shackles are removed again, and then there's always some tidying left to catch up on. At 12 the food arrives. At 1 we're shackled again, and this time has to be used for things that would be better done with two hands, such as writing, reading with looking things up, and activities of that sort. At 1 I finish reciting my Bible passages, maybe start a hymn as well, then sit down atop my table, the bolster behind my back, a blanket under me, and your lovely blanket around me, my feet on the chair, and read. From time to time, once or twice a week, I read through my notes about my statements. On the other days, I systematically read the hymnal, write notes for myself in the Bible and hymnal. By the way, when I'm sitting, I definitely start by reading several chapters from the Old Testament before the Psalms, from the New Testament after the Psalms, from the Gospels and the Epistles. That's how the afternoon always begins. At 4 our shackles are taken off again; then I keep on reading if I have nothing else to do, at 5:30 there's supper, and at 6 we have to be ready for bed and the shackles go on. Then I read the hymns for evening worship, and if I'm in good shape, I ponder things, and if I'm not, I read the hymns or Psalms until I'm sleepy, punctuated by thoughts of you, my love, and go to sleep early. That is the day. So far it has never really been long enough.

So, my love, I've been shackled since the fifth line of this page, and now we're getting ready to go out. Farewell, my love, full of gratitude for the great blessing of these weeks, full of confidence that He will guide things in the way that is best for us, full of confidence, full of prayers that He may watch over you and hold His hand over you, and watch over us and hold His hand over us. Jäm.

1. Farewell letters to those close to him. Of the four letters one for Sister Ida Hübner (see Appendix: Additional Documents) and one for Freya's mother, Ada Deichmann, survive. A third was for Harald Poelchau; the addressee of the fourth cannot be discerned. 2. They were permitted only the Nazi publication *Völkischer Beobachter*.

FREYA TO HELMUTH JAMES, OCTOBER 26, 1944

Thursday afternoon

My dear love, today is the day that I can reply right away to what I get from you when I'm at the friends' house. I love that. It won't be much longer until I head out on my highly cherished path. This afternoon I typed many short things, including the passage from the book of Wisdom, which, once again, I liked so much. I also typed the excerpt from Freisler's speech,[1] and when I take in these confused and diabolical contents, I can't believe that this could go well for you.

What a world, what an outlook, where is all this leading, quite apart from what happens to us!?—Tomorrow morning at 11 I'll be at Steengracht's. His wife will be here as well. That is useful, because I can't make much headway with Dieter [von Mirbach]. I suspect he's not ready for a commitment. Maybe that's wrong.

—I have now received all the lovely letters and of those to the others I've read only the one to Sister Ida [Hübner] so far. I find it quite lovely and comforting for her. Isn't it strange that since yesterday I have also once again started to regard your death as the far more likely outcome! This feeling became clearly palpable to me yesterday, to the point that I felt the need to call to you again to embrace this outlook, because it is without question a blessing to be able to die with such awareness and say goodbye with such awareness, and we mustn't, my dearest, let this opportunity to see and live it fully slip away from us by hoping against hope, and we're not letting it slip away, but that is exactly what I have to keep thinking and saying. My dear, how wonderful that I had grown onto you,[2] how wonderful, how comforting. My dear love, how I enjoy your still being here, that I still stand hand in hand with you, that you're still there, that I can write to you and your dear eyes roam over my words, your dear eyes. Oh, Jäm, help me if I have to remain alone. I have to stay really and truly alone in order to keep you. But maybe the solitary path ahead of me won't be so long. Who knows! The only thing that matters is the readiness to accept what God has given us. May He grant us—us both—the strength we need, may He make us small and Himself large within us, and then all this will work out. Good night, my dear love! Sleep well. I embrace you, and I am and will forever remain your P.

1. On October 21, 1944, Freisler gave a speech about the jurisdiction of the People's Court. Freya copied excerpts for Helmuth. 2. Refers to Helmuth's dream of the Siamese twins; see his letter of October 26, 1944.

HELMUTH JAMES TO FREYA, OCTOBER 27, 1944 [UNDATED, BUT FOUND UNDERNEATH FREYA'S LETTER OF OCTOBER 26, 1944]

I'm eating mountains of honey; last night in particular I ate up a whole spoonful of honey, when my throat was very scratchy. The honey is so much my Pim's own product, no butcher, no creamery intervening.

Freisler's presentation is interesting, but it eliminates any last doubts. It is clear as day in many parts, and is targeted directly at me.

HELMUTH JAMES TO FREYA, OCTOBER 28, 1944

Tegel, 28 Oct 44

My dear love, I want to spend a bit of time on a quick chat with you. It's the afternoon and we don't have shackles on because we're supposed to be scouring, and I've already done that. I assume you went home this morning so you could celebrate Casparchen's birthday. I guess that means you're now on the train somewhere between Liegnitz and Kreisau, although I have no sense of what time it is, because it's raining and so dark that the light's been on the whole day.

I really felt like talking to you because I was sad. There was no reason at all. But living this way, between death and life, is exhausting. Once you're finally totally ready and prepared to die, you can't make a permanent state out of it. Unfortunately that doesn't work; the flesh doesn't play along. So you bounce back to life, maybe only a little, you build a house of cards and then, when you notice it, you tear it down again, and the flesh doesn't take well to that. It's also an instance of practice not making perfect; it always remains unpleasant to the exact same degree. That's how it is today all over again; then two nasty air raids during the night—always so close that you hear those big chunks hurtling down and the windows shaking during the explosion—then darkness and rain. The Old Adam just isn't willing.

It's especially difficult these days because I'm working on my defense and then have to summon up within me confidence that I'll be able to mount a successful defense, and that results in an unpleasant split in a center layer of my consciousness. On the top, my powers of reason say: "Nonsense"; the center says: "God can help, and my attitude isn't so wrong," and at the same time: "Maintain your readiness for death or else you'll undergo spiritual crises." And deepest down is this: "For whether we live, we live unto the Lord; and whether we die, we die unto the Lord: whether we live therefore, or die, we are the Lord's." And unfortunately, this deepest layer doesn't always hold sway over the two higher ones.

So, now I've laid it all out for you, and that has already made things a little bit better. You know, my major sin is black ingratitude. Not only for my life as a whole—no, it's for the day-to-day things. What marvelous weeks I have behind me; I have been given so very much. And then I act as though it would be a misfortune for it to stop. I'm certainly not entitled to more! Instead of humbly accepting every new fortunate day, I tremble with worry about whether there will be another one. Why should I actually—from my standpoint—go on living even one more day: I have enjoyed more true happiness and, most of all, love than anyone else I know. Why should the happiness of these past weeks go on for even a single day more: Who else has enjoyed this?—As far as I can see, there is only one reason for me to need to go on living: in order to get my share of chastisements.

My love, I'm writing this to you in part so that you can pray for me to learn humility and gratitude and that God's grace is with me throughout the ups and downs of these days and I never lose sight of the firm foundation.—And that you pay careful attention to this with the little sons: Humility differs from modesty, and gratitude needs to be a permanent condition. By the way, I think Casparchen will have that.

When I look back upon these years, I find the image of the sower a fitting one. The seeds are scattered, and I'm certain that they will sprout someday, because no thought is lost in God. We cannot know whether an earthly connection will be apparent, whether our death will mean something. Maybe it will, among other things. It would be good, as that would accelerate everything. Of all the agricultural figures, the sower is the most fortunate, because he is full of hope, and no hail, no storm, no drought has yet come to curtail his hope; everything is possible. That is part of what makes sowing so wonderful.

My love, I, too, hope that we will bid each other farewell in full awareness of this life, and that we won't spoil this precious thing for ourselves by clinging to false hope: but we must always remain vigilant that the train doesn't leave the station, you might say, while we happen to be looking elsewhere. I'm now fully back in a parting frame of mind, thinking about your and your sons' future lives. Sometimes I focus on the great moment of death; I tremble at the thought that creaturely fear will overpower me then, that, you might say, I will miss out on this moment that is all about keeping the faith. How very weak we are! Only grace can help us keep the faith and see the Redeemer. Poelchau would probably chuckle at that and call it pure romanticizing; he would say that it all happens quite soberly and that one is so little in control of oneself and one's senses that nothing whatsoever can be of help. Well, I'll have to wait and see.

I'll quickly jot down a few hymnal verses I'm working on and learning: 208, 5 + 6 [and] 222, 7–12.[1] And now I'll stop. I hope all of you have a lovely birthday celebration. I thank you, my love, because I'm now quite consoled. J.

1. Verses that focus on death and the afterlife.

FREYA TO HELMUTH JAMES, OCTOBER 28, 1944

Saturday noon

My dear love, my train will now leave from the Schlesischer Bahnhof. But that doesn't matter at all; I'm not going until 5, and even then only as far as Liegnitz and I'll see where I can lay my head down so that I can really be home early tomorrow morning. I had to wait at Steengracht's for too long; he was working, I waited for forty-five minutes, and I had no more time. But the advantage is that I can write to you, tell you once again about the great, warm love I'm trying to surround you with. I am struck by my closeness to you innumerable times every day; the way I belong together with you is an exhilarating feeling I experience over and over: your being anchored next to and above me! It was a rushed week, though not a frantic one, and I wasn't able to sit and consider and read and contemplate often, yet I lived quite close to you. Of course, the delightfulness and beauty of these weeks is defined largely by the peace I am experiencing. My Jäm, I'm quite certain that you have to die, that your path has to lead to death, just as $1 + 1 = 2$, and still I know quite as certainly that you can be saved and more of our life together on earth can be granted to us—not *will* but *can*—because it's not inevitably the case that $1 + 1 = 2$. I don't know whether after the ups and downs of the past few weeks I am now hoping for too much after all, I really don't know what's happening inside me, but I'm not despondent, I don't cry so much anymore, I'm quite calm and feel—and now I'm going back to the beginning again—my great love. You can't imagine how happy the Siamese twin keeps making me.—My Jäm, think of us and your beaming Casparchen on Monday at 11, and at 4 lots of children will be coming to eat cake!! My love, my dear, I'm sending you a tender embrace. Live in peace and tranquillity, and surround yourself with love. I am and will forever remain your P.

HELMUTH JAMES TO FREYA, OCTOBER 30–31, 1944

30 Oct 44

My dear,

1. So, on Wednesday morning I'm going to ask to be brought in for a dictation session so I can dictate my written defense, which means that I can be brought in on Thursday afternoon at the earliest. Let's see how that turns out.

2. The question of how to set aside my own confession of guilt is very much on my mind. It's a complication. But if a defense involving

my prior knowledge should come through at all, we'll get past this lesser obstacle as well. Time, good advice, and a rationale are vitally important.

3. Müller had suggested submitting a petition for clemency to the Führer. Question: *a*. Couldn't Carl Viggo [von Moltke] bring up this question with Freisler? Rationale: Family, name, disgrace of all family members, a death sentence that is carried out represents an irreparable stain on the entire family, whereas a death sentence that is not carried out, with later arrangements made on the occasion of a general amnesty, or a verdict that grants freedom or an act of mercy allows for a *reparatio*. Carl Viggo can do a good job of representing this family interest, while you can't, because he's close enough, yet distant enough. In all this, of course, the relinquishing of Kreisau. *b*. If Freisler doesn't want to—which I assume—couldn't this sort of petition for clemency go by way of Bürkner–Keitel with or without Freisler's approval?

31 Oct 44

My love, I spent the hours before and after 10 and from 4 to 6 immersed in very tender thoughts about all of you, especially about Casparchen. I'll bet he was overjoyed and hopped about like a flea. Then, at night, when we were awakened by two alarms that were harmless by our standards, I looked for you on the train. I hope your trip went well, and now you may already be with the friends. I just wanted to tell you that my soul is where I prefer to have it: way down deep, but on bedrock. If only I could keep it there; the ups and downs are always draining. For the trial, though, I'll also need a strong boost, but preferably in a different layer of myself, because the line of defense we've now chosen is difficult to hold to in many spots, and will require every bit of strength, perseverance, and constant ideas and improvisations. I'll need to pray for that, and I'm also placing my hopes in Ulla [Oldenbourg]. Let her know if you find out when the trial is.

My dear love, the relative security of the fourteen days is over, and now we're back in a period that makes us feel, more strongly than ever, that every word could be the last one. So be it. No matter how repetitive it may get, we don't want to be deprived of the precious opportunity to keep saying to each other "till I see you again, till I find you again, till I'm never separated from you again." That is a treasure that encompasses more for us than happiness on earth; it has become a means of revelation, and should remain so. My dear love, may the Lord watch over us both; may He preserve both of us in His mercy "both in this world and in the other,"[1] and, if this should be the last word: May He hold His hand protectively over you and the little sons and send you His Comforter. J.

1. From the Lutheran hymn "Abide Among Us with Thy Grace."

FREYA TO HELMUTH JAMES, OCTOBER 30, 1944

Monday evening

My dear, any moment now I'll be leaving with Hans [Deichmann] to come to you. Once again, as on each of the past Mondays, I am full of longing and eagerness to see how I will find you, my love, my dear. Tomorrow I also have to go to see Schulze, of course, and I'm dreading what I'll find out there. I'm dreading the end of these weeks, my love. They've offered so many treasures and have spoiled me in many ways, my dear. God willing, they have also strengthened us. The odd thing is that here in Kreisau the notion that you have to die just can't take hold. Here I live together with you too much in all kinds of practical matters, here I simply cannot believe that you should no longer be living here with me as part of this world. In any case, that's how it was once more for these two days. I haven't done much, my love, because I had a cold and was taking care of myself.—But today was the birthday, and we enjoyed it to the fullest. It was a great party! Casparchen was already quite excited yesterday, quite fidgety and beside himself, and today things started up in the boys' bedroom at 5:45 in the morning. The highlight was the afternoon, with all the children, but in the morning there were little garlands and flowers and buns, and, at 11 on the dot, the birthday cake and table with the presents. It was very full. From us a book and slippers and socks; from

Asta [Wendland] the highlight: an old alarm clock that still works; from Carl [Deichmann] a charming case with a fountain pen, pencils and crayons, eraser, and everything the heart can desire. Then there were all sorts of games and pictures, etc., so that it looked quite bountiful, and your letter was in the middle, surrounded by little flowers. He was very pleased. We ate early, at 11:45, with Hans-Viggo [von Hülsen];[1] there was thick soup and apple strudel and we clinked glasses with strawberry juice. Then the young gentlemen headed off to school and I went to the farmyard.—Just after 3 I was home again, and then it was high time to prepare for the party, because when Casparchen came home just after 2, he brought Hans-Viggo, Clem, and Rita along with him, and by about 3 there was infernal noise and the height of bliss in the living room. Until snack time they played one round of Air Raid Alarm after another. When snack time arrived, the hullabaloo came to a halt and yielded to a purposeful silence, for they were utterly absorbed in the business of working on countless pieces of cake. There were eleven of us, and Ulla [Oldenbourg], Asta, Hans, and every so often I, too, sat at the lower end of the extended table. Casparchen held court in my usual seat, crowned with flowers around his plate, flanked by tall burning candles, and asked for Hans-Viggo and Dietel to sit next to him. They all ate up a storm! Tarts, poppy-seed cake, apple pie, weak tea, milk, and sugar. Casparchen was beaming. There were all kinds of flowers in the garden, and his little garland was made up of the last zinnias and snapdragons, and mainly marigolds. In the center of the table was a vase with the last lovely bright red geraniums. When they had eaten their fill, the mob jumped back into action, and we had fun with musical chairs, Hit the Pot, Old Maid, Blind Man's Bluff, and more things of that nature. There was infernal noise and utter fulfillment, until I threw them out at a quarter to seven. Casparchen enjoyed it immensely. Little Konrad, the only younger boy, ran around somewhat apart from the others, but contentedly. He was essentially playing by himself, but he talked about Casparchen's birthday quite a lot. Casparchen just about made it into bed, exhausted and unprotesting, while Konrad still felt like talking. I listened at the door to him say that now— This is where the train came, and I won't get to that until tomorrow, my dear love, because I'm already at the friends' house. With love, your P.

1. A son of Leonore and Karl von Hülsen.

HELMUTH JAMES TO FREYA, OCTOBER 31, 1944

31 Oct

My dear, thanks for your letter. Everything sounds really lovely. Ulla [Oldenbourg] should not be led astray by the safe atmosphere in Kreisau and stop working. She has to bear in mind that from a human standpoint there is no prospect for things to turn out well. As far as I'm concerned, the main thing is for me to get the written defense and the letter to Müller, the cover letter, as quickly as possible. Dix should work hard on the revision, because once I hand it in, I have to stand behind it and can't deviate from it again. That's why it is necessary to include the confession of guilt from the outset as well. Don't go too easy on him; he should take pains with this.

How wonderful that you're here again, my love. That's always so pleasant. My dear, how warmly I am held inside you, and I'll remain that way. If only I could warm you too—I mean, warm you forever: that is my wish. My love, we are truly not entitled to more life, because we have had so much good come our way.

I'm sending you an embrace, my love. Tomorrow is the beginning of a new month, and it will likely bring my death; we should never forget that, so as not to feed foolish hopes. May God protect us. J.

FREYA TO HELMUTH JAMES, NOVEMBER 1, 1944

Wednesday morning

My dear, my dear love, my Jäm, yes, today is the beginning of a new month. I set foot in it as well, and in order to do this, took my courage in both hands. I wonder what it will bring us, my dear husband! Even if it is so likely, my husband, that we will have to part within the four weeks to come, I still firmly believe in the possibility that we two will be able to exit this month again as well. Along with the prospect of what lies ahead for us, my love, I'm always also overwhelmed by the feeling of being comforted. This feeling is an inestimable treasure. Last night I got quite a few things and haven't fully analyzed them yet, but I did read everything, and took in all that was for me. How good, my dear, I understand every word of what you wrote on that sad day.[1] Even though it is incomparably easier for me at this stage, your feelings are exactly my feelings and your fluctuations are mine as well. There can't be great heights without deep valleys, my poor husband. I can't spend too much time writing today, because as you know, I have a lot of work to do. At 3:30 I'll be with Dix; now I'm coming out to you, and then I have to keep an eye out for an address I already have. Schulze wanted me to call him this morning so he could tell me when he's submitting the written defense.[2] Just now, at 9:15, he didn't answer. I'll try again in a minute.—I was just going to tell you about Konrad talking to himself in bed when I had to leave off with my letter. It was nothing special, just a way of showing you that he is truly already a little person with his own ideas and reactions. He said, "Now Reyali is going away again and leaving us all alone, she's leaving us alone with Astali, and then we have to live alone again. She's taking the cake (birthday cake) and going to Pa." It went on in this vein for quite some time.

I have to get going now. Farewell, my dear. May God watch over you, and I love you and I am and will remain your P.

1. See Helmuth's letter of October 28, 1944. 2. Freya presumably means the indictment, since Schulze was the prosecutor.

FREYA TO HELMUTH JAMES, NOVEMBER 1, 1944[1]

Berlin, 1 Nov 44

How are you, my dear?

I'm happy that I'm able to write you a word or two like this.

Everything's fine at home.

There will definitely not be a trial this week. The indictment is drawn up, but it's still in Herr Schulze's safe. That's what he told me.

What else is there for us to say! We agree completely on all the issues. I'm deeply devoted to you in love.

What things are you missing?

What would you like to have?

Today I should be getting news from the prosecutor about my call asking when the indictment will be submitted to the court, but so far I've been unable to reach him.

1. Letter accompanying the exchange of laundry.

HELMUTH JAMES TO FREYA, NOVEMBER 1, 1944

1 Nov 44

My dear, business first here too:

1. It seems to me that Carl Viggo [von Moltke] has to come at once. It would be best for Carl Dietrich [von Trotha] to contact him right away, because it seems certain to me that Freisler now knows every detail. The indictment won't be presented—even to the court— until everything has been discussed with Freisler.—The appeal for clemency is a difficult process and will take some time for Carl Viggo as well. He needs to try to enlist Bürkner's aid in getting him through to Keitel. Ask him to grant us this time.

2. For the same reason, Steengracht–*Round Table*[1] is now urgent. It absolutely must function as a means of slowing things down. Steengracht should write only what he considers right. But maybe you can call up Illemie [Steengracht][2] and say that the matter is likely to come in the next few days, so haste is essential.

Ceterum censeo[3]: Carl Viggo should see Freisler this week, and the letter should be relayed from Steengracht to Kaltenbrunner this week as well. I would also go ahead and discuss the issue of clemency with

Illemie. She's clever, doesn't let Steengracht off the hook, and has some insight into the system.

3. It looks as though a Bavarian I barely know, Sperr,[4] is incriminating me, claiming that I was nursing thoughts of overthrowing the government. Frau Reisert ought to tell her husband that if Sperr really did try to pin on Delp or me something that could be interpreted as an attempt at overthrowing the government, he has to recant his statement in the trial and say he mixed up the conversations, because it's simply not correct. Reisert will be sitting next to him and surely will also have a chance to speak with him while being transported to the trial.

My dear: 1 and 2 take precedence, however. Don't let anything else sidetrack you from these two things. Even the tiniest stone that contributes to building up those two positions is more important than anything else. It will take several rounds to get something in place. Please focus your complete concentration on those two.

My dear love, the stories from your two sons are very beautiful. The duck was delicious. The elderly guard today thought, however, that you didn't give me much to eat, and I replied that you knew it wasn't permitted, but he thought that some more wouldn't have done any harm. Yes, this month will likely bring a certain decision. We have to await it with confidence. In any case, I feel quite safe and sound at the moment, and in comparison everything else is inconsequential. The month of October 1944 will thus go down in our annals as a truly important month, and we can look back on it only with gratitude. And who could have prophesied that when I began it in a depression. We never want to forget that we owe our gratitude for this important month not only to God but also to Poelchau. A Christian. J.

1. See Helmuth's letter of October 14, 1944. 2. Illemie Baronin Steengracht von Moyland, the wife of the Nazi secretary of state, an anti-Nazi herself. 3. Latin for "furthermore, I am of the opinion." 4. Sperr was tried with Helmuth and did not present incriminating evidence against him.

HELMUTH JAMES TO FREYA, NOVEMBER 1, 1944

Berlin-Tegel, 1 Nov 44

My dear, tomorrow is Casparchen's birthday, but I first want to congratulate you on your first little son, for whom you fought so hard. Not only did you persuade me completely, not only would the present moment be far more difficult if I left you without knowing that you would be looking out for one another. No, the point is rather that I absolutely cannot imagine my—our—life without the little sons.[1] My love for the little sons has become a part of me, and when I leave this world, I'll take it with me. My love, you achieved that with a great deal of grit and determination and without any support from your husband. Seven years ago today, I was at Eileen [Power]'s[2] home, staying there, and got your telegram on the evening of the 2nd, and on the morning of the 3rd we spoke on the phone. The ugly little creature in Bonn has now become a little person with such a dear, tender heart that one cannot be grateful enough to be in the company of something like him. I'm utterly confident that when I leave you, you'll be the beneficiary of his baptismal verse,[3] and he'll be a blessing for you. May God preserve his good heart in the face of all the wounds a heart like this must suffer.

My dear love, today I was very happy again, and kept warm by your presence in this house. That was quite beautiful. You are very close by, my dearest.—If I now get my written defense behind me, I'll be set. I get the feeling that my insides are prepared for both battle and defeat; I have said my goodbyes to everyone, I have had my debts waived, I have the certainty that we will stay together and that you will not lose me either, I feel so ready to go.—I want to point out two more things to you: Luke 10:38–42 and hymn 296. Goodbye, my love, now for this night, but if need be, for this world as well. May the Lord watch over you.

J.

1. Helmuth recalls his earlier refusal to have children; see Freya's letter of September 29, 1944, note 6. 2. Helmuth was in England staying with Power

on the day of Caspar's birth. 3. Genesis 12:2: "And I will make of thee a great nation, and I will bless thee, and make thy name great; and thou shalt be a blessing." In the farewell letter to his sons, dated October 11, 1944, Helmuth provided a condensed version.

FREYA TO HELMUTH JAMES, NOVEMBER 2, 1944

Thursday morning

My dear, the document now has Dix's approval. He didn't change anything at all, apart from a couple of minor matters we discussed together. I pointed out to him once again that you were looking for harsh criticism and that part II might be cut a bit more, but he said no. Still, he also regards the confession of guilt as an obstacle, and said that Freisler would belabor these kinds of matters. He said, incidentally, that this is an old police tactic. He told me he knows these brief summarizing confessions quite well, and that they always turn out to be ominous, so you absolutely have to mention this issue in the defense statement that *Freisler gets*. He suggests writing something like this at the end: "May I mention one more thing: I am distressed by the summarizing statement I made on September 25, 1944,[1] which I wrote in a state of deep depression, and in the brief summarizing manner desired by the official who was interrogating me, although I'm not intending in the slightest to suggest that he applied any impermissible pressure on me. When I talk about 'guilt' in this summary, I am of course referring first and foremost to the accusations leveled against me. In addition, I truly feel guilty in the human sense, on account of the unhappiness I have brought upon myself, my relatives, and my family name. I ask that my explanations at that time be understood in this light; they may conflict with my explanations above strictly in terms of the wording, but not in the meaning given here." I'm not sure whether that really belongs after part I or ought to go at the end. By all means, go ahead and make changes to the rationale and the diction, since you know the details of the background story; this is just to show the thrust of the defense.—We all consider the letter to Müller a bad one, in both form and content. And it's still too deferential. Here's what's left of it now that we've worked on it:

> Gruppenführer! Attached please find the defense document that you kindly agreed to forward to the People's Court. I ask you to bear in mind that I have no knowledge of the accusations that have been made against me.
>
> Even if it should prove necessary to present new perspectives after the indictment has been scrutinized, the basis of my defense remains the same: that I haven't violated any duties of allegiance.
>
> You have accused me of not having taken the initiative to pass along to you what I knew after July 20th. I was quite horrified to learn about the events of July 20th in the daily newspaper. But once the deed was done, and every detail of the guilt of those involved had been made known to the Gestapo, I thought there would be even less of a question regarding any obligation on my part to inform the authorities. It will be understandable that I had misgivings about taking the initiative of communicating my knowledge of the above-mentioned details to the Gestapo back then. I was hesitant to get involved in this matter—innocently, in my view.

I personally am not sure whether that is quite right with respect to the content. I'm formulating it that way, but you can of course change it again. In any case, Dix also thought that your letter ought to broach the subject of your disloyalty to the SS again, but not say too much. He kept telling me that you shouldn't admit to anything, that you shouldn't be pinned down.

My love, I slept at the friends' house! That, too! So I went to bed just after 10. That's how tired I was. He has to leave right away, so I'll just say quickly: The indictment won't go out before the 13th. Another respite! Why, we ask in delight! On the 10th I'm supposed to see Schulze again. Then he may grant me *a face-to-face meeting*!! Only if I had good reasons!! "But you do have an estate..." So it's quite likely!—I don't think Frau Reisert knows much. I saw her only briefly, but today again between 1 and 2. He, Reisert, did not incriminate you in any event, but she doesn't know about Sperr.

My love is great and my time is brief. Yesterday I had a very heavy schedule, not today, today only Steengracht. In the evening I was too tired to write. There is much in my heart, much love, happiness, and gratitude. You know that! Forever yours, P.

1. At other points, Helmuth dates this to September 28 or 29; see, for example, his following letter, dated November 2, 1944; see also his letter of December 10–12, 1944, which indicates that he may have been interrogated under the influence of administered drugs on various days.

HELMUTH JAMES TO FREYA, NOVEMBER 2, 1944

2 Nov 44

My love, what a surprising new respite. It is very valuable, especially for the issue of Carl Viggo [von Moltke]–Bürkner. Don't let anyone rush you, not even your husband. It is even more important for matters of this kind to be done well than to be done quickly. Especially don't see Bürkner without Haus.[1] No one else is reliable. Just don't be too modest in asking for other people's time. Since we have never asked anything of anyone, we can now easily afford to be somewhat demanding.

So, now I feel totally prepared. The unfortunate statement on September 29 just has to be taken in stride. Given the infinite number of obstacles that will likely trip me up, one more won't really make any difference. Regrettably, I have an unfortunate compulsion for objectivity that always makes me see the opposing point of view. That is hardly beneficial for these proceedings. Well, God is able to accomplish what He wishes with even the most unsuitable instruments, and I have no desire to change.

My love, the prospect of a face-to-face meeting is heavenly.—But if it doesn't work out, that is fine too. When all is said and done, we don't need it, and we don't need Herr Schulze.

Goodbye, my love; I take you in my arms. May God watch over you. J.

1. A loyal fellow employee at the international bureau of the Abwehr, the German intelligence organization.

FREYA TO HELMUTH JAMES, NOVEMBER 2, 1944

Thursday morning

My Jäm, now somewhat more detail about Herr Schulze. I have no idea why the completed indictment is in the safe and an adviser has to be called up and then I'm given the information that it will definitely not be handed over before the 13th, and on the 10th I can come back, at which point he'll have a clear idea, although a delay might still be possible then. I asked that if it did take so long, might it be possible for me to talk to you? Yes, he explained, but it would depend on the reasons, which would have to seem sufficient to him, but I have an estate, and that could easily yield something. No, not just yet, but perhaps next week there could be permission for us to talk. I was told that I shouldn't come for it as early as Tuesday, but rather wait until Friday. Once again he was very polite to me, almost friendly, but he is a stony individual.—At the moment I'm sitting outside quietly, and now that I've sewn my dress, I'm sitting at the desk reading your letters again. I don't think you've been so ungrateful. I actually find that gratitude can't be expected from very young people. They have to grab at everything that comes their way as a matter of course. Gratitude is a feeling that comes with maturity. My love, be grateful that this beautiful feeling is being bestowed on us so abundantly now at such a difficult stage. And you *are* grateful, so pay no attention to ingratitude; instead, take pleasure in your gratitude!—My Jäm, it is my heart's desire, too, for you always to continue to be allowed and able to keep me warm. It's all up to me, but I'm often afraid as to how I can manage to keep you close to me. Ulla [Oldenbourg] was able to do it, but she is a far more intellectual person than I and has lived a life of the mind. And what about me!! I could, but I don't, or rather, I do too much. Oh, my Jäm, what a task.

I'm at the friends' house. We had a talk. There were very beautiful and delightful letters. They showed me that you're doing well, and that is the most beautiful thing for me. I got a very moving letter from Mütterchen Deichmann.[1] She obviously understands what is happening with us quite well, and she had a friend have a mass said for you in Cologne in the crypt at St. Gereon's Basilica. I'm very pleased about that. My beloved, I belong to you—I am and will forever remain in abiding love, your P.

1. Ada Deichmann, Freya's mother.

HELMUTH JAMES TO FREYA, NOVEMBER 3, 1944

Tegel, 3 Nov 44

My dear, today I wrote to Müller and asked him to call me in for dictation. In the meantime, though, I'll very slowly write the written plea in ink and in my best penmanship so I'll be prepared in any case. If Müller doesn't have me called in by the 7th, I'll send him my defense handwritten in ink on the morning of the 8th.

My love, I have absolutely nothing new to write. I'm doing very well; it is so pleasant that the weather is nice, because on cloudy days nothing at all can be seen in the cell, and we don't get light throughout the day. Right now I'm quite busy with the written plea: the writing is going very slowly, because I have to write rather as if I were writing to Casparchen, and I'm still continuing to make improvements here and there in form and content. I do want to make sure that it reads well, and easily.—I think it would be best if Carl Viggo [von Moltke] could get Freisler to postpone the trial until the plea for clemency to Hitler has been submitted. That would be petition I; petition II: Imprisonment only, based on Freisler's own plenipotentiary decision; petition III: If a death sentence, postpone the execution until a decision regarding the plea for clemency has been reached.

How, by the way, is your head cold? Is it all over? You might as well go to Kreisau, seeing as you'll most likely have to stay here next weekend, since the plea for clemency will surely not move forward very quickly, even if Carl Viggo should get through to Freisler soon. By the way, there has to be some consideration of whether Müller needs to be informed about the plea once it is in motion. At any rate, Müller or Freisler have to know about it. But Sack[1] is in the best position to judge something like this.

Farewell, my love, how beautiful are these days with you, precious pearls. If I should leave you, which is, of course, to be expected, we will have been well rewarded. May God watch over you. J.

In any event, send me another writing pad.

1. Helmuth did not yet know that Sack, a jurist, had been under arrest since August 9, 1944; see Freya's letter of November 6–7, 1944.

FREYA TO HELMUTH JAMES, NOVEMBER 3, 1944

Friday noon

My dear love, yesterday evening I got two particularly beautiful little letters. I've just read them again at leisure and with a great deal of happiness. If only you could stay in this good, beautiful mood. I've had a very peaceful morning, didn't budge from my desk, and now it's 2. Just before a quarter to, I have to get going. I want to get the letter to Steengracht, one to you via Schulze,[1] which I've written, pick up a permit for Poelchau, and at 5:30 I'll go to see Frau Reisert, who asked me to come by. I wonder what she wants to tell me. Yesterday I communicated your request to her. She didn't know anything negative about Sperr. I just jotted down a couple of notes about what, in my view, needs to be in Carl Viggo [von Moltke]'s petition for clemency, and I'm sending you a carbon copy. Let me know if something better, or additional, occurs to you or what you'd like to see changed. Tomorrow Carl Viggo should then come here with a finished draft. That's how I arranged things with him this morning.—Steengracht was quite overwhelmed with work yesterday, and although he had been carrying around the letter for three days, warmly crumpled in his breast pocket, he hadn't done anything with it. I myself am for leaving off the somewhat explicit sentence at the end, because in effect "my" thought is already implied by the description of the facts of the case, without being expressly stated. The letter won't be quite as flowery then, but it's enough. Steengracht agreed. He's quite willing to lend his support because your life is at stake, but he's clearly had a lot on his mind. Dieter [von Mirbach] walked by when I was waiting in front of Steengracht's door. He said only that today I wouldn't have much of a chance of seeing him, that he, Steengracht, was very busy, he didn't stop, nor did he ask or do anything, so I don't feel like dealing with him either. The kind Schlitter at least gave me a gentle look but didn't know anything and got nothing out of me either. That is already [a] piddling place[2]—but this remark doesn't apply to our case; it's just a general observation. I have to set off, my love!—I'm at the friends' house. Reisert can't get to Sperr and thinks that a policeman will always be standing in the way. We'd now like to try doing it by way of the lady who looks after him, because Reisert was just as appalled at the prospect of this sort of statement. I can't keep typing any more this evening; our friends here have to go to bed, so you won't get the copy until next time. I still can't visualize the Carl Viggo project: I can see the petition for clemency, but I can't picture him going to Freisler with the pleas.[3] It won't come to that anyway, but we shall see. A great deal also depends on Carl Viggo's bearing and dedication. Only Carl Viggo can do all this—I understand that—but I still feel that I would need to appear before Freisler in order to complement you, as with Neuhaus, although that proved pointless. I'm not for doing it together; if it's done, each should go alone, but as I've said, I'm not really clear about this whole matter.—My dear, when I see Frau Reisert, I realize how good we two have it. I'm doing quite well, and I feel happy and so firmly united with you that I go about like someone who is in a good, happy, carefree marriage. How is that possible with prospects like ours! My mind doesn't grasp it. Today, two people who knew nothing about our situation have told me that I'm looking well. How can that be? I don't want to stop and leave you, but I'll forever remain your P.

1. The reference is to an official letter sent via the People's Court. 2. By "piddling place," Freya means the Federal Foreign Office. 3. This refers to the wishes that Carl Viggo would be relaying to Freisler; see Helmuth's letter of November 3, 1944.

HELMUTH JAMES TO FREYA, NOVEMBER 4–5, 1944

Tegel, 4 Nov 44

My dear, I'll start my little letter in any event. I'm now spending most of my day writing the defense but doesn't have a single copy completely finished yet and the earliest I can get the first copy done is this evening. I'm actually quite pleased with it now, and that's already a bad sign. But it's a truly daring defense, which is: "I have always and openly held an opinion contrary to your regime's, and am hence exempt from punishment." But in essence it's the truth, and it is the only argument that offers any reasonable line of defense. But that assumes I do well at the trial and successfully reinforce this line while defending myself against individual attacks. In any case I'm eagerly anticipating it.—Good interaction with Bürkner will also be a key to success if they follow up with him, and that can be assured only by way of Haus; talk to Poelchau about the extent to which you can involve him. He has to make certain all the explanations concerning my case that are made in court or to the police go through him; since he was an attorney, there is good justification for it. But he has to know what I need, because Bürkner can destroy my entire defense if he provides misguided information.

As for the Carl Viggo [von Moltke] petition: I think the correct procedure is this: *a.* Draft of the petition to be discussed by Carl Viggo and Sack. *b.* Then meeting, Carl Viggo with Freisler. *c.* Then meeting, Carl Viggo with Bürkner. *d.* Then preparing a cover letter, chief of the Armed Forces High Command[1] to Hitler by Haus, Oxé, Sack; but maybe that won't work out and has to take a different course;

Sack certainly knows best. *e.* Afterward Carl Viggo's visit to Keitel with a request to pass along the petition with his support.

All this will not go quickly and cannot be accomplished in passing, but will take a couple of days. I'm sorry about that, but it has to be done well, because we have to be right on the mark.

You yourself must do as little as possible on the substance of the matter, just prepare the people by having preliminary discussions; get them together and light a fire under them. Most important, you need to think carefully about the issues so that you'll notice when mistakes are made; but your thinking process cannot stand in for the work of Carl Viggo or the other men.

It's very important for me to have a good defense counsel, preferably Dix.

My dear, I always have so many suggestions and wishes that it must be overwhelming. Many of them might be idiotic, but I do think that you ought to write down all the various ideas so that you have them together on one piece of paper. Naturally I have the most productive brain in this arena because I have a great deal of time to delve into all the options; on the other hand, I don't have a clear picture of reality on the outside.

My love, I'll stop here and continue writing my plea. I hope you're doing better and you've had a good night of sleep. Take good care of yourself, my love, these strange times can impose heavy demands on you at any point. I embrace you, my love, J.

5 Nov 44

My dear, yesterday I forgot something else: If you have time, give Vikki Bausch a call at some point—telephone Schoeller & Bausch. He takes care of Haubach. If he should see Haubach, it would be good if he would inform Haubach in detail about what I've said on the subject of his and Carlo [Mierendorff]'s attempts to notify the authorities.—I don't know what the delays mean; maybe no trials pertaining to July 20th are taking place at the moment? Since there were no executions, it's easy to assume that. Maybe basic deliberations about how to treat these cases are still taking place. Maybe they pertain to our case as well, either because there is too much else to work through or because they're waiting to see if they can capture Rösch as well.[2] But we can only guess, and that serves no purpose; we can't influence what's going on, only Carl Viggo may be able to get the trial suspended until the clemency proceedings have been resolved.—I find Mütterchen Deichmann very touching.—My love, your remarks about the right of young people to lack gratitude have given me a bit of comfort about my own behavior. Maybe you're right, and maybe I'm much older in that respect than I myself know. That's what I think sometimes when I realize how indifferent I am to many things that I really ought not to be indifferent to, from an overall human point of view.—I now gratefully savor every day and every night: they give me time to think, to understand, to fathom the situation, to learn, and to love my Pim. I always notice the bafflement that greets me once the staff realize that I don't want to have any books; I seem to be the only one in the whole prison. But the truth is that I have absolutely no time to read. The day is always over before I'm finished, and I have to force myself to read over my statements again from time to time, or rather my notes about them, because I'm so pressed for time. Sometimes I concentrate on one line for quite a long time, such as Job 5:18 and 19 or "Their soul in Your hand, may become smaller and cleansed of all impurities, focused only on You."[3]— Then I go back to thinking about how my Pim will cope with it all and how I might best pray for her. It is quite difficult to pray in the right way, and one doesn't always capture it as well as King Solomon (2 Chron. 1:10); then I spend an hour reciting to myself, reveling more in the way it all hangs together and harmonizes than in the individual ideas; sometimes I don't think at all as I recite, because I know my feelings perfectly well. That's how I spend my days. Then I work on my defense, thinking about how unsuited I am for a defense of this kind, because I see the worthlessness of the arguments on both sides, including those of the indictment: how false, how hollow, how deceitful! And then I think that the people must see that themselves, and then I have to strain to recall that they really don't, and that their view of the world is so different from mine, as though we were sepa-

rated by thousands of years.—I've completed the first copy of my
defense but don't want to start the second one today; instead I'll
  [The letter breaks off here.]

1. Field Marshal Wilhelm Keitel. 2. Rösch had gone into hiding but was discovered and arrested on January 11, 1945. 3. Hymn 107, "Jesu, der du bist alleine."

HELMUTH JAMES TO FREYA, NOVEMBER 6, 1944

Tegel, 6 Nov 44

My dear, this time around I have only two concrete things to say: *1.*
On the issue of what to include in the petition, that has to be left to
a man who knows his way around these kinds of petitions, that is,
Sack, who is the best choice, otherwise Dix. We're all amateurs. *2.* Be
careful in the matter of Sperr! The woman who takes care of him has
to be very reliable, cautious, and good, otherwise it's too risky. Delp
says that Sperr said two things: *a.* Sperr told him, Delp, about Stauffenberg's plans; *b.* Sperr talked with me in general terms in '43 about
overthrowing the government and not only about postwar plans.
Both of those things are false, and he has to renege on these points.
Last night I once again had no desire to die; not that it tormented
me, but I simply had no desire and found the prospect of the kingdom
of God quite vague and unclear and not really tangible. Luckily I
now laugh about these tribulations when they assail me, at any rate
when they come in this innocuous form, and I don't really take them
seriously. If I were to continue to be plagued by doubts, they would
have to beset me more thoroughly and stem from deep down: With
the help of God and the Holy Ghost, the banal "flesh"-based doubts
will no longer hold sway over me. The only sad part is that our mind
is such a sophisticated instrument that if it wants to it can always
reach down even a level deeper than one expects, and it can also rise
higher than one thinks. This expansion of its capacity, which, unfortunately, always occurs simultaneously in both directions, is a process

that brings about growing pains in the very same way that I had them in my body between the ages of fifteen and sixteen.

Yes, my love, your future: If you can live on two levels—a busy one and a contemplative one—that is good. Only you can decide whether that is feasible. In that case, the contemplative level is simply open to the Holy Ghost for primordial reasons, for reasons we don't know. If you achieve that, it is presumably still better, because it is something more certain than the spiritual capacity that a person like Ulla [Oldenbourg] has. You can then do without that capacity, or if you have it, it's an added bonus. You know what I mean: I think you might have the ability to carry God as surely within you as you carry me within you, without ever devoting a thought to Him. That is certainly possible, and a state of grace. But there is no doubt in my mind that you could also achieve it through your intellect and spirit if you were to force yourself, go to great lengths, work on it systematically. But that requires time, strength, and calm; I don't know whether you will be granted any of these three things when I leave you. You have to wait and see about all that and commend your soul to the Lord. He will give you what you need.

My dear love, how wonderful that you were in Kreisau and visited your little sons. I very much hope that Frau Pick stays with you in any case; under no circumstances should you let her go for financial reasons. Until the end of the war you have to find your way through it all however you can and not pinch pennies. Mütterchen Deichmann will help you out. Later it will be different; then you'll have to make do with what you have. Does Frau Pick know that most of the men whom she has cooked for are already dead: Carlo [Mierendorff] and Peter [Yorck] and Adam [von Trott zu Solz] and Haeften,[1] etc.?—I hope events won't force you out of the Berghaus. If you can stay there, I think you'll always be content and provided for. Your bees, the fruit trees, so many things we've planned will prosper and help you. Besides, these days we're doing so well financially overall that I don't think you'll have trouble. How good it is that we stayed modest in every way and now no great change is necessary.

I'll stop now, my love, because we're eating soon, and also you'll soon be arriving in Berlin. Oh yes, I ought to write you what I need: two shirts, handkerchiefs, one towel, thick underpants. I have enough of everything else.

Farewell, my very dear, my very dearest love, may God watch over you. J.

1. Members of the Kreisau Circle.

FREYA TO HELMUTH JAMES, NOVEMBER 6–7, 1944

Monday afternoon

My dear, I'm back here, and very glad to be so close by. First of all the news from Frau Reisert from a very reliable source—she'll be telling me more details about it tomorrow—that there won't be a trial in the week of the 13th to the 20th. So now we've slid all the way to the 20th, and this time, my dear love, still belongs to us. What good fortune! I've been in such good spirits for many days now and can't suppress them for more than a very brief time. I'm not filled with actual hope, but for some inexplicable reason I'm utterly carefree. I keep wondering why that is, and whether I'm actually being frivolous, but I can't keep it in, and everybody is telling me I sound and look as though things are going better, even though that's not the case at all. It surely stems from the good fortune we've enjoyed these past weeks. I keep having the feeling that we're going through these weeks hand in hand, and I think more in terms of "we" than I have in all these years. Oh, my Jäm, what great good fortune to be so close to you. I wonder how you spent the three days. I'm sure you wrote quite a lot. That is certainly strenuous business. How I'm looking forward to hearing from you again.

Please think over what reasons I should be presenting in getting permission for a face-to-face visit. It has to be the kind of thing that can be taken care of only in person. I have the balances of all of our bank accounts with me, the estimate for the new crops, our old financial statement, which I worked hard on yesterday. I've thought about saying that I couldn't figure out the various bank accounts and the money transfers into them and needed clarification from you as to what kind of money was where, and what kind of money transfers. Yes, I understand you so well when you say that we ultimately don't need Herr Schulze, I agree with you completely, but if Herr Schulze only knew what happiness it would give me, no, us, my love, to look at each other, he wouldn't grant me the permission, because he wouldn't want us to have that, since he regards you as an enemy of the state. My Jäm, what happiness it would be for me to see your beloved face and your hands. Oh, how I feel my love for you as I write this!

It's now— That is where I went to bed, and now I'm sitting at the friends' home on Tuesday morning. I've barely read anything, but I fear that he has to leave right away. So in addition to my love, I'm just quickly sending you the news that Sack has long since been arrested,[1] so Dix is the one who remains for me to go see.

1. Sack had been arrested on August 9, 1944.

HELMUTH JAMES TO FREYA, NOVEMBER 7, 1944

Tegel, 7 Nov 44

My love, Carl Viggo [von Moltke] will likely be coming tomorrow, and then we'll know whether Freisler will see him at all and what he'll say. I'm eager to find out.

I'm continuing to do quite well. Yesterday your November 2 letter arrived.[1] I think I'd forgotten to tell you that I sent Casparchen a second birthday letter by way of the People's Court; I thought that was the right thing to do.[2]—Yesterday afternoon I read two beautiful Proverbs. I find that one verse brings me pleasure on a given day, and on a different day it's another. Yesterday it was Proverbs 14:32 and 15:15.[3] The great appeal of all spiritual truths is their everlasting nature, regardless of whether they're two or 2,000 years old. And considering how quickly everything else gets outdated, it's hard to grasp why the humanities are in such a bad state and so less highly valued than any form of technology. This is not a recent development; it was already the case when I was a university student and most likely before 1914 and even before the turn of the century. The heyday of the humanities came to an end with the end of restraint, and now technology dominates us. Will our little sons be part of the generation in which the tide turns back once again? It is truly high time! Why didn't we see that for what it was long ago? I've basically always had an antitechnological disposition, but as a student I didn't realize that, otherwise I'd have studied differently and explored different subjects. I had a clear understanding only of the negative side but not of the need to drill down with all our might to the depths of the humanities and pierce through to its buried source. At least one generation, and maybe even a second, will pass before that can bear fruit, and if we're being honest, there is no beginning in sight as yet. We can embrace the hard times that lie ahead if they serve to show us the path to our goal. But will they? It always strikes me as so familiar when I read how Judah or Israel are punished for abandoning the Lord and following other gods made of wood or metal. Might we, too, have to go through Babylonian captivity for seventy years? The truth is that the first commandment is the key to everything else. Christ does say so [in] Matthew 22:34–40, Mark 12:28–34, and Luke 10:25–28 as well, but we must continually bear in mind that any devotion to God's creatures can be idolatry. In any creation, be it physical or mental, you can love only the creator; loving a human being, a nation, an idea for its own sake, even in the most sublimated form, is idolatry and violates the first commandment. Can that be taught to children and teenagers? I used to regard as foolish old fables all the stories about Baal[4] and Ashtoreth and all the other deities the ancient Jews fell for, because no one really explained their symbolic content to me. The first commandment seemed natural and unproblematic to me, and difficult only for the ancient Jews, because we wouldn't even be tempted to pray to other gods, apart from Mammon and the belly. Gradually this commandment fell into place for me, but it was only in Ravensbrück that its key role became clear. It is the commandment of all commandments: if we truly bear that in mind, we may go astray in all the other commandments, but we'll always find the proper corrective. But if you go astray in the first one, you're unlikely to notice the rest.

My love, I've been chatting on and on, don't have anything else to write other than that you delight me, that I have every reason to thank the Creator for you, that I love you, my dear, and can only pray that the Lord may hold you in His hand and watch over you, with and without J.

1. Presumably the official letter Freya mentions on November 3. 2. To avoid suspicion of the ongoing clandestine correspondence. 3. Proverbs 14:32: "The wicked is driven away in his wickedness: but the righteous hath hope in his death." Proverbs 15:15: "All the days of the afflicted are evil: but he that is of a merry heart hath a continual feast." 4. Baal was a heathen deity. Freya remarks on the unshaken reverence of Nazi believers in their false god.

FREYA TO HELMUTH JAMES, NOVEMBER 8, 1944

Wednesday afternoon

My dear love, yesterday you wrote me all kinds of beautiful things, which I enjoyed so much. I also quite like what you write about the humanities. What is likely to come of everything that matters so much to us? My disposition is of course also quite nontechnological, and I've often wondered whether that isn't a major shortcoming of ours and could become dangerous for our children. It is clearly a task for the future to redress the overemphasis on technology, but that is possible only after a certain process of digestion, and when it comes to the two of us, I get the feeling that our nontechnological disposition won't even let us digest it because we won't consume it in the first place. That is a mistake.

My dearest, I'd wanted to take care of the factual part first, and instead I dove right into enjoyable musings. So now I'll get to the report: We want to get to Sperr by way of Frau Reisert, who already made a meal for him today and sent greetings. Frau Reisert knows the practices at Lehrter Str. quite well, and I think she can be entrusted with that.—I was at the 1st court. Freisler had a trial, and his friendly secretary said that it was not customary for him to meet with anyone before the trial. I said I would sign up in writing, but then I left it alone so as not to take away the opportunity from Carl Viggo [von Moltke]. All we know is that Carl Viggo also has to show up there "on his own behalf" if he is to be at all successful. And I'm quite skeptical as to whether he will be. Additionally, on Friday there is certainly a trial, but the order of the visits doesn't seem too important to me. Yesterday afternoon I spoke to Oxé, Haus, and Pfuel in the department; the latter (not my case) acted self-important and hard-working, but also fully involved, to the extent that his own interest allows for that, while Oxé and Haus are truly devoted and concerned. *1.* I tried to tell Haus how he should brief Bürkner today at noon as far as you're concerned. He said to me in regard to this point that there was no doubt that Bürkner considers you an outstanding, or, as he said, *important* worker, and that your possible death would "upset him *greatly.*" *2.* They considered the idea of going through Keitel a bad, very bad one; he would surely do nothing at all, they said, other than alternating between trembling and "hollering 'July 20th.'" So after a lengthy back-and-forth, they suggested sending the clemency appeal via: Bürkner, Hewel, Hitler. But we ought to discuss that with Bürkner. Steengracht could also put in a word with Hewel, whom I hadn't heard of. They also heaped praise on this man Hewel and said that the Führer listens to him. That's where we are now. Carl Viggo will come on Friday at 8, and then we'll see. I've forgotten to mention that during the visit at the court, I was sent to a very unpleas-ant Saxon senior administration official regarding an attorney's ques-tion. He said right away that Dix was out of the question, and there were only seven eligible names. I could choose one of them, he explained, and he would designate him the official attorney. Dix is for Hercher[1]: He's reputable but elderly. Frau Reisert's office manager praised Hugo Bergmann. Fundamentally the choice is between these two. But now I'm determined to write another letter to Freisler next week about this issue, when things with Carl Viggo are complete. I want to try to see Freisler, even though it's unlikely that I'll be able to.

What you write about the first commandment is very much on my mind. You're quite right. Sometimes I used to think about how I wasn't able to love God the way I love you. That seems very difficult to me, although I've made great progress. I was always aware that a very great, strong love carries within it the hazard of limiting one's ability to love God or other people. But I never saw it as clearly as you describe it.

Now, my Jäm, I'll head off to bed. It's 9:30 again, and the friends should be getting to bed early. I'll send you the Steengracht text. Good night, my Jäm, my love, my beloved. I'm sending you a tender embrace. I am and will forever remain your P.

1. The attorney Wolfgang Hercher.

HELMUTH JAMES TO FREYA, NOVEMBER 8, 1944

Tegel, 8 Nov 44

My dear, that is quite a delicious turkey! You got it to mature quite quickly, or was it an emergency slaughter? Can you eat an animal like that every Sunday? That would certainly help us out quite nicely.—You know, our apples are so incomparably better—in both taste and nutrition—than any that Poelchau brings me that it is downright astonishing. They are so beautifully uniform. It is a true joy and likely a result of the way we've cared for them. If you can remain in the Berghaus, you definitely ought to take up bird care, then you'll get splendid fruit.—Now back to a concrete issue that occurred to me. I might be asked whom I told why I need the information of a macroeconomic, etc., nature. I actually told quite a number of people. I think I should name Carl Dietrich [von Trotha] and Einsiedel. It won't put them in any more danger because I was asked to provide detailed information about those two a full three months ago, and I assume that the district attorneys are waiting for my trial before deciding whether they want to arrest them. That's why I think it won't entail any additional risk. On the other hand, however, it improves their defense quite significantly if they can say it was for my work at the Armed Forces High Command.

Before my execution I'll still have a chance to write you a letter. I don't know for certain whether I will make use of that, especially because it isn't certain whether you'll receive it. All these letters that go through the censorship are somewhat untruthful, and I can imagine that I won't want to write you a slightly fraudulent letter at a time like that. So don't draw any conclusions from the fact that there is no letter or that there is one that strikes you as distorted or troubled. Everything has been said between us, my love, it wouldn't contain anything new. If I should happen to think of a turn of phrase that is true and persuasive, yet would pass censorship, I'll certainly write it. It may also be that I write because I'm afraid that it will attract attention if I don't, or because that's the only way that the guard sitting next to me will leave me alone and not disturb me. It's not as though I can recite Psalms aloud in his presence, which would certainly be my preference. For all intents and purposes, I believe, my love, that I will already have left you in that moment and can seek you only in God. I've given that a great deal of thought, and I wish I could anticipate my death mentally, so to speak, and not push it away in my thoughts, but instead turn to what lies ahead. Maybe this is all nonsense, and maybe we're so caught up in the procedures and operations that we're unable to think of anything else; or maybe the reality or rather the unreality of the process is so enormous that any preparation blows away like dust. I don't know, and no one can tell someone else, because it's bound to be different with each of us. I'm writing this to you only so that you don't draw any wrong conclusions.

Well, they're now getting me for my haircut. Farewell, my love. May the Lord watch over you and us, and, should it please Him, may He save my life. J.

FREYA TO HELMUTH JAMES, NOVEMBER 9, 1944

Thursday afternoon

My dear, not much happened today, but Gentz, the old criminologist, has advised me to go with Hercher, as Dix has. He told me he's worked with him. Pfuel has yet to comment. Marion [Yorck] was very impressed back then by the humane way he conducted himself. He is what is referred to as an elderly gentleman, someone who surely lacks Dix's stature and skill and quick-wittedness. But I don't think we'll get him. I'll have to decide soon. Then I spoke to Haus on the telephone again, who isn't leaving for the west until today, and he told me he spoke to Bürkner yesterday over lunch. Bürkner evidently already knows that we're coming with the petition, has approved of the approach via Hewel, and is prepared to take over its delivery. Haus said he wanted to tell me that "to ease my mind." It was also gratifying to learn that Bürkner said he already knew that Steengracht was prepared to support the matter wholeheartedly. I am quite pleased that this worked out without my putting in an additional appearance. Now things can start tomorrow. Lansstr.[1] at 3:30. Bürkner and Dix at 5. In the morning an attempt to get to see Freisler, while I visit Schulze. But I'm sure that Freisler has a trial. First Carl Viggo [von Moltke] will come here to have breakfast, and then we will likely type up the draft of the plea. I'm somewhat fearful how all this will work out.

My love, when I think about how you are now standing by me with such fortitude, come what may, equipping me for the road that lies ahead for us, how strength and serenity and confidence flow from you to me, I'm not only full of admiration that you can do this but I also get a definite feeling of how God's strength, God's peace, and His love reside within you. Yes, we will remain united and close, and we will live on and find each other again and belong to each other forever, but dying is hard nevertheless, and one always faces death alone. I'm not supposed to go with you quite yet, my beloved dear, but maybe the executioner wouldn't really be able to kill you because the right side has to stay alive![2] As God wills, my love. I'd like to keep my hopes up because I find it too wonderful to live with you, and we can also keep our hopes up ever so slightly because we want to fight—and gladly. My Jäm, I love you so much. I've loved you passionately for so long. I still understand why I was moved to tears—which Mami and Asta [Wendland] didn't understand—when I had to be apart from you before our wedding. Everything in life seemed pointless if it wasn't at your side. Since then I've learned that physical closeness is not what matters most—it also matters because we are such weak creatures, but it's not the only thing that counts—but my life still seems pointless to me if it isn't connected with yours. Back in Grundlsee, I already, and instantly, felt that I existed for you. I believed in the blade of grass around your left thumb. That's how it is. May God help me go on truly loving you! I'm sending you tender embraces and saying what you've known for a long time and what I still say again and again from the bottom of my heart: I am and will remain your P.

1. Helmuth's former office at Tirpitzufer had been relocated to the school on Lansstrasse due to bomb damage. 2. Refers to Helmuth's dream about the Siamese twins; see his letter of October 26, 1944.

HELMUTH JAMES TO FREYA, NOVEMBER 9, 1944

Tegel, 9 Nov 44

My dear, what delicious things you brought me yesterday! That was truly splendid. In any case, your gluttonous husband is greatly enjoying them. Herr Gissel[1] was also quite delighted and very obliging, which made me think that he expected something from these packages as well. But he's a kind old man.

One month ago, I was quite nervous about the oral trial. Not only did I not see how it could turn out—I don't see that today either—but I was also in a state of complete uncertainty about how to defend myself, indeed, if I'm being honest, whether I ought to make any serious attempt at defending myself. I have Pim, Poelchau, and above all the dear Lord to thank for that getting better, and I'm now calmly awaiting the trial. I now have to remain in this state of mind. I don't know whether anything substantive depends on this trial, even in its indirect effects; maybe it's just one of those maintenance stops, stops at which the conductor has to ring the bell, but getting on and off is not allowed. Still, that's not the point: I simply have to try to convey at least the impression that I'm espousing a reasonable opinion. Of course this would all be far easier if I weren't fighting for my life but only for the matter at hand; the combination is what's making it so hard. But I'm now quite confident. I have the feeling that the trial will have some surprises in store for me, things I'm unaware of, maybe statements from Goerdeler, maybe from Leuschner. Well, I'll have to wait and see, it's just an unfair game, but I always knew that: with your right hand tied behind your back, you're supposed to defend yourself against attacks from many sides without having the slightest idea in advance where they might come from; and the key witnesses are dead, which means that their incriminating statements can't be combated effectually, and their exonerating statements can't be extracted. Goerdeler as a witness will say nice things about me; rumor has it that he undoubtedly knows more about me than I do.

So I bless this month every day: however I look at it, it is always a tremendously precious month, and we have to give our thanks for it on a daily basis, on an hourly basis. Yesterday I came across Proverbs 18:14[2] for my Pim. And for your little sons, especially for Casparchen, I'm hoping for Proverbs 20:11.[3] May his heart remain unchanged and not be hardened by an idiotic education—not by you. He himself has to get harder than he is now, though he'll do that, but his heart needs to remain as it is. The anguish this will bring him, the wounds that a heart of this kind must suffer, are a precious treasure; he must learn that as well. I shudder at the thought of the educational principles now in force and think of Casparchen. The only good thing is that in the end, practical experiences and life are more powerful than those sorts of principles.

I embrace you. J.

A quick note about the letter I just received: *1.* As far as the choice of attorney goes, I think it's right that you try to get Dix. But make sure there's a decent alternative. The most important thing is for the man not to stab me in the back, so under no circumstances take the one that the councillor wanted. *2.* Keep Pfuel out of it: he's stupid and a blabbermouth and ruins everything he touches. *3.* Hewel is good. Not the man himself but the Bürkner–Hewel route is good because Hitler is known to actually pay some heed to Hewel. However, the imprint of the military would then be missing...[4]

1. The head guard at Tegel prison. 2. Proverbs 18:14: "The spirit of a man will sustain his infirmity; but a wounded spirit who can bear?" 3. Proverbs 20:11: "Even a child is known by his doings, whether his work be pure, and whether it be right." 4. The normal official channel for passing along the petition would be via Field Marshal Keitel, but their advisers suggested he would be a bad choice; see Freya's letter of November 8, 1944.

HELMUTH JAMES TO FREYA, NOVEMBER 10, 1944

Tegel, 10 Nov 44

My dear, my thoughts are with you on all your difficult and cumbersome travels today. Just don't be too disappointed if not everything goes the way you want it to. That's always the case. I'm wondering whether you've heard from Herr Schulze today. Might you get permission for a face-to-face meeting?

Yes, my love, dying is and will always be unpleasant, and any preparation for this event does nothing to change that. We always need to be keenly aware of this reality so as not to be overwhelmed all of a sudden by the unpleasantness of the process. Well, it's ultimately a peripheral process, and somehow I'll cope with that—not only because I have to. In the deeper sphere, the problem of death is only a matter of faith. Coping with this matter is incomparably more important and difficult. It seems to me that even though one might be plagued by doubts throughout life, the one and a half hours from my arrival in Plötzensee up to the moment of my death have to be shielded from doubt. That, above all, is what I have to pray for. "Now faith is the assurance of things hoped for, the conviction of things

Letter from Helmuth to Freya, November 10, 1944

not seen," Hebrews 11:1 tells us. "Conviction" is the vital point. The bad part is that in people as overbred as ourselves, the devil always has points of entry, so I can imagine him suggesting to a person something along these lines: "The only reason you're not doubting is that your flesh is afraid and has no other way of enduring the thought of death." I'm seeking to gird myself to face these and similar doubts as well as I can; but any attempt at girding is mere vanity, because at times like these, only the Holy Spirit Himself can help, giving one the strength needed to say: Get away from me, Satan! Everything else recedes anyhow. My love, I'm writing this to you so that you'll know exactly how you need to frame your prayers, because I don't want to do without my dearest as my supporter. If you are nearby, I hope to be able to stand close by you, quite close, my love.

I hope to be able to stand by you. And I don't want you to slip away from me either. Imagine that: what a possessive husband you have. Now it's coming out. Just don't grow impatient with yourself, my love. This is not an intellectual question but a spiritual one. It can be tackled not with work but only with prayers, innocence, and a humble heart. Everything worthwhile takes time and strength and effort. And an asset as valuable as a tranquil heart is no exception. The only advice I can give you is to take the time to make your heart tranquil and open and secure, just as you have to take your time when darning your socks. Sometimes it will work and sometimes it won't, and you have to accept that, but you always need to struggle to achieve it.

And why would your husband slip away from you? Don't you have a totally clear answer in 1 Cor. 13:13,[1] that three things remain when all else is ephemeral: faith, hope, love. That is the great trio, and why shouldn't your otherwise good-for-nothing husband be the modest instrument that God sent to teach you that? My love, don't consider it a shortcoming that you're not a "spiritual" person. In your situation, that could be very dangerous, and beguile you into embracing a cult of the dead. No, my love, I'm with you and will remain with you and stand by you and be within you without any need for ballyhoo. You know, it probably won't be any more difficult for you to find the right path than it was before; on the contrary, it may be easier. We always go astray, quite a bit, and the two of us have also gone astray quite a bit, and if your husband now precedes you out of the realm of time, you're less likely to go astray than before, but the demands you place on yourself to find the right path will have grown, so you won't even notice that you are going along more steadily.

And another thing, my dear: we read in Psalm 90, "So teach us to number our days." It's not easy to think in those terms. No one can always bear that in mind; even in my situation one constantly forgets it, because the flesh refuses to accept it. Even so, that is a very wise statement, because it gives you a fixed pole, the way a compass points to the North Pole. A realistic knowledge of death separates everything into large and small, important and unimportant, and bears out 1 Cor. 13:13. If your husband is gone before you, it will be much easier for you to set your sights on this constant. That is the pole pointing forward, and gratitude is the pole pointing back. Between the two, it seems to me, one can make it safely across the river, like a *ponte*.[2]—I'm getting too chatty, my love; this sheet of paper is making me stop. J.

1. "And now abideth faith, hope, charity, these three; but the greatest of these is charity." Where the King James Version translates "charity," Luther uses *Liebe*: love. 2. A wide ferry.

FREYA TO HELMUTH JAMES, NOVEMBER 11, 1944

Saturday afternoon

My dearest, my Jäm, you're sure to be waiting in suspense for the outcome of these days, and to sum up, I must say right off that I'm not able to see any great improvement in the situation. It may well be the case that we can do very little and that death has to be what we keep in our sights. It's probably best if I tell it chronologically, but I'll say from the outset that I *have* a permit for the face-to-face meeting. That is a great gift for us, my love. I'm so happy, my love, and am already afraid of having to part from you again. But that is just part

of our fortune, and I mustn't let that diminish it for me. So I'm carrying the permit in my pocket and haven't come racing over yet today:
I'd like you, too, to know in advance that I'm coming, and when, and
I'd also like to enjoy knowing that it still lies ahead of me. I'll discuss
the day with Poelchau. I'd also like to have some quiet beforehand.
My preference would be to come on Monday.—So, now I'll tell you
everything. Carl Viggo [von Moltke] didn't come until almost 9:30,
and by the time we'd had breakfast and he'd shaved, it was after 10.
But there was coffee, and right after breakfast Carl Viggo and Carl
Dietrich [von Trotha] drafted the first part of the petition for clemency together, with additions I brought up. Then we left it at that
because I had to see Herr Schulze at 12. Afterward we spent quite a
while at the People's Court. Freisler was presiding over a trial there.
His secretary said he had appointments from early to late on all six
days of the week. She noted Carl Viggo's wish, but wasted no time
in pointing out that he had a court session today as well, and this
morning, when Carl Viggo called at 8:30, she hadn't spoken to him
yet, and he was gone again. Carl Viggo is now writing from Schätz
before any more time elapses, saying that he wants to submit the
petition for clemency, and he wants to take part in the trial, so that
Freisler at least knows about it. I don't think he'll agree to see him.
In the meantime, Schulze, for whom I'd been waiting, came back
and agreed to see us. He began by telling me that "yesterday or the
day before yesterday" the charges were brought, but that the trial
would certainly not take place before the 20th, and most likely later,
and granted me the permit to see you, then I left and Carl Viggo
stayed. I hurried over to Thiele, a councillor who is much higher up
in the Nazi hierarchy than in the judiciary; he schedules the trials
and appoints the attorneys. I was terrified by the thought that he
might have assigned you Weismann[1] at his own initiative following
our previous discussion. But that was not the case; he actually said
that he wouldn't be making assignments until the trial date had been
set, and that process would take quite some time, and would not take
place until the very end of the month or perhaps, indeed most likely,
not until early December. Again I said that I wanted to be nearby,

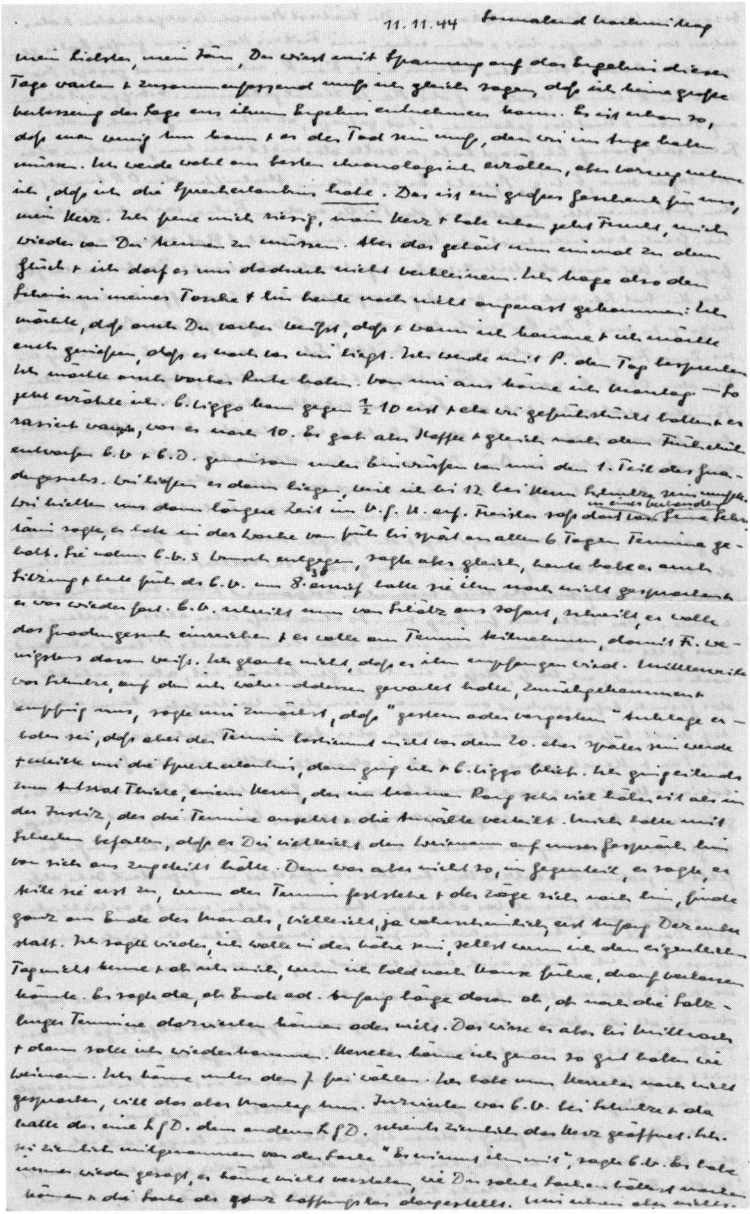

11. 11. 44 Sonnabend Nachmittag

Letter from Freya to Helmuth, November 11, 1944

even if I didn't know the actual day, and asked whether I could rely on this time frame if I went home soon. He told me that the scheduling for the end of this month or the beginning of the next depended on whether the Salzburg trials intervene,[2] but that he would know by Wednesday, and I should come back then. He also said that I could just as easily have Hercher as Weismann, that I could freely choose among the seven. I haven't talked to Hercher yet, but I want to do so on Monday. In the meantime, Carl Viggo saw Schulze, and the one lawyer had apparently poured his heart out to the other. It seems Schulze was rather unsettled by the whole thing. "It upsets him," Carl Viggo said. He kept saying that he couldn't understand how you could have done such things, and depicted the matter as utterly hopeless. But as I saw it, nothing especially new seemed to be coming out. They have established that you had organized meetings—quite a long time ago, in fact—and Fritzi [Schulenburg's] map[3] appeared to have played a central role. Frau Reisert once told me, in a similar vein, that in Reisert's case they kept coming back to the map. Carl Viggo then turned to the subject of Kreisau and the Moltkes, and asked whether he recommended sending a petition to the Führer, whereupon Schulze said that not only *should* he do so but also that it was even his—Carl Viggo's—*duty* to do so, and that he ought to submit copies to the chief Reich prosecutor[4] and the minister of justice[5] and request that they be presented to the Führer. As a rule, the minister takes less than one hour to rule on the issue of clemency and the sentence is carried out two hours after it is pronounced. We know how that works! Schulze said very favorable things about Kreisau, evidently because he's taken a liking to me! This charming man told Carl Viggo that the best thing about you is your wife! If only that helped! But Schulze doesn't want to suggest that the chief Reich prosecutor seize Kreisau, and was totally in favor of it remaining in possession of the family and likely of the little sons.[6] That was not the case with the man at the Ministry of Justice Carl Viggo went to see today, but more about that later. At home we finished up the petition for clemency, and afterward I spent a long time typing it, because I had to make it error-free. Then we slept here, and I couldn't go to the friends, which was hard for me. I couldn't even go this morning, because I had to have the petition at Lansschule by 9:15. Carl Viggo had a 10 o'clock appointment at the Ministry of Justice, and the people there were evidently quite unpleasant, gruff, and surly. He spoke to two men: First Prosecuting Attorney Pieper and Undersecretary Dr. Franke, who both said that the minister would certainly not present the matter to the Führer because it was about the July 20th plot. Carl Viggo insisted that this was not the case, but he replied that as far as he knew, you had made direct preparatory actions for July 20th. (But that is objectively *not true*!) It is just really unfavorable that you are sailing under that banner. Kreisau, he claimed, would certainly be confiscated, and if we tried afterward to keep Kreisau for the family through a petition for clemency, which in this regard would certainly be successful, it would be better not to claim it for the sons.—How is my love feeling after these digressions? Are you depressed, or had you wisely not got your hopes up? After I saw off Carl Viggo on his train—for the time being, he can't actually do anything—I was quite depressed, and went to great lengths to find our bedrock, then I went to see Frau Reisert, where I saw Haubach's girlfriend too,[7] and both women were so touchingly delighted to have me visit, and both had such an obvious need to seek comfort from me. It's strange; I keep telling them: Figure on death, there's no point in doing otherwise; and yet I always seem to give them a breath of fresh air and hope, even though I was in a very bad frame of mind today, but apparently theirs was worse. In Reisert's case, I have to say that I can't believe there will be a death sentence, but Frau Reisert expects it. She's a nice woman, smart, lively, and has a gentle heart, and she's also nice-looking. Today, though, she just looked miserable.

I send you a big embrace. I'm living quite close to you and am deeply united with you. I'm doing well, because I can rest assured that we're so secure. The other people have it much harder. In abiding love, I am forever your P.

1. On November 8, Thiele had recommended the public defender Arno Weismann to Freya, but Poelchau dissuaded her. 2. Freisler presided over trials

throughout the German Reich. Freya refers to the fact that he may not be in Berlin. 3. Fritz-Dietlof Graf von der Schulenburg. This appears to refer to the map on which the members of the Kreisau Circle marked the administrative districts (*Gaue*) and the military districts (*Wehrkreise*) for which they had specific state administrators in mind. 4. Ernst Lautz. 5. Otto Georg Thierack. 6. In most cases, a death sentence resulted in a seizure of assets. 7. Anneliese Schellhase.

FREYA TO HELMUTH JAMES, NOVEMBER 12, 1944

Sunday morning

Good morning, my dear! I'm very close by and will probably stay here until noon in order to get a reply from you. I can eat here, and then I'll go to see Carl Dietrich [von Trotha] again. I spent a good and lovely night here,[1] my dear love! Yesterday evening I was exhausted, not physically but emotionally. All the activity had filled me with hope, and then this activity struck me as unsuccessful, the impressions I had taken with me now depressed me, I found the situation disgraceful, and then all of a sudden I had no more hope. Even though I know this is the right place for our hearts, I was simply unable to keep my heart there, and the plunge hurts all over again each and every time. Now, however, I'm settled in down below again, and I'm back on firm footing—I think I can say that with certainty.

The dear good friends could already see from far away that I wasn't on an even keel. It must be easy to recognize, you would have seen it instantly too, so they kept me in this splendid haven, and I gave vent to all the gentlemen of Verona.[2] That was quite beneficial, and soon I had plucked up my courage again, found you—no, I always had you quite firmly, but found the true, indestructible, everlasting connection to you—and then I slept well and gratefully. May God grant that you aren't having a more difficult time of it! You will of course be tested far more in your cell, my dear. The fact of the matter is that the most beautiful thing we have been granted during these past few weeks is our shared preparation for your death, my beloved husband. That is the great gift.

Another thing became clear to me last night, or rather, overnight: We will not see each other as though it's the last time, my Jäm. We don't know that, we can't know it at all, and we'd make things too hard on ourselves otherwise. I'd wondered whether we oughtn't to make a point of seeing each other as though it was our time to part. I very much doubted that my heart could endure that, hence my fear. But this morning I know for certain that I have to see you in the pure happiness of being able to see you, filled only with joy and not with pain and with the fact of *life*. That's how I'll come, my Jäm, that's how I can be terribly happy. Do come to me in the same spirit, and don't let death enter into us. It has no business being with us yet. I've known it for certain since this morning.

My Jäm, I love you! You surely feel that with every word I write. I am and will always remain your P.

1. At the home of the Poelchaus. 2. That is, to tears, an allusion to William Shakespeare's *Two Gentlemen of Verona*.

HELMUTH JAMES TO FREYA, NOVEMBER 12, 1944

Tegel, 12 Nov 44

My dear, I've been thinking of you tenderly and a great deal, and hoping that you haven't fallen into a pit of depression because the tasks you are undertaking are strenuous and at times quite unpleasant for the soul. Right, it just occurred to me to tell you that I've been edifying myself in particular with a verse that is different from the one you know: 232, 4: "There my spirit knows no darkness, / Love remains when all is gone— / Sorrows crushing body and soul / Do the heathens know alone— / Resting in Christ's blessed light, / Fears she not the earthly night." That, my love, is something we have certainly both learned, and now we are told to remain in the blessed light. It is easier said than done, because it is not a possession you can simply carry home; instead, you have to achieve it anew every day, indeed, every hour.

Now I'll keep on writing my defense statement because I want to get it done today and then finish a new copy for the attorney at the beginning of the week. I would, however, very much like to see him, the attorney, ahead of the trial. Farewell, my love, I embrace you, may the Lord watch over you and the little sons and keep you in His blessed light. J.

HELMUTH JAMES TO FREYA, NOVEMBER 12–13, 1944

Tegel, 12 Nov 44

My dear, no, I'm not depressed at all. I hope you saw that I had already warned you about reacting to a return of depression.

My written defense will be sent off tomorrow, and I assume it will get to Schulze by Wednesday or Thursday at the latest. I think you ought to go to see Schulze again at that time on behalf of Carl Viggo [von Moltke] and ask whether he can find out if Carl Viggo can get to see Freisler. Maybe while you're there, you can get some sense of whether the written defense has made some sort of impression yet.— And please make sure to hand in Carl Viggo's letter to Müller in the outer office; do it yourself, but not until Friday, so that the written defense will be there as well.

Have you found out from Steengracht whether Kaltenbrunner has his own man at the trial or has to rely on news from Lange and associates? . . .

No, my Pim, you have it harder than I: the turmoil, the stress, the inevitable hope, the disappointment about people, the joy about people—all of that is far more stressful than staying in a cell. When you are misled into getting your hopes up, and the problem springs from within you, you wind up chastening yourself. Being on the outside, you have it harder, which is why you have also had it harder than Marion [Yorck], Clarita [von Trott zu Solz],[1] etc. But you'll also be richly rewarded for it. We shouldn't ever compare ourselves with others, because what really counts isn't how hard people have it but rather the relation of weight to the capacity for bearing it.

My dear love, I am full of happiness as I think about tomorrow. How wonderful it will be to see you. The question of whether it'll be the last time is totally unimportant. For years now, I have always left you feeling that I won't see you again; that is nothing new to me. Every time I've left Kreisau I've felt the same way. I'm happy when you're here, and I'm happy when you've been here, because then I can add a new image to my treasure album. In August and through early September, my broadsheet of Pim pictures spanned Grundlsee to the Fürstenberg train station, then it extended to include the courtyard in Tegel, and starting tomorrow it will extend again to Tegel prison, Building I. God willing, He will continue to add something more—not that we have any actual right to it—and we can be grateful in any case.

I basically don't have anything else to say, my love. Today I feel like a rock, and as soft as the most exquisite down. As long as the Lord sustains this frame of mind for me, I'll be untouchable for Herr Schulze, Herr Freisler, and the executioner, and I am receptive and filled with gratitude for every ray of sunshine, for every friendly thought, for the jingling of the keys in the lock when Poelchau comes, for a letter from Pim, and for Pim's presence. Look at how rich I am, immeasurably rich.

Farewell, my love, sleep well. J.

13 Nov, morning

My love, how delighted I am about this day. Such good fortune is being bestowed on us once again.

Since I assume that the director[2] will be coming shortly to pick up my letter to Müller and the People's Court, just a word about something that occurred to me during the night. I would direct the letter to the SS Reich Leader [Heinrich Himmler], without delay, and write something along the following lines:

> On behalf of the Moltke family I am enclosing a petition for clemency for my nephew Helmuth James von Moltke to the Führer, and request that you, SS Reich Leader, endorse this petition to the Führer.

If I am directing this request to you even though I know that you were already willing to show consideration for the name Moltke,[3] it is for the following reasons:

The Moltke family is a very close-knit family that has always felt like a single entity, a single clan, whose center was the Kreisau estate, which belongs to my nephew. The family as a whole has done great things for the Reich, not only in the past but in recent years has also committed its most brilliant member of the older generation to serve the Greater German Reich as the ambassador in Warsaw and Madrid.[4] In this war all the men in the family who were fit for military service have been soldiers: one was decorated with the Knight's Cross,[5] a brother of my nephew was killed in action.[6]

The proceedings at the People's Court and, as we have been told, the death sentence that is the expected outcome will deal a heavy blow to the entire family and all its members. Carrying out the death sentence would, however, make this blemish on the family take on an irremediable, irreversible character. The family therefore requests that it be protected from such an action and that the death penalty not be carried out on its now guilty member so that he can later be given the opportunity to be granted amnesty and not die in dishonor.

We are requesting a decision of this nature, which would be made not as a show of mercy for the family member who has incurred guilt but rather in order to soften the blow that an entire clan would feel.

Another idea: If it turns out not to be possible to endorse the petition now, it is requested that an opportunity be provided to revive it after the verdict, once these indeterminate questions have been clarified.

1. The wives of those involved in the plot were excluded from any communication and learned about their husbands' executions only after the fact. 2. Kurth, the warden of the prison. 3. See Editors' Introduction. 4. Hans-Adolf von Moltke was the ambassador in Warsaw from 1934 to 1939 and the

ambassador in Madrid from January to March 1943. 5. Johannes Helmuth von Moltke. 6. Helmuth's brother Carl Bernhard.

HELMUTH JAMES TO FREYA, NOVEMBER 13, 1944

Tegel, 13 Nov 44

My dear love, what a wonderful half hour we enjoyed. I feel a bit richer, safer, happier again. I was so glad to see that you looked well, and how lovely your little foal[1] turned out. My love, we have slid just past melancholy a few times, and I enjoyed even that because it gave us a way of feeling the lava under and within us, which we wouldn't have noticed without these dangerous moments. My love, how grateful, grateful, grateful we must be once again that this good fortune has been bestowed on us. And, my love, have you noticed that we have no need to worry, secure in the knowledge that we will always go together on our seemingly separate paths, you with me into eternity, and I to the warmth of you, on the path you continue to follow in life. I'm writing that without providing any alternative because I want us to build on this basis and not lose ourselves in picturing a life together. But we want to believe with all our might, my love, believe that the Lord can preserve me. We have not only a right to do so but a duty, because everything is based on this belief. Luke 17:20, for instance. We must not believe that God wishes to rescue me; so we need to pray to Him, and, depending on His resolution, He may hear our prayers. Yet we have to believe, and not doubt for a moment, that He *can* rescue me. Have I written you about hymn 230, 2? "Your spirit is never bound to human laws of reason and good intentions. Your sword can sever and undo the knot of doubt, according to your penchant. You tear the strongest bonds in two; whatever resists cannot come through; a word can break the strictest view; then you'll move ahead anew." The certainty that if I die, He wanted it to be so, and if He wanted it to be so, it was for the best, for you and for me, is grounded in the firm belief that for God, wishing and achieving are one and the same thing. Why? How can that be? What would have happened otherwise? These are questions that we are not entitled to ask. We read in hymn 178, verse 6, "And should you see no further trail, faith will prevail." You know it too, my love; I'm writing this not to instruct you but rather to affirm you, especially if you should think you can't see the proper path ahead. If the Lord calls me to Him in ten or fourteen days, anyone can easily see that it may be, and even from a human standpoint quite likely is, for the best. But in your case it is so much harder to see how this could be for the best. My love, fasten the rope you use to steer you across the stream to two stakes: "gratitude" behind you, and "faith" in front of you, and somehow or other you'll make it across the stream. And if you ram in the two stakes quite firmly, you ought to be able to laugh at the waves, no matter how high they may rise.

It's so lucky that you are so at home on Afrikanische Str.[2] Farewell, my love, I'll stop now, and I have to wage a little battle with Satan, nothing too bad, just a bit. I'm sending you an embrace. J.

1. Presumably an article of clothing. 2. The Poelchaus lived at Afrikanische Strasse 140 in Berlin-Wedding.

HELMUTH JAMES TO FREYA, NOVEMBER 14, 1944

Tegel, 14 Nov 44

My dear, last night I waged a terrible battle with Satan, and only the glow of your visit yesterday was there as a laurel wreath to reward me at the end of every struggle, and then I fell asleep again and again, filled with such tender thoughts of you that I was almost able to bless the struggles, which, in my weariness, conjured up the image of my Pim, so beautiful to look at, red, kindly, soft, beloved in her little gray foal.

The battle was about the issue of clemency, and eventually I came to the conclusion that the petition is bad and the path we have taken is wrong. I'm saying that so brutally, my love, because I think you can take it exactly as well as I can. The Lord has ordained this, and who knows whether it isn't for the best. The mistake is partly mine, partly

Carl Viggo [von Moltke]'s. I want to pick it apart because we have to try to fix it.

1. The approach. In my opinion, Keitel will not submit it. I would stay in touch with Erika [von Moltke] about that, and she should contact Bürkner for precise information. I think it's better for Keitel not to submit it. If he does, everything will have to work according to the current plan, and we need to leave the outcome to God. But I do ask you to say this to Bürkner: If Keitel doesn't submit it himself, but instead wants to pass it along to either the minister of justice or to Himmler, then he, Bürkner, should bring back the petition. In this case, we would pursue this approach directly. This wish regarding the approach is mine.

2. The contents:

a. I cannot appear in it at all, because the petition for clemency has to proceed on the assumption that I'm guilty and deserve to die. No earlier merits, no mitigating factors. Himmler and the minister of justice know about those and they are worthless.

b. There is only one argument: We are one of the major families in the country, and if the family unanimously—in writing—stands with me, the following argument can be made: Because of the family's closeness, with this one man the others are implicated as well, and together they can point to such great accomplishments that these merit clemency.

Make an entirely new petition with Dix tomorrow and discuss in detail with him how it ought to be presented.

My love, I've now subdued Satan, and my only concern is for you. Subdue him. I first thought I would spare you by keeping silent; but then, if in the middle of next week Bürkner happened to tell you that Keitel had rejected the submission, you would have fallen into a pit in a very different way. Just fight your way through. God's will shall be done, and if He chooses these paths, He has His reasons. J.

FREYA TO HELMUTH JAMES, NOVEMBER 14, 1944

Tuesday morning

My dear love, it was such happiness, such sheer happiness, to see you. Oh, my Jäm, how beautiful it was. This beautiful time is sparkling within me. You looked so well, so good, so right, the way you have to look, just like my Jäm, just like always. I was familiar with everything and saw this with delight and saw that everything was well wrought and well appointed from within. It really was as beautiful as could be, my love, and I know that you were content as well. My Jäm, there is no question that we are as one and united, but it was so palpable that God is prepared to stand by us, now and in the future. He is truly with us. He has also helped us—helped me, in any case—to achieve this beautiful state. For while I was on my way to you, I suddenly became afraid of what my heart might do, until I recalled a beautiful passage I had read on Sunday here at the friends' house: 1 John 4:18.[1] Do read it. From that moment on, I was no longer afraid, and then, after waiting so long at first, I got to be with you surprisingly quickly, and I felt nothing but happiness, even though I certainly bore in my heart the possibility that I would have to part with you in this world. My dear Jäm, my dear love, my beloved, my husband, we have to bear it in our hearts as well. I say it again and again. I saw that you do, but I do too. That's the way it should be, and you said, quite beautifully, that we mustn't hope but believe. My Jäm, the many precious words you've given me to go on these weeks were all confirmed, illuminated, and irradiated yesterday by the beloved sight of you. Yes, you are like a rock and like the most delicate downy feathers. How eager I am to pray for it to stay this way, for your faith to stay strong. I can't, I simply can't have any doubt that it will stay as it is and that God will help you. But there is nothing I would rather do than pray for it to be so. My Jäm, my Jäm, how beautiful it was and how grateful I am. I'd often told myself that it wasn't the least bit necessary for us to see each other, but seeing you was actually such an exhilarating confirmation of everything we have learned and lived through and experienced. You looked exactly the way that I hold you securely in my heart, and everything was just the way I know and love from the bottom of my heart, so dearly, so tenderly. Afterward it occurred to me that I wasn't just watching your mouth on its own; I was so filled with the entirety of you, I saw only the entirety, all of which was in your eyes and brow. I had no need to find out how dearly I love it all—I knew that—and so it was nothing but a deeply gratifying confirmation, a generous gift. My Jäm, yes, we are as one, and God does not want death to split us apart. I know this for certain, and will be able to carry this knowledge through any sorrow, any pain, and any tears throughout my life, down to the end of my days, so I'm sometimes truly confident and joyful and know what does and doesn't count, know the poles before and behind me. You wrote so much and so beautifully in your last letters to me. Go ahead and be quite chatty. That is my good fortune and reward. But our time together also proved that we are in complete accord in our very foundation and that this needn't be elaborated in words!

My Jäm, I slept at the friends' house again. I didn't get here from Nikolassee[2] until late. Wilhelm [von Moltke] didn't come home until shortly before 7, and I couldn't really pull what we wanted out of him[3] in just five minutes. He has grown incredibly old and diminished. I was quite shaken by the sight of him. They had all visibly aged. Karin and Heini Rittberg also came by soon after. Four days ago, he became a lieutenant colonel at the age of thirty. Just looking at him tells you that he might well have a brilliant career ahead of him. He is clever and cold, a fervent soldier, no clear-cut character, and utterly undeveloped on the human level. His wife is far ahead of him in this arena, though, she's the way a woman ought to be. He would surely never do anything whatsoever for us. He claimed that he had consciously steered clear of everything, that his precarious position required him to steer clear of everything. I have the impression that his sympathies lie with the SS. He clearly liked your letter to the SS Reich Leader the best by far. I don't know whether your petition to the Führer makes any sense because the Führer has anyone killed who has the remotest connection to July 20th. It is uncertain whether he'll discover that this isn't the case with you.

Poelchau has to leave in a moment, so I'll say farewell, my love. I love you very much and I'm full of gratitude and keenly aware of the words by which the two of us live. I am and will remain your P.

1. 1 John 4:18: "There is no fear in love; but perfect love casteth out fear: because fear hath torment. He that feareth is not made perfect in love." 2. The Berlin residence of Wilhelm von Moltke. 3. His signature for the petition for clemency. Helmuth and Freya used pro-Nazi relatives to appeal for clemency.

HELMUTH JAMES TO FREYA, NOVEMBER 14, 1944

Tegel, 14 Nov 44
My dear love, Poelchau had to go, but he'll come back again, and since I've always turned my struggles into a letter to my beloved, I'll go ahead and start one. Maybe it isn't time yet and the letter certainly won't get finished.

You can see that your proud rock has split apart once more and has again spent some time in hell. One thing is certain: If I were to spend several more months in this situation, I'd know hell better than I know Kreisau, for I've discovered that each time you penetrate hell more deeply than the time before. This time I was driven by my haughtiness, my lack of humility, and if Satan didn't appear to me last night, complete with tail and talons, it is only because the light in my cell stays on at night. Your beautiful, precious, magnificent, invigorating visit, this splendor, which seemed, once again, to sum up my entire life, had made a center layer within me keenly aware once more that such a conscious parting from life is simply not an act of reason, a mere formality, but a cut into the living flesh. The flesh's yearning for life was accompanied by insight into the hopelessness of my situation in regard to the flesh, and my thoughts ran to the petition for clemency and what I had written about that, and from then on I suddenly felt dependent on Hitler and Keitel and Bürkner and Müller and Himmler, and poof, I had fallen from the hand of God, or that is how I felt. I have learned quite a bit in the past few weeks, recited Psalms and songs and biblical passages, and as an old hand, so to speak, I always knew precisely what was needed next, and then there was Psalm 139, then the redemptive penitential prayer, and then the opening words of the sacrament of the Holy Communion, and now, I said to myself, I ought to be at peace, and I stood before the good Lord feeling so certain about my request: Now I've done everything, now hand over that peace of Yours. And this haughtiness, this very routine of fighting off the devil, was my pitfall; things kept going lower and lower, and the good Lord had no intention of doing as I wished but instead had me tortured by the devil, so much so that October 10 (?) was a celebration by comparison.[1] I realized that my routine—all I had learned about these questions— was the scourge. If, at the time, Psalm 139 could pull me out, I now knew it too well, and all the resources failed for the very reason that I didn't receive them with a simple heart but instead "used" them. And in my haughtiness I was not able to find simplicity. I was so haughty, my love, that you might say I was proud of my suffering, and told myself: How few people in all of Germany are capable of such suffering. I was unable to retain my faith, so I returned to gratitude, and then the image of my beloved looking so lovely in the little gray foal came to me, and I fell asleep gratefully. But I soon woke up again, and the whole thing started all over. Suddenly I was alone with my fear of being hanged—something that is downright antiquated—and alone with the devil, who cast doubt on things that had seemed utterly fixed and absolute during the tribulations I faced in October.

I hope and pray that it's over. I'm writing this only because I believe and feel that it's basically over. I can still feel my insides trembling, but I think that's just a sign that it's dying down and will soon be over.—My love, I'm also writing this to you because although I believe once again that God can preserve my life, I also know that I can't count on that in either the human or the spiritual sense. And so I want you at least to share in the fruits of this struggle and it may be of help to you if you should face temptation. But I just believe that you, my love, have the very simplicity that I lack, that you can never have my haughtiness, but instead you give yourself over to God's will with much greater humility. May God preserve you in this and spare you the trip into hell that I must take.

Will I be able to gain control over my haughtiness before I die? Do you see that the very act of posing this question is haughty? I'll leave the question in place anyway, because you might as well know it, and the good Lord has to forgive me so much in this arena that He will forgive me this thought as well. Humility is now more important for me than faith, for in the state I'm in, my haughtiness can rob me of my faith. I have learned one thing: Hell is deeper than we think, and if I should come back out of it today, the next fall might become even steeper. Somewhere it says, "Work out your own salvation with fear and trembling," and in Psalm 51, "a contrite heart, O God, thou wilt not despise." My dear, bless your simplicity and pray for your husband. These are hours that make me long for the hangman, can you imagine that.

Poelchau told me this: No subjective remedy can help. We have to know, even if it is only with our reason, that objectively we have become God's children through baptism, that objectively Christ died for us and that this is how it is, even if we don't feel it, if we fail to detect the subjective presence of this insight, even if, for that matter, we deny it. He referred me to Isa. 43:1+2.[2] He was right. But for a haughty soul it's very little and very bitter because it means that I'm on the exact same level as Heinrich Himmler and Adolf Hitler, provided that they are baptized. What a humiliation! But he is right, and I have to learn it, and until I have taken this into myself completely, there are no more new heights ahead either. Pray for me, my love, that God in His grace and in His mercy grants me humility and that I don't lose it again.

My love, it's all well and good to say "if I make my bed in hell, behold, thou art there"[3] as long as one isn't there, or at least not deep within it. But if all faith and all certainty are taken away, it becomes very difficult to say: I may not notice it, nor can I believe it, but it is objectively the case.

So, my dear love, the letter is finished after all, and I've poured out my heart to you. My love, you see how great yesterday's happiness was when I tell you that the gratitude for it and the happiness of seeing your image have repeatedly granted me the serenity that my "wisest" thoughts could not provide. The fifth stanza of "The Moon Has Risen" has that lovely line, "Let us become simple." Imagine how nice it would have been if I hadn't known the poem and had just come across it yesterday; but I did know it. I recited it to myself more than ten times, and it didn't help, precisely because I knew it and recited it for the effect I was anticipating rather than in a simple manner. Gruppenführer Müller would call that a complicated man.

My love, what a world I'm leaving you to. The things you write me about Dieter [von Mirbach][4] and Hans-Heini Rittberg can make your heart freeze. What catastrophes must there be before this mentality is eradicated. Stay as you are in this world, my love, and don't let your little sons get like that. I don't want to be like the Pharisee in Luke 18:9–14, but I'd rather suffer any wounds than fall into the hard-heartedness of people like them; they will never understand 1 Corinthians 13[5] and will wind up as poor human beings, but we, my love, are rich, rich beyond their imagination. Keep up this capability in the little sons. I do think that they have it, unless their upbringing drives it out of them.—I don't mean the way you bring them up. That's why you should keep them away from technology, by which I don't mean technological professions, although those are dangerous. But Dieter and Carl Viggo [von Moltke] are just as much technicians as a foreman is.—And, my love, for the hundredth time: Don't let this throw you. We now know what is big and what is small, what is important and what is unimportant; stay with this gauge, and I hope, my dear, that everything we've been able to write each other over these weeks will help you to do so.

Until I see you again, my love, in this world or in the other. Help to believe that the Lord can also save my life if He wants to, and that if He doesn't want to, it will be for the best. May the Lord watch over you and us. J.

1. The date in question is October 11, 1944; see Helmuth's letter of October 12, 1944. 2. Isaiah 43:1–2: "Fear not: for I have redeemed thee, I have called

thee by thy name; thou art mine. When thou passest through the waters, I will be with thee; and through the rivers, they shall not overflow thee: when thou walkest through the fire, thou shalt not be burned; neither shall the flame kindle upon thee." 3. From Psalm 139. 4. See Freya's letter of November 3, 1944. 5. See Helmuth James's letter of November 10, 1944, note 1.

FREYA TO HELMUTH JAMES, NOVEMBER 15–16, 1944

Wednesday noon

My dear, poor love, my Jäm, what a hefty price you had to pay for our beautiful time together, as that was clearly the trigger for this terrible fall. I'd been steeling myself for quite some time for the low that I feared would follow your radiant high. It would have come even without the visit, but not as abruptly and not—maybe not—as agonizingly. But it's conceivable that it was also a source of consolation for you. My love, it's not the case that I've been made unhappy by the conviction that I was the cause of this fall. I was able to squelch thoughts of that sort right away. I know too well that the visit was also a great source of happiness for us both, and will remain so, and I understand all too well the entire process within you. The toll it has taken was expressed in every word, and yet I can't even begin to gauge it, my poor love. Suddenly, I can now understand what I hadn't been able to grasp before: the scope of struggle and anguish experienced by our people of the greatest faith. My heart writhes when I picture it, yet it's clear that our greatest minds have faced and had to endure the toughest battles, for the very reason that they are great minds and haven't been able to be humble and simple before God, and they have to struggle terribly to achieve what Mamsell[1] carries within herself all on her own. You poor souls! Mamsell needs to pray for you! So do I, my Jäm, so do I, with so much love, but this beautiful simplicity and especially humility aren't very well developed in me—if anything, simplicity more than humility. The way of the world is that the highs and lows alternate. As long as we are in this world, we can't step out of it anymore than we can step out of time. It is just as certain that a low is followed by (at least) a higher ground as the other way around.

The only question is whether it goes like this: ∼∼∼∼∼ or this: ⌒⌒⌒⌒⌒. My love, all you need to believe is that God loves us and is merciful to us. He will hardly expect you to love Him as much while in your hole as you would at other times, in which case you would already be out, but if you are still able to believe while down there that His love is great and He is simply far greater than our own hearts, then Satan can go ahead and rage, but he can't accomplish much of anything. He's unable to do so anyway. Of course you know all this yourself, my love, and God willing, you are resting in His lap once again by now; you surely fear, though, that a low will hit you in the hours when you can't afford to have it. But only trust in God helps against that fear. I, my love, cannot think that way. He can test you but not abandon you. Don't forget the garden of Gethsemane[2] or Christ's last words on the cross.[3] It isn't easy, and it won't get any easier, but you will triumph anyhow because God will not forsake you. This I firmly believe, my dear love. It is quite evident to me that this is all very difficult for you, my truly complicated husband: We belong to the Pharisees, or at least to the wealthy, and so the way is especially difficult, because we have to divest ourselves of all our proud goods and burdens, which in many ways are the source of the sublimest earthly pleasure. Oh, my Jäm, I know! It's quite clear to us that we are effectively on the very same level as Himmler, Hitler, and Freisler. I don't dare to assess their functions and their weight on the scales of God. It cannot be so simple that God condemns the paths they take just as we do. This, at least, remains: "Father, forgive them; for they know not what they do." It seems to me, my beloved heart, that I'm also quite the Pharisee, the way I'm talking to you even as I stand with you, hand in hand, and, like you, await our fate from His hand. I want to descend to hell with you and come out with you yet I'm not at all capable of that; I'm far too primitive and cannot feel such things as intensely as you can.[4] All that truly remains in the end is just faith, *love*—and hope, my beloved Jäm.

Now, my Jäm, I need to write about practical matters.

The way I see it, the greatest danger in regard to the petition is that Hitler will have the wrong reaction because it will be coupled with July 20th, in which case Hitler will pay no attention to what it actually says. If Keitel doesn't work out, as we certainly assume, then we'll wait to see how the Steengracht–Hewel route goes. I think it's a mistake to intervene and push that again now that it's in motion and Freisler does know that it's in motion, and I have the impression that you had an exaggerated view of it because of your depression. Your letter and petition to the SS Reich Leader are also now en route. Müller's adjutant told me that Müller had forwarded the letter immediately and it would probably reach Himmler as early as today, or tomorrow at the latest. The egg has now been laid, and we have to put up with its scratches and splotches. A new petition would have new slipups. It is certainly favorable to our case that the cover letter to Himmler is better than the petition.

My love, all this doesn't frighten me so much, even if you give me new tasks. I'll do what I can and what I manage to accomplish with my limited strength and with the best possible guidance. Clearly my love and my threatened happiness are what spur me on.

Now I have to go to see Dix first. This is where things stand: Carl Viggo [von Moltke] saw Freisler today, and he will meet with me tomorrow at 8:30.—My beloved, now I have to hurry off to bed. Now where am I again!? My body is tired today and I'm glad I don't have to travel any more. So I'll leave from here to go to see Freisler. I'll just quickly fill you in on a few more things. Freisler was very friendly to Carl Viggo but hadn't read the files. Carl Viggo presented the petition, and Freisler said that the trial would be held no earlier than the week after next anyway. But of course he was aware of the overall situation. He wanted to have Carl Viggo come to the trial as well, but *Lautz* opposed that idea. He was very chilly, very reserved and dismissive, and wondered why the family would want to protect its black sheep. Quite the opposite of Freisler. On the subject of Kreisau, Freisler said he might not even declare that it be confiscated. So he was quite affable, but I don't get the impression that Carl Viggo made much of an impression on him. Haubach's fiancée, who went to see him this morning and wanted to have Dix, didn't accomplish anything. He beat around the bush and wrapped things up quickly. I won't accomplish anything either, but I'll go there. I'm not afraid yet, but I probably will be.

Dix thought the petition wasn't bad, and said it doesn't contain anything that Hitler would object to hearing. He made the good suggestion to follow up the copy that the minister of justice has with another cover letter saying that it has been given to Hitler and *Himmler* and to please suspend the verdict (carrying out the sentence), so that in the event that nothing has been decided yet, it can be deferred until such time as there is a decision. He thought that in the end they would be afraid to enforce the verdict without notification.

I hope you're already asleep, my dear, and that no Satan is tormenting my dear love. I'm going to sleep soon too. I'm wearily getting into my bed without hope and braced with many comforting truths. I belong to you, my love, and both of us belong to the Lord. Good night, my dearest. My will and the will for you to go on living are great—let us believe. I'm sending you an embrace, and I am and will remain your P.

Good morning, my love. I'm still eating breakfast, and then I'll go. I don't think it can help much, but it's right for us to do everything. How glad I am that Poelchau is coming to you again today. But I'm confident that you've found your balance once more. In abiding love, your P.

1. Nickname for Ida Maerkert, the longtime cook at the Berghaus. 2. Matthew 26:39: "O my Father, if it be possible, let this cup pass from me: nevertheless not as I will, but as thou wilt." 3. Matthew 27:46: "My God, my God, why hast thou forsaken me?" Luke 23:46: "Father, into thy hands I commend my spirit." 4. Freya could also suffer profoundly; see her letter of January 13, 1945.

HELMUTH JAMES TO FREYA, NOVEMBER 15–16, 1944

Tegel, 15 Nov 44

My love, I'm praying to our Father for you to withstand the anguish I caused you last night, that it was not too awful, that you get a full experience of grace once again. Forgive me, my dear, but today we are more married than ever before in the past thirteen years, so I cannot spare you my pain. God grant that I may help to carry your pain in the times ahead, oh my dear.

I just want to continue my story so that you get to hear not only about the drowning part but also about the gradual return to dry land. I think it's over, and He has once again sent me His grace. He didn't make it too hard either, as He preserved in me the gratitude I have for you and your closeness in even the worst moments. Yes, I hope it's over, I don't yet dare to move on the solid ground I've regained, I fear for my own safety, and my heart is still quivering, but I think it's over.

Last night, fearing I might make demands of some sort, I didn't put my prayers into words, but instead hoped that the spirit would represent me "with groanings which cannot be uttered."[1]

When I woke up in the morning and thought of my Pim, I felt better again, except that I couldn't bear the wait to get up out of bed, seeing as I couldn't bring myself to pray or read the Bible or hymnal, and then a little panic attack came over me about the petition for clemency. But it was merely a little—very little—rearguard action, and it struck me as more of a confirmation that He wished to let me feel my presence in His hand by showing me that I would be able to cope with it once again.

That's where things now stand. I've thoroughly tidied up my room, and afterward we'll be bathing. I won't be doing any reading again in the morning but instead will quietly work away on my defense, and simply wait until He calls me again.

Does that all make sense, my love? Since we are as one, I want to leave you with the fruit of our torments. Farewell, my dear. J.

16 Nov 44

Your letter has since arrived, and it really gratified me. I agree completely with all the practical issues; when it comes to the petition for clemency, it's basically the case that the less I know about it, the better. The only thing I want is for you, too, to feel as little stress about this as possible.

Now comes the interrogation I had today: I was taken to dictate my written defense, which was a very accommodating gesture on their part. I responded that the handwritten defense was now already on the way and that I didn't have my draft with me. I'd thought I wouldn't be questioned anymore.

Then an interrogation about Steengracht and Illemie [Steengracht]: odd and not an entirely pleasant line of questioning. Final question: Does Steengracht also belong to the Kreisau Circle and did he participate in the meetings?[2] Considering that the questioner regards these meetings as high treason, it's really a bit much to be asking something of this sort about an active secretary of state. The examining SS major, however, came across as rather foolish, and he was not well prepared. So it's possible that this was only an error in judgment and that they only wanted to clarify why Steengracht is speaking on my behalf.

The latter point is interesting, and then we got to the crux of the matter: Willo [von Moltke], Mami, connections with grandparents during the war, my intention of moving to England in the event of war. The latter particularly presumptuous in view of the fact that I'm here. I allegedly feel more like an Englishman than a German. The basis for that claim was the photocopy of a two-page typed letter, but they very carefully kept it away from me. One question led me to believe that the letter claimed Carl Bernd [von Moltke] was not dead but had defected to the British. I can think of only one source for this claim, and that is "Pension" Annie [von Moltke].[3] What else would explain the snide remarks about Mami, alleging that we were brought up British by our mother? Since I was able to give convincing answers about everything and concede the black mark that is Willo,[4] but said he was lost and written off as far as we were concerned, and we had only Red Cross correspondence with the grandparents, he wrapped up the matter without taking minutes and intends to work his way through the previously unknown personal details about me. I assume that I'll be called in again. Nice, isn't it? Luckily, I don't care a bit about it.

So, my love, I'll stop now. I'm well. Farewell, my dear love. May the Lord watch over you. J.

---

1. From Romans 8:26. 2. Steengracht, a committed Nazi, had no ties to the

Kreisau Circle. 3. Helmuth's father married thirty-five-year-old Anne Marie Altenberg in late 1937 after the death of his first wife, Dorothy, in 1935; Annie was not accepted by the children of his first marriage. When Helmuth's father died in 1939, a court dispute ensued, with a ruling in favor of Dorothy's children. The second wife was dubbed "Pension Annie" because her demands to the family were supplanted by a pension. 4. Wilhelm Viggo had gone to America with Helmuth's support, which, for the National Socialists, meant that he had "defected."

FREYA TO HELMUTH JAMES, NOVEMBER 16, 1944

Thursday afternoon

My dear love, what terrible weather. I wonder if it's really getting on your nerves in your cell, my dearest. I've done a lot of splashing about in the mud, but luckily with little galoshes on and so I'm dry down below. Even so, I don't feel very comfortable, and when the body is weak—it's not an illness, just weakness—the poor soul is far more vulnerable to dangers than otherwise. I already know this, but you know that the best knowledge is of no use. On days like these, my life without you at my side seems terribly dismal, and I regard myself as ill equipped for the task of continuing to live with you even though you have hurried on ahead of me. It's not overwhelming, but it's there, and I already know that I don't start to feel better until I'm sitting on the bench with the friends. They are the only ones who know my life, our life, so I'm safe and secure with them. I'm writing you this, but it needn't weigh on your mind. You know that it can't always go easily; I'm just telling you about it.

What should I tell you about Freisler? He was very friendly as well, but he doesn't want Dix, and he explained that everything having to do with the 20th should remain within as small a circle of attorneys as possible. If Dix were on the People's Court list as a public defender, he said, then it would be acceptable, even if he had himself added to the list, but understandably Dix doesn't want that, because then he'd have no time left for his private clients. So: no. Then I tried to get on his good side, but even if I managed to do so, it's of no use. I know him. He's a dangerously erratic man, but somewhere in there he is also human, although he's one to constantly playact and is said to be phenomenally smart as well. A very dangerous man, but only in certain circumstances. At any rate, instilling respect in him really matters for his verdict. I'm well aware that Carl Viggo [von Moltke] wasn't able to make any headway with him. He told me that there are also acquittals; Bismarck was acquitted. A judge, he added, must never convict wrongfully, and other platitudes of that sort. So it wasn't unpleasant, but it didn't accomplish anything. Afterward I spoke to the councillor[1] again and didn't hear anything new, but his whole manner suggested that he truly intended the recent advice he gave about Attorney Weismann as good advice. He's not wickedness personified. There's no such thing. They worship their Baal with an absolutely clear conscience and full of conviction.—So I took Hercher and went to see him at 10 and had a very good impression of him. He will do everything he can to help you. He won't stab you in the back. He's spirited—the kind of person you meet in Berlin—and elderly, but not the least bit crotchety. He is without question a respectable old man and a decent one. You can work with someone like this. He has a sense of human probity. In short, I liked him. I don't know yet when he'll be able to come to you. His schedule is awfully crowded next week, and even though the president of the court said that he would be coming to see you in the next few days, that's not correct. He can't come to see you until the trial date has been set, usually two to three days in advance, but I'll see to it that he makes it the week after next; after all, I have the president's word on that.

I would like to have the strength for the coming weeks. I would like, my dearest, not to miss the precious days. I would rather endure distress and suffering and have to struggle, yet be able to stand by your side and be as close to you as possible for the final weeks and days. May God help us do so. It won't work without His help. I'm sending you a tender embrace, my Jäm, and I am and will forever remain, full of love, your P.

1. Thiele.

FREYA TO HELMUTH JAMES, NOVEMBER 17, 1944

Friday afternoon

My dear love, I just got a call. Freisler didn't leave, as he'd intended to. The trial may be sooner than expected after all, because he'd planned to be away for six days. I called up the court right away, but no one is there anymore. So tomorrow I won't be going at 8 but will wait until 10:30 because I have to have the information, and if I'm not certain that next week things will remain calm, I don't know whether I'll be chasing after Steengracht tomorrow to find out how far along he is in this matter. I'll spend the day of the trial alone. I don't want to be distracted. I'll see if I can get Hercher to call me up right away when the judgment is rendered, so my thoughts and my prayers can be with you afterward. You shouldn't think about me anymore, but I should be thinking about you. The only people I could see on that day are the Poelchaus. I think I shouldn't make any attempt to come to the superior court. The sight of me could only distract you, and it is highly unlikely that I'd see you at all or you'd see me. For that to happen, I would have to do a careful study of the premises and the question of whether you would be coming to the courtroom by way of the corridor or directly. I can find that out from the secretary in the attorney's chamber; she's nice, and I know her from Reichwein. I'd like to have your opinion on this. As I wrote you yesterday, Councillor Thiele told me, "I've been to every trial so far. A person's demeanor and comportment are all that is needed to reveal guilt or innocence." I'm sure that your inward composure is critical not only for yourself but in every respect. I don't think, of course, that the trial is *merely* a comedy; tragedy is more appropriate. At least your composure is important for how the case proceeds. I'm so glad that you are taking a firm line, and that this line is a bold one. That makes it easier to keep your composure. My Jäm, I'm not ambitious on your behalf; the gravity of this day is hard for me to fathom. But I have faith that you will weather it well. I'm asking God to give you strength and power and serenity, Moltke serenity. In the end, they can take nothing from you but your life! Whether you lose it at the age of thirty-eight or forty-six is of lesser importance than that you die a rich man: you know the whys and wherefores; you will die in the faith that you are dying after a brief and beautiful life. You will leave me stronger, you yourself were able to help get me this way, you know that life basically comes easily to me; and we both know that we will never lose each other because our love unites us forever. All hells and all torments, all tears and all sorrow can do nothing to change that: "There is no fear in love; but perfect love casteth out fear."[1] Do you find that so comforting and so beautiful too, or is it beautiful only for me?—My Jäm, at Christmastime you'll still be quite close to me, and then you'll really have to help me, because otherwise it will get too hard. So, my beloved love, now I'm heading to the friends. On the way I'll pick up another letter from Mütterchen Deichmann. When Haus called earlier, I was really happy that this nice man was here again. But next week he's going to Godesberg again. I want to ask Jowo [von Moltke][2] in any case; maybe Haus will be there too. But most important, the Poelchaus are there.—Poelchau wisely said I might as well go to Kreisau at 8. Dorothee [Poelchau] will make the telephone calls, and if the information turns out to be very unsettling—which none of us assumes—I will be informed. Poelchau doesn't think it will go that quickly.—I feel dumbstruck about your interrogation! I'm not upset about it, but it certainly is astounding. I didn't think that such evil individuals actually exist![3] I need to give some more thought to Steengracht. But I didn't think that was possible either. I hope you were able to explain that clearly to the interrogator. It seems to me that my second letter was taken the wrong way, but we can't really know that either. In any case, they see you in a totally wrong light, and that almost upsets me.—My dear, and yet it is all *Kappes*,[4] and we fortunate people know what counts. My dear, my love is abundant. May God watch over you, my love, watch over us. I am and will forever remain your P.

1. In Freya's letter of November 14, 1944, she refers to this passage from 1 John 4:18. 2. Helmuth's brother Joachim Wolfgang stood by to help Freya and Helmuth at any time during these months. 3. Freya refers to the apparent

false accusations Helmuth had been questioned about by the Gestapo; see Helmuth's letter of November 15–16, 1944. 4. Rheinland slang for "nonsense."

HELMUTH JAMES TO FREYA, NOVEMBER 19, 1944
[OFFICIAL LETTER]

Berlin-Tegel prison, 19 Nov 44

My dear, last week there was no letter from you,[1] so now I'm hoping for the first days of the new week. But, my dear, how happy I was to be able to discuss the most important matters at least with you, and to be of at least a bit of help to all of you. The issue of the fertilizer really worries me, of course, because there is only the choice between reducing the intensity of the entire operation or taking a considerable risk in the grain harvest. But I think we have to choose the second course. We just have to hope that the weather helps us and that we'll have enough laborers to work the fields and make up somewhat for the lack of fertilizer.

Overall, I'm continuing to do well. My feet got wet from my worn-out shoes and I caught a cold, which has been traveling through me and at the moment has taken on the form of lumbago after gracing my head and throat. But it's not bad at all, and I'll be over it in a few days; I'm mentioning it only for the sake of full disclosure. Apart from that, my body and soul are healthy and in balance.

The days fly by like a storm; they're so short because we stay in bed for so long and sleep so very much. Today begins my eleventh month of detention, and a year ago was the last time I came home for three peaceful days. Asta [Wendland] was in the hospital, and before I arrived in Berlin on the morning of the 23rd, Derfflingerstrasse[2] and Tirpitzufer[3] had burned down, and after that there was only an indescribably great amount of work—though it was a success—until Jan. 19,[4] when the great calm set in.

When you went back to Kreisau, did you find that all was well and in order? November and early December are always our treacherous time of the year, in which everything tends to go awry, and with the constant rain that certainly poses a danger. But I hope Frau Pick will take good care of your sons. In the late winter it won't be so bad anymore. Did you get fruit trees this fall? What is the situation with chopping wood this year? It would be best if Zeumer could finish up the front part of the wooded areas between the fields, but would need to plant there for the spring. Are you still able to get plants? It would be absolutely essential to finish that; it's just that it would conflict horribly in the spring with the necessity for the most intensive field work and cultivating the winter seeds. The less you're able to accomplish with fertilizer, the more you have to hoe.

My love, the sheet of paper is used up. I'm leaving a mountain of work and responsibility to you. Don't let anything get to you; stay confident and joyful. J.

1. A statement meant to mislead the censor. Freya and Helmuth had to make use of the authorization of a weekly official letter in order to avoid raising suspicions about their secret correspondence. 2. Helmuth's apartment in Berlin. 3. The seat of several ministries and high commands; Helmuth also had his office there until November 1943, when his department was relocated to Lansstrasse. 4. The day of his arrest.

HELMUTH JAMES TO FREYA, NOVEMBER 19, 1944

Tegel, 19 Nov 44

My dear, don't come to the Superior Court.[1] A farewell glance would not make us happy: if we miss each other, you'll be unhappy; if I see you, I won't know whether that will give me strength for the trial. I sense that I'll be most secure if I put everything behind me beforehand and just gear up for this battle and its consequences. A backward glance can be dangerous under these circumstances.—Stay home in peace and quiet, or at the Poelchaus'; support your husband with deep serenity. Don't get distracted that day, and don't go running all over the place unless an extraordinary situation should crop up. But on the whole, this is where things stand: anything that hasn't been prepared by then won't be effective anymore.

This morning, my love, when the rising bell died away at 6:30, I thought of you all with great tenderness, the way all three of you were now probably lying together in your bed. What a lovely image that was. I hope you're finding that all is well at home. A year ago today was the last time I came home feeling truly at peace, because the shock about Asta [Wendland] was already fading.[2] On the 21st the three of us were in the hospital, and on the evening of the 22nd we were both in Breslau, where I spent the night; when I got to Berlin at 11, Derfflingerstr. was burned down. What a year for my Pim, and how well she has weathered it. May the Lord keep you in His grace, so that you withstand everything that lies ahead with the feeling that you are in His blessed light.

I feel quite ready for the journey ahead. But that doesn't change the fact that dying doesn't come easily to me, nor should it; but the odd thing is that each time I prepare myself for it again, it gets harder for me to take my leave. It's like screwing in and unscrewing a wood screw again and again and making the hole somewhat looser, so that when you screw it in again, you have to screw it one rotation deeper, which gets harder every time. It doesn't matter, and I don't put any stock in it; it's also a sign that the will to live, which I need for the trial, is there; I just want you to know that this is not the kind of thing one gets used to. For Stauffenberg, and for Peter [Yorck], it was much easier: speed is a relief.[3] Nevertheless, I'm grateful for every day, and if I still have to be at Prinz-Albrecht-Str. after my conviction, I'll enjoy every day there as well, there is no doubt about it, but a quick death after the sentence is an act of charity. I don't know whether that is an absolute principle or whether it's a function of age; it's certainly not an individual matter; I get the impression that only very young people—those up to the age of twenty-one or twenty-five—have a much easier time dying; the older you are, the harder it gets.

Yes, Christmas worries me too, if I were just recently dead. Think about whether one of the women would be able to bribe Herr Thiele. He's definitely open to bribery. Maybe he can shift the trial until after Christmas. After all, Christmas would be easier for you if I were still alive.

Farewell, my love. You know my thoughts, and so I needn't say more. J.

1. At times the People's Court convened at the Superior Court. 2. Asta had had a stillbirth. 3. Stauffenberg was executed on the very day of his attempted assassination of Hitler; Peter Yorck was executed on August 8, 1944.

HELMUTH JAMES TO FREYA, NOVEMBER 21, 1944

Tegel, 21 Nov 44

My dear love, I'm a little listless today. It's not too bad; it's a mixture of a bit of leeriness, a bit of a cold, a bit of stress from the darkness in the cell and the constant wind outside. I guess that's the way it has to be. At the same time, it's nothing worth fighting off in any serious way; it's on too silly a level. This afternoon I won't be writing;[1] I'll just let them handcuff me and I'll read the two books in the hope that by the time the evening comes, this feeling will have passed. It's probably also because right now I am waiting for the interrogations, which I'm anticipating with some concern, and have to prepare myself for the prospect of being brought to Prinz-Albrecht-Str. for this purpose.[2] This should not, of course, weigh on me, since I'm ultimately resting in God's blessed light at Prinz-Albrecht-Str. as well, but "how difficult it is for flesh and blood to strive for the eternal good."[3] I'm telling you this only for the sake of truthfulness in my reporting.

I've been spending these days—Monday, that is—just whiling away the time, feeling lackluster, with no particularly nice thoughts in mind, and really frittered away the day. Since I've been working seriously on my defense, every now and then I end up spending many hours on this garbage, unfortunately. But I feel that I need to do it and prepare, at least in the technical matters, all that can be prepared.

It's just that it's wrong to devote so much time to these things in the few days that I am likely to have left to me.

This is not a lovely letter, my dear love, and you actually deserve a very lovely one on the occasion of your return. But even though I'm listless, I love you very very much, my dearest heart, my part of myself, whom I won't be leaving whether I live or die. J.

1. He is referring to the document he was evidently unshackled to work on. 2. He had to anticipate abuses at Gestapo headquarters on Prinz-Albrecht-Strasse. 3. From the Bach cantata "Ach Gott, wie manches Herzeleid" (Ah, God, how much heartache).

FREYA TO HELMUTH JAMES, NOVEMBER 20, 1944

Kreisau, Monday afternoon

My dear, your thoughts must be seeking us out here so often. My dear love, you are so very here with all of us. Casparchen has kept discussing the question of whether you'd be let out by Christmas; everyone is thinking of you so full of love and full of hope. I found the reflection of my own good mood from when I was here the last time, now in everyone else. They all believe that things look better: Zeumer, Sister Ida [Hübner], Aunt Leno [Hülsen], Fräulein Hirsch, my—your—whole house was more lighthearted—for no reason, but it was still so very nice that they were all that way. How they are all thinking about you! How they love you, how they are praying for you! I so wish I could communicate that to you. My third thought when something nice happens is always: If only he could see it!—our Casparchen as he stood at the train on Saturday with his schoolbag, in his green loden coat and pointed cap, with a grubby mouth and mud-spattered legs, and how his face beamed when he saw me. We then headed home together, and the first thing he told me was that he had thought about bringing galoshes to school for me!! He has changed quite a bit again, not in his nature, which is wholly unchanged and very childlike, but he treats and regards school in a completely different way. He's working much faster and more precisely and, as a matter of fact, quite well. He writes quickly and neatly and knows how to do his multiplication tables up to 4 quickly and well. He has now understood it; it's working out. In the very same way that he used to think he couldn't do much, he now thinks, objectively and calmly, that he's able to do much more and has greatly improved his standing in his class. He also made sure to tell me that the soldiers are taking away Krause's tractor, and he can now bring nothing but sugar beets to Weizenrodau, and all sorts of other things. He's very grown-up in his heart, and a great, dear friend, and in all other respects still a playful toddler. He and Konrad sat on the floor in the living room yesterday after supper and played with old decks of cards. You know how and where. They were both engrossed in what they were doing and were talking eagerly at the same time. Then I thought again: If only he could see this! Konrad, the poor child, has poor man's rash[1] on his head and is wearing an odd hood. It doesn't bother him too much, but it is quite distasteful, and instead of his nice curls he has greasy strands of hair on his head. It doesn't disturb me. The little sons were the best part here. Apart from them I also felt at home and close to you, but nothing special was going on, yet I was feeling what the little sons mean to us in this menacing situation and was happy about them. They are also so overflowingly affectionate with me, neither wants to leave my side, and that is very comforting for me and quite pampering. Kaiser has now lost his fourth and last son. Isn't that awful? His brother, who fled from Cologne, will move into 14 and 13 in the Schloss. Schmudke's fourth son was also killed in the war; did I write that already? What suffering for all these people!— On Saturday afternoon I went right to visit Zeumer with Casparchen. He wasn't doing badly, and he's now driving his sugar beets to Weizenrodau because it's impossible to get hold of any wagons. The potatoes are out and ready. He plowed quite a bit, but the beets aren't all out yet—still, they'll all come out this week. Seventeen more acres have to be harvested. Once again, the fall was too wet for the beet harvester. We'll surely harvest a good eight tons of beets. Zeumer hasn't yet calculated exactly how many potatoes there will be. It's hard going with the constant rain, but in these two weeks he has managed to do quite a bit, and what is particularly pleasing

[The letter breaks off here.]

1. Impetigo, which is contracted mostly by children.

FREYA TO HELMUTH JAMES, NOVEMBER 21, 1944

Tuesday afternoon

My dear, yesterday afternoon I'd sat down to write with the serene feeling that I had a great deal of time ahead of me, but a leisurely letter of this kind takes up quite a bit of it, and before I knew it, there was Ulla [Oldenbourg], who now spends a lot of time living and sitting in my room, because Asta [Wendland] also sleeps in my bed, and shortly afterward high tea and Casparchen. But after eating, we had to head off right away, because there was singing at 5 in the Schloss at Aunt Leno [Hülsen]'s. While the children were singing, I left; but I did sing a couple of songs with them first and said to myself and felt that no matter what happened, the two of us would and could affirm the meaning of "Oh How Joyfully"¹ together on Christmas just as we do today. So while I was singing and looking down at my happily stuttering Casparchen, I had one of those exhilarating moments in which I experienced everything the two of us have gone through as grace in all its grandeur, warmth, and ability to fulfill us completely. Do you know that feeling? I don't even need to ask. I know that you know the feeling. Casparchen was a bit sad when I went. I had a quick visit with Sister Ida [Hübner], then left at 5:42 p.m. I've now given up traveling second class, even at night. I slept for a long time, and well. For the Poelchaus I brought a giant box with a goose, cake, flour, apples from farmer friends; for you, my dear love, I have all kinds of lovely things, and mountains of them. I hope you'll get all of them. I brought them along full of happiness, and then I also got a lovely package from Davy [von Moltke]: orange marmalade, gingerbread of the finest sort, eggs, pears, and some quince bread.

It's been so long since I've answered your letters that I have to say how grateful I am that you tell me about yourself in such detail. I also understand quite well what your poor soul has to suffer, and why, and when you describe it, I am nothing but glad that I can take part in it.

I'm happy that we're also agreed about me on the day of the trial. Yes, I will stay at home quietly, and I'll do everything to stand by you in a state of deep composure. My dear, my Jäm, my husband.

Yes, all three of us were in bed on Sunday, for a long time, too. It started relatively late—not until 7—with a shout from Casparchen, who wanted to keep Konrad, who was rushing forward, from waking me up, which happened quite late as a result. Then there was snuggling, reading, studying, and singing.

My love, that is quite right: it is getting harder and harder for you to prepare for dying. That is the burdensome part of this long waiting period. It has to be that way. The initial impact is far, far easier. You needn't explain that to me at all, because I'm well aware of it. We humans cannot manage always to live at this kind of height or intensity. We keep sliding back down. I've also spoken to Poelchau about that. Question: Would you like to return to the world again to the extent that you read something else so as not to be constantly focused on death? I don't know myself whether that is a piece of advice, but it strikes me as too great a strain to have to wait so long even though it is obvious that we are happy to wait for a long time, and that you should take it as easy as possible and relax. In stark contrast, Eugen [Gerstenmaier]'s optimistic calm is almost incomprehensible to us.

My Jäm, I'll stop for now, write to Mütterchen Deichmann, and go to the friends.

1. The traditional German Christmas carol "Oh du fröhliche."

HELMUTH JAMES TO FREYA, NOVEMBER 22, 1944

Tegel, 22 Nov 44

No, my dear, I don't want to take my mind off things. I'm too afraid to miss out on precious time. Every hour is precious, and I have to use it *a.* to gird myself for my death and *b.* to reinforce my trust that God might preserve my life. It makes no difference whether that's hard or easy; we are living here within the bounds of time, and I have to use it. I know that this is not an argument in the eyes of God and that I cannot earn His grace; that He is just as likely to grant it to me if I read Karl May[1] as if I study the Bible and hymnal. But I want to think it over, even if I know that I can't understand it. I also get the feeling that I'm of more help to you that way, and I do enjoy every day in spite of the hardships.

My dear love, how wonderful that you're getting pleasure from your little sons and that they are a help to you. My dear, dear love, I wonder if you'll get permission for another face-to-face meeting. It's really unlikely. Let's never forget that parting on this earth is something quite concrete, so that we're not taken by surprise. It's a matter of "watch and pray." And let us never forget that God can preserve my life in a hundred ways and that we have a right to ask Him to do so. And we give thanks for what we have had. Farewell, my love—pray for your husband. J.

1. Karl May was a popular German author of adventure stories set mostly in the American West.

HELMUTH JAMES TO FREYA, NOVEMBER 23, 1944

Tegel, 23 Nov 44

My dear love, your wonderful coffee and the Holy Spirit made for a lively and tasty afternoon for me. Rarely have I so enjoyed a cup of coffee. Even so, I hope it was less the coffee and more the Holy Spirit.

In any case, I sat atop my table, read, and compared hymns and the Bible and delighted in the beautiful thoughts and feelings that seemed to surface at random.

My love, I paid for that tasty coffee with an inadequate night of sleep, but of the thirteen hours I spent in bed I surely slept eight: Only where I am does that seem inadequate; besides, I was very content in bed. But my lumbago is acting up like crazy, and I want to go to the doctor tomorrow. What a nuisance that I let it act up again after it was already subsiding. As long as nothing is demanded of me, it doesn't matter, but if I need to move with a suitcase or stand for a long period of time during the trial, it would be quite bothersome. Maybe the doctor will give me something to rub on it.

Now a few more requests and suggestions:

- Delp asks that, if possible, Sperr should be told that he, Sperr, did not tell him about his conversation with Stauffenberg until after July 20th.
- Is anything known about Peters? Maybe Einsiedel can look for him: air force operational headquarters I c or in his apartment.
- Any news about Husen?
- The more I think about it, the more important it seems to me that I see Hercher before he studies the files so that we can discuss what he needs to focus on.
- I want to write to Müller about the interrogations, and I'm enclosing the letter. Let me know.

My love, I have to finish up because they're about to shackle me. Farewell, my dear, how precious is every day, every minute that I can still write, say, think this. My dear, I think I have the right to say to you: I will stay with you until you follow me. J.

I've just noticed that I'm acting as though I'm dying. I'm doing that with every letter because it can be the last one. But I'm very strong in the belief in my life. Stay strong too, my love. Let's not have me flounder as I face these people, not for a second. But we don't just want to surrender to God's will, but instead greet it with a joyous "yes." J.

FREYA TO HELMUTH JAMES, NOVEMBER 24, 1944

Thursday morning[1]

My dearest, now it's finally the true hour for writing once again. It's 6:15. I wonder whether you're already awake. Certainly! And you've certainly already sent your loving thoughts to me. My love, how safe and secure I feel when I'm near and with you; it's only on occasion that I become fully aware of that, because I usually take it for granted. I am in very safe hands with you. How is your lumbago, my love? All that comes from the cold. In such a wet autumn it's inevitable. Just wrap yourself up really well. I'll send you the black scarf if I'm able to. Wrap it around your lower back. I told Gissel right away to make sure you stay warm, and he said he was doing so, and that they were doing whatever they could, and things weren't too bad there. I gave him another nice big piece of Kreisau sausage; I think that's his favorite. He's even more softhearted with Brigitte [Gerstenmaier], but he does do a great deal for us, and yesterday he accepted a virtual mountain of food from me. We've already agreed to meet next Wednesday, "so that I'm there too."

My Jäm, once again you have written many lovely things. I can well understand that you were listless, and maybe still are. That's sure to pass. I grew warm and happy when at the end of the rather sad letter I found the beautiful thing you wrote about your love and that you won't leave me, dead or alive. My Jäm, please don't ever spare me, and do go on writing me—as long as we still have the great good fortune of writing—exactly how things stand with you. I'd like to go on sharing the dark hours with you, since I'm also able to experience so much that is wonderful with you. But the passage in your letters that was most beneficial to me and greatly helped me along in my thoughts about you was your reference to how our waiting should be seen as a period of "watch and pray." I was so worried about how you could endure this for so long, but that is the right way to look at it, because you're saying that it is not only death that you need to focus on, nor is it just life, but rather you affirm the inevitable tension between the two poles and take it upon yourself and live within it as well as you can. That is quite beautiful and gives me great comfort! My Jäm, I'd like to write more, but I have to get going. I'm unable to finish a fully complete little letter in less than two hours, nor do I need to, and this evening I can deliver another one. I'll be at the friends' house again. For now I just want to say that I phoned Hercher yesterday. He was told: mid-December. But next week I'll try to make sure that he comes to see you; this week he's booked solid. I'll wait for tomorrow to look into getting permission for a face-to-face meeting. I had to let some time pass first, because I'd said I wanted to go home again and for that reason wanted to have some idea of the trial date. I can come in again only if there is urgent business. I'm actually quite confident that I'll get it. Today I'll see Frau Reisert and Frl. Schellhase. They are very hardworking, and I'm hoping to get tips from them.

My dear, my love, my Jäm, my dearest, my part of who I am, I'm sending you a tender embrace, with love. Do you feel this love, my beloved, my husband? Oh, surely you do, for it is big and strong. May God help and protect us, you especially, my dear sweet husband. I'm P., yours alone, no one else's in the world.

1. This should probably read "Friday morning."

FREYA TO HELMUTH JAMES, NOVEMBER 24, 1944

Thursday afternoon[1]

My dear, you write that we're more married than ever in the past thirteen years. How wonderful for me that you feel that way; how wonderful. It's true that you tell me more about yourself than you ever have. I've sometimes wanted to know more! How happy and how deeply grateful I am for that. Never think that you could burden me with anything. You can only make me happy. The significant element is that for my part everything is as it has always been. My Jäm, I've already been loving you all these years with all the strength that is within me. Maybe the contents of my love, its prospects and its goals, have changed over the course of these precious weeks—yes, they have!—but not the intensity. Oh, my Jäm, it is so wonderful to be able to love this way. Little Schellhase told me today how much Haubach and she have grown to love each other over the course of these weeks, how her being there for him so completely and loving him so much brings happiness to Haubach, that he is amazed, to be experiencing it after forty-six years and in a situation like this, and she herself is amazed as well, for in spite of it all, she has never been so happy. I was also full of amazement about how much happiness these weeks hold for those two as well, and once again also abashed and full of gratitude about how good things have been for us over such a long, marvelous period of time.

I'm reading what you wrote about your faith, that you're not entitled to the security and grace of faith, that you're afraid about whether it will be preserved for you. My Jäm, I'd like to say something about that and don't quite know myself what. I understand what you mean, and yet something is not right here. But what is it! It is unquestionably a great, the greatest possible grace, but I believe that God really likes to bestow it. He would much rather give grace than not give grace. He does indeed love us, or rather, it is in love that He exists. He certainly does not want to abandon us. One is just often incapable of taking hold of grace. It is actually always there. It's likely all due to the fact that your situation is far more complicated and difficult than mine and that you are now living in it far more consciously than I. You're far more alert and pray much more; I let myself be cradled, which is much easier. But how would I fare if I were the one in the cell!! I don't know. One thing is for sure: For these worries you really do need intercessory prayer, so that it can be light and bright and easy within you and you needn't torment yourself.

My Jäm, today was one of those gray, gray days again, which means that it is dark in your cell, and that's hard to take, my Jäm. I hope it wasn't too hard to bear. November is in itself the most difficult month of the year. By the way, I was offered pills that have an energizing and invigorating effect, famous pills.[2] Do you want to have four of them for the trial? They're a kind of stimulant, like coffee or tea. Do you feel like having something like that? Or better not? I wasn't entirely sure of how you'd react to this option. Please let me know about it.

Now you're going to bed already, my love; it's 6. I hope your heart is content and calm, you feel my tender thoughts, and your shackles don't disturb you. Good night, my dearest love. I am and will remain your P.

1. This should probably read "Friday afternoon." 2. Probably Pervitin, a psychotropic drug composed of the stimulant methamphetamine; see Helmuth's letter of December 10–12, 1944.

FREYA TO HELMUTH JAMES, NOVEMBER 25, 1944

Saturday morning

My dearest, it's not very early. I'm at the friends' home, and we've just had breakfast. Poelchau is out, and I want to write a little letter for my dearest that will get to him tomorrow morning. On Monday at 11 I'll be with Hercher, and before that I want to go to the People's Court. But yesterday afternoon was wonderful! I had planned to use the day to run a couple of errands in town. I wanted to find something nice for our soldiers' packages, but that was totally out of the question. All I got was a few nice little books along with a couple of pads, some endpaper, a couple of jumping jacks, and that's all for one whole morning. But I set aside that day for shopping, tried one thing after another, and have now done my part. I'm not really worried about Christmas, the gift-giving part, I mean. In Kreisau I still have so many old things, fabrics, and a bit of this and that, that I can take care of Christmas giving by taking things out of storage without looting my own things too drastically. But I have no intention of spending money on trash. That's about it. My dear, how do these reports from a very uninteresting and dull world strike you? It's all so poorly suited to what is happening within us and in the other world, in the west and the east, I mean. But I tell you about it because it is quite simply part of my life and thus belongs to it. When I got home, my legs were tired, but I wasn't exhausted. Oh yes, what I wanted to say earlier, though, was that I have always been taking you along within me, firmly and securely, on all my walks. I felt quite calm and fine. I was totally preoccupied with you in the beautiful and strong certainty of our inseparability. That is a gloriously pleasing feeling! With these feelings, your last letter, and the book, I settled in on a sofa and stayed there for two hours, read the passages you had specified for me, then read them again, and others as well. For me it's positively lovely to see all the hidden treasures that still lie in store for me! I thought of you, read for you, and spent a happy afternoon like that.

But I wonder how things are with you! I'm greatly looking forward to getting news from you again, I hope tomorrow at noon. How is your lumbago? Did you sit atop your table and feel comfortable? I liked the letter to Müller. I wonder if you've been brought in, but it probably hasn't happened yet. I look at all the police cars in the city, thinking you might be in one of them. How you found it when all of a sudden you were outside your cell and riding through Berlin. In principle, my Jäm, you're now living like a monk, and you *should* live that way and enjoy the fruits of that sort of life. And you're doing so, but the love of your Pim keeps pulling you back into the world. That complicates things for you, but I can't do anything about it, because I know all too well that you are made to have a wife, and that wife, my Jäm, is me. She may distract you, but her great love will keep bringing warmth to your life and warm you as long as you still have that life. May God grant, my dear, that it is restored to you once again.

I'm sending you a tender embrace. You know whose I am and will remain: your P.

HELMUTH JAMES TO FREYA, NOVEMBER 26, 1944

Tegel, 26 Nov 44

My dear, something new has occurred to me. You could present the following project to Konrad [von Preysing]—after a very thorough preliminary discussion with Poelchau my line of argument is this:

Following the occupation, the church is the main support of Germanness. Now that the first German territories have been occupied,[1] the Catholic Church offers its protection in the occupied territories to all, to the National Socialists as well as their flock. The bishops will give the pertinent instructions to their clergymen that all internal political differences in particular need to be abandoned, and that help will also be extended to those who have previously attacked the church; and beyond that resistance to all separatist tendencies.—The explanation was that it would otherwise be difficult to gain the support of the clergy for a resolute adherence to this line since they have been attacked everywhere in some way, and everyone from this group knows someone who is in a concentration camp or has been executed, so the following can be expected of the National Socialist state: forgoing the execution of convicted clergymen and forgoing the execution of the "Moltke people," whether they're Catholic or Protestant. For the following reasons, I am very comfortable with this position:

a. because I have always taken the stance that the church needs to be a secure base and I've acted on behalf of that belief; in the episcopate I'm known to have won over even the most active Catholics, the Jesuits;

b. because along with my head, the heads of Delp, Rösch, and König will likely roll (since Wienken was told that Rösch and König were captured,[2] it is clear that it will have to be extended to the three of them);

c. because I'm a cause célèbre[3] that the SS Reich Leader has dealt with and because the only Catholic Church involvement in the July 20th uprising is tied to my name and my case is also being dealt with in the church division of the Gestapo.[4] Thus it is easy to get a precedent-setting decision since the case is known and serves as a precedent for all other clergymen, because if the Jesuit provincial stays alive, that will apply a fortiori to the others. [Marginal note: *d.* because through me they may be able to get to the Catholic bishops, since many depositions confirm that I have spoken to them.]

There are, of course, infinite objections. First it needs to be clarified whether Preysing would go along with something like this.

My dear love, you wrote such a nice beautiful little letter. It was so wonderfully tranquil and limpid, and it delighted me. My love, may the Lord preserve your steadiness, even when He calls me to Himself. Today is the last Sunday before Advent, when we commemorate the dead, and I began the day with 1 Cor. 15 and John 20+21. We naturally focus our commemoration on those who preceded us, but today the two of us are bearing my death in mind even more. When I woke up last night, I felt close to, not alienated from, death, yet later I found it very unwelcome. We are, after all, a trembling reed,[5] and it's crucial to see new work on a daily and even hourly basis in order to remain upright in any wind. The last crisis took away all my joy in being upright, no, not all my joy but all my pride. Up to that point it had been rather a point of pride that no weakness waylaid me. But the Lord did tell me quite emphatically, "My grace is sufficient for thee." So I am grateful for every moment in which I feel this grace, knowing that I haven't earned it and praying that it may remain with me.

My love, my thoughts are forever seeking you and always finding you. It sometimes seems to me as though you are my heart, which keeps on beating resolutely and quietly, come what may, because it does not depend on my nervous system but instead draws its strength and stability from other sources. Do you understand that?

My dear, I wonder if you could bring me some sprigs of fir on Wednesday. I would like to do something for Advent, especially if it is my last one. Next Sunday at home will surely be quite lovely. Do enjoy it, because I enjoy it through you.

My dear love, I'll stop here. Be well; I really burden you with an awful lot of tasks. Don't take on too much responsibility, so you won't have to blame yourself later for anything that went awry. You have to promise me once and for all that you'll never think: If I'd done this or that differently back then, my Jäm might still be alive. I can expect you to do all these tasks only if you make a firm promise about this. Farewell, my very dear love. I embrace you. J.

Another thing about the issue concerning Konrad: Even if nothing comes of the whole thing, it could still be enormously important for me if the officials in the Gestapo get the impression: a grain of Moltke's seed is germinating in a way that is interesting to us. All it would take to achieve that would be an absolutely unofficial tentative exploration.

1. Allied troops had taken the first German towns and cities near the Belgian and Dutch borders. 2. Rösch was not arrested until January 11, 1945; König was never caught by the Gestapo. 3. Used here to mean a trial that attracts a great deal of attention. 4. Meaning Karl Neuhaus, a former Protestant theologian and the Gestapo officer in charge of ecclesiastical and related matters, who was responsible for Helmuth. 5. Reference to Friedrich Schiller's *Wilhelm Tell*, 2.1.

FREYA TO HELMUTH JAMES, NOVEMBER 26, 1944

Sunday evening

My dear love, tonight I'm with the friends again. They're already in bed, but I'd like to write you now because Poelchau wants to go tomorrow morning, and I do as well. When I arrived today at midday, your little letter was here. I read it, but not until after the meal—your letter to Konrad [von Preysing], too. I typed it up right away to simplify things for him and headed right off to take it there. It is a beautiful letter. His Excellency was at home, sitting unassumingly in one of the hospital rooms of the big, modern, and undamaged hospital in Hermsdorf. Since he was there, I went up to him, preferring to hand him the letter myself. When he heard: a letter from you, he said it would have to be burned on the spot, and he read it immediately. I waited and observed him (as he sighed deeply, twice), his surroundings, his beautiful shoes and ring, and his clever clerical head. I must say in advance that the whole way he treated the project did not convey a hint of fear; as you can tell from what I just wrote, he, too, is unquestionably sympathetic to you and wishes to help, but he initially turned down the project, for two reasons. The first and most significant reason, he told me, was that the church doesn't have anything to offer, as they have no contact with or influence on their clergy in the occupied territories. They no longer had any knowledge about the bishop in Aachen, for example, and the same would soon be the case with Cologne and Trier. The SS, he went on to say, is not the least bit interested in what happens to the Germans in the occupied territories, and so even if it has objective value, it is of no interest to them. Second, for the past twelve years now, he has seen again and again that when the Catholic Church intervenes with the SS, the outcome is both detrimental and useless. In this important case they would surely be highly satisfied that the church was evidently willing to ante up for this matter and it would therefore have been a real coup for them. That could only confirm for the SS that it was dangerous, and besides, it would be sure to be interpreted as a sign of weakness on the part of the church. Finally, it would be virtually out of the question to spur the cardinal[1] and Wienken into action. So this was a wholesale rejection of the line of argument. However, he did state that he will consider the entire matter carefully, and if a better approach along these lines occurs to him, he will inform Dix. That was the visit. He said that not a day goes by without his thinking of you and all the many others, and he is counting on your not being killed but rather neutralized because of your name. Maybe it would have been better just to hand over the letter for the time being and to go later with Poelchau, but given his nature, I hardly think that the outcome would have been much different.

My Jäm, what you wrote about the heart that I should be makes me very happy. I think I also understand what you mean. How I would love to keep on beating for you, and how wonderful that's what you sometimes feel. As I was sitting here peacefully at the round table and deciphering your letter, which is so dear to me, written in your dear little handwriting, and I came to that lovely sentence, I was once again struck by the strength of our great good fortune. What riches we have been given, my dearest Jäm, and what grace to be able to feel that in all its beautiful abundance. The pains of parting truly pale by comparison, and what remains is the feeling of a precious possession that will never be lost. Tell me, my love: Do Matthew 18:18+19[2] also pertain to us?

I have to go to bed soon and would like to let you know quickly that I came back from my excursion at about 7, and the friends came soon too. We then ate and sat around. Poelchau read us a lovely sermon by Gollwitzer, from which I learned quite a bit, including the fact that other people don't seem to have an easier time of it in their ways, because the sermon was about prayer. My Jäm, I'm so close to you here, and in such a safe harbor! How would all this be without the friends! Why do they hold me so close, as though I belong to them completely. I also take big fat pieces of the cake they're always offering me. I'm not even ashamed. I'm just grateful and utterly convinced that one can only accept friendship like this without ever being able to reciprocate in kind. Strangely enough, it is also a sign of much greater humility to take without thoughts of payback. I'm a vile Pharisee by nature, and would always like to have given more than I've taken, and edify myself in the process. Before God that is no better than keeping everything for yourself, especially if you recognize what you're actually doing. My pleasures are far more refined than those of primitive egotists, seeing as I can still stand tall before others! That's how it is, my Jäm, now don't you try to gloss over your Pim's shortcomings with a gentle hand. I do know where to position them!

My Jäm, I love you, I love you with every fiber of my being, and would like to keep you. I probably don't need to say that, and I also know that's not the decisive point. Tonight, however, I can still write to you: Sleep well, my love, and I embrace you. That, at any rate, is a nice thing. I'm your P. forever.

1. Adolf Cardinal Bertram, Archbishop of Breslau, who tended to appease the Nazis all along. 2. Matthew 18:18–19: "Verily I say unto you, Whatsoever ye shall bind on earth shall be bound in heaven: and whatsoever ye shall loose on earth shall be loosed in heaven. Again I say unto you, That if two of you shall agree on earth as touching any thing that they ask, it shall be done for them of my Father which is in heaven."

HELMUTH JAMES TO FREYA, NOVEMBER 27, 1944

27 Nov 44

My dear, Konrad [von Preysing] is a very smart man, and his arguments are certainly correct aside from one thing: I meant less that contact should be established with the now-occupied territories as that the clergy in endangered areas should be given the general directive before the occupation. I'm not in a position, of course, to judge whether he's right apart from that, because it depends on the current situation. Three months ago, I would have judged it that very same way, and it won't be possible until the rulers feel as though they are in a somewhat precarious position. Naturally I can't say when that will be the case. But I do believe that the idea is generally correct that one has to try to stop the lion from lashing out maliciously in the throes of death.

Matthew 18:18 isn't apt, but 19 certainly is. In my opinion, 18 refers to being bound on account of sins.—My dear love, I've been keeping an idea, a wish concealed within me in case you're able to arrange for a face-to-face meeting, but since I didn't dare to hope for one, I haven't mentioned it yet. But now I hear that you may possibly be coming within the next few days. This idea is whether we might be able to take Communion with Poelchau after our face-to-face meeting. We've never taken it together, and it would be such a keystone on the path we've traveled thus far. But the central question remains whether Poelchau thinks that will be possible. It mustn't endanger either him or us, and we could celebrate it together in our minds as well. But if he thinks that the warden would permit that without it turning into an incident, that would be wonderful. I didn't talk to him about it because you really have to want it, not just to please your husband.

Farewell, my calm, dear, strong love, J.

FREYA TO HELMUTH JAMES, NOVEMBER 27–28, 1944

Monday afternoon

My dear, for you it's already the evening; it's 5:30. I'm finished with my tasks and I'm sitting in the farthest corner of the waiting room. I'll probably stay here for a while, because I can't show up at the good Poelchaus so early, and I'm sitting here quite peacefully and undisturbed. I can't go to Carl Dietrich [von Trotha]'s at this point. That's too far. My Jäm, here's the best part: I have in my pocket a new permission slip for a face-to-face meeting. Herr Thiele liked my lovely request as much as Herr Schulze had previously. "Yes, Frau von Moltke, you shall have permission for a face-to-face meeting," I was told, but not until today at noon, because today there was again a major trial in the courthouse and all the gentlemen were there. As a result, I didn't get a chance to speak to Stier,[1] and I'll try again tomorrow morning, but for now I'm happy that I'll be seeing you again. Oh, my Jäm, how happy I am, how beautiful it will be to let my eyes take you in, to touch you, to see you once again. How wonderful, my Jäm! My dear! I don't yet know whether I should already come tomorrow. If it's to be at the warden's again, I can't exchange any laundry, which means I can't bring any food, and I want to do it on Wednesday as always. So only Tuesday and Thursday are left, and since you may be brought in after all, it's probably better to try for tomorrow. I'm happily taking a bit of pleasure in the possession in my pocket. We've been granted half an hour!

When I found myself standing in front of the People's Court at 9 without having achieved anything, I decided to pay a visit to Frau Lukaschek; Fräulein Hapig recently told me about her being there and utterly abandoned and desperate. I was appalled by what I saw. I barely recognized her. She saw Lukaschek[2] once and said he had been tortured horribly, mainly, it would appear, in Breslau, and he turned as white as a sheet and wept. But it seems to me that on the whole, he's not faring badly; he just wanted to give vent to his feelings for once. He can read and smoke, and is at Lehrter Str.; his file's not yet at the court, but she's afraid that it will go quickly. She sees everything as far worse than it needs to be seen and has no one to comfort her. Her helplessness can break your heart. I spent an hour consoling her, but I didn't get the feeling that it did her much good. The poor woman! We have to stay in touch with her. By the time I was back with Carl Dietrich, it was 12. There I found out about a call from Fräulein Hapig saying that I should come again. Since I wanted to go to Thiele beforehand and afterward to Hercher, I had time only to make myself some cream of wheat, eat a couple of sandwiches, and set off again. After that, things all went smoothly with Thiele. Frl. Hapig had moved away from her project and now had a new one, namely to get me together with Frau Planck. Why not?! She has passed on her requests to Himmler via Frau Himmler, but I still believe that Planck senior was the reason.[3] Incidentally, she doesn't have it in black and white yet. All these things took place on Grosse Hamburger Strasse. I'm gradually getting to know Berlin quite thoroughly, since the morning visit was near Kottbusser Tor. I'll see Frau Planck tomorrow between 1:15 and 1:30, and that was arranged through her father confessor, who, incidentally, is a brother of Frau Kleinert in Gräditz!— Here, it was said, there was "trouble brewing,"[4] whereupon I promptly set off. In any event, I did arrive, and it was harmless, as you also noticed. Poelchau isn't here this evening, but I found your lovely little note. Yes, my dear, you know I want to.[5] I would find that very beautiful. I believe that I'm wholly prepared for it. No, not in order to please you, no, I couldn't do it for that reason. I share and affirm your wish from the bottom of my heart and say "yes" to it. But Poelchau will have to say whether it will work out. So I'll leave the little slip of paper there for him and won't come tomorrow unless Poelchau tells me to, because it either will or will not work out.—Now I'll come back to Hercher. He said from the outset that he wouldn't get the permission for a face-to-face meeting until shortly before the trial, but when I said that I wanted to go to Stier for that, he was instantly ready to come to you if he got permission that way. Tomorrow morning it's Stier's turn.—Brigitte [Gerstenmaier] is quite willing to have a go at bribing Thiele, and she has some talent in that sort of thing. She should entice him with a goose, but first we have to discuss the project in detail with Poelchau. Today he[6] told me there was no certainty about the trial as yet, and looked pensively at the schedule, which, he said, he had just drawn up. Herr Thiele is the local group leader[7] of Rengsdorf; he is gaunt and pale and Saxon, but when he is shown respect, he is very friendly. So far I haven't felt the slightest bit of unfriendliness anywhere. But because I go with my head held high in this matter, it makes unfriendliness difficult. It could still come, but that doesn't matter to me at all.—My heart is full of love and full of happiness, because I belong to you completely and I'm so firmly and finely connected to you. P.

1. Martin Stier, the head of the district court. 2. Hans Lukaschek was also a member of the Kreisau Circle and survived the war. 3. Erwin Planck, a son of the famous physicist Max Planck, had been in custody since July 1944 and was sentenced to death on October 23, 1944. Frau Planck is Nelly Planck, his wife. His father had tried to get him pardoned by writing letters to Hitler and Himmler petitioning for his release, but he was executed on January 23, 1945. 4. Shortly before an air raid. 5. Freya's reply to Helmuth's suggestion about taking Communion together in his letter of November 27, 1944. 6. Councillor Thiele. 7. He was an Ortsgruppenleiter, the head of the Nazi party in the locality, a powerful position.

HELMUTH JAMES TO FREYA, NOVEMBER 28, 1944

Tegel, 28 Nov 44

My dear, how happy I am about the permit for the face-to-face meeting. I hadn't dared to hope for one. It would be very nice if afterward we could take Communion with Poelchau, but it's lovely in any case.—Once again I have a couple of minor details that have occurred to me: *1.* If you (we) keep Kreisau, something has to happen to honor Carl Bernd [von Moltke]'s memory.[1] I had always thought of placing a big boulder at the corner of the new family plot and inserting a plate with a view over the valley rather than of the path. Or putting a plate into the low stone wall near Mami. *2.* I'd like to ask you to bring a new pad; this one will still last for a little while, but if I continue writing so diligently, I may need another one later after all. 3. Every day I read 3 chapters from the Gospels and am now, that is, as of yesterday, at Matthew 19–21, just where you were yesterday. So today it'll be 22–24. Since you're also at this place, I thought maybe we could keep reading together, and wanted to tell you that.

Everything you write, my dear love, is so dear and restorative, and gives me a feeling of comfort. I only hope you'll be able to keep your balance through all the possible adversities. It is a grace that has been given to you—no, to us—and for which we must ask anew with each passing day.—Poor Frau Lukaschek. Yes, if you have time, try to help her. Maybe sometime she'll be able to find out what Lukaschek said about me. I didn't say anything that could incriminate him, other than that I talked to him about factual questions regarding self-governance and church and state, and that when he asked me in 1942 who Herr Goerdeler was, I advised him not to see him. But I'm afraid that he has recently been dragged into the matter in some way.

Yes, my love, all of you need to talk about whether we should be working on a postponement of the trial. I'm not really capable of judging that. One thing is certain: The war situation is precarious again and the later our turn comes, the more it can help us as an argument. But human eyes cannot gain insight into this question because an enemy advance over the Rhine might lead to hurried sentencing of all pending cases, and I only have any sort of chance if time is devoted to me: as a rule of thumb, I will have to be hanged. This entire discussion is a bit awkward for me, and it makes me see how I really have changed somewhat. I see too clearly that these are all matters of lesser account, that I am in God's hands and live and die in Him. But discuss the question. The primary human feeling is that time can be precious because the enemy quite obviously wants to break through now, and will do everything in their power to achieve this. If the Allies do break through somewhere, everything can go quite quickly.

My love, I'm not going to keep on writing, because I hope you'll come, and then we will comprehend with our eyes whatever I could still say now. I'm hoping for that. Farewell, my very beloved heart, embrace your children when you see them, and say hello to everyone. J.

1. His brother Carl Bernhard had been killed in action on December 30, 1941. The memorial was supposed to be close to the grave of their mother.

FREYA TO HELMUTH JAMES, NOVEMBER 29, 1944

Wednesday evening and afternoon

My dear love, I am still full of what we experienced together this morning.[1] It was very beautiful for me—it was purely beautiful, not sad. The truth of the matter, my love, is that I'm incapable of saying anything about it. I'm different from the way I was before, yet I don't know why. Since I've known that we would be able to experience this together, I've kept thinking it over and especially this morning have been gathering my thoughts only for this. I was harboring a great fear that in spite of it all I might not be worthy, but then I saw clear as day; in memory of the death of Christ, in the willingness to recognize his path as the only true path to God, and through His intermediation and His help to accept for ourselves whatever He has decided for us, most particularly, however, to allow ourselves to be united through Him.[2] I was fully ready for that, and when the time came was unable to think of all that anymore and felt only our great willingness: what a gift, my love, to be able to kneel next to you and be able to receive this from the hand of our friend. My dearest, I can't say as yet what has taken place within me and what will grow within me. I felt as though I, too, had crosses on my forehead. Poelchau did it so beautifully and lovingly. He knows so well what goes on in our hearts between the Sunday before Advent and Advent itself. It wasn't about your death at all; it was about our two lives. We have had our union sealed beyond death, and come what may, this seal will always remain with us. Did you also read the three chapters 25, 26, and 27[3] this morning, the ones that suited our celebration so beautifully? I'm very happy to keep reading the three chapters with you. That really pleases me. I also read the little catechism.[4] My love, I'm sitting here, my heart brimming over, and I can tell you only about my love and the certainty that we are sheltered for all that may come.—You know, of course, that it was wonderful to be with you earlier. I didn't have a feeling of limited time at all, right from the outset. I feel as though we spent a good long time together, and this togetherness was nothing out of the ordinary but rather a familiar state. Often your presence is so strong and concrete that I don't feel the separation at all. This is why our parting wasn't so painful for me, because you weren't taken away from me. My dear, that is the precious fruit of these weeks: I now know for certain that we are inextricably linked. At first I had to keep reminding myself of that, but now it is an integral part of me. Just like you, I keep being unnerved by the richness of these past weeks, including this day, at a depth I have yet to plumb.

My dear, here's how my day went: When you were gone, Poelchau told me I should eat at Dorothee [Poelchau]'s and meet him at about 2 for the visit with Dix. I did that because here I could be alone and compose myself. I wasn't distraught but full of tears, actually tears of gratitude, but I am as incapable of describing them as I am of describing my state of mind as a whole. My visit to Dix wasn't really successful. Poelchau can give you his shrewder assessment of it. He clearly saw the supra-Moltke possibilities in the project but didn't know how to tackle it. He considered the letter you're planning to send to Himmler not bad in principle: But of course the form will make the crucial difference. Then we turned around together and I stayed here again. Now it's the evening, and I'll go see Carl Dietrich [von Trotha] when the letter is finished. I'll pack there tomorrow morning and come to Tegel again, where I left my gloves. There I can probably then pick up another letter from you, which I'd like to take along with me on the trip. Poelchau thinks that I ought to travel at noon because that's less exhausting. So that's how I'll do it. Even though two dear little sons are awaiting me, I'll tear myself away with difficulty from being near to you. I would rather stay, but it is right and necessary for me to go. We are close regardless, and even though the little sons are rightly in second place and don't need me all that much, it's only right for me to be with them for the first of Advent. We agree on that. The days with you were once again very beautiful, very precious ones. I feel blessed for our future life together: I feel very rich. I embrace you in tender love. I am and will forever remain your P.

1. Taking Communion together. 2. This sentence is fragmentary in the original German as well. 3. Matthew 25–27 with the description of the Last Supper. 4. Martin Luther's introduction to the Christian faith.

HELMUTH JAMES TO FREYA, NOVEMBER 29–30, 1944

Tegel, 29 Nov 44

My dear, I don't want to let this day end without having spoken another little word with you. My love, our farewell ceremony—for that is what it was, and it will remain so even if you should come again—has given us a new element of richness, a new treasure to take along as we head toward what God has intended for us. Now that we have had more time, we are again a bit better equipped to endure anything that may be inflicted on us. The bond we have formed, a bond that ties us together even beyond this time, indeed, beyond all time, has received an outward seal, although the word "outward" is actually wrong on the face of it: it is meant only in the sense of a seal that can be clasped and grasped. My love, we will take it along on our path, which will remain our communal one—a communion—even if we can no longer see each other with these eyes, hear each other with these ears, and touch each other with these hands. We'll go where He leads and sends us. Take a look at the twenty-first chapter of the Gospel of John, verses 18–23.[1]

I sat here in the dark for another hour and thought about the riches we share, filled only with happiness and gratitude. Our time together is of course a good part of that feeling, which was eclipsed only by the celebration. You look well, my love, and so wonderfully free of grief. I sometimes think about how difficult everything would be if I left behind a grief-stricken wife and might already see the traces of grief on her. Sorrow is good, grief is bad. Maybe something else new will occur to you in fourteen days that you'll need to talk to me about, and maybe I'll still be alive then. I don't dare to hope, but I do hope that you will try, in any case, and maybe you'll be able to overpower Herr Thiele.

My love, I asked Poelchau to give me a candle and a holder. On Sunday at 5:30, when I go to bed, I'll unscrew my bulb, because at that time there are no patrols, and light the candle, because all of you will probably be singing at that time, and then I can sing along with you;[2] although I'll be whistling for the most part. By the way, it occurs to me that I've yet to give you a description of my current cell.

1. bucket = toilet
2. clothes closet and two open shelves for washing utensils and dishes
3. lamp
4. table 80–50 cm
5. chair with backrest
6. water pitcher
7. folding bed 1.95 x 1 m quite good
8. my suitcase

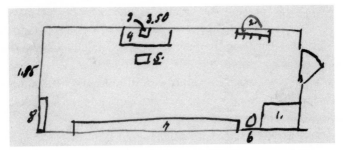

Helmuth's sketch of his prison cell in his letter to Freya from November 29–30, 1944

The window, which used to be very good, maybe 75 cm, has been replaced by a plywood board with a small 20 x 20 little window. The window begins at 2 meters up, the cell is about 2.75 high. When I lie in bed, this is what I see:

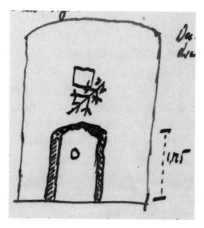

That's where the candle should go.

Enough for today, my dear; just one more thing: Make an appointment with Dix for next week; by that time I'll have developed something new. I embrace you, my love, and the little sons too, as the one joined to you.

30 Nov 44

Good morning, my love. Since early this morning, I've been thinking about you so much, and with such intensity; after a good night in which my pains have eased a bit, this morning the pain of parting loomed large once again. It does not matter, my dear, and it is only a sign of the value of what I possess; I had anticipated it and am telling you about it only for the sake of completeness. It wasn't even a pit of depression, just the pain of parting.

I'm enclosing the draft of a letter to Himmler; it'd be best to discuss it next week with Dix. I don't know what's smarter, to do nothing or to actively oppose the goad of "scorn." In any case, this basic question has to be settled before we say how to construct the letter. But I'd like to make this problem a topic for discussion.

1. Jesus to Peter: "another shall gird thee, and carry thee whither thou would-est not ... Follow me." 2. Sunday was the first of Advent.

FREYA TO HELMUTH JAMES, DECEMBER 4, 1944

Monday evening

My dear, I'm writing on the first sheet of the pad I'll be bringing you. I hope, my dear love, it will get safely into your hands and you will be the one writing on it. I was so carefree during those days in Krei-sau, and now I wonder, doubly anxious and uneasy, how I will find everything tomorrow. How glad I am to be close to you again. My heart is full of love, my Jäm! I'm writing this in the writing chamber of the Reichshof Hotel in Liegnitz. I'd actually intended to be at Asta [Wendland]'s now, but I missed the connection in Königszelt and had to ride straight through. I left Kreisau by 7:30 in quite a hurry and would very much have liked to stay two hours longer, but as a result I now have a good deal of leisure time in this writing chamber, which I had already discovered on the trip to Kreisau, when I missed my connection and didn't arrive until 2:30 at night. The moon was shining brightly when I got there. Arriving is now always difficult for me because it's not worth anything to me without you, and yet it was so beautiful, and this beauty caused me pain as I came to the moonlit path from the train station. But I forced myself to change the subject, and took off my things and went to see the gently sleep-ing little sons. Casparchen woke up full of love and was touchingly delighted, little Konrad was having a good snooze.[1] I then did the same in my own treasured bed. Asta was still in the house. In the morning both little boys came in, and we cuddled and read quite contentedly until Asta came and sat down with us. On Sunday at lunch, I said to them, while we were still eating at 1:30—the meal actually lasted until 10 minutes to 2—"Now Pa thinks we're already finished eating." "And," said Casparchen, "he's thinking about how I can eat with you today." When the telephone rang during the day on Saturday, when he was doing his homework next to me and I was sitting at my desk, he said—and I already knew what he was going to say when he began to speak—"How nice it would be if that was Papa and he said he was out of prison and would be with us tomorrow!" Oh, my Jäm! I'm so happy that he loves you so truly, all of his own accord, unprompted by me, and so much. The little one speaks about you quite often, because he knows that I travel to see you and that those are eggs for Pa, he says all on his own, but he doesn't really know you.

I saw Zeumer only briefly in the courtyard on Friday. He's still busy with his beets and hasn't spread the fertilizer yet, but he was in high spirits. On the 6th he's celebrating his silver wedding anniversary.

On Saturday I made gingerbread while Frau Pick gutted nine young chickens! Afterward I also made paper angels for the singing children. It was a lot of fun for me, but I hadn't expected it to be such a success. You'll get one too. I made nine, and the funny part was that they all had different expressions on their faces. It was truly delightful to see them all next to one another.

On Sunday morning we celebrated as usual. Soon we'll know "Break forth, O beauteous heavenly light, / And usher in the morning." After breakfast I went out with both sons. The sun was shining and Kreisau was wintry but lovely. Then we went to see the Schmolkes. Our two sons happily headed off to the pond while I visited with the poor careworn Schmolkes. They both look so sad and so old. When I'm with people who are faring as poorly as they are, I'm almost glad that we aren't having an easy time of it either. I couldn't say anything in the face of so much pain. The two living sons were there, and I eventually talked to them about the national militia,[2] etc., while their poor parents sat there impassively, looking so sad. Then I retrieved our little sons, who were quite happily armed with cattails, and we went home to eat. There was a princely meal, chicken with the wonderful endives that grew so abundantly this year. Then Konrad went to sleep and Casparchen went outside to play noisily with the papers looted from Zeumer, and I started my preparations for Advent. We have quite a lovely wreath made of evergreens this year. Fräulein

Hirsch brought them all the way from Ludwigsdorf and said we didn't have evergreens anywhere near here. Is that true? I don't know where they might be, but that's no reason not to think they're there. Aunt Leno [Hülsen] and her children[3] and the grieving Reichweins all wanted to come so that you, my beloved heart, would find us at the Berghaus. We sang in the big living room, where we had lots of candle stubs. First we sang with the piano from about 5 to 5:30. That was the best kind of singing as far as I was concerned, because I only had to think of you and not keep the children in line. So I sang and felt everything we have experienced during these precious weeks. At 5:30, Aunt Leno and her children left, to keep on singing for Aunt Ete [von Trotha] down below,[4] then we sang with you, my love, without a piano. Casparchen was absolutely thrilled that it was almost as if you were there. It was so beautiful that way! Was it that way for you too, my dear love, or were you homesick and sad? This question was very much on my mind. I so wish you weren't sad.—My Jäm, I have to get to the train! What a shame. I'm not even close to finished. All the important things still need to be said, but I have to go now!

1. Helmuth and Freya frequently used the family expression *pümpeln* to denote snoozing. 2. The regional National Guard, to which all men between the ages of sixteen and sixty had to report beginning in October 1944. 3. They were in fact her grandchildren, both parents having been killed by bombs. 4. "Down below" refers to the Schloss, which is downhill from the Berghaus.

HELMUTH JAMES TO FREYA, DECEMBER 5, 1944

Tegel, 5 Dec 44

My dear, Hercher was here on Saturday, and I was able to skim the seventeen-page indictment. If at all possible, I have to get it back as quickly as possible, ideally a copy I can keep, because there's so much utter nonsense in it—saying that I wanted to supplant Goerdeler with Beck and take Goerdeler's place—that I simply cannot remember it all. My love, the indictment is astonishing: the charge is utterly false. There is no talk of serious knowledge of Goerdeler in my case—apart from a single conversation—and almost none in the case of the others. There is no mention of preparatory actions for July 20th; in my case they've actually given up even the possibility of high treason, and only defeatism remains. The following must be noted in that regard: *a*. Defeatism, if it is presumed to be a proven fact, is also sufficient. *b*. The truth of the matter is not so very important to Freisler. *c*. If it starts out with "unrestrained defeatist" and "fierce opponent of National Socialism," then that is sufficient. *d*. In the end, they can introduce new facts during the trial, at least in support of the two addenda. So: there are no grounds whatsoever for hope on a human level. But, my love, we need to identify this process as a sign that God hears us; it would be a vain lack of faith not to do so.

Just now your letter arrived, but I want to read it later because I'm full of things I want to ask of you, things I want to get off my mind.

1. Right now I basically need only butter (+ salt), anything else is an extra; I still have enough sausage in particular.

2. Clothing: I need to ask for two shirts, handkerchiefs, warm long underwear, maybe one pair of pajamas.

3. Dix: please
   a. Examine the letter to Himmler.
   b. My draft for a statement: Is something like this better at the beginning or the end? Attack on the indictment or composed counterstatement? Is what I said about the war situation enough for me to come out from under the charge of defeatism?

4. Information from Haubach and Steltzer is important, but the women should not be running over there.

5. It's important to find out, if at all possible, how much more time we have. But Brigitte [Gerstenmaier] can do that.

6. Hercher: If at all possible, I would like to have a copy of the indictment next time. Think about how to tell him that.

If time is running short, he should send the copy of my written defense for the record if it is not there.

New consultation soon.

7. Haubach: Perhaps his confession refers only to
   a. Knowledge of government formation Goerdeler in June '44.
   b. Knowledge of illegal trade union organization and not to Kreisau.

Air-raid warning. I hope nothing happens to you. Poelchau is in the building. I always pack everything away at times like this, but since it takes so long, I'll now write on my knees and pack it away only when it comes close again.

8. It would be good if Lukaschek could clarify what he said about me.

9. I'd like to have my baptismal and confirmation verses.[1] The pastor's wife can track them down.

My dear, I just read your letter during the breaks in the alarm. A very lovely little letter. Thank you, my love. Since Poelchau will be here momentarily, I'll add just a word: Advent was very nice for me; the candle burned nicely, my thoughts were with you, and I whistled Christmas songs; here and there I also sang a little verse.—Unfortunately I'm quite stiff, I'm having particular trouble standing and can barely walk; I always slump forward. Today my whole chest is painful as well. At the same time, when I'm resting the pain is much better than before. If I should still be here on Friday, I want to see whether the doctor will put me in the sick bay so I can stay in bed for two days and sweat. So although it doesn't bother me at all, it would be quite detrimental for the trial.

My love, I'll stop now, because a nasty guard has just taken over at the station. Farewell, my dear, be well. Keep praying for your husband and keep loving him. J.

1. See Freya's letter of December 15–16, 1944.

FREYA TO HELMUTH JAMES, DECEMBER 5–6, 1944

Tuesday afternoon

My dearest, how awful it must have been for you again this morning. There were so many planes. My poor husband! Were you shackled? Was it very agonizing for you, or did you feel too sheltered in His lap, my love? I was with Dorothee [Poelchau] and thinking of you and hoping that you didn't find it too agonizing. For us it wasn't much of anything. We just heard the many, many planes, and we actually thought that the prison[1] had been spared. The steeples looked unscathed and peaceful when we viewed the situation from the roof.

Tegel prison: Cell Block C in 1969

However, Borsig got badly damaged once again,[2] although to a far lesser extent than "Argus."[3] My love, how horrified I was when Dorothee told me that the prison had been hit hard again.—Wednesday. I'm sitting and waiting for Gissel to take the things off my hands. Brigitte [Gerstenmaier] is sitting next to me: she has permission for a face-to-face meeting, for the second time, like me. It's crowded here today, so the atmosphere is not as good as it might otherwise be. My love, I'm sitting quite close to you, and you don't know it yet. Poelchau is also coming afterward and when he does come, he'll get this little letter. I'm not very far along yet with my various tasks. I'll be speaking to Dix at 2:30. Haubach's case has advanced pretty far, but I have to meet with Fräulein Schellhase about it again. The alarm has made everything grind to a virtual halt.—Now Gissel has come back down, and I have the good news that you're doing better, my love! How glad I am, but I'll still get the medication from Poelchau's friend, the physician, as well as pain pills and stimulants. Then you can see whether or not you need all that. Brigitte just went to see the warden, and I shook hands with Eugen [Gerstenmaier] in the hallway. I'm waiting for her, and maybe I can leave the letter for Poelchau here then. So I'm still near you, my dear love, and once again, you don't know it!—My Jäm, did you read the first chapter of Luke yesterday as well? It makes me happy every day that we do this together! When do you always read it?—My love, I'm afraid I have to go, otherwise I won't get very far. I hope I'll be able to write in peace again. It's not yet certain whether I can sleep at the friends' home, because Brigitte may be coming in the evening. Farewell, my dearest, I'm sending you a tender embrace and feel close to you in every way. I am and will remain P.; I'm yours completely.

1. Tegel prison. 2. Borsigwerke in Tegel, which was involved in armaments production, was largely destroyed during the war. 3. Apparent reference to Argus Motorenwerke, also an arms factory with forced laborers, as a satellite concentration camp in Reinickendorf.

HELMUTH JAMES TO FREYA, DECEMBER 6, 1944 [UNDERNEATH FREYA'S LETTER OF DECEMBER 5-6, 1944]

Today I'm on Luke 4–6. I usually read after eating my meal. I had a very nice talk with Poelchau about the problem of "unbelief," which was of great help to me. I hope you're able to convince Hercher that I have to speak to him again soon. Please go over the question once again of whether and, as the case may be, how the trial can be postponed past Christmas. With Poelchau, of course, not with Hercher. Maybe Frau Reisert can help with that. I'm feeling better, but I have to be very

[The note breaks off here.]

HELMUTH JAMES TO FREYA, DECEMBER 5, 1944

Tegel, 5 Dec 44

My dear, the warden was just here and ordered me to be unshackled on account of my rheumatism, as per my request. He wants to talk it over again tomorrow with the chief Reich prosecutor,[1] and I hope he doesn't object. In any case I now have the gift of the evenings, because I can now go to bed when I want to and so I want to use this additional time to write you, my love, in peace and quiet.

At my best moments I now feel like a little heap of iron filings lying on a smooth surface and being moved about by a magnet. Then everything is easy: whether I see myself, in my mind's eye, heading to the gallows, handcuffed behind my back, or I picture myself making my way from the train station to the Berghaus, the two options seem equally merciful to me, even though my flesh wants only the second option. But if I wish to pray, everything gets complicated: if I ask only for my life, it feels like presumption and a lack of surrender to God's will on my part, and if I also ask for mercy for the path to the gallows and for my entry into His kingdom, that strikes me, according to the signs He has given me, as a lack of faith and impermissible and wrong. "Too complicated a person," Herr Müller would say.

Is that truly too complicated? Am I lacking in simplicity and humility? That question has tormented me in the extreme this afternoon: not an unpleasant sort of torment but just in the way that something of this sort has to torment one.—If I think, "He wants to keep me alive" and "so you have to pray," I tell myself, that's your flesh talking; if I think, "I commend myself into His hands just as readily at the gallows," I say, that's unbelief. My love, you surely do that a lot better than I, so do pray for me; help your weak husband. The line "For whether we live, we live unto the Lord; and whether we die, we die unto the Lord,"[2] which is spiritually and intellectually satisfying as well as simple, is in reality very difficult, if you don't have the humility, acquiescence, and simplicity that are so sorely needed. "Sell all that thou hast, and distribute unto the poor... and come, follow me"[3] applies just as much to all spiritual gifts as to material things. Parting with those is sure to be even more difficult than relinquishing material objects, and it is possible only through God's grace.

I've already written you that my first day of Advent was nice. Never have I been as prepared for it as I was this time. But during the day, I sometimes quite happily look at the branch. It's certainly lovely, it's from Kreisau, and it adorns my cell magnificently, and yet it's so wonderfully spare. It so beautifully, so harmoniously expresses the all-embracing simplicity, beside which any magnificence and glory of the world amount to nothing. And in precisely this way it expresses the tremendous abundance that is bestowed upon us. Also, when I look at the branch, I see you amidst all the children. I'm so delighted, of course, that Casparchen thinks of me in such a moving way. I find everything you tell me about the little sons so beautiful. Let's just hope that Casparchen stays healthy over Christmas.—My love, it'll be very close to Christmas if I'm killed now, and I tremble at the thought that in this case you won't yet have processed my death at all. If the proceedings aren't over by then, or if I'm sentenced to death and not yet executed, it will actually be even worse. Brace yourself, my love: "Sorrows crushing soul and body / Do the heathens know alone— / Resting in Christ's blessed light, / Fears she not the earthly night."[4] I hope you will be capable of this, for the many children do have the right to a merry Christmas even if their fathers have just been killed.

Actually, the prospect of the trial does scare me. I can't deny that at all. Whenever I get word that it could come any day now, I get a bit startled. I see the end of our dear, intimate, tangible union, and I see Prinz-Albrecht-Str. with the horrors it may entail, and I see the trial on which my life depends. And every time it takes new effort on my part to realize that these are all accidentalia, and everything essential is written in the Holy Bible. We are simply weak human beings, appallingly weak.—Most of the time an evil thing turns out to be far less terrible once it arrives than the image we had of it. If I go there with a serene soul and with faith in God, it will work out.

My love, I don't want to take with me the card you gave me. I'm leaving it in the hymnal. I'll soon also give all your letters and the photos of the children to Poelchau. People shouldn't be in a position to find out anything about me, and the very idea that your card could wind up in the files of the chief Reich prosecutor is ghastly for me. When Poelchau recently asked the executioner how he was doing, he said: We had ten figures again. If I'm to be hanged, I want to be a figure too, and nothing else. I am carrying all of you, my love and the little sons, in my heart, and I don't need you to be anywhere else.

But you, my love, I commend into God's hands. J.

1. Ernst Lautz. 2. Romans 14:8.3. Luke 18:22. 4. Verse 4 of hymn "Wearily My Spirit Sinketh."

FREYA TO HELMUTH JAMES, DECEMBER 6, 1944[1]

Berlin, 6 Dec 44

My dear, today is St. Nicholas Day. He's bringing something for you too, my dear! First and foremost, though, you'll find two pieces of candy from Casparchen wrapped in a little piece of paper, which he made a point of sending you.

How is your back? Please give me all the details! I'm in touch with a doctor.

With the gingerbreads there's dried fruit, all of it from home, of course.

They're saying the trial is scheduled for the 20th/21st. Hercher, however, seemed to know nothing about it.

My dear, I'm not bringing anything else special, apart from my love, but that love is grand and blazing and tender.

1. Letter with the exchange of laundry.

HELMUTH JAMES TO FREYA, DECEMBER 6, 1944 [UNDERNEATH THE LETTER WITH THE LAUNDRY EXCHANGE FROM FREYA, DATED DECEMBER 6, 1944]

My dear, today substantially better and no real discomfort anymore; I hope it'll now get better. Most important, hardly any pain except when I make awkward movements and uncomfortable only when walking upright.

I'll give back the pajamas and handkerchief again in case I am moved. I won't need either until next Wednesday.

Otherwise everything is the same as always. J.

HELMUTH JAMES TO FREYA, DECEMBER 6–7, 1944

Tegel, 6 Dec 44

My love, two things have occurred to me: Kleist, a fellow prisoner, was released today. You may have heard from him that Herr Claus, my head guard, is very nice to me. Talk to Poelchau about whether you can, or should, get him a few peas.[1]

The other matter is more important. If I were you, I wouldn't go to see Frau Kleinert. It seems to me that the right way is for Poelchau to suggest to Fraulein Hapig, by way of Frau Kleinert's brother and possibly by way of a Catholic clergyman in Schweidnitz, if Hapig should have a good connection there, to circulate a legend about me[2] along the following lines: He has absolutely nothing to do with the events of July 20th, but did do something to bring about an accommodation between the denominations and was particularly close friends with many Catholic clergymen. That has been a thorn in the side of the Gestapo, which is why they want to use the opportunity presented by the actions of July 20th and take liberties with the facts to get Moltke out of the way. By the way, that's actually not so very far from the truth. But give some more thought to what's best to say. Under no circumstances can you be seen to be part of this action, not even by Hapig; she needs instead to draw on her wellspring of knowledge. This kind of support from the Catholics in the area would also assure you the support of Krebs and similar people and have a beneficial effect, particularly in a preventive sense regarding my conviction in the framework of the July 20th plot; and I truly have nothing to do with that. If one were to put the bustling Hapig on it and make it clear to her that this can be very important for your standing in the area and can offset the disadvantage of my execution in this respect, it should work out.

7 Dec 44

Good morning, my love. I hope nothing has happened to Afrikanische Str. tonight. Well, I'll hear about it in the course of the day. It wasn't as bad here as on Tuesday: I saw only one bomb, that is, the trail of fire it left behind, heard two in the air, and a total of about three or four explosions were close enough to make the building rattle. By our standards, that's not bad, and we're always afraid anyhow as soon as we notice that they've chosen this area. As long as the intense noise continues, I can't get past that feeling. I generally recite something aloud to calm myself. But it's very quickly forgotten.

My dear, if you should go back home this Sunday, do bring a new evergreen branch with you. If I should actually still be here on the third day of Advent, the one I have here will be too dry and too liable to catch fire, so I'd like to replace it next Wednesday.

My dear, I actually don't have anything left to say. I spend a lot of time thinking about how you and the little sons will fare after my death. How you'll live. Actually I'm not the least bit worried about it. I just get the feeling that if you are able to come through my execution in good shape, "the bit of chaos" won't daunt you either.[3] And I feel certain that I *can* expect you to come through it in good shape, because I feel it's so evident that of all my prayers, that is the one that God is most pleased to hear.

My love, I'll stop now. Farewell, my very dear love. Will I see you again? I'm presumptuous, but I hope that I'm also grateful; in any case, I'm endeavoring to be grateful for the cornucopia of grace that has been poured out over us. But I'm embracing you. J.

1. Because of the food shortage, peas were a welcome gift. 2. An attempt to circulate information selectively in the vicinity of Kreisau in order to pre-empt negative propaganda from the Nazis. 3. This prediction would turn out to be entirely correct in 1945.

HELMUTH JAMES TO FREYA, DECEMBER 7, 1944

Berlin, 7 Dec 44

My love, by local standards, this is certainly a wild night life; it's definitely after 7 p.m., probably just before 8. I'm also quite tired already since I worked like mad today because I finished the written defense for the People's Court; if Hercher doesn't come in the foreseeable future, I'll just send it off. Likewise, the letter to Himmler will go off unless I hear that Hercher will be returning in the foreseeable future, in which case I'd rather use him as a courier because otherwise I'm too afraid of the official channels. I'm actually quite satisfied with both written pleas: there is a great deal in them, even though they're short, and maybe Herr Freisler will notice that the written plea reads better than the prosecution's drivel. I also get the impression that the censors[1] were quite content. If I have enough time tomorrow morning, you'll get copies of both, so that you have everything.

And meanwhile my poor love is hard at work on behalf of her husband, always, always, in the certainty that it's of no use and the feeling that everything has to be done anyway. When I think of all the errands you have to run, in a constant race from one to the other, while I do nothing but concoct my tiresome chores for you...Just don't get your hopes up, my love.

It seems to me that the gentlemen at the People's Court are already putting up a smoke screen about the issues, and one day they will spring it upon us. But tomorrow I'll get updated information: I would greatly appreciate it being extended beyond Christmas, in which case I might be able to incorporate the Saar region into the number of territories in which my form of resistance ought to be blossoming now.[2] At any rate, new arguments could keep coming my way as time goes on. After all, the Alsace-Lorraine situation has arisen in just the past three weeks, and that already sounds better than only Eupen-Malmedy and Aachen.[3]

Tell me, my dear, you keep coughing up bacon and geese and butter and chickens and eggs and sugar, etc., etc., etc., for your husband, indirectly and directly. Aren't you starving as a result? That was all fine and good when we thought this whole thing would last three weeks, but it's been going on for two months now, and it can't continue this way. Don't you at least want to do your part by cutting back what the glutton himself gets? He really can get by with less, he wouldn't need, for example, eggs, butter, chicken, and would be very well-fed with just honey and sausage and an apple every once in a while.—The coffee was wonderful. I now always drink half of it warm and leave the other half for Thursday morning. It's still very good even when it's cold, and besides, it doesn't really interfere with my sleep. You still have enough coffee, don't you?

When I look at the people I'll be sentenced along with—I'm counting Delp as well—it seems safe to say that there could hardly be any other team of eight in this complex that is such a patent example of "positive Christianity"; even Haubach rejoined the Protestant Church a year ago and received Holy Communion from Gerstenmaier at that time. Steltzer, Gerstenmaier, and I provide a good representation of the Protestants, and Delp and Reisert of the Catholics; at the same time, everyone knows that Rösch is missing there, because they don't have him,[4] and that one Protestant and four Catholic bishops are very well disposed toward us. Taken together, it's better after all than being killed with Goerdeler and his people; these are all quite silly considerations, of course, but I'm mulling over how our death, if the dear Lord has ordained it, can at least be capitalized on, and that is possible in this manner. One just needs to underline this clearly, and it's the Catholics especially who must do so.

Now, my dear, I just want to eat my stewed fruit, which I've had soaking in water. I'll write you tomorrow to let you know whether that worked. And then I'll go to bed. May God watch over you, my dear love, and us. And He will do so; we can, we may, no: we must rely on it. J.

1. He is presumably referring to Dix and Poelchau, who had reviewed the draft defense. 2. The Allied offensive on the French border into Germany. 3. Western areas near the Rhine that had been captured by the Allies. 4. Rösch had gone into hiding after July 20, 1944; see Helmuth's letter of November 4–5, 1944.

FREYA TO HELMUTH JAMES, DECEMBER 8, 1944

Friday morning

My dearest, it's 6:15. I'm with the friends, but I already know that I won't have enough time to write everything I wanted to by the time Poelchau goes. Last night I got another little letter that was so lovely and so long, and I'd like to say so much about all of it. Yesterday morning, after I came back from seeing Hercher, I should have written right away, I had time until 3, but I had all sorts of other things to do and to write, of an urgent nature, and afterward I slept for an hour. I've had some lack of sleep this week, and I have to catch up on that as soon as I can: last night I went out at about ten with Brigitte [Gerstenmaier] because she needed to go, and we first got stuck at the Friedrichstr. station for fifty minutes, but halfway there we came to a complete stop because of an unexploded bomb on the tracks and then had to make our way to Lichterfelde Ost by way of detours, and mainly on foot, well guided by two friendly railway workers who were headed the same way. We got there at 1, and at 6:30 I had to leave so I could get to Hercher in time with my goose on my back. You'll be most interested in how that went: He told me quite a lot, holding nothing back. He happily indulges in that guilty pleasure of old people, talking up a storm. He told me a good deal about the Goerdeler issue, which he considered the most dangerous. The way I see it, he has the exact picture of you that he needs to have: he considers your ideas highly impractical—in particular he deems impossible any involvement of the church and finds all of this to be pipe dreams (my term, not his), but he regards you as a pure idealist utterly devoid of ambition and far from any interest in striving for some sort of power. This is true. He has also worked hard on your documentation already, but hasn't gotten through the notes about the Goerdeler issue. He's not making a copy of the indictment, but he said: I have to go there again so he can read it once more. It looks as though he will be defending Delp as well. We have to ensure that he lets you read the indictment when he comes for his first visit with Delp. After that I went to see Poelchau's friend, a physician. She has eight children, seven of whom are alive, and a thriving practice. She prescribed something for external and internal use, which I'll pick up today; but when I asked about the stimulant's effects, she also gave me a stern warning: it does pep you up and generates a kind of need for self-affirmation, but at the same time strips away any inhibitions about speaking. The Russians gave a similar substance to the accused in their marathon trials! So you're not going to get it, even though I already have it in my pocket. "I hate that stuff," she said, and she makes quite a formidable impression.—Oddly enough, I was already concentrating on your latest project, concerning the air raids,[1] but actually in a purely negative vein. If it's unsuccessful, it spells your immediate death, and I consider it very likely to fail. The fact that I was so fearful of the consequences of an instantaneous death made me realize once again that behind my back, my level of hope has risen quite high again, in defiance of my own will. It's the old, difficult, difficult art of keeping it at the right level. The Henssels no longer have an apartment in Berlin. As far as I know, Frau Sarre[2] has a house full of Rhinelanders, but I'll find that out. It's possible that they would put half a million on your head![3] After all, you've seen that this almost always works. In short, I'm afraid, but maybe I'll think of something better and my fear will subside. You're awfully conspicuous.[4]

My love, how good we still have it, how close we are to each other. How wonderful that is! I love you very much and I am and will forever remain your P.

1. Freya refers obliquely to the idea, which Helmuth had probably discussed with Poelchau, to attempt to break out of the prison in the chaos of a bomb attack and go underground. 2. The wife of Helmuth's former law partner, Friedrich Carl Sarre. 3. Goerdeler tried to evade capture following the July 20 bomb-plot failure and was found when a price was put on his head. 4. Helmuth was six feet five inches tall.

FREYA TO HELMUTH JAMES, DECEMBER 8, 1944

Friday noon

My love, I'm so relieved that you're now unshackled; it must really help your poor body relax, especially during the night.—You're quite right about the gifts of the spirit. We are absolutely in the ranks of the rich and so we have a very tough time of it.—I also liked the meagerness of the evergreen branch.—I'm now filled with hope that you won't have the trial before Christmas. Who would have thought that possible in early October!

Of course you're fearful about the trial, my dear. I shudder to think what that means for you and what the day will take out of you, but, my Jäm, I know that you can ride it out with God's help; I don't even know myself what "ride it out" might mean in this case, but the day will reveal that. I recently read a sermon by Gollwitzer, a friend of Poelchau, and found in it, essentially, the idea that if you fear someone, that person becomes the master of the fearing individual. Too bad I can't find the text right now. I found it quite illuminating and encouraging. But the very idea that Freisler is your master is absolutely out of the question!—Now Poelchau has gone as well.—By the way, I, like you, find everything having to do with the approaching trial quite daunting and sad, but, my love, we must let ourselves be borne along and believe and know that we're not alone. But we tremble at our own weakness, oh, my love.—I don't think that Prinz-Albrecht-Str. will be especially horrible; Poelchau doesn't think so either.

Just like you, I was afraid that it was just smoke and mirrors about the trial, but I don't think that's the case. Yes, if only it would take quite a long time!—I would be distraught if I voluntarily deprived you of the tiniest little bit. Bacon and sausage are all still from the old pig; the new one is already waiting to be slaughtered.[1] A small number of the young chickens are already laying eggs, so I have eggs. The chickens had to be dead before the December 4 count.[2] My household ate a good ten chickens. They eat their fill and the cooking is good and solid; there's no place for luxury. You've been eating my butter for close to a year, and that is a source of my happiness; don't spoil it for me. I was quite sad when I had so much butter to eat in Sept. I sometimes eat butter here, most of the time, in fact, at the expense of the household, I can't do anything about that. They're not in prison, and in town they would only have half anyway. The children get plenty. The Borsigs donated a big bag of sugar—you've had some of that, too—so it wasn't much of an accomplishment on my part. Yes, I still have tea and coffee. I'm trying to conserve, but the reserves are of course shrinking bit by bit.

Today I also ate dried stewed fruit for lunch. I hadn't read that you had made some for yourself, and said to the Poelchaus, "Helmuth ate the same stewed fruit today"; but that was yesterday.

My Jäm, the day before yesterday Thiele told Hercher that the case would be coming up before Christmas! That needn't be correct, but it could be, and Brigitte [Gerstenmaier] has to go to see Thiele on

Tuesday after all. How can this all make sense?! Once again, it really got under my skin. It's also quite unpleasant for me to be worrying you with this. The truth is that you have to be prepared. Hercher thought he'll find out more on Monday. He told me all kinds of things besides this. He had the petition for clemency at home, and we went there together. He also said something that seemed important to me: With Freisler, you can always tell how serious things are right from the start. In general, the sentence is passed before it starts, so it is even more vital that he gets the second defense statement beforehand. That has to go out, as does the letter to Himmler.—My Jäm, my love, my beloved, how will this all go for you! My heart trembles, but I'm confident. Above all, we need to remain where we are in good hands and submit to God's will. Sleep well, my dearest. Good night.

1. Agricultural operations were subject to monitoring of what was consumed on the premises. Authorization was required to slaughter a pig. Pork was an important nutritional element in Kreisau, and the slaughtering of pigs and their consumption had to be planned out carefully. 2. There were limits on how many chickens could be kept privately at certain dates.

HELMUTH JAMES TO FREYA, DECEMBER 8, 1944

Berlin, 8 Dec 44

Yes, my dear, the major additional difficulty signified by the emergence of a glimmer of human or quasi-human hope is indeed major, oddly major. Death is no longer as much of a natural and familiar and thus dear companion as it was before. That's a great pity, because it means that when I want to—or have to—confront it once more, I'll have to battle my way there all over again. We joyfully accept God's will when it seems to suit our plans, but surrendering to a path that is unpleasant for the flesh is far more difficult. That may be an exaggerated way of putting it, but unfortunately there's quite a bit of truth to it.

In the face of all this confusion, there is only one firm position to keep coming back to: For God, everything is possible. If He wants to preserve me, He can do so in a hundred ways without our having any inkling in advance, and if He wants to call me to Him, He will let a bomb fall down onto my head once my acquittal seems a sure thing. If we were able to keep this awareness, which frees us from the whims of Herr Freisler or the random chance of a petition for clemency or something similar, ever present and vivid in our minds, we would be a crucial step ahead. But the impulse to work on the "hopes" muddies the issue and keeps creating turmoil in our hearts. We are nothing more than a very big dung heap, and in a situation like this, we relearn that time and again. Anything that is not bad within us is already an act of grace, and this awareness would be a great deal more beautiful if it were always within our grasp. But even that is unattainable.—Enough moaning and groaning, my love; all this doesn't torment me—unfortunately—as much as it really ought to.

Of the issues I've touched on in earlier letters, I just want to remind you of these: propaganda,[1] Peters, Steltzer, Husen.[2]—In the end, I think we have to ensure that our attorneys work together, and each of us has to tell his attorney that he may not gain advantages at the expense of a codefendant. But it is even more important for the attorneys to coordinate their activities and exchange information about the defense. In any case, I will require Hercher to do so, and this issue has already been discussed with Fugger and Eugen [Gerstenmaier], so you need to win over only Lehrter Strasse.[3] So, my love, my dearest. I imagine you're at the friends' home by now, where I know that you are safe, and I'll go have a snooze. Are grains of wheat always this intractable under such circumstances when they are to be lowered into the earth?[4] In spite of it all, I do know that His will is good and for our salvation and that I want to submit to it joyfully; I also believe that when the time comes, I will not be found wanting.

1. He is referring to the propaganda in the village of Gräditz. 2. The information for Theodor Steltzer, who was being held in the Gestapo prison, and his

Kreisau friends Hans Peters and Paulus van Husen, who did not have a trial impending yet. 3. His codefendants Theodor Haubach, Theodor Steltzer, and Franz Sperr were held in the Lehrter Strasse prison. 4. An allusion to John 12:24: "Except a corn of wheat fall into the ground and die, it abideth alone: but if it die, it bringeth forth much fruit."

FREYA TO HELMUTH JAMES, DECEMBER 9, 1944

Saturday afternoon

My dear, I haven't read your letter yet, but I did get it and am still sitting on my buried treasure, full of happiness. I've just arrived at the friends' house and don't have very much time left. It's 4:45 and at 6:02 my train leaves from Zoo. On the way here, I was able to fit in a quick talk with Frl. Schellhase. She brought Haubach's answer. She would like once again to inform Hercher about your line of defense in somewhat more detail. Can you write up a brief note about it? I will include the papers for you. It all refers to Goerdeler, and the attorneys seem to regard only that issue as dangerous. Write a little note to Steltzer too, with what you want to say. I'll type it up.—Now I've had a chance to read your beautiful letter. My poor love, how stressful it is for you. Eugen [Gerstenmaier]'s absolute certainty makes it easier on him.[1] But I don't approve of it. My dear, you're totally justified in having all this going on inside you, and you mustn't judge yourself too harshly. The good Lord knows that, too, that we are poor and weak people, but He is prepared to reside within us!—I have to stop. I'll be there again soon. My love stays here, as do all my thoughts. How I love you, my dear! I am and will remain yours. P.

I'm here! The train was canceled. I'm with the friends! Poor Casparchen! I just put in a telephone call!

1. Gerstenmaier was firmly convinced that he would survive the ordeal.

HELMUTH JAMES TO FREYA, DECEMBER 9–10, 1944

Tegel, 9 Dec 44

My love, I'm going to get a quick start on writing a little letter "in a minor key," because that's also part of it. Hercher has just left. I'm very pleased that he was here, because we were able to make a bit of progress once more.

He thought we'd definitely come before Christmas, emphasizing that Thiele had said so quite definitively, with the explanation, "Hermes, Fehr, etc., will not come until after New Year's."—He also said that after working his way through my documents, he considers the case quite grim, because the court "will surely have no interest in hearing my explanations," which is why he is anticipating a death sentence. That's not new, but it's just the thing to destroy the somewhat more optimistic versions. He also told me that the sentence would surely be carried out right away, even though there had been some exceptions as well. Vote on the whole: I will not get to experience Christmas. In spite of the minor-key mood stemming from these statements, at the moment I feel secure with our Father and pray that He may preserve this feeling in me—not this feeling but this certainty. My love, He will also hold you in His grace.

From this angle, Steengracht is both important and urgently needed.[1]—Now it's time to eat.

Evening. I just finished my supper, and the guard has already said good night to me. I'll now write before I continue reading. Hercher's opinion, based on my documents—he wants to have a look at the court file early next week—is as follows: Danger no. 1 is this single conversation with Goerdeler and Beck[2] plus my confession of guilt; danger no. 2, defeatism;[3] danger no. 3, individual points from the conversations centered on Kreisau, in particular the map. Each of these things can be lethal, and taken together, they actually must be lethal. He didn't say all of that so pointedly, but that's what it is, and it also tallies with my opinion. The earth is nice and hard under our feet once again, and the pink clouds have scattered; nevertheless, an indictment this bad is an advantage, though Hercher said they were always this bad.

My love, don't think I'm downhearted. No, I'm not. But it is only right to be focused completely on my imminent parting and not to get lost in all sorts of hopes. There is only one hope and that is our hope for the Lord. Over these past weeks, He has blessed us so appreciably that we have every "right" to expect more, as we know from the saying, "For He that hath, to Him shall be given." We may expect more because we have noticed that He hears us. Do you know, my dear, why I like writing you so much about this topic? Not only because I love you, not only because I would like to tell you and myself as much as possible before I depart, but also because it makes my soul feel light and airy. I then see before me, in black and white, how things need to be; once I have told all to my beloved, it is so much easier to say to the horse who at times grows weary: *hic rodus hic salta*.[4] If I didn't know about the struggle in Gethsemane, I would condemn myself to hell on a daily basis. But then I tell myself, if Jesus grieved and despaired, I guess you can do so as well. What a colossal reality all these words have taken on. You know, before this I hadn't known what grieving and despairing were in this context; nor did I know what was behind it when he says "so I will drink it, thy will be done." I'm learning this now, and it pains me to think of those who don't have that model, that light; they can only despair, or scurry past it, conceal it from themselves. I'm grateful that I don't need that: every evening, as I fall asleep, he stands before me fully visible, and my first thought when I wake up at night or in the morning is of that walk to the gallows, a walk I may have to take in ten or fourteen days. That is what spurs me on to "watch and pray," and it does require some spurring; the disciples had no choice but to sleep, because they lacked this prod. Other than these thoughts, and thoughts of what will happen to all of you afterward, I dwell solely on my defense, again and again. I still read the newspaper from beginning to end, but sometimes only two days later; I read it only when I'm waiting for something and don't want to concentrate or I'm restless and can't concentrate or I'm tired.

In our free hour I now always walk at a snail's pace in the inner small circle, abreast of Delp and Eugen [Gerstenmaier] in the large one, and we always have the same conversation about faith. They claim that one must pray for one's life and believe that this prayer will be fulfilled, while I keep saying that is going too far: I can't prescribe what God should wish for, not even by invoking my faith. I can only believe that He wants what's best for me and for you and for the little sons. That's as far as it goes. New arguments occur to all three of us at night, and in the morning it continues.—Incidentally, Delp will have his trial with us, Hercher said, which means that they're no longer counting on getting Rösch and König.—It is a true joy to me that Delp was accepted into the Jesuit order yesterday.[5] Not only because he was able to do so in prison but, more important, because I'd spoiled his chances in the early part of 1943, as I'd told Rösch I found it wonderful that the Jesuits, of all people, had such an undisciplined brother; I didn't know at the time that Delp had yet to take the big vow, and Rösch then told me he would again defer his vows. This was not intended.

That's enough chitchat for today, my dearest. I hope you'll be home soon and don't miss the connection in Liegnitz. Might I see you next week? May the Lord watch over you and us, my dear love. J.

10 Dec 44

Good morning, my love, it's 7 o'clock, and I picture you now with the two little sons in bed, reading and studying with one of them and keeping the other one quiet. What a lovely image for me. I've just finished getting up and making my bed—because I'm unshackled, I'm doing this half an hour earlier—and now I just want to say, in black and white, that my thoughts are very tenderly with you all. For I have next to nothing to tell you. Actually I do have something to say, maybe three things: There was an air raid, which was of medium intensity where we were—at one point it was terribly bright above us, I saw four bombs and maybe a dozen impacts that were strong enough to make the doors and windows rattle quite a bit—but that is mercifully over.—Second, the following has occurred to me: Since you're making a new petition for clemency with Hercher, just be sure that if this one is handed in after the verdict, it doesn't supplant the other one, because a petition for clemency after the verdict is a pure formality and has to be rejected. It must clearly indicate—it shouldn't matter if it's in the text or the cover letter—that the main petition for clemency is already with the Führer and the SS Reich Leader. Please discuss that with Poelchau and then with Hercher. I'm fine with anything you do, and I'm not inclined to panic at the moment, the way I did a month ago; I simply wanted to point out the chaos that might ensue. Another question: How would it be if in some way—for you can't be the one to do it—a message were introduced into the SS channels, maybe via the reserve army, maybe via Keitel: if you don't want to give the man a reprieve and leave him in jail, then give him the reprieve of a suicide mission, as it is done with a soldier sentenced to death. Talk that over with Poelchau.

Farewell, my dear, my dearest love. May the Lord watch over you and us, and we shall joyfully submit to His will. I cannot say more, farewell. J.

1. This is a reference to the petition to Hitler for clemency, which Steengracht had agreed to endorse. 2. On January 22, 1943, in the apartment of Peter Yorck; see Helmuth's letter of December 21, 1944. 3. The National Socialists regarded a lack of faith in a final victory as a serious offense, which could warrant the death penalty; see Editors' Introduction. 4. "Here is Rhodes, jump here." The phrase, from Aesop, essentially means: Show what you can do, here and now! 5. Delp had a fellow Jesuit administer the final oaths of admission to the Jesuit Order in prison. Delp had set great store by this accomplishment. See Roman Bleistein, *Alfred Delp: Geschichte eines Zeugen* (Frankfurt am Main: Josef Knecht, 1989), 331. Helmuth had meant the "undisciplined brother" comment as a compliment, but Rösch, Delp's superior, decided to defer his final oaths as a result.

HELMUTH JAMES TO FREYA, DECEMBER 10-12, 1944

Tegel, 10 Dec 44

My dear love, I've just blown out the candle on the evergreen branch over my door, which brings my celebration of the second Advent to an end; it's about 6:15, and I've got the urge to talk to my dearest once again. My love, your beautiful angel is next to me and shields me from above with his wings. Thank you, my love. I lit the candle just after 5:30, along with a piece of branch, so it smells like Christmas, then realized that the branch is dried up and droopy, and it would be nice if I could get a fresh one in case I'm still alive for the third Advent. Then I put your big candle on my table, your angel along with it, and read the beginning of the Gospels of Luke and John, that is, Luke 1:26–56 and Hartmann's Advent songs from the hymnal, then I just sat quietly, watching the light and thinking of the coming of the Lord, of my Pim, and of our sons until it was time to blow out the candle so that some of it remains for next Sunday if I still need it. Oh, right, I also read Isaiah 59:16–21 and 60.

Please let Ulla [Oldenbourg] know that it now appears to be heading into the final, critical stage. Tell her I'm so thankful for her help so far, but she continues to be crucial, for with human eyes there is still no hope in sight, but only a totally mechanical process from the departure in Tegel to the chimney in Plötzensee, in which the People's Court is no more than a maintenance stop, a stop where the conductor has to call out "make way," but no one can get on or off.[1]

One more thing: Did Poelchau tell you I had the idea that my idiotic statements[2] were induced by Pervitin? After my second sleepless night, they got me at 10 again and made me sit there until 2, claiming it was because the senior councillor wasn't back. Then they came up with the suggestion that I might want to eat something, and a large dish of very thick soup was brought "from the cafeteria." It could have contained that infernal stuff; right after the meal the questioning started, and I clearly recall feeling a need for self-affirmation, which I'm not normally subject to. On the 28th they did the same thing again.—I don't know this for a fact, of course, but that's at least a rational explanation for my almost incomprehensibly foolish behavior. Still, it could also have been a combination of stupidity and nastiness, with stupidity predominating.—Finally, I had a long talk with Claus today and introduced our legend of the church's attitude as the true cause. And that caught on; his interest was sparked, because he too, and this one and that one, had been hampered in their advancement because they went to church and had their children confirmed, he told me. That came out like a torrent and showed me that the cover story rang true; now it just needs to be circulated with a vengeance.—May the Lord watch over you and us. J.

11 Dec 44

I've spent the whole day looking forward to the evening, when I'll be chatting with my dearest again. At the same time, there's nothing at all to report. But I see my hourglass running out and I'm thinking: Talk to her while you still can.—During the day I wrote a medium-length set of notes about my line of defense, and want to ask you, if this would work, to deliver it to all four of the men at Lehrter Str.[3] with a request to point out any discrepancies. I would be especially grateful to hear from Sperr about what he actually said. Sperr also needs another reminder that he did not inform Delp about his conversation with Stauffenberg until after July 20th. Finally I would ask for a copy of this, my line of defense, on thin paper so that Eugen [Gerstenmaier] and Delp can see it in black and white.

My love, I'm terribly worried about your Christmas, but there's nothing I can do about it. I tell you quite bluntly that I think I take precedence, unless it's definite that we won't be up before Christmas. Your presence in Berlin is extremely precious to me, especially at the time of the trial and afterward. I want to have the feeling that you are standing by me with an undivided heart and undivided attention. Do you understand that?—My dear, all this is very demanding for you, but I think the matter is so important that I can say this. I'm going to spoil your Christmas somehow or another, no matter what, and last year the little sons saw to that;[4] you really are surrounded by tactless men.

My love, if I'm dead by Christmas, which is, after all, in line with prior standard practice, it won't be so nice either to go home and celebrate Christmas. My poor love, all this weighs me down, and I would be very happy if we could put it off to the new year. In any case, give it your best effort. I can only keep hoping that after the long preparation time the Lord has granted us we are both truly so well equipped now that we can cope with all this, with His grace. Think about how it would be if I had been executed with Adam [von Trott zu Solz] on September 9, as originally planned. The world would look very different for you, and I would have departed in a different manner.

12 Dec 44

Good morning, my dearest, I've just heard that we will be tried a week from today. Fugger's lawyer told him that. If I only remain firmly in God's hand, and you as well, this day will certainly be a day in God's scheme of things like any other, without any fright. The Lord was merciful with me, as Fugger just told me, and it didn't scare me in the slightest. I only hope I can remain with Him, but I'm relying on that. Whatever that day may bring for us, my love, it cannot touch our love; instead, this love will conquer all the events of that day, too. Farewell, my love. J.

1. A metaphor from certain tram stops where leaving the tram was not permitted. 2. Helmuth appears to be referring to his interrogations in August 1944 in Drögen or in the last week of September in the Lehrter Strasse Gestapo prison; see his letter of October 1, 1944. 3. The reference is to Theodor Haubach, Franz Reisert, Franz Sperr, and Theodor Steltzer. 4. Because of illness during Christmas 1943.

FREYA TO HELMUTH JAMES, DECEMBER 11, 1944[1]

Monday afternoon

My dear, the big writing pad is at the friends' home and since it will be coming to you on Wednesday, I won't be writing more on it anyway. I have to get another one in Kreisau, or shall I say I *would* have to, my love, because I fear that the long letters I so enjoy writing will be few in number. It doesn't appear altogether certain that they'll be finished with you by Christmas. They'd like to be, but it's far from sure that they'll be finished with their schedule next week. It seems certain that it won't be this week anymore. It's an exceptionally strenuous week, the week before Christmas. How will all this work out, my Jäm! That is not an expression of despair; it's just a sigh. It'll all work out somehow or another. We must let ourselves be borne along and comply with what God has imposed on us. There is a certain happiness, a prospect of easing the tension in the precious certainty that we are utterly united, utterly inseparable in God's keeping. So I see distress, pain, sorrow, and a difficult path for you ahead of me, but no despair, and down to the end, my faith that God is capable of keeping you alive will remain unshakable. My Jäm, how much richer you will be leaving me behind, if you have to die, than you would have three months ago. We have a rich, happy, harmonious, blessed, never troubled life together behind us and have appreciated it full of gratitude and happiness, we were rich in view of the past, but, my beloved heart, now we're rich in regard to the future.

Yes, my love, we will be able to see and speak to each other once again this week.[2] That is a beautiful and cherished and precious prospect, my dearest. However, if I'm the way I feel now, all my strength would leave me and I would let my streams of tears flow. But that's not an option because that is not nice for you and, God willing, it will turn out differently, I'd rather leave the way it turns out to Him, because that is actually our hearts' desire.

My Jäm, your little "letter in a minor key" is lovely; I'm happy to have it. Yes, my own little pink clouds have scattered as well. I am basically doing well and feeling safe too, and I'm so close, so close to you, my love. I understand so well that you want to keep telling me what holds and binds us. I cannot hear this often enough, and time and again, I'm grateful and happy about every word you say to me.

I am and will forever remain your P.

1. Only a copy of this letter has been preserved. The date that was added later, 18 Dec 44, is unlikely. 2. Shortly before this, Councillor Thiele had promised Freya a face-to-face meeting for the following week.

HELMUTH JAMES TO FREYA, DECEMBER 12–13, 1944

Tegel, 12 Dec 44

My dear, in all likelihood, that is, according to purely human calculation, I will already be dead at this time in a week from today. I was thinking today about my old farewell letter to you[1] and thinking about how I ought to write you a new one and realizing that I actually can't do so now. I'm not at all in the mood for parting; the fact of the matter is simply that the very thing I should consider to be the most decisive farewell appears not to be a farewell. May God grant that this certainty remains firm and steadfast for you and for me; if He retains this certainty in us, He will have given us the greatest gift He can bestow. If He were to take away my creaturely fear of dying, I would go to Plötzensee quite cheerfully in the knowledge that He is calling me and I will see Him, live within Him, go on loving you and finding you within Him. At the moment, the 31st Psalm has become my daily constant companion, and I read it two or three times a day.

My dear, once again, something practical has occurred to me: It is possible that the hyenas[2] who want to snatch up the loot will show up in Kreisau before you, since you might wind up being detained here. You have to give Asta [Wendland] and Zeumer clear instructions for this day, explaining that the Berghaus does not belong to me and that the items in the Berghaus don't belong to me either, so the people have no business being there. Asta has to stay in Kreisau after my sentence until you come, because Ulla [Oldenbourg] can't defend the house on her own. She'll simply have to do without her Wend [Wendland] at that time. Once they've emptied out the pantry and surrounded the rest of the house, it'll be hard to do anything. Asta has to stand up to them and say, "I'm a co-owner, I'm a co-owner,"[3] and Zeumer has to support her in that.

13 Dec 44

Imagine, my dear, Poelchau, who was just here, showed up unexpectedly. I had an enormous desire to write to you, looked at the angel standing in front of me, and he said: No, because otherwise you'll ruin your evening, when it's so much better to write. And then Poel-chau came.—My love, the main sensation is that our trial will appar-ently be not on the 19th *or* 20th, but on the 19th *and* 20th. Should that prove to be true, as I hardly dare hope, that will offer us an op-portunity, because it means that Freisler will hear us out. If that is true, it's probably a result of my written plea. Still, I'm happy that news like this doesn't set me in upward motion;[4] I just need to be able to bear in mind always: "My times are in Thy hand." My mind and my faith are both telling me so, yet it's certainly not easy to remain aware of it all the time. The creature that we are is definitely despicable.

My love, your "laundry exchange" was splendid today. The footmuff keeps me exquisitely warm, the chocolate candies are simply heavenly, I hope you ate some too, and the little card very sweet. I've likely now got everything I'll need for the rest of my life. Don't bring me anything else on Monday, not even coffee, because I have to sleep well on Monday night. I don't need any more clothing either, not even long underwear.

Now I come to Christmas again, under the assumption that the trial is on. There are three possible decisions: death sentence, no death sentence, postponement. You'll leave if there is a postponement, or no death sentence, or a death sentence that is carried out. That is quite clear. The problem arises only if the outcome is a death sentence that will not be carried out before Christmas. If this is the case, you should, I think, go home at midday on the 23rd, and be back here on the 27th. If this state of uncertainty drags on for an extended period of time, let's say past January 6, without a decision and without my reappearing anywhere, and it is clear that there is nothing more you can do, and the situation only torments you, you should go home. If I haven't been executed by the 21st, make sure to get through to me on the 22nd. By then I'll need some fresh clothing and some food. You'll surely be able to do so, even at Prinz-Albrecht-Strasse.—You'll have to set up a grapevine regarding my execution so that in any event you can find out about it right away. I'd like to assume that if I remain in Gestapo custody, Neuhaus or Lange[5] will be in charge of me, and Müller in any case. If I'm to be incarcerated by the judicial system,

I'll probably be brought to Tegel, but however that works out, my location won't remain hidden for long.—So if I'm kept in custody, I'll try to get us a face-to-face meeting, and you can try to exchange my laundry—just a little at a time.

Claus was very happy about the bacon. I told him he would have received a Christmas package, but because I would now be away and my wife didn't feel like coming back here after my departure, this gift came offhandedly. Claus is really afraid for us. He was even more agitated about our trial than we are and quite pale. "It would ruin my whole Christmas if you didn't come through." He's also very unhappy that he probably won't have the section next week because he has to do the night shift, and that's why he can't see us off at noon.

At this time I'm not trembling at the thought of the trial at all; I'm actually glad that we have now survived this period. I think a postponement would be rather unpleasant for me now, even though I'd be pleased about it in some respects. But all the earlier times that I thought the trial was just around the corner I was afraid and was constantly at risk of succumbing to panic that this or that step had to be taken beforehand, while there was still time. That's all gone now. I can only keep praying that I can hold on to this sense of security.

My love, on Tuesday we'll read the Passion from the Gospel of John together, as well as the magnificent twenty-first chapter, which says: both are disciples: the one who follows him to the cross, and the one who doesn't need to follow. And on Wednesday we'll read Ascension and Pentecost. And on Tuesday you'll read for me the story where Balaam is summoned to curse, but instead has to bless.[6] I'm not in a martyr-like frame of mind, not a bit, but I now understand that it was not so incredible that the early Christian martyrs sang as they were thrown to wild animals to be torn apart. It really is quite a bit easier to comply with something like this in song than to grumble. But whether one sings or grumbles is an act of grace and not something that one can will. However, this can't actually be understood by people who aren't in a similar situation or at least able to bear witness to it.

Whatever will the little sons say about these things one day? Will they understand these kinds of problems? Will they learn something from our efforts? They will indeed in any case, because after the experience of these three months you will raise them differently from the way you would have without these three months. That is quite certain, as long as they come to grasp the underlying causes. I sometimes think about whether our little sons will read these letters and understand them someday. Do you know what important thing we're still missing: the awareness of belonging to a visible church. We're still too individualistic in these matters. Maybe that, too, will come in time, and if it does, the institution of the church will also flourish once again.

Another thing occurs to me. I'd like to bring honey to the Prinz-Albrecht-Strasse, but I'm not allowed to take glass or metal to the Prinz-Albrecht-Str. Maybe you can get hold of a jam jar made of papier-mâché (is that the way it's spelled?)? My liniment will also be used up by then, and I need to ask you to get me another bottle. I'll then repour it into prison containers and hope that the Prinz-Albrecht-Str. permits me to have it. As it is, I may well find that on Tuesday evening I'll have racking pains from standing so long and will have to be on my toes again on Wednesday. For it is completely clear that I will have to fight the main part of the battle: if I ride it out, it will be half won for the others, even if they kill me; if I let them get the best of me, it will be all over for the others, and the positions of Carl Dietrich [von Trotha], Einsiedel, and Husen, etc. will be in jeopardy.

My love, I'll stop now, because all I can say is the same thing again and again. May the Lord watch over you and us, or, as has been said for thousands of years: "The Lord bless thee, and keep thee: The Lord make his face shine upon thee, and be gracious unto thee: The Lord lift up his countenance upon thee, and give thee peace."[7] J.

1. Presumably Helmuth's letter of October 1, 1944. 2. The reference is to the members of the Gestapo after a seizure of assets. 3. Helmuth had inherited the Berghaus jointly with his siblings, as separately held assets. 4. Helmuth is referring to the upper emotional registers in which he experiences hope; see his letter of October 30–31, 1944, where he writes that he prefers to have his

mind "way down deep, but on bedrock." 5. See Helmuth's letter of September 30, 1944, notes 14 and 15. 6. Numbers 4:22–25. 7. Numbers 6:24–26.

FREYA TO HELMUTH JAMES, DECEMBER 14, 1944

Thursday morning

My dear love, I'm at the friends' home and I slept wonderfully. I enjoy your letters incredibly. They're so lovely, and like conversations. It takes quite a long time to read them, and I keep finding new things. Yes, my dear, dear love, we really can't write each other any more farewell letters; there is nothing more to say but the same things again and again, and both of us are eager to hear them again and again. May the dear Lord help us to live out what we have experienced. It will not work out without Him, but I'm full of confidence in His help, just as you are.

What are you writing, my love, about claims surrounding Christmas? That is all nonsense. I belong to you. As far as I can, I will go *with you* along the path you must travel. I almost have to laugh when you worry about my Christmas. I'm of no interest whatsoever here. The relatively happiest Christmas would be celebrated close to you, but of course the little sons have to be taken into account, and I have to go to them, if at all possible, on the 24th—and only on the 24th. All the other days are of lesser importance. I'll come again as soon as possible after the 24th, if the case is going in a way that makes this the right thing to do—and your description of the options is so right.

So, my dearest, now you need another report. The exchange of laundry was nice. I'm so at home in your building there! It's strange how homey even prisons can become. The waiting room, Poelchau's room, the warden's room, and across the way, Gissel's room, where I always hand over the items; these rooms are very dear to me. The place behind the door leads to you, and every clank of that door connects me to you a little. I always have a little urge to run over and look up to see whether I can spot you, and I keep on seeing you as we saw each other for the first time, going up the stairs there and turning around to me. I talked to Gissel about picking up my belongings. I mean: I'll come again on Monday, but I'll leave those things there for now. I'm still hoping that things may work out without Prinz-Albrecht-Str., right from "home." You ought to have all the little conveniences as long as possible. They are already part of your inventory in "25."[1]

I got to Steengracht too late, because early in the morning, Fraulein Schellhase had made me wait in vain for thirty minutes, so I fell behind. When I was at your place, I didn't rush at any point; I took my time talking to Gissel, which was more important to me. As a result, I had to wait at Steengracht's, and spent the time writing to Mütterchen Deichmann. I'll have a connection to her again now that Haus has an office in Godesberg. Steengracht was friendly, cordial, and full of sympathy for me. He's turned the petition over in his mind again and again, and is totally willing to do whatever would be most beneficial for you. But he was not in favor of the route from the Foreign Office to Himmler. He thought that if Himmler received the same petition, which was not addressed to him, so often it might have an adverse effect. He felt that if I do this, it would be better to go by way of Keitel, because there is a clear line of authority; he also thought that I myself ought to write a few words to Himmler again and discuss the possibility of sending it with Müller, and that I ought to find out what Uncle Peter [von Moltke] accomplished in his inquiry. Evidently Hewel said: Yes, but I definitely have to wait for a good moment. Steengracht did not know whether that had occurred. But he felt that if it still hadn't, one should withdraw the petition. That's how it went. Does that disappoint you?

The secret message transaction[2] hasn't gotten very far. It's written—Frau Breslauer is in Munich, but I have her typewriter—and today Eugen [Gerstenmaier] and Delp are getting it, but it strikes me as somewhat extensive for Reisert and Sperr. Haubach is likely to get it, but I first have to see whether Steltzer's old friend is willing to accept it this morning. I'm a little afraid of being careless at the last minute. Frau Reisert isn't coming back from Bavaria until later today. Apparently Carl Dietrich [von Trotha] and Einsiedel also looked it over last night. Today at 1 I hope to meet with Peters.[3] I think that's the most important part. I've yet to deal with the propaganda.

Claus and Gissel will get a Christmas package in any case. Gissel is also afraid of the trial. Yes, I knew that two days are scheduled.

Stay calm, my beloved Jäm, my great unlosable love, my love. Tomorrow, I think, I'll be visiting you! You know how much I belong to you: I am and will forever remain your P.

1. Helmuth's cell number, no. 325, on official correspondence. 2. See Helmuth's letter of December 10–12, 1944. 3. Hans Peters, who was willing to go and see Freisler. See Helmuth's letter of December 10, 1944, in Helmuth James and Freya von Moltke, *Abschiedsbriefe Gefängnis Tegel: September 1944–January 1945* (Munich: C. H. Beck, 2011), 301.

HELMUTH JAMES TO FREYA, DECEMBER 14, 1944

Tegel, 14 Dec 1944

My dear, the most important thing as far as I'm concerned is that on the day or days of the trial you and Ulla [Oldenbourg] and everyone willing and able will pray for me. No matter how things turn out, I'd like to have the feeling of being held close during these hours; that is incredibly important to me, because so endlessly much depends on my not growing weak, and not only for me. Think of the parable of the pleading widow.[1] It will surely go according to God's will, but perhaps—no, definitely—He wants to be asked. I'm not talking about the outcome here but rather about the process. I have to succeed in cutting through the first thrust of the offensive like a breakwater so that they don't have any desire to stir our pot anymore, because that will spill over onto too many others. They mustn't be able to surmise any further knowledge on my part either.—I'm not nervous at the moment, and am praying for the Lord to keep me in this state and let me withstand the trial in this state, but I really cannot get nervous.—My love, I have so many reasons not only to be grateful but also to look to the trial with trust in God. Now that I think about it, I have had nothing but hopeless cases to deal with in my life, and He has always steered me through: from the work for Waldenburg,[2] all of which was considered impossible to carry out, to the financial rescue of Kreisau,[3] which not a single expert considered feasible, to my work as an attorney, which provided for us in a miraculous way, to the Kempinski case,[4] which was utterly lost when I started working on it, down to my work at the Armed Forces High Command, which ought to have plunged me into all kinds of moral conflicts in this state. So I have every reason to know that He can steer this process marvelously as well if He considers that right—but He could also think that I've now learned quite enough.

—After all, if He has never forsaken me in eleven months in prison, if He let me be tormented only three times over the course of these months and afterward taught me why, because, as I learned, the hardness and stupidity of my heart did not realize things it ought to have realized—why would He forsake me in the superior court or at the gallows in Plötzensee?

My love, I think I'll stop for now. Tonight I continue writing. May the Lord watch over you and us. J.

1. Luke 18:1–7: the parable of the persistent widow and the unjust judge, and encouragement to pray, which will be heard by God. 2. See Biographical Note. 3. See Biographical Note. 4. Helmuth was the legal adviser of the Jewish Kempinski family.

HELMUTH JAMES TO FREYA, DECEMBER 14, 1944

Tegel, 14 Dec 44

My dear, it's the evening, and although I wrote you a detailed letter this morning, there is truly a great deal of news, and I have a rich field ahead of me. Let's start by hoping that January 8[1] isn't a ruse but is actually true. And then it'll go on. If this is true, we can only echo Psalm 118: "This is the LORD's doing; it is marvellous in our eyes."

There's no doubt that this postponement not only is a pleasure for us but is also an objective advantage. Incidentally, at first I was not as excited as I ought to have been because I am, and was, so prepared for the 19th, 20th.

Now we have to rethink everything. I'm now in favor of your going to Kreisau on Saturday and not returning until after Christmas for the final sprint, with fresh energy. I'm not in favor of your traveling back and forth again; it's too strenuous, and you ought to save your strength. The following things need to be considered: my provisioning, the exchange of secret messages, the petition for clemency, discussion with Haus.—My provisioning is unimportant, although you refuse to believe that. Just have someone come from Kreisau. Maybe Lenchen can do it. She should bring the necessities, and you can get them to me if you like; otherwise Brigitte [Gerstenmaier] will surely do it. I have food and laundry up to and including Thursday the 21st. For the time afterward, honey and sugar are all that will be needed, that's it, no clean clothing.—There's time for the exchange of secret messages once it's definite that we are rescheduled past New Year's. Just don't do anything careless and don't induce the others to do so either; they should do only what seems absolutely safe, because a slipup can make everything go haywire for us.—The petition for clemency. First issue is your talk with Steengracht. I don't know where things stand as a whole, and don't want to interfere; just make sure it's not bungled. We don't need a decision; we're not in a rush for that, but we have to make sure that the petition is so effectively circulated and well known that the Gestapo and the Ministry of Justice don't carry out the sentence before a decision is made on the petition. I think you have to discuss that with Hercher and first run it by Dix.

My love, the 8th of January means that once again, we have the gift of three full weeks, of which you have to devote one to the little sons and the home front, so that you can begin the final sprint with a totally free mind. In any case, we have to be enormously grateful. It shows us, time and again, that He is with us, and so we may also hope that He continues to let us feel His presence.—My love, I'm overwhelmed with fatigue and have to sleep. Sleep well, my love; I imagine you'll be speaking with dear Jowo [von Moltke] today on the phone. May the Lord watch over you and us. J.

1. The trial had been postponed from December 19–20 to January 8.

FREYA TO HELMUTH JAMES, DECEMBER 15, 1944

Friday morning

My dear, dear love, you're getting only a few words instead of a long lovely letter, because yesterday, after my indescribable happiness about the additional reprieve, I was totally submerged in a lethargy brought on by a headache, more completely than I have been in a long time. I did see Peters, who was very nice, very amenable, and very pleased that he could do this with a stretch of time ahead of him, and then I went home and lapsed into lethargy. The best sign of that, as you'll see, is that I didn't go to the friends. I went to bed at 6. Incidentally, I already had the symptoms in the morning, but luck was evidently too much on my side, and I was unable to keep going. I'm a bit fearful that you, my beloved heart, were so prepared from within that the changeover is causing you stress. I'm not sure about that. I, my love, am simply overjoyed! And so grateful! Grateful to the dear Lord for lending us aid! It was already set for Mon/Tues, and on Wednesday Hercher had Hermes, and his turn really is coming up, that truly weighs me down, because things look bad for him too,[1] Hercher says.—My dear, I'm now writing on the commuter train. Poelchau wants to leave early. Even though I got up early too, things didn't go quickly, and I had to make myself some oatmeal and tea, and then I got a call from Asta [Wendland] after I sent her a telegram with the news. They were all overjoyed too.

Now it's just after 7. But yesterday afternoon I was totally unable to write. And I have to catch up on reading our three chapters together with today's. Now I also have to tell you how things went with Thiele yesterday: I said that I was coming for permission for a face-to-face meeting, since I feared you would be taken to Prinz-Albrecht-Strasse as early as Saturday. Herr Thiele said, "Yes, but the trial isn't taking place now. The director had to go to Klausenburg on urgent business." "Then it will be between Christmas and New Year's." "No, no! No sooner than early January! Some will be quite happy about the postponement." "I'm one of them." Then there was a conversation about the children. Herr Thiele has a two-and-a-half-year-old son he's quite attached to. After that I pulled out my application regarding the fertilizer and said that I wouldn't be going to see you until next week, at which point I was given thirty minutes of speaking time—it doesn't matter to him when I go. Then a stranger came in, full of Christmas spirit. He wanted to know when the court sessions would begin again after Christmas. "Oh, not before early Jan.! Wait a minute!" Then he had a look at the calendar: "Not before January 8 for major matters; maybe for minor matters, we'll have to see." Then the stranger left, and so did I. I hadn't been this happy in a long time. I immediately made a telephone call in the booth and reached Poelchau, so you probably heard about it between 10 and 11. I'm also going to tell all the other women right away, feeling like a Christmas angel. I was so overjoyed. I hope you're pleased as well. I'm eager to find out what Poelchau will say next. Oh, my Jäm, it is so wonderful to still be celebrating Christmas with you, and, God willing, to ring in the year 1945 with you as well. Since you wrote to me last year at New Year's that we could be thankful if we all left 1944 together, I've never let go of that thought. Now the prospects are looking good for us still to be together. Even though we won't be close by each other this year, I may actually be closer to you than ever. Isn't that a miracle as well? Oh, my Jäm, how grateful we really must be.

Now for a technicality: I can't travel between the 22nd and 24th. All business travel stops then, and only urgent family trips are permitted, so I'll have to leave here on the 21st. But I also have to go to Kreisau again to get all sorts of things. What should I do, then: Take a short trip this weekend and then again on the 21st? So should I visit you on the 21st? What would work best for you? I can then stay with you over New Year's. Now there's just the interesting question of

when the pig dies:[2] before the trial or not until afterward. I have to
be home for two to three days that week, without Lenchen. That is
a lovely problem to have, but of burning interest in providing food
for the Berghaus.

This letter isn't tidy, but my love and gratitude are immense. You
know that. P.

1. Andreas Hermes was also sentenced to death, but his execution was postponed several times, and he was eventually freed when the Soviet troops entered. 2. See Freya's second letter of December 8, 1944, note 1.

FREYA TO HELMUTH JAMES, DECEMBER 15–16, 1944

Friday evening at Carl Dietrich [von Trotha]'s third Advent! 5:30!
My dear, my beloved Jäm, I was well aware what would go on inside
you if you had to adjust to a respite once again, now that you were
totally prepared for the journey, for the battle. For me, this shift was
easier than for you and more "just pleasant." For you, my love, the
renewed transition to "relaxation" is far more difficult. In spite of
your will to live, you were so close to death again, and well acquainted
with it. Now everything is starting up anew. My love, this whole thing
is a difficult test for you, quite a severe one, and right at the outset you
decided to delve straight into it, in whatever form it takes. That's why
it's harder for you than it is for Eugen [Gerstenmaier], who is so sure
of his hope, and harder than Delp, who has nothing that binds him
to life as much as your living Pim binds you. The same difference holds
for the women involved. But you also have lots of help, you're given
lots of strength, you're never abandoned, and you'll follow your path.
My love will go with you as far as it can, my dear, dear heart. In any
case, this postponement is yet another astonishing act of providence.

No, my love, I don't want to go away from you now for more than
one week, no, no. I will travel tomorrow at 10:30, without having your
explicit blessing; I'm in very good shape, and anyway, it's not so
strenuous. I had expected that Poelchau would be with you 2 times

and bring me a reply from you. So I'll be in Kreisau at 7, and on Sunday night I'll come back so I can be back with you until Thursday. Then I'll be able to fill you in on everything at home and bring you the things you can eat and something that the Poelchaus may enjoy. Poelchau thought I shouldn't travel, but this morning Casparchen's voice sounded so urgent when he asked "Are you coming on Sunday?" that I said yes right away. The very idea of being away until after Christmas makes my heart turn over in my body. This is where I live with you, this is where I belong, and I have to visit the little boys. I just hope you agree.

I won't write any more about practical matters tonight, aside from one thing, because I know it'll make you happy, my love: today Frau Pastor wrote me your baptismal and confirmation verses, and they are so particularly beautiful and they are so well suited to your life and its current paths that it is a joy to read them: baptism: Romans 8:38–39,[1] see hymn 150, 11–12; confirmation: 1 Corinthians 15:58.[2] That will surely please you! You are really flanked by beautiful verses, without and with P. Good night now, my dear love. It's after 11. I hope you're already sleeping well!

So, my love, I'm now at the friends' home. I don't actually have anything more to write, but let's face it, when could I stop writing: I could talk to you all the time. My dear! You need to recognize clearly that the little sons and I are the only ones making your current situation truly difficult and stressful. If you put us out of your mind, dying will be quite easy for a man like you, in spite of the blossoming apple trees and the sun over the mountains in Kreisau. I am keenly aware of it, because it is still important to me, in spite of it all, not to delude myself. I've known all along that my existence makes your life easier and more bearable, but that I also bind you to this world and its joys. I'm far more a creature of this world than you and quite far removed from the spiritual realm. This is why the good Lord will take care of me, because I am also part of His creation, so the connection to Him can be quite close, but I pull you back down onto the earth, making you more suited to life and happier to live in this world, while binding you to it. It is true that our love is more than that. I know and believe it. It also helps you to die, yet Pim in a little foal, who can be touched and seen, is making it hard for you! My poor, sweet, dear love, even though I know this, I still affirm myself at your side; I know that I make things hard for you and don't want to change that at all. It just is difficult for you. God knows that too, and has joined and united me with you. When we met, I rushed to your side with elemental force. If that was not destiny! For me, there was absolutely no other choice; when I saw you, my heart opened up, and that's where you live and remain. If we hadn't married, you'd still be there, and I knew that from the start. I've often told you that. But now I'm like a millstone around your neck and have even enhanced my earthly power with the two little sons. Just be quite clear about this; maybe this clarity will help you.

My love, I'll now tear myself away! May God watch over you, us; may He not leave us alone. I'll come back to be close to you as quickly as I can. But nothing changes even at a distance.

I am and will forever remain your P.

1. "For I am persuaded, that neither death, nor life, nor angels, nor principalities, nor powers, nor things present, nor things to come, Nor height, nor depth, nor any other creature, shall be able to separate us from the love of God, which is in Christ Jesus our Lord." 2. "Therefore, my beloved brethren, be ye stedfast, unmoveable, always abounding in the work of the Lord, forasmuch as ye know that your labour is not in vain in the Lord."

HELMUTH JAMES TO FREYA, DECEMBER 16, 1944

Tegel, 16 Dec 44

My dear, if it weren't for a miracle, I'd now be sitting at Prinz-Albrecht-Str., unable to write to you, so I'm writing this letter with a special feeling of gratitude.—This letter comes too late for making plans. The only thing I want is for you not to run yourself down traveling back and forth, because January will pack quite a punch, and your breakdown, although it was a minor one, over the release from the pre-Christmas trial is a clear sign that you need to take care of yourself.—Better to leave me without some items than to make the trip twice; but it seems to me that there ought to be someone who could be found to bring you what you need.—I would arrange to have the pig die before me, because it's possible that you'll still need to attempt some things here after the trial, and it's also possible that you will then no longer be regarded as an agricultural producer, or in any case you won't be able to get to the pig. It will all depend on the mercy of the Silesian Gestapo, and you shouldn't be dependent on their whims. Can't you borrow Sister Ida [Hübner] for the two days of the slaughter? She surely has two days to spare at this time of year. I think it best if you do all that right after Christmas rather than making your way back and forth, assuming the pig is fully developed. Maybe the butcher will slaughter it for you before Christmas, although that would involve a rush, and is thus not likely. So I'm in favor of your going home on the 20th at the latest, taking care of the slaughter on the 27th, 28th and getting back here on the 29th or 30th.

Now there are unfortunately a great many technical matters that will create some work for you again: Yesterday I was brought to Lange for questioning. Lange was extremely friendly—which is always a bad sign. I even had to shake his hand again, an act I had been exempted from for four months. The questioning has to have been a mere pretext, because it was about a man I don't know at all, someone who certainly had no case against him, and Lange was clearly indifferent to what I said; the entire written record amounted to twenty lines. But beforehand he told me he had received my written defense from the section commander—it was in front of him, clearly well thumbed—and he was told, by Müller, to let me know that he had not ever experienced such a brazen act as invoking him as a witness for the defense;[1] he evidently couldn't imagine that this was an ingenious kind of defense. Of course, he explained, they would pass along the written defense; it didn't matter to them at all. They hadn't known anything, of course, and if they acted as though they did know something, that was hardly a reason not to report the matter. I replied that I wasn't able to believe that for two reasons: first, I thought too highly of them and their intelligence, and second, Müller himself confirmed it to me.—Then came the questioning. Then he said I'd be questioned about Mami and Willo [von Moltke] later too, and then, maybe a half hour after we had finished the subject, he asked whether I had anything else to say about my written defense, to which I replied: No.—The whole thing was very strange. At any rate, it was clear that they hadn't yet passed along the written plea; in fact, the copy, the duplicate I'd included, is now at the People's Court, which evidently—as I'd hoped—the chief Reich prosecutor had picked up right away and kept there. I hope they don't find out. It's certain that the plea intrigued them in some way, because if it hadn't, this copy wouldn't have been so well thumbed. If my listing Müller as a witness merely angered him, it would be foolish, but if it also confirmed their image of me as a naïve utopian, it could come in handy.[2] In any case: *alea iacta sunt* [sic],[3] and now I can't bat an eyelash but have to stick to this line without wavering.—Still, it's clear that they don't regard my written plea as putting the death sentence in jeopardy, or else they would have gone to greater lengths to plant mines to counteract it.

Hercher was here today; most of the time he talked to Delp, but gave me the indictment to read. The conversation with him made it clear that he'd only glanced through the court record. I asked him certain questions, mainly in order to find out whether records of my interrogations might be missing. Do call him up again; tell him that when he examines the court records, he should please find out whether all the records about me are there, along with my two letters to Huppenkothen,[4] and also whether the Kiep records are in the files.—He also explained that he did not regard the knowledge on the part of the police as a defense; the obligation to inform the authorities was an absolute one. I referred him to Dix. Please call Dix and tell him that. Tell him I urgently request that he put a real fire under Hercher, because it would be dire if he strayed from my line in his oral defense. Dix should really prime him. Now on to the indictment. My impression has stayed the same, namely that it's hard to understand why the attack is so misguided. There is only one point in which a careful study has turned up a new complication; my major burden of incrimination comes not from Maass but evidently from Steltzer. A great deal of what my first impression had suggested came from Maass actually came from him. Under these circumstances it would be important *a*. to familiarize him with my line of defense, and *b*. to get a clear description from him how he can conform to this line. Maybe Frau Graf (?) can see to that even during all the hustle and bustle of the Christmas season. Maass is the source of several very stupid accusations and quite an idiotic depiction of the discussion in Kreisau "in August '43." That's what we'll have to deal with. Steltzer started the garbage about "steering committee of bishops and unionists" who were supposed to represent a kind of replacement for the government or the Führer. On top of that, he claims—according to the indictment—to have traveled to Munich on my instructions.—So we have to try to get a commitment from Steltzer that he can shape his statements in such a way that they harmonize with my defense, because I have no desire to have Freisler get me into a conflict with Steltzer. As far as I can tell, Sperr's and Reisert's statements mesh quite nicely, and of the whole crowd, only Steltzer appears not to line up.

Now to my health: Yesterday's excursion went miserably for me. At the Prinz-Albrecht-Str. I was so stiff that I had the greatest difficulty climbing the stairs; the problem was restricted to my sciatic nerve. The rest of my rheumatic pain is gone, but the sciatica reacts instantly to cold, damp weather or heavy strain. I would love to do something about that, because in my current condition I can't remain standing for fifteen minutes at a stretch. And while we're on that subject, another thought has now crossed my mind. We have to keep on trying to postpone the trial, for the fact remains that every extra day is a gain for us. Question: Perhaps you could speak to Thiele in early January, tell him I'm so bent over that I can't stand, but don't want to go to the sick bay, because the trial is imminent and even treatment in the sick bay wouldn't fix me in time. If you learn that the remaining time would be at least as much as I need, I would follow up with reporting to the sick bay on Friday, which is always the physician's day; but that would make sense only if I could spend at

least fourteen days to three weeks in bed; anything else is useless.—
That's the end of the practical part, I think.

My dear love, your collapse upon hearing the good news and the
relief it sparked once again made it quite clear to me how stressful all
this has been for you, my poor thing. This has been going on for two
and a half months already, and it horrifies me to contemplate how
you may fare when the probable ending arrives and I am killed. My
poor dear, the fact that your happiness at us gaining these three weeks
wore you out so thoroughly shows that you have to take it easy. Rest
up until New Year's Day. During that time nothing concrete can get
done, so this is the time that you're least indispensable. Only the
secret message transactions must be prepared by you in such a way
that they can be handled during your absence.—Oh, right, that pig
Weber who came to get me asked whether you'd already had permission for a face-to-face meeting. Maybe that was nothing but chattiness
on his part. But please be careful, especially with our letters. You
basically always have to anticipate your arrest, even though it is no
longer likely now without special grounds. In any event, if you should
get arrested, be prepared to ward off any harm.

Yes, my dear, of course I'm happy and grateful about the postponement, although I get the feeling that it has less of an effect on me
than on Poelchau and you, Eugen [Gerstenmaier], and Delp and
Claus. I felt so sheltered that I was awaiting the trial free of inner
tension and strain. I was very grateful for that and can only pray that
He shelters me once again when the trial approaches. As a consequence,
though, it was not such a relief. Yes, I'm also happy to be able to live
to see Christmas once again, and despite all the uncertainty it's
easier on you and the others in Kreisau than if I had just died or been
sentenced to death but not yet executed.

Incidentally, don't come to see me on the last day, because it's always
possible that I will be brought in for questioning. Farewell, my love,
I want to snooze. Sleep well. May the Lord watch over you and us. J.

1. In his defense statement, Helmuth claimed that the Gestapo knew about
Carl Friedrich Goerdeler's activities and there was thus no obligation to re-

port him. 2. Helmuth hoped that the People's Court would regard him as an idealistic theorist. 3. The die is cast. 4. In March 1944, at the Ravensbrück concentration camp, Helmuth wrote two letters to the Gestapo in connection with the interrogations about the Solf Circle and Otto Carl Kiep. See Helmuth James von Moltke, *Im Land der Gottlosen: Tagebuch und Briefe aus der Haft 1944/45*, edited by Günter Brakelmann (Munich: C. H. Beck, 2009), 98 and 103.

HELMUTH JAMES TO FREYA, DECEMBER 17, 1944

Berlin, 17 Dec 44

My dear, at 5:30 I lit my candles on the branch, spread a bit of good fragrance by burning a twig, set up and lit the long candle behind me, switched off the electric light, read, sang, or whistled either Advent hymns or Christmas songs and just stared at the candle, and during this whole time had fond and tender thoughts of you and the little sons, picturing all of you singing with all the other children. Eventually I put out the big candle and watched the candle on the branch burn out. Only then did I write the Christmas letter to Casparchen, and you see what I'm doing now.—This evening was very nice and will remain so, and I appreciate that especially because I had a "weary" day, mentally weary. I wasn't actually sad; it was just that my head, heart, and soul no longer wanted to play along; they didn't want to do anything at all, and that is always bad, because the vacuum that results is inevitably filled with thoughts of the trial and its utter hopelessness and of the military situation, which doesn't offer a ray of hope one way or another either.[1] That is always very dangerous, because that is the upper end of a slippery slope. Can you picture a "weary" day: the way I feel at moments like this, I'd like to stay fast asleep right up to the trial; anything but once again going to the intellectual effort of tackling the material and presenting it comprehensibly, anything but once again having to produce a readiness to fight alongside my readiness to die; just nothing more until the time has come.

As far as other things are concerned, I am being ungrateful, because the day has had two more highlights: Poelchau came again, as he now does every Sunday; and then he brought a letter. Poor Poelchau cut his upper lip quite dreadfully, but he seems to have avoided major damage. The letter made me very happy, my love. I'm tremendously pleased about the baptismal and confirmation verses. Both are part of my basic repertoire, and I've recited them to myself many hundreds of times in the course of this year without knowing they were my verses. Have you also noticed that my confirmation verse is closely allied with little Konrad's baptismal verse[2] spatially, and spiritually even more? In any case, the two are especially beautiful verses, and I now feel so close to them.

I don't think I entirely accept what you write about your function in my life, which has an overestimation in my favor. But I don't want to say anything more about that, because I know myself less than ever before today. At the moment I don't understand myself, and the more I have seen of myself under pressure, the less I'm able to make rhyme or reason out of myself, to be honest. If I die, I'll have to rely on grace anyway, and won't have to grapple with my own mysteries; should the Lord preserve me, all this will once again shift and fit into some sort of framework.

My love, may He watch over you and us. J.

1. This assessment could be referring to the Battle of the Bulge, which had begun the previous day; it was the last attempt by the Germans to penetrate the ring of the Allies in the west. The phrase "one way or another" is in English in the original German text. 2. 1 Corinthians 16:13: "Watch ye, stand fast in the faith, quit you like men, be strong."

HELMUTH JAMES TO FREYA, DECEMBER 18, 1944

18 Dec 44

Good morning, my love. Did you have a very bad night? I shudder at the prospect of this journey for you and always think that with all the strain you're under during this time, this trip will take a lot out of you. Just get a good rest. I'll now write you the opening lines of the indictment; that will be enough for you to get a sense of its tone:

Count von Moltke has been an enemy of the National Socialist Reich all along. Given his strong church affiliations and
owing to his bizarrely mixed, partly federalist, partly reactionary, partly Marxist views, he has for years been an unrestrained
defeatist, and has been able, since 1940, to gather a series of
opponents of the state of various schools of thought around
him. This circle was composed of members of the nobility, such
as Yorck, Schulenburg, Schwerin, Haeften, Trott, Einsiedel,
Trotha, and Husen[1]; clergymen from both Christian denominations, such as Delp, König, Rösch, Gerstenmaier, and Steltzer, who have deep ties to the church; and old Marxists and
union officials, such as Mierendorff, Leuschner, Maass, Reichwein, and Haubach. Moltke repeatedly brought together his
politically like-minded friends in the years 1941 to 1943 for
gatherings that often lasted several days at his estate in Kreisau,
where numerous political issues were discussed in deliberate
opposition to National Socialism and were markedly defeatist
in outlook. Over the course of time, he endeavored, more and
more doggedly, and with evident success, to align the participants in these meetings, who had initially shown up with highly
diverse opinions, to come together in solidarity and agree on
a single platform that reflected the subversive view he was
advocating. In addition to the meetings in Kreisau there were
numerous smaller discussions on the same subject with different sets of participants in Berlin, at the Moltkes' and Yorcks'
apartments, and in Munich. In all these meetings—the number of which can no longer be determined—Moltke relentlessly
propagated the idea that Germany would definitely lose the
war and hence the Führer and National Socialism would be
removed. He went on to explain that it was imperative to prepare for this time right now, and toward that end to set up an

emergency and safety-net program. He thus developed the following plan: In lieu of National Socialism as the foundation of the People's Community, the Christian churches of both denominations would become the organizational elements that would outlast the political events of the moment.

I didn't get any further in that passage. Afterward there's another awful passage concerning Steltzer, which says:

In the late spring of 1943, Steltzer, on behalf of Count von Moltke, held a meeting at the apartment of Father Delp in Munich, in which Dr. Mierendorff, Rösch, Reisert, and Fugger also participated. In his introductory remarks, Steltzer explained that in response to instructions by Count von Moltke, he would be contributing a report about the military situation from the viewpoint of the Armed Forces High Command ... (conclusion: war lost). Moltke was also envisioning a German defeat, which would be tantamount to the downfall of the National Social- ist regime. To prepare for this eventuality, he found it essential to set up a structural plan right now. The idea was for a popu- lar general to serve as a Reich administrator to try to salvage the situation. Then there would need to be people in all the provinces ... Strictly federalist constitution with considerable autonomy for the constituent states. Moltke's ideas could be realized only in the framework of a military dictatorship.

It would be important to inform Reisert about this rubbish, and Steltzer if possible. But it's crucial to come up with some kind of sign with Steltzer and Sperr to indicate that they received the secret mes- sages, even if they can't give any response.

Farewell, my dear love, I want to get a little work done for my new meeting with Hercher. May the Lord watch over you and us. J.

1. Helmuth wrote "Hülsen," which was undoubtedly an oversight.

HELMUTH JAMES TO FREYA, DECEMBER 18–19, 1944

Tegel, 18 Dec 44

How was your trip? Poelchau hasn't had any news, but it occurred to me that you thought he was in Brandenburg, and maybe that's why you didn't get in touch with him. It would be quite annoying if you had to spend the night in Liegnitz. I suppose I'll get news tomorrow morning. I imagine you'll be coming for a face-to-face meeting tomorrow or the day after tomorrow or Thursday, and I'm already looking forward to that very much. How wonderful, my dear. Don't forget to mark my forehead with little crosses at the end. You did that back in Grundlsee, and if the Lord intends for me to go to the gallows, I want to go with a little cross from Pim.

My love, can you bring me another fresh evergreen branch for Christmas? They get full of dust so quickly here and turn gray instead of green. The Christmas celebration is at 2 here, and you'll probably be setting things up just then, for a tiny Christmas, since Asta [Wendland] will likely be in Breslau too, or will it be possible to get Wend [Wendland] to Kreisau?

My love, I have nothing more to write but that I have to keep cautioning you to bear in mind that I am absolutely certain of ending up at the gallows, according to all human insight, so all the accomplishing and doing and running in the world will not entitle us to get our human hopes up. The only thing we can do is pray, and God determines it the way He wishes, regardless, and He can save me; we can pray for Him to want this. But in addition, my dear love, I can remind you that He gave us the certainty that no death can part us and that we are ultimately one single idea of divine creation. That's how it is, that's how it was, and that's how it remains. J.

19 Dec 44

At night the following occurred to me. A tough battle may flare up about the extent to which the fact that the Abwehr and police knew the situation can work as a defense if Freisler doesn't simply say they didn't know, basta!, in order to dodge this discussion. How does Dix assess the situation if it cannot be regarded as verifiable that the police knew, but it is established that the Abwehr did? Even on Friday, Lange didn't deny to me that the Abwehr knew. Isn't a member of the Wehrmacht[1] automatically exonerated if he knew that the military authority in charge was informed? Does he have to notify the police on top of that? Might there be rulings on these issues that you could read up on?—Furthermore: How much can I take cover behind Haubach's notification[2] if it is established that he went to the police on my behalf or in accordance with me? Can you please go over these questions in detail and quite technically with Dix and write up a report for me? We're well aware that this is not really about an issue of jurisprudence, but even so, it's better to have precise knowledge of the legal framework. I'll have them give me the Dalcke that they keep here in the library.[3] Please give Dix a good kick in the pants to make sure he does it carefully, even though he's not representing me. I have the impression that this issue will trigger the fiercest battle.

Farewell, my love, I'll be waiting for news once again. I hope you're well and strong. J.

1. Helmuth was a member of the Wehrmacht by virtue of his work at the Armed Forces High Command. 2. Theodor Haubach had filed a notification with the security services in 1943; see Helmuth's letter of December 21, 1944. 3. Albert Dalcke, *Strafrecht und Strafverfahren* (Criminal Law and Criminal Proceedings), a compilation of the key laws of criminal law and criminal proceedings, which had numerous print runs.

FREYA TO HELMUTH JAMES, DECEMBER 17–18, 1944

Sunday evening

My dear, I'm curious how the writing will be on this curly paper. Casparchen left this pad on his sled, and a friend of his let the sled slide into the ditch on the bridge near the pine trees, so the first sheets got wet, though only the first ones. But Casparchen had attached great importance to bringing the pad up himself. It was a beautiful winter's day with a warm sun and blue sky and now in the evening bright stars; there was also a thin covering of snow, but still thick enough for both little sons to come along on the sled and for Casparchen to go outside after lunch and disappear into the sun on skis, sliding around quite happily. You can well imagine, my poor dear love, how beautiful Kreisau looked. I didn't go very far—just from the Berghaus to the farmyard and to Sister Ida [Hübner]—but everything was bright and beautiful. In the farmyard there is great sorrow: Krause is missing. No sooner was he at the front than he went missing, and nothing is known about his whereabouts. Plätschke, who was drafted with him in September, was killed in action, and Kammel from Wierischau is missing too. Poor Frau Krause is distraught and unhappy, and rightly so. There is very little to say that would be of comfort to her. It is surely quite a consolation for her to know that I have grave concerns too. While the boys were playing in the sun with their sled in front of the Schloss, I had a long conversation at Ida's with her, Frau Krause, and Frau Rose. All three were touching and full of genuine devotion to you. I learned that Gustav asks about you in every letter. They say you always helped everyone, that they grew up with you here, and so on and so forth. No one says anything bad. I got a lovely goose for the Poelchaus there and then twenty little brown eggs, fifteen of which I have here in my bag for my Jäm. My dear, I'm looking forward to the visit with you so very much and will try to come tomorrow. My Jäm, how splendid is the prospect of seeing you. The thing I don't love about Kreisau is that for me it's much harder there, at times impossible, to give you my full, undivided attention. That is obvious, because there's too much to do, and once I'm there, I do want to keep everything together and use the time for the children and for everything. I know that you are always within me, I don't lose you for a second, and the connection to you sometimes arises consciously in me with a warm certainty that makes me happy, but that's not enough for me now. I want to live focused on you in a more concentrated way, and I can only do that here.

I also have to tell you that Romai [Reichwein] visited me for a while after dinner. Her demeanor is beautiful and dignified and not as closed off as it seems. She is a brave and capable woman. If only she doesn't harden toward the world, or rather, to her inner self and its possibilities! That is the danger. She needs to manage it for the sake of her composure, for she suffers greatly from her grief. Marion [Yorck] is far more open, and continues to be deeply connected to Peter [Yorck], while for Romai, the separation seems to be much harsher. She's looking for work, Marion for contemplativeness, which is quite a significant difference.

Good night, my dear love, good night. I'm so glad to be close by again. Sleep well, my love, safe and secure. You know whose I am, and although there's nothing new between us, the old is good and strong. I'm sending you a tender embrace. I am and will forever remain your P.

HELMUTH JAMES TO FREYA, DECEMBER 19, 1944

Tegel, 19 Dec 44

My dear, now the precious half hour has been added to our possessions, and how it differed from the earlier ones! They were alike in only one regard: This one, too, was exhilarating and wonderful. My love looked quite well and fine, not exhausted, not overworked. My love, for me, the main difference between these and the earlier face-to-face meetings was that from the first to the last moment, I had not just the will but the complete certainty that I would live on with you. I'm writing all this to you only because I feel certain that it won't build up your hopes; I can't tell you where this certainty came from, whether it was from above or from the creaturely will to live that is always stirred up powerfully by the sight of you. And it doesn't make the least bit of difference, because I'm too certain that I have to blindly entrust myself to God's guidance and that He has no intention of revealing to me in advance where He wishes to lead me. Because I know this with such certainty, I believe there won't be any setbacks.

So, getting right to corrections regarding my statements about my health: Today the pain is almost nonexistent as long as I stay bent over. The need to stay bent over is real, the report about pain was tinged *ad usum Delphini*.[1]

My dear, your news from Kreisau made me so happy, because on the whole all sounds good.—Now to Romai [Reichwein]. Please tell her that we are all greatly pained by Master Reichwein's death and our pain is not alleviated in the slightest by the fact that we probably have to follow behind, no, it's really not. Tell her, too, that we know quite well that this is far worse for the wives than it is for us, and we can only pray that they maintain a sense of peace within them and that all of our wives stick together as well as they can, transmit our spiritual inheritance, and help our children gain a proper outlook regarding their fathers' executions, as hatred or resistance aren't tolerable attitudes. We don't know, of course, how what we wanted will be judged one day, we don't know whether the seed will sprout despite our death or perhaps for that very reason; we have to wait and see.

My love, this is the Christmas letter for an odd Christmas. Divine providence has kept me alive, while I normally would likely have been killed about three hours ago, and, God willing, I'll still be alive for Christmas. I wish you, our sons, your house, and everyone who is a part of it a merry Christmas celebration. This year, the celebration will mean more to us than ever before, because we know far more exactly than before what this birth means for us, for you, for me and the little sons.—I, my love, will certainly celebrate a merry Christmas, and will not be melancholy on Friday afternoon or on Sunday at 2 during our celebration, but instead will happily think of all of you.

Sleep well, my love, after this lovely day, which is ushering in the twelfth month.[2] Tomorrow I'll write a little more, before you get the letter the day after tomorrow.

1. "For the use of the Dauphin": The gist of this phrase is that it has been adjusted for the recipient. Helmuth's description of the pain in an official letter of December 17, 1944, was "tinged" for the censor and/or others who read it.
2. Of Helmuth's captivity under Gestapo control.

FREYA TO HELMUTH JAMES, DECEMBER 20, 1944

Wednesday morning

My dear love, it was so wonderful to be with you. But I couldn't even think about a parting; I felt nothing out of the ordinary while sitting there with you because I am so astonishingly close to you. Seeing you is a great joy, but it is not the most important thing in and of itself. I know all too well how everything looks, it is so indubitably a part of me, I love it so very much, it is mine and I am so close to it, the dear heart; that is the greatest happiness. But one happiness is added to the other, and so it was a great and lovely gift. It would only be even more beautiful if we didn't need to say anything, because we fill up the time with talking and could be sitting and looking at each other. That would be the best thing. I was somewhat dismayed by how bent over you were, and after reading the little letter I got last night, I don't know whether there was a little faking going on. Other than that, you looked right, the way you are on the inside, too, and I gazed upon all this very tenderly. Oh, my dear love, that's how I am: I clearly feel us standing together before God, with my heart open and ready for anything that lies ahead for us, and I'm calm and very happy when I'm with you, yet since we have a bit more time now, your death has been pushed into the distance once again, not because I have a great deal of hope but because there's still some time.

I was also thinking about your little crosses before I found them in your lovely little letter. There was one time when you didn't get them, when we saw each other the first time in Tegel. But in Grundlsee you got a kiss on the forehead. I don't know either when the little crosses began, but I have an exact recollection of the kiss on the forehead—as we were standing in the room that faced toward the back and you were tending to my sunstroke. It was my initiative, and you probably thought it was heading elsewhere, but I wanted to go there only because it hadn't occurred to me yet that I might be able to kiss you somewhere else. I was already terribly fond of you and was shivering with excitement for the first letter all the way to Cologne! Oh, my Jäm, that's just one in the flood of the tenderest, dearest memories. Recently, in some dark hour, I suddenly recalled our first stroll on the mountain meadow with the two squirrels. Do you still remember that too, and how beautiful, dear, tender, yet unpretentious that was? We've had it very good.—Poelchau just gave me the envelope for Christmas. How delighted I am. My dear, I love you with all my heart, and with all my soul, and with all my mind. How happy you have made me with the "single idea of divine creation."[1]

Off now with your P.

1. See Helmuth's letter of December 18–19, 1944.

HELMUTH JAMES TO FREYA, DECEMBER 20, 1944

Tegel, 20 Dec 44

My dear love, I was very happy to receive your letter and to get you the one I started. Please take the letter to Ulla [Oldenbourg] with you and give it to her without Asta [Wendland] noticing, otherwise she could be offended that she doesn't have one, and I don't want that. But I can't simply write a normal letter now and send it via this path, which poses a risk to Poelchau's life,[1] and I don't have anything else to write to Asta. So please see to it that there isn't a slipup.

Yes, my dear, in recent days I've been recalling the route to Adler, the path to the mountain meadow, the ring of grass, the excursion to Aussee on the day after Daisy [Freyberg]'s departure, the way to the cliff, and things of that sort.[2] I always imagined it was a little cross and a kiss on the forehead, but maybe I just slipped in the cross in my thoughts.

I spent this morning feeling rather upset, because one of our people here, Wentzel-Teutschenthal, was being prepared at 7:30 for his execution, I knew that Poelchau didn't plan to come and they kept poor Wentzel-Teutschenthal waiting until 12:30 p.m. with an open cell door in which Herr Claus or some other official was standing, only to tell him that he would be picked up at 2 p.m. In the meantime, however, Poelchau came, which was good, and Wentzel has been gone for half an hour and will probably be hanged any moment now. Tell Zeumer that Wentzel is dead, and Scholz-Babisch may interest Zeumer as well.

Claus just came with the news that a ninth man is joining our trial. If it's Husen, then he has to get my line of defense very soon.

My sciatica is somewhat better again today. The pain has subsided in the course of the past few days, but I have to stay bent over; standing up straight is very stressful and painful if it goes on for too long. During the holidays I want to stay in bed and see if that makes it any better. On workdays I'm so reluctant to be in bed because I would be so unprepared if they were to come for me. Yes, interrogations are now always possible for me, and it's an unpleasantly disconcerting feeling. It may be, though, that they will put them off until after the verdict, because they can then run roughshod over me as much as they like. Fortunately, it is in God's hands whether that does or doesn't happen, and if that is what He intends for me, He will also give me the strength to bear it. I can only hope that He won't let me fall into the feeling that I am dependent on Müller or Freisler, let alone on Lange. As long as I have the feeling, "A Christian man is a free man and subject to none,"[3] everything will be all right.

Well, my love, Poelchau will be coming very soon to pick up the letter, and I'll stop so that you won't get one without a closing again. Have a good trip, my love, get back safely, send my love to everyone at home, the little sons and Asta and Ulla, Frau Pick and Liesbeth, etc., etc. I wish everyone a blessed Christmas celebration. "Rejoice in the Lord always: and again I say, Rejoice," it says in Philippians 4:4, and that, my love, applies to us as well. My dear love, I am and will remain for all time your J.

1. Helmuth was aware that Poelchau was risking his life with *every* letter. 2. All memories of their first meeting in the summer of 1929. 3. Martin Luther.

FREYA TO HELMUTH JAMES, DECEMBER 21, 1944

Thursday morning

My dear love, last night I was very busy with your Christmas item—which really can't be called a gift—and afterward with preparing the goose—which is nice and fat—and then with my own fatigue, so I put off writing until the lovely early-morning hours. So here I sit now—just got dressed—the friends are still sleeping. My dear, I'll get the factual part out of the way first. So far, your messages have not reached any of the men on Lehrter Str.[1] It is so large. [Frau] Graf and Schellhase have it in their hands. Reisert is mentally ill and utterly unable to absorb anything. Frau Reisert is going to have him brought to a psychiatric clinic. He keeps attempting suicide; his condition is serious, and he may well not make it to trial. Poelchau is holding on to Husen's. The Christmas cakes are really the true means of transport. I wonder if it's really Husen! Not pleasant! We've left out Sperr. He says he hasn't gotten a secret message yet! So he must have eaten it![2] Yesterday afternoon there was a lengthy visit with Dix. It's such a shame that he isn't supporting you, for he's tempted, and then he starts in right away, and whatever we might say against him: he's excellent at that. Well, he's not our man!—Of course he will spur on Hercher significantly. As for knowledge by the Abwehr, he affirmed your exculpation in this respect, too. If you knew that your immediate military superior knew, and that this was the very department in charge of such cases, it had to be sufficient for you as an officer. You were able to assume that Canaris[3] notified the authorities, otherwise you would have had to assume that he is an enemy of the state, "Are you accusing me of knowing that Canaris did not pass along this information!" But there are no decisions on this question. Dix thinks that you also have cover via Haubach, if he really notified the authorities with your knowledge and approval. (In that regard there is the following piece of paper I got from Haubach yesterday: Helmuth: my second item of information on Gestapo Winter '42/'43. Our conversation, spring '43: Helmuth: "I can no longer look on at the criminal and preposterous goings-on of the

Goerdeler people. Want to inform the authorities." Me: "Isn't necessary, have already done so." Helmuth in full agreement, including
with the mention of Kreisau {his comment: the Gestapo has of course
known this for quite some time—and we have nothing to hide},
promised complete silence, and kept his word.)

I have to stop now, and I'll come to visit you afterward.

P.

1. This discussion is about the distribution of secret messages to Steltzer,
Haubach, Reisert, and Sperr, with the one for Husen (still free) in Poelchau's
hands. 2. The secret messages were inside the cakes. 3. Admiral Canaris, the
head of counterintelligence and Helmuth's ultimate commanding officer,
was also an opponent of the Nazis.

HELMUTH JAMES TO FREYA, DECEMBER 21, 1944

Tegel, 21 Dec 44

My dear, this morning Gissel came with all kinds of treasures, and
then I knew that my dear love was in the building, quite close by, so
I was doubly delighted when I unwrapped the treats that my darling
had brought for me; how sweet and glorious that was. Then there was
quite a magnificent branch, truly an exceptionally beautiful one,
which now adorns my doorway, along with the white candle that is
awaiting the 24th.

The matter with Theo [Haubach] is different. In the fall of '42,
probably November, after Kreisau[1] in any case, I said to Carlo [Mie-
rendorff][2] that we had to scare Leuschner[2] so he would ditch Goerdeler.[3]
For this reason, a formal notification would have to be made at the
Gestapo, even though that would be pointless, because they knew
full well why they weren't going to make a move.[4] Still, he or Theo
should do this so as to be able to inform Leuschner about the reaction. Two weeks later, Carlo told me that nothing of any use came
out of the visit to Prinz-Albrecht-Str. because they said, "We know
about this, it's being watched, there's nothing further to do." I no

longer recall whether either Theo or Carlo was there, or both were. Then came the conversation with Theo along the lines of how he is describing it, but to the best of my knowledge we went on to talk about how another foray ought to be made, which one of them would want to make because they know the people. For me it's pretty significant that the first initiative originated with me, and Carlo is sure to have said that to Theo.

In 1940, between the Norwegian Campaign and the Battle of France, I heard the first rumors about plans by Beck–Goerdeler. They came from Peter [Yorck] via the Abwehr. These rumors got thicker and more frequent in the following years, without my ever having knowingly associated with any Goerdeler man or having heard anything about these plans from such a person. Everything always came from the Abwehr or police sources. In the fall of '42 there was my request to Mierendorff to inform the authorities in order to scare Leuschner; and at roughly the same time, the letter from Canaris to Bamler, in which Canaris states that he has spoken to the SS Reich Leader about this. Then came the conversation with Schulenburg, in which Schulenburg essentially claimed that Beck and Goerdeler were seriously contemplating plans for a coup and wanted to recruit me. Once I had rejected that, he said that at least in the case of a defeat, a clarification with Beck and Goerdeler would be good. I rejected that initially as well, whereupon he said that Beck was not at all committed, and it was entirely possible that I would discover that he rejected the idea of a coup just as much as I did, which is why there should be a discussion about the concrete problems. He then arranged for the Beck–Goerdeler–Popitz–Hassell–Peter [Yorck]–Adam [von Trott zu Solz]–Eugen [Gerstenmaier]–me meeting,[5] which I wanted to use primarily to dissuade Beck from any subversive ideas and make it quite clear that, as far as we were concerned, this was out of the question. This is why I began with a sharply worded attack against any coup and asked Beck to declare his solidarity with this position. He didn't do so, and after some idle chatter, we went our separate ways, so on this evening I was the only one to have broached the subject of a coup. Two days later, Beck communicated to me, in the name of the other older men: *a.* that they were highly indignant about my attack; *b.* that he had determined that no one besides me spoke about a coup; *c.* that he rejected in no uncertain terms the allegation that any of the older men had thought in terms of a coup; they had no intentions of this sort, and he asked me to take note of that fact; all other rumors lacked any basis in reality.[6]

Question: Does the conversation with Schulenburg imply a concrete obligation to inform the authorities? Does the meeting among the eight of us again imply such an obligation? After all, the police and the Abwehr knew nothing about these two meetings. What they did know was only that Goerdeler and Beck had been contemplating plans for a coup. So they knew only what had made me suspect it and triggered my attack, but no reaction followed.

All these considerations make me see one thing, at any rate: Every day we can gain to mull over these matters is infinitely valuable, because a swarm of complications has to be taken into account; basically our work is far from done. Since October 22 or 23, when I began to get a sense of the very first arguments for a plausible defense, hardly a week has gone by without my coming up with something new. If only Hercher were better! But ultimately the most important thing is that he needs to be a decent human being and not stab me in the back.

Good night, my love, I hope you're already making your merry way from Liegnitz to Kreisau. I'll stop for today. Sleep well, and may the Lord watch over you and us. J.

1. Helmuth is referring to the second plenary meeting of the Kreisau Circle in October 1942. 2. Wilhelm Leuschner was a Social Democrat who switched from the Kreisau Circle to join Goerdeler, to the dismay of other Social Democrats. 3. Goerdeler was the mayor of Leipzig from 1930 to 1937. 4. Members of the Kreisau Circle did not opt to notify the authorities until they knew that the case was already known to the Gestapo. Mierendorff, a key actor here, had died in an air raid in 1943. 5. This meeting Helmuth had was a key charge against him in the indictment submitted to the court by the Gestapo. 6. For an evaluation of the Goerdeler connection, see Editors' Introduction.

HELMUTH JAMES TO FREYA, DECEMBER 24–25, 1944

Tegel, 24 Dec 44

My dear, I need to have a word on paper with my dearest before the candles have to be blown out. It's about 6 o'clock, and my thoughts, which have been with you the whole day, have spent the past hour seeking you out as you're singing, reading, and gift-giving. My love, a manger, corona, and a little songbook arrived from you, and I've just opened the package. The manger, which you constructed quite splendidly, is on my table, looking down at me, I attached the star with the corona to the edge of the table in a way that I can look straight at it when I'm lying in bed, and I've read about two-thirds of the little book by the light of the big candle behind me, which is also casting its light on me for this letter while the Christmas candle burns on the branch over the door.—Since yesterday, I've been on total bed rest, and will stay that way until Wednesday in the hope that my leg will take well to that.—Today at noon I listened to the Christmas celebration, which Poelchau organized quite nicely.—I'll stop now, my love, because I want to blow out the candles and turn the light back on and so call an end to the Christmas celebration, which is probably my last. I'm not sad, no, I'm grateful that I get to experience it once more, because the very feeling that it is probably my last makes the gift of this day doubly great and doubly happy for me.—All my thoughts are with you, my dear, and I pray for God's blessing for us. J.

25 Dec 44

Yesterday evening, and during the night, I read the prophet Isaiah all the way through, for the first time in my life in a single sitting. One thing is quite clear, namely that you have to do it again and again that way, because piecemeal reading makes you lose too much of the context. But it is very difficult reading, far more difficult than even the Gospel of John or the Pauline epistles. But I think it's even greater, even more powerful. You'll be astonished that I'm saying this. But isn't someone who doesn't see and knows that he won't be getting any humanly tangible confirmation greater than someone who proclaims what he has seen or objectively experienced? The complete certainty of the Redeemer who has in no way been revealed, a certainty with which Isaiah is suffused and which keeps him safe from all doubts even in the face of hostilities, a certainty that does not abandon Jeremiah when he is thrown into the snake pit, and that lifts the soul of Job: Is it not stronger, more powerful than what comes after the birth of the Redeemer, precisely because it doesn't rest on any proofs but only on promises made many hundreds of years ago? It makes you sad to see what has been bestowed on people and how hard we have to struggle for far simpler things.—I want to read the Gospel of John tonight and plan to read Isaiah again in a few days. One would have to read him fifty times to begin to understand him. The beautiful thing for me, particularly in Isaiah, but also in Jeremiah, is that nothing out of the ordinary takes place, the way it does in Elijah and Elisha, David, and Jonah, etc. They are all quite prosaic, unmelodramatic stories.—The more I have read over the course of these months, the more firmly I have come to be convinced that the compilation of "New Testament and Psalms" is a monstrosity.[1] No one should be kept from knowing the Old Testament. And no matter how incredibly difficult the Old Testament is for us, I still think that it is far easier for humble hearts than it is for us, and certainly easier than we believe.

And with that, my love, we are back again with ancient wisdom. And so I can only pray that I am truly, "whether I live therefore, or die," the Lord's. J.

1. The edition of the Bible that was customary in the Third Reich, which did not include the Old Testament.

HELMUTH JAMES TO FREYA, UNDATED, DECEMBER 1944

My love, this isn't very good, but I wanted you to know how it looks here before I move out. In order to make sure you recognize the objects, I'll tell you: The circle is the lamp; your star is hanging underneath it, exactly at eye level, below that your manger and your angel to the right of it, then farther to the right the hymnal, to the left of

Helmuth's sketch of his Christmas table in an undated letter to Freya from late December 1944

the candle the inkwell, and on the far left, the open Bible.—Despite the amateurish quality of the sketch, I'm happy with it, and I won't make a second attempt, because I'm sure that your loving eyes will recognize that although it's "cell-like," it's still endearing and not forlorn. And that's exactly what I was aiming to convey. You have to accept the table's crooked and uneven legs, etc., etc. The star is exactly at eye level when I'm sitting, and I gaze at it steadfastly when the need arises. It's quite an important prop.

FREYA TO HELMUTH JAMES, DECEMBER 24–25, 1944

Kreisau, 24 Dec 44

My dear, the day has come to an end. My thoughts have flown to you a thousand times, and they found you every one of those times. I hope it went the way I wished, that you were calm and content and secure, as was my heart's desire. Oh, my Jäm, it wasn't a hard day, for I felt you so close to us, so close that I wasn't even wistful. It was a happy day, because I was always and forever filled with gratitude that you are still there and your life is so connected with us, filled with gratitude for—you know what for! But it was also happy in view of the two beaming boys. The only truly sad part was that I enjoyed it and you couldn't get a look at this lovely scene. It was a day for the two of them, through and through, and now that it's evening, I am happy to be able to reflect peacefully, and probably won't report every detail I'd like to tell you at this point: that remains for tomorrow. This day should not come to an end for us without my having written you a word of love, my beloved heart. Your loving thoughts have surely kept me from having to spend this evening in a state of agitation. I was able to finish up everything quite nicely, though I spent part of two nights on it as well, but this way I had a very peaceful day today, with many thoughts of you. Now I want to carry them on a bit further, taking your lovely gift and the gift from the friends into bed with me and celebrating a bit more.—Now it's the 25th, just after 7. I've been awake for only half an hour and spent it pleasantly, enjoying your present, thinking of you, of all our friends, reading our three chapters and feeling close to you. I had a good long sleep. For once, both boys are still sleeping off their happy exhaustion. My love, I'll first tell you about yesterday: In the morning I had to carry around the presents in the farmyard, and I took both sons along. The sun was shining over a very cold morning and it was incredibly slippery. Both boys are not only well but look positively glowing. The November crisis is over, the sharp frost and sun are good for them. Little Konrad, whom Maria [Schanda]—she came the night after my arrival, as I wrote via the People's Court—and I have been pushing a bit hard, marched along bravely, Casparchen played skittles, ran, hopped, both with their red-rimmed pointed caps and Konrad already wearing your coat with the lining. Casparchen abandoned us near the Schloss by the Peile,[1] where it was quite alluring. Then I kept on going, just with Konrad. This year I gave Zimmer and Kaiser each a pair of old boots from Papi, and Störcher as well, and all three were simply overjoyed. I also took in the reaction of the gift-giving at Sister Ida [Hübner]'s and found that they afforded real pleasure, which I hadn't been expecting at all. More than anything, though, I talked about you, for a long time and in great detail, and communicated your best regards to everyone, and they all gave a cordial response, full of sympathy, concern, and varying degrees of outrage, but always with a great deal of devotion to you, which was so spontaneous that I found it sincere and pass it along to you without embellishment, totally objectively. You know that I've always been skeptical about "people's" devotion. But I have to say that I experienced a natural, unpretentious, neighborly feeling of friendship, which made me very glad for our sake, but especially for yours. I went ahead and said that I'm quite worried about your future, and also mentioned Reichwein, who hadn't done much either, and who was very popular around here. So I was kept quite busy, my love. After we ate, the children went to sleep. Even Casparchen went willingly, if for no other reason than to kill time, the terrible time! They both slept like a log, and Maria and I had lots to do. You know that all my thoughts were with you after 2, while I was decorating the tree. Oh, my love! I was picturing it so clearly! My dear love. We have a gorgeous tree. If only you could see it! It's graceful, and now that we've raised it up a bit with books, it goes all the way to the top of the mirror, it's quite, quite well proportioned, quite, quite slender, quite full, quite charming. Not only are tinsel and white candles hanging on it but also a good many of the tiniest red-cheeked apples that you, my love, always eat these days. That looks gorgeous and is so truly from Kreisau. The evening before, I had grown desperate at the thought that your old train set might be nothing but a wreck now, in spite of all the repairs, but we set it up little by little, and of course it turned out that it is wonderful in so many respects, including that every so often the locomotive manages to go backward without cars in tow. The cars can just be pushed along—more about that in a moment. But we had a very lovely and very devout celebration. First we sang "Ihr Kinderlein ..."[2] That was especially nice, for contrary to my expectations, and totally in line with yours, Konrad sang the first stanza quite correctly and enthusiastically along with everyone. Both boys were sitting on the little bench from Cologne wearing white shirts and neckties—even Konrad insisted on that. The candlelit Advent wreath was between them and me. Then they sat next to each other and sang: Casparchen was loud and boyish, Konrad a bit behind him but full of enthusiasm. It was such a beautiful sight, and my heart went out to you, because I would so have wanted to treat you, you, you, my love, to all this. They are truly such dear little boys! Then Ulla [Oldenbourg] read aloud, you know how lovely that was, and Konrad climbed onto my lap. Then we sang "Stille Nacht"[3] and Casparchen, uninhibitedly and quite fluently, and with an endearing look on his face—he would have loved to keep his hands in his pockets—recited "Brich an du schönes Morgenlicht."[4] Then we sang "Oh du fröhliche,"[5] and I left them while they sang "Kinderlein" and "Vom Himmel hoch"[6] again. Then the door opened and happiness set in.

My heart was still and grateful and remained that way, near to yours. We have every reason to feel like that. I read your gift, I read the beautiful verse with the picture of the friends. How lovely of them that they first had it in your cell. Yes, it's actually your verse, but for that very reason it's mine, too. This is exactly what makes me so happy: that your verse can be mine as well. But now, in addition, I am collecting the outward riches of Kreisau without you, and I would so like to convey to you the love and comfort of home, the splendor of Christmas, everything that has made our years past so wonderful, and I'm sad that you can't see it in your cell, otherwise I'm nothing but grateful.—Now, my love, I'm going to get dressed and keep on writing as soon as I can, because there's still a great deal to tell, and you'll be pleased, but at least the most important things have been said.—It'll soon be 12, when Carl Viggo [von Moltke] and his wife want to come, and they'll leave by 1:30. They plan to pass along this letter then. I cleaned up, had breakfast, played with Casparchen, and visited Ulla. We had a long talk there about you, Mami, and our faith once I was able to read your letter aloud to her, which evidently made her very happy. My love, it is in fact a very beautiful letter. It has everything in it, it's a lovely, clear picture of you in your difficult situation and how well you are sheltered in spite of it all. Ulla had read it two times already, and I only gave it to her yesterday.—I have to tell you about

Casparchen: his first cry of joy about the train set! Followed by "You can even slow it down!" (You can hardly do anything else with the locomotive.) Then, today, when he was asked what was the nicest of all: "The train set!" It is unrivaled! "The railcars run better than the locomotive." Remarks like these help you gauge the objective quality of the gift. But he spends the whole day sitting on the floor and working on his tracks and fiddling around with the little old cars, onto which the wheelwright mounted new roofs.—So, now Carl Viggo is here, and we've had a very good meal, and I had everyone drink a toast to you. That doesn't accomplish anything, but they mustn't forget for even a second that you're here, you belong here, decide things here, and remain here: you and what you represent. We were sitting there, your little sons and I, and you were right there with us! I'll stop now, and will soon write the next letter about Sister Ida and everything else.

Full of tender love, I am and will remain your P.

1. The local river. 2. "O, Come, Little Children." 3. "Silent Night." 4. "Break Out, O Beautiful Light of Morning." 5. "O Joyful." 6. "From Heaven on High."

HELMUTH JAMES TO FREYA, DECEMBER 27–28, 1944

Tegel, 27 Dec 44

My dear, during the days I spent in bed[1] I may have thought of you and your little sons even more than usual, because I sometimes spent long periods of time lying around in bed, which I ordinarily never do. So I traced your goings-on, thinking about whether your bed or the Christmas room had the greater appeal for the little sons on the morning of the 25th, if you all went outside, if you had nice weather, etc. I was happily occupied the whole time. Now I'm quite eager for news.

I've been mulling over the path that God's grace has been leading us along since Sept. 28. The many proofs of His presence, His benevolence, His love, which He has let us feel; how He has shown us that He can hold us and carry us even in the misfortune of my death, even in the contemplation of this misfortune, how by means of an abundance of individual small "chance" occurrences He made it possible for us to gradually construct a defense from the utterly hopeless and futile facts of the case, a defense that as long as I can maintain and make convincing the contention, which is in fact a correct one, that all the news came from the police and the Abwehr, offers us for the first time a chance even from a human standpoint. All this is a miracle, and we have to accept it gratefully. If only I didn't have the two wild theologians,[2] who are always trying to talk me into believing that they've caught a glimpse of God's cards and therefore know how the game turns out. Other than that, they are very dear to me, but they're unbearable in this respect.

My love, we have to count on having time only until the 6th, and because the week begins with the 2nd, you have very little time to fit in your many tasks. Maybe we'll get more time, but for now we don't know. It strikes me that the most important issue is Dix and the exact line of argument, then Haus; everything else won't come until relatively far into the distance, although I'd also like to have Freisler's documents, though just a selection, only what is relatively germane. See what you can do to deal with all that. The best thing would be for Herr Thiele or his boss to delay the trial once more. Might my sciatica be an argument?

Want to know something that's making me especially happy? That the sun is now shining and I can always sit without an electric light in the afternoon for one or two hours. This continuous bad electric light is hideous, particularly as it's on at night as well. On Dec 21 I marked the position of the sun at 3 in the afternoon and I'm delighted to see that the sun is already visibly below the mark, meaning that it remains higher in the sky.

28 Dec 44

There's nothing new, my love, apart from my loving you so very much; that continues to be new for me every day. I'm especially eager for news from home. You know, one year ago today is when I last left home. Or was it on the 27th? We headed into town at 3 to the home of the district administrator for tea, and from there to Breslau, where we had a look at Casparchen,[3] and then I left. At the moment I have a level of confidence—which I myself find scary—that one day I will find my way back again, and I'm only waiting for something to put a damper on it. It's so hard to stay in the proper equilibrium; to achieve that, you'd have to pray the whole day, and then it's also a question of grace. Do help me, too, my dear, I need it badly. J.

1. Helmuth kept to his bed from the 23rd to the 27th in order to rest his aching leg. 2. Alfred Delp and Eugen Gerstenmaier. 3. Caspar spent Christmas 1943 in a hospital in Breslau.

HELMUTH JAMES TO FREYA, DECEMBER 28, 1944

Tegel, 28 Dec 44

My dear, as a result of the many letters, briefs, and drafts I've had to produce, most of them in multiple copies, in short, as a result of the substantial production this December, my pad is running out of paper again, and I have to be sparing with it until I get a new one from you. That's why you're receiving this half sheet of paper today.— Your splendid letter about the 24th arrived today. It all made me very happy, especially, of course, your description of the little sons. I'm so glad that you appear not to have discovered any new things to be concerned about in Kreisau, and that—and this is the most important thing—everyone was healthy. Things are now improving and illnesses aren't as nasty. Nice that Maria [Schanda] was there, otherwise the group of you would have been quite small, and she is a big help. But I have yet to receive the letter via the People's Court; in fact, I haven't heard anything through them since November 22. You need to tell them that I asked you at our face-to-face meeting why you don't write anymore, otherwise this may be a trap, even though I don't really think that's the case in a civilian institution. Which reminds me— although this doesn't belong here—how pleasant it is to be in a penitentiary. The atmosphere still gives off a whiff of justice, and you don't get the frightening feeling that there could be traps, informers, wiretapping devices everywhere, sudden interrogations at impossible hours of the night, etc. I truly had it good in Ravensbrück, but I prefer it here and would feel that way even without Poelchau.

—I'm also happy that everything was nice and bountiful again. What might Christmas '45 be like? The store of reserves has to run out at some point, after all. Of course, even relatively measly presents grow more and more precious as the general impoverishment increases, and by next year your whole suitcase of old shoes may be a gold mine. —I'm also glad to learn that you spoke with Ulla [Oldenbourg] in depth, which I find quite important; I'm eager to hear what she thinks.

For me, a strange year is coming to an end. I actually spent it among people who were being prepared for a violent death, and many of them have since suffered that death: Kiep, Frl. v. Thadden, Langbehn, Hassell, Peter [Yorck], Schwerin, Schulenburg, Popitz (?),[1] Maass, Leuschner, Wirmer, and surely ten or eleven concentration camp inmates. I've lived in a building with all these people, shared in their destiny, listened as they were taken away for interrogations or when they were carted off once and for all, spoke with almost all of them about their cases, and saw how they coped with everything. And here in Tegel about ten, I think, from my group have already been executed. Death has become such a steady companion during the entire year. And though at first I got awfully upset when "Emil" was summoned for a "walk around the camp," these violent killings have become such an everyday occurrence that I've accepted the disappearance of individual men with sorrow, yet like a natural phenomenon. And now, I tell myself, it's my turn. Can I accept it like a natural phenomenon in my own case as well? That's the frame of mind in which I came here; actually I only thought the detour via the People's Court was a nuisance, and if anyone had told me that death sentences could also be imposed at the request of the accused by means of an order of summary punishment and be carried out at once, I would have made that request in late September. That's how caught up I was in the atmosphere that it would not be right to make any fuss[2] about dying by execution. And where am I now? The landscape is simply unrecognizable. Now I most definitely do not want to die; there's no doubt about it. This constant work on the arguments to prevent that outcome has stirred up a powerful will in me to get around this thing.

So this year, which I have spent in close and familiar, I'd even venture to say intimate, proximity with death, is now coming to an end in a spirit of resistance that is far more resolute than it was even on January 19.[3]

I now sometimes think—as I haven't for months—about how it would all be if I were to remain alive, and I wonder whether I would forget everything again or whether one actually retains a realistic relationship to death and thus to eternity from this period. I'm coming to the conclusion that the flesh and blood would do everything possible to suppress this knowledge again, thus requiring a constant battle to hold on to the fruits of this period. We are a wretched species, without a doubt, but we generally don't have the slightest idea how wretched we are. Now I also know why Paul and Isaiah, Jeremiah and David and Solomon, Moses and the evangelists will never be obsolete: they were simply not as wretched; they had a stature that is unattainable for us, even for people like Goethe, and indeed even for Luther. We will never fully understand what these men underwent and came to know. Good night, my love, may the Lord watch over you and us. J.

1. Johannes Popitz was not executed until February 2, 1945, in Plötzensee. 2. Helmuth uses the English word here. 3. Helmuth was arrested on January 19, 1944; see Editors' Introduction.

FREYA TO HELMUTH JAMES, DECEMBER 26–29, 1944

Kreisau, Tuesday evening, Christmas
My dear love, Christmas is now coming to an end. I wonder how it was where you are! I have such a clear idea of how I wish it were for you. I'm wondering whether you really stayed in bed until this morning, whether you had tranquil, peaceful, grateful, Christmassy feelings,

whether your thoughts were close to us and our peaceful hubbub! Quite apart from thinking about our personal fate, I have often been dismayed, these days, as I ponder the difference between the terrible war in the west and the spirit of the Christmas holiday at our home. Here it's utterly peaceful—so far! For the children, these were two ideal Christmas days. Little Konrad thought so too last night when he was tired and happy and came out with: "It was a beautiful day this morning!" Both days full of sun and cold and the evenings full of playing children. Even Romai [Reichwein] couldn't stay away. I think she and her children are quite content in the Schloss, even though it is really not easy for them on a practical level up there.[1] But when I go up there and see the pictures hanging on all the walls, with an evergreen branch tucked behind them, pictures of this lively, spirited, nimble man, always ready to spring into action, feelings of fury, heartache, and pain keep rising up within me, yes, even fury— a rare emotion for me, and certainly a false one. Oh, my Jäm, what lies ahead for you, and for us! There's only one thing to be said about this and we know what that is!

Friday—My dear, I'm here again! How have you been, my love? I felt far too carefree during all these days. I don't like that. I didn't think of your death at all; I was incapable of taking it in, I had a certainty within me, although it barely reached a conscious level, that you would live; it wasn't conscious hoping—not at all—but this strange certainty. Don't think I have faith in that certainty; quite the contrary, I'm afraid of it, but throughout the Christmas days it was present. And then the all-important vigilance is missing; inner wakefulness is so important to me, and I'm not able to achieve it in Kreisau as well as I would deem right and agreeable.—I wasn't able to slaughter the pig because the butcher is busy with his own matters between Christmas and New Year's. He is now booked until Jan. 19th. I set things up with him for that date. If necessary I can also have it killed at short notice and it can die without me. There was no other way of arranging this. It already weighs four hundredweights, and all the others have already done their slaughtering, but in terms of my stocks I'm in no rush.

Marion [Yorck] is doing well. It's truly lovely and very gratifying to see, because it's not just outward composure but something of substance; in Romai's case, it's merely composure. And Marion isn't quite herself either; she is in far better hands. She is more like a vessel, and that is very nice. She is not at all destroyed, and consequently the continuity is secured. Nowhere is there a rupture. That is a miracle!

So, my love, soon I can set off. Now I'm knitting another thumb on my gloves, since I don't have any more woolen gloves. They're all torn.

I'm sending you a tender embrace. May God keep on protecting you! That is my greatest wish! P.

1. After Rosemarie Reichwein's apartment in Berlin was destroyed in August 1943, she and her four children lived in the Schloss and, beginning in the spring of 1945, lived with the Moltkes in the Berghaus until both families left Kreisau after the end of the war.

HELMUTH JAMES TO FREYA, DECEMBER 29–30, 1944

Tegel, 29 Dec 44

My dear, even though now isn't my writing time, I'm so pleased about your detailed news and your visit and the treasures you've sent me again, and the clear winter day is making the cell bright, so I don't need light, and the window is open because it's so mild outside that I can afford to open it, and I have to try out the new pens, and the manger, the star, and angel are looking at me so encouragingly—you'll admit that these are compelling reasons to write to you although I've just now, right after our meal, finished putting away your treasures. My dear love, whatever may await me "over there," I'm still so grateful to have been here to experience these days and hence your entire Christmas. That is a great treasure, one I'll be storing in my treasure trove. Here I have such a nice amount of time to be quite deliberately pleased, whereas when I was on the outside, I could also be pleased but at the same time I always had something else to do.—So, I'll continue this evening.

30 Dec 44

The evening calm has set in, and since I'm hoping for a means of transportation tomorrow, I'll want to write in peace now.

I'm glad the pig is so fat, or so heavy, at any rate. The 19th is of course a risky day, but as of the 8th every day is, and it's better to have a day at the end of the week, like the 19th, because you can safely leave on Thursday if I'm not taken away, for then there's nothing until Monday, whereas surprises are always possible at the beginning of the week. Well, we'll just have to wait it out for now. The race between the pig and me is thus not yet, as I assumed, decided in favor (?) of the pig, which presumably shares completely my opinion about death: that 4 hundredweights is not a sufficient reason.

I'm enclosing the warrant.[1] I made a copy for myself, but thought that the original might possibly be useful for you even though it doesn't have an official stamp. You just have to store it safely, because it is generally considered "Secret Reich Business," the most highly classified material for the civil authorities.

First I'll tell you that I wanted to speak to the doctor yesterday and relayed the message to him that the main thing I hoped for was for him to issue me a medical certificate so I could sit during the hearing, because standing would be absolutely out of the question.—My condition is such that I feel nothing when I'm sitting and very little when I'm lying, and my pain is basically quite minimal, but walking and standing just won't work. After three rounds, which amount to about 100 yards, I have to sit down.—We might consider whether we can use that to get a postponement or rescheduling of the trial.

My love, I get the feeling that in the last two letters I've painted too rosy a picture of the way things stand. I definitely want to correct that. If someone were to ask me today how I see the trial unfolding, I would say without reservation: death sentence. We need to stick to that, right? But I do admit that on a purely human level, I figure the chances are higher than 1 percent today, not much higher but higher nonetheless. Of course I'm going on the assumption that Steltzer's statements can be interpreted to mean that I cannot be held liable and that there are no other snags I'm unaware of caused by, let us say,

Husen, or because König is captured, or something of that sort. I'm now working primarily on the Goerdeler complex, because Hercher considers it the worst part, but if I get the feeling that at least Hercher sees the light, then I have to turn back to the Kreisau issues, because that's where I personally see the danger of defeatism as the most challenging. That is why time is important and every day we gain is precious, so we have to at least try to capitalize on my sciatica. If we come down on the list of relatively urgent matters, we're sure to gain another one month to six weeks.—Because you surely couldn't get anything done yesterday or today unless you talked to Haus, you have quite a week ahead of you, particularly if it is our turn at the beginning of the week after next.

My dear love, I'll write again tomorrow, and I'll be celebrating New Year's with the old branch and what's left of the candle tomorrow at 5:30 as well, that is, the close of the year plus the post-Christmas days. And then the new year begins.—I'll write tomorrow; now I don't want to append more new thoughts—that is, old ones—to the letter, which has taken a very different turn. Those thoughts can be left for tomorrow.

Good night, my love, sleep well. May the Lord watch over you and us, He to whom we already owe so much gratitude. J.

Your People's Court letter dated December 7th arrived.

1. See Appendix: Additional Documents.

FREYA TO HELMUTH JAMES, DECEMBER 30–31, 1944

Saturday evening

My dear love, I'm at the friends' house. They're also writing, to my right and my left, at the round table where we once ate together. I'm sitting on the little sofa under the lamp in my usual seat. My love, I don't know a thing about Jeremiah, Isaiah, Ezekiel, and Jonah! But as time goes on, you'll fill me in. It has certainly impressed me that you regard these men as *so* important. Isn't wisdom so timeless only because human afflictions, despondency, worries, and torments essentially always remain the same and these men found the way to cope with them, a way that is unchanging? But I can't, and shouldn't, pass judgment on that and for the time being will listen to it with amazement.

My dear, what you said about December 28 of last year is true. The only part you forgot is that we went to Asta [Wendland]'s home to sleep and slept together in Wend [Wendland]'s big bed and you didn't leave until the next morning. I brought you to the train, we had to wait quite a long time for the train from Vienna, and walked back and forth. I can still see you ahead of me as the train started up and you were waving—as always, my love—and I saw you off feeling composed and calm. That's how it was. Soon afterward you wrote to me that your future prospects for coming to Kreisau were quite dim, and that we would have to cling to the past. Oh, my dear, dear love, if only you were permitted to find your way back! I don't even dare say that.

My love, I haven't gotten around to doing anything since I've been here. Yesterday I spent all my time sitting here. After eating, I slept, but was still sleepy afterward. Frau von Truchsess came for supper with the youngest Bonhoeffer's[1] very nice chubby fiancée, who is related to Dietz von Truchsess and looks after him here on a regular basis. That was a very nice supper. We talked about all kinds of fascinating things, and I really liked her as I had before. Do you like him too? Is he also so unpretentious and straightforward? At the same time, she has a great deal of charm and verve and an intelligence that comes from the heart. I'm quite humbled in her presence, but I'm content to be humbled. The warden seems to be quite taken with the couple, as they spoke for sixty-five minutes! I don't think we've ever had more than forty-five, but I never look at the clock. For the Truchsesses, Maria von Wedemeyer (the fiancée in question) also does this.[2] But the time we spend together always seems long to me, not short. Does it seem that way to you too? The Truchsess case is milder, of course, but even apart from that, I hope with all my heart for everyone to have a "long" time.

Sunday, still in bed: my dear love, I went to bed shivering and with a sore throat and woke up feeling well and happy after a long and

Helmuth and Freya in
Grundlsee, Austria, 1931
with Eugenie Schwarzwald

Freya and Helmuth on
their wedding day, 1931,
with Freya's mother, Ada
Deichmann, and Helmuth's
mother, Dorothy von Moltke

Drawing of Helmuth James by M. Schneefuß, 1930

Freya on the steps of the Berghaus in Kreisau

ABOVE: Helmuth in South Africa, 1937
RIGHT: Helmuth on the train

Freya with her son Konrad, speaking to Frau Rose in Kreisau, December 1944

Helmuth and Freya in England with Lionel Curtis

Helmuth and Freya on the steps of the Berghaus with Helmuth's siblings Jowo and Asta in the background, the American journalist Edgar Mowrer in front, 1933

Harald Poelchau (1949);
as prison chaplain at Tegel,
Poelchau smuggled each of
these letters into and out of
Helmuth's cell, risking his
own life in the process

Freya reading a newspaper

Helmuth at the People's Court

Helmuth at the People's Court conferring with his attorney

ABOVE AND BELOW: Helmuth at the People's Court

ABOVE AND BELOW: Helmuth at the People's Court

Freya after her move to the United States in the 1960s

Freya at her house in Vermont,
during the 1980s

Freya with her two sons, Caspar (l) and Konrad (r), 1959

Aerial view of the New Kreisau / Krzyzowa

The Berghaus today in the New Kreisau / Krzyzowa

delightful night. Yes, I woke up again exceptionally happy and grateful: the whole richness of my life—of our lives—was instantly and fully clear to me, your closeness and our great feeling of being sheltered. So I was able to begin the final day of this year in a lovely, gratefully peaceful frame of mind—with you, and firmly in God's hands. My love, may He give you the power, strength, and peace to endure everything that lies ahead for you with His help. I'm quite confident of all that. The year 1945 will be even more difficult for us than 1944, but our strides have become far more confident because we are less supported merely by ourselves as we take them. While anxiety, fear, suffering, despair, and death rule the world, we fortunate ones know whose hand can help us through it all. So I'm heading into 1945 with you feeling full of hope, not full of concrete hope but with an indefinably contented and grateful feeling of confidence that knows nothing of what may be your imminent death. How odd! As a result, for us the beginning of the new year unquestionably falls under the heading: "Watch and pray"! How wonderful that I can be with the friends, that is, with you. Quite close, quite close! We are both likely to be sleeping as the year 1945 begins. Regardless of whether we live or die in it, we will stay together, yet we are not ours but the Lord's. He must help us put the realization within us into practice. May God watch over you and us. I embrace you, my dear love, and am and will remain your P.

1. Dietrich Bonhoeffer. He was imprisoned in Tegel for nearly eighteen months, looked after by his fiancée, Maria von Wedemeyer. He was executed in the last days of the war. 2. In Tegel, Maria von Wedemeyer also looked after Baron Dietrich von Truchsess.

HELMUTH JAMES TO FREYA,
DECEMBER 31, 1944–JANUARY 1, 1945

Tegel, 31 Dec 44

My dear, this is the final evening of a year that has been so momentous for us, that will stand out from our lives with great radiance, whether we live or die, because it gave the two of us the gift of something that I hope we will never lose: a solid faith. It has certainly been the most important year of my life, and when I consider that it passed under circumstances that are commonly regarded as an ordeal, I ask in amazement: Where is the ordeal? I had three days in this year that were harder for me than anything has ever been: March 24,[1] October 10,[2] and November 13.[3] But afterward I always saw that it was the price that had to be paid for surmounting a new stage, and besides, these days had nothing to do with the imprisonment or with the uncertainty surrounding what lay ahead. No, my love, I can't complain about the year, nor can I regard your fate this year as bad, although it was worse than mine, because you had to live in a state of constant uncertainty. Truly we can only look back on 1944 with gratitude.

Whatever comes now is in God's hands, and we will accept it joyfully and confidently from these hands, even if it should turn out to be my death in a matter of days. In this case, my love, I will leave you feeling that the past few months have so well equipped you to bear up under this, even under this, that no misfortune will befall you. And in order to accustom you to my beloved Isaiah, I want to tell you what the Lord promised through him in 46:4: "And even to your old age I am he; and even to hoar hairs will I carry you: I have made, and I will bear; even I will carry, and will deliver you." Let us pray, my love, that He gives us the ability to lift ourselves up, to be carried and delivered, and whether it is at the gallows in Plötzensee or in the cellar of Prinz-Albrecht-Str., in the uncertainty that may be your fate, and in a wild band of soldiers and a burning Berghaus.

Since Christmas, the close proximity of my death, which I'd actually been feeling on a constant basis since July 20th, is no longer there. I don't know quite what to make of that. I'm not entirely happy about that, because I have the feeling that it stems from a weakness of the flesh that is fed up with "watch and pray." But there is no doubt that my inner disposition has undergone a transformation. I can't see any reason for that on an intellectual level, and I certainly expect to be put to death next week; but there is an enormous difference between the "expecting to" and the palpable presence of death.

Now I'll get back to Isaiah. No, Isaiah did not express anything about the human condition, nor did he find solutions for human afflictions. Isaiah has something altogether different in mind, namely God's will with the world. Job speaks about human afflictions and surmounting them by means of faith, as does Jeremiah to a degree, but the greatest of the prophets, Isaiah, is not interested in the hardships humans face, because he is reporting about God. The man is too elevated above human woes, at least when he speaks as a prophet. I greatly prefer Daniel and Solomon and the Psalms to Isaiah, because I'm simply a little blade of grass eagerly seeking and obtaining solace and help. I'm no hero. However, I see the greatness of Isaiah beckoning, just as a blade of grass in the valley looks over at the peaks of the Himalayas in the sad realization that a blade of grass can't grow in those regions.

Well, that would truly be a letter for Herr Freisler. I wonder if he'd understand it. He would be obliged to have me killed if he didn't understand it, and all the more so if he did.

My dear, strong, good, bravely beating sweetest of hearts, stay with me. May the Lord watch over you and us. J.

1 Jan 45

My love, I now wish you a blessed new year. I've just read Romans 10–12, our passage for today, and it contains several very lovely verses for us and for this year. So let us begin it with confidence and receive from God's hand what He sends us, be it death or prison or freedom, be it hardship or a wild band of soldiers or destruction or dispersion or peace. The range of possibilities that this year is visibly spreading out before us is colossally large, and we can ask for only one thing, that we may continue to feel that we are in God's hands and that He does not withdraw His grace, His succor from us.

Farewell, my love, may the Lord watch over you and us. J.

1. The three dates represent days of great suffering for Helmuth alone in his cell. The first was after the Gestapo advised him that they were going to try him as part of the Kiep treason trial that had caused his arrest. See Helmuth's

letter of March 26, 1944, in Helmuth James von Moltke, *Im Land der Gottlosen: Tagebuch und Briefe aus der Haft 1944/45*, edited by Günter Brakelmann
(Munich: C. H. Beck), 2009, 224. 2. Helmuth here means October 11, 1944,
when he had written his farewell letter to his sons; see his letter of October
12, 1944. 3. Helmuth again struggled mightily on November 13, 1944, after
his first face-to-face meeting with Freya; see his letter of November 14, 1944.

HELMUTH JAMES TO FREYA, JANUARY 1–2, 1945[1]

Tegel, 1 Jan 45

My dear, serious times are now quite palpably close again, and we
have to come to terms with the fact that I may be killed in little more
than a week.

We've said everything about the time after my death in matters
both economic and noneconomic. I'm assuming that you either jotted it down or can reconstruct it, so I won't go through that once
again. I want to repeat only this: A dead hand cannot rule, that is,
everything from me is only a suggestion, and you mustn't feel duty
bound to follow it.—As for Kreisau, I'm of the opinion that you ought
to and will be able to defend the Berghaus resolutely, but that in all
other matters preserving dignity is more important than the outcome;
luckily you don't depend on Kreisau for your material well-being;[2]
but I would defend your claims to Kreisau.—As soon as the opportunity arises, you should all do everything in your power to take full
advantage of our deaths, politically, and, if there is a usurper in
Kreisau, whoever that may be, economically as well.

If I'm sentenced to death and not executed right away, you should
do everything that's still possible, as we had agreed; the question of
Hewel strikes me as especially acute, and the path to the SS, whether
it be to Müller directly or by way of Kaltenbrunner. The best thing
would be for you to talk that over with Dix in advance and let both
Steengracht and Dix keep a time slot open for January 11th so that
you can really launch things immediately. Clearly the chances will
be no better than 1 in 100,000. But it should be tried even so. It remains to be considered, however, whether you ought to ask Carl Viggo

[von Moltke] or Jowo [von Moltke] to come for the 11th in any case, because I always find that you are too much of an implicated party and that only the arguments regarding the Moltke family can hold sway,[3] and you really can't be the one to represent them.—In Plötzensee, all of you and Buchholz have to come up with a well-defined means of getting messages back and forth so that you can be informed by telephone about my execution; he can't say it officially.

If I'm held at Prinz-Albrecht-Str. after the sentencing, you have to try, first by way of the prison, then via Lange, and finally via Müller's front office, to get permission to exchange laundry. Maybe Hercher can help too. But there should always be very little laundry so that it's soon needed again. And always bring me one of those little books published by Insel, and I'll try to give you news by marking it up. To make sure it's not too easy to decipher, let's plan for me to mark up quite a number of pages, but only the even or only the odd ones count. You have to figure out which ones.—Give me an Insel book right away, but it can't have any markings because I don't have an eraser.

Can you imagine: When I was writing to you the other day, I actually forgot our cherished night on Arndtstr. last year, and our last unfettered walk on the train platform. At the same time, I recently found myself fondly reminiscing about that evening, as I have several times over these past months, and how we played Mozart's Requiem, although not to the very end. And before that, we also played "Dans un coin de mon pays."[4] You surely recall that one quite well too. It was so lovely.

My love, do you have Lindi?[5] I'm a bit unhappy that this is coming at a rough time for you. It is very important for me to feel that you feel totally safe and secure and that you are standing by me with your thoughts and prayers from your mighty fortress.[6] The best part in that regard is the thorough preparation and the three days.[7] If I can resolve the contradictions in my earlier statements in a reasonably persuasive manner, and I think that's possible, thoroughness may afford me the chance I need. From the National Socialist point of view, I'm damnable on the surface and quite damnable in the true depths; but between those layers there is a thin—very thin—one in which I'm acceptable, or marginally acceptable. I think it's out of the question for Freisler to get down into the true depths; he'll get no more than a hint of what lies there, but if he does make it there, well, at least I'll be dying for the right thing. It's more likely that he only penetrates the surface, and it's conceivable that I can make him see that the thin intermediate layer is plausible.—Incidentally, one thing is certain: It is better to be hanged by Hitler than to die from a bomb. It is more meaningful.

I hope, my dear, you notice that I am quite reassured. Of course the prospect of my turn coming up in a week from today isn't a pleasant one, but no one is expecting me to feel that way. The trial is weighing on my mind with immense force, and in my head the difficult, sensitive points keep popping up, the ones that Freisler is sure to pick apart. In all the days ahead I will be dealing with that constantly, as you'll notice in my letters as well. But you have to let me do this.

Now good night, my dear, may the Lord watch over you and us. J.

2 Jan 45

My dear, I was just at the doctor's. He examined my back and determined that it is just the nerves that are causing the neuralgic symptoms. He wants to prescribe additional light baths and write me a doctor's note stating that I'm unable to stand and will need to sit. That is quite reassuring as far as it goes, but it's too little to effect a postponement of the trial. Still, you can try to make inroads, and no one can hold that against you; that is undoubtedly one of the privileges of being a wife.—In my view, the question of whether sitting is a clear advantage for me is too close to call. It is much harder to shout at a sitting man, who is better able to dodge the psychological pressure of these kinds of actions, and I can also keep refreshing my memory by glancing at my notes, which can be useful. In short, try to get a postponement, but if you can't, it's not so bad.

I'm doing well, my love. I'm quite confident and joyful, and fully aware that things will go according to God's will. As long as I have no doubts on that score and don't start to feel dependent on Herr

Freisler or the executioner or Herr Müller or Heinrich Himmler, all is well. You have hard work ahead of you this week, my love. May the Lord watch over you and us. J.

1. This letter was accidentally left on Harald Poelchau's desk in the Tegel prison for one night. 2. See Helmuth's letter to Freya of January 10–11, 1945, for further detail. 3. On the status of the von Moltke family name in Germany, see the Editors' Introduction. 4. A 1940 song sung by Jacques Pills. 5. The reference is to menstruation. 6. The word "fortress" is often used to refer to Freya's body and its dependability. 7. The three days scheduled for the trial.

FREYA TO HELMUTH JAMES, JANUARY 2, 1945

Tuesday morning

My dear love, I'm writing in bed, because the temperature conditions have deteriorated dramatically at the friends' house as a result of a lack of coke. Only in the evenings is the temperature bearable, and at night the heating stops again altogether. But this is why I've lived here most of the time since my return, and it has been quite delightful. A little bit of freezing can't hurt. I keep going outdoors and walking to warm up. The friends are taking very good care of me, and I think they find my presence very natural and it doesn't stand out, you might say. I really hope so.—My love, I got quite a lovely letter from you to launch the new year. Yes, that is how things are, my love. We're such different people, and yet we're so united and get to belong to each other so unreservedly. I love you so much, but I can see you with a certain degree of objectivity, and the way you appear to me then, my dearest, odd husband, makes me love you all the more.

Poelchau came to eat at 12, and we had a good lunch in hats and coats during an alarm. Dorothee [Poelchau] cooks well and quickly and full of variety. It was rather strange. When my dress was ready, I went to see Fräulein Schellhase, Dorothee went three-quarters of the way with me and we had very bad luck with public transportation. Sometimes the trip goes splendidly, and other times it takes twice as long. The attack the day before yesterday created minor disruptions everywhere. Today I'll see about Husen, have lunch with Henssel, and go to see Dix at 4:30. I've already prepared almost everything I'll need. I just have to type the written plea for Hercher.[1] I think that Hercher will always be tough to influence. He does only what he wants. Old people are obstinate, no matter how willing they actually are. I won't get to Steltzer until Thursday morning. I'll speak to Haus today.—Meanwhile, the

[The rest of the letter appears to be lost.]

1. This refers to a supplement to Helmuth's written defense.

FREYA TO HELMUTH JAMES, JANUARY 2, 1945

Tuesday evening

My Jäm, my dear love, my husband, and again my Jäm, my dearest, I have to write you all these names with joy, with gratitude and happiness, and with tender love, because I can't write you many letters by Monday, my sweet, my beloved heart. In spite of everything, I can't yet comprehend the possibility that today is Tuesday and you could already be dead in one week. I quite plainly don't believe that this will happen. That has nothing to do with hoping, nor does it signal preparedness (or rather, a lack thereof); I don't believe that they will kill you right away, even if they sentence you to death. Apart from that, I feel that it's now coming, that we now have to be prepared, that we now have to rely on all that the past few months have given us. I know, my love, what my part will be. I'll tell you again what you already know, that I will stay at home on both days, alone. You told me that I ought to be in a deep state of calm: may I be helped to do so by God, to whom I will pray for you. In the evenings I'll go to the friends, but I'll hardly be able to sleep there, because I can't have Brigitte [Gerstenmaier] traveling home alone on those days. But that is immaterial, and also depends on the verdict.

It's now 11, and the friends are already in bed and Brigitte went home. Poelchau seems to have left today's letter on his desk and will pick it up tomorrow, so tomorrow you'll get this little letter.

Now I want to write only about some concrete issues, the most important being Dix.

The discussion ended with Dix's urgent, determined, detailed warning to you *not to be too complicated*. Just don't raise any formal legal questions, or any issues of jurisprudence, or anything too intellectual! Don't rub the fact that you're a complex person in their faces, my dear love. It will be hard for you, but you have to make an effort. Yes, that was Dix.

You're already sleeping, my dear love, and I will be sleeping soon too, at which point I'll be close to you and in sleep united with you. I'm sending you a tender embrace! You know whose I am and whose I will remain.

HELMUTH JAMES TO FREYA, JANUARY 2, 1945

Tegel, 2 Jan 45

My dear, I've just read your letter again at the beginning of the evening; it stayed here because the orderly came to get me "for the light bath." The remaining evenings are few now. Apart from today, there will be at most three more on which I will be able to put my conversation with you down on paper, and then begins the tightrope walk that is likely to culminate on the gallows in Plötzensee.

Sometimes I think about the fate of our long written conversations, and whether you and the little sons will find them worth reading after ten, twenty, or more years. They originated in a situation that most likely has rarely been captured in writing, because normally the contact winds up being ruptured or monitored. When this time is over, when true peace has been restored, what will people say about these kinds of reflections? Will they be understood? Will it be believed that these were extreme situations that made people hysterical, will people be able to grasp the notion that a human being, this curious animal, can grow accustomed even to being executed? I know that I didn't understand when I first met Poelchau how he could stand to accompany many people to the scaffold, week after week. And now it no longer surprises me.

So, now I can come to the events of my day. (Right, another thing: Tomorrow we'll begin with 1 Corinthians, won't we?) The orderly, a guard named Mittelstädt, came to get me at 11 o'clock "for the light bath." The doctor was away at the moment, and we went to the custody prison. Mittelstädt sat down on the doctor's chair, invited me to have a seat, and then it started up: Why did the July 20th attempt have no follow-up, and wasn't something new going to be formed soon, and the war was lost anyway, and it was crucial to realize that immediately and act accordingly, and the speech[1] had been outrageous, not a word for the dead, and only the nation is suffering, but the gentlemen up there, they didn't notice anything, well, if that were to change, there would be quite a rude awakening, and the fact that the old families had taken such a stand would not be forgotten, but the medical health officer hates us and thinks nothing is bad enough for us, and he doesn't care in the slightest if I have something worse than neuralgia, he wouldn't think of offering any real help, and Budapest[2] and the air strikes and the many executions, etc. He told me that of course he could not say a word to the medical officer, and there are several 100-percenters[3] among the guards as well, but most of them think the way he does. By 11:45, he had poured his heart out, and graciously returned me to the cell, letting me know he would come to get me after the meal for the light bath.

When he got me, he said he had grown tobacco but didn't know how to ferment it, so I told him you could give him advice, and he should have Herr Gissel let him know when you're here again. Then we headed to the sick bay.

There I was looked after by a trusty working as a health-care aide, who spoke to me in the same vein as Herr Mittelstädt and praised him to the skies too. He said, "Here we're all of one mind; we just have to make sure that the medical health officer doesn't notice." I have to say that I have hardly ever witnessed such open, albeit self-interested, hostility, and I get the impression that the sick bay is a little collection of enemies of the state who, under the protection of the unsuspecting medical officer, feel quite safe and secure. It doesn't appear to be difficult to trick him, and as long as that works, everything will be fine.

It was also nice that Herr Mittelstädt was disappointed to learn that I was insufficiently subversive: "Well, of course you now have to embellish your case, but if you pull through, maybe we can talk about it again." Another lovely remark: "When the tide turns, there will be a massacre; there won't even be anyone of the Brown- and Blackshirts[4] left to mourn their pals. Do you believe that?"—He was saying all this to a man who may have been wearing an identification tag associating him with July 20th—which for Herr Mittelstädt was tantamount to a medal—but whom, before he got started, he had known all of ten minutes.

I see the days dwindling away. In one week, at this time, I could already be dead. Whether Friday evening is still nice depends on whether Poelchau comes again on Saturday. But I'm not the least bit melancholy about it; I just note that this is the way things are. We have had our full measure of grace; we may pray for more, yet know how to be content if our prayer is not answered. If I die now, I'll die with the feeling that my house is in good order, because the heart of my Pim is well equipped, because I am certain I'll be able to continue to stand by her, because I have been able to bid farewell to everyone and everything, because I have completed all the tasks that have been assigned to me thus far. Should God wish to have me carry out a new task, I will accept it with gratitude, but I am not departing with a feeling of having left things unfinished. Somehow I am finished, at least in one chapter. I am very glad that you will not need to grapple with material difficulties, because I also believe that you would somehow be able to deal with them.—But if you should decide to remain in Kreisau, you will have to use all your might to try to stick to this decision and not to let either friend or foe drive you away. Together, Romai [Reichwein] and you would surely be quite a protective force.

So, my love, another evening has come to an end. Now there are three more at most.[5] Farewell, my love. May the Lord watch over you and us. J.

1. This presumably refers to Hitler's New Year's speech. 2. Apparent reference to the Siege of Budapest, in which the Red Army encircled the city on December 25, 1944. 3. Guards who believed strongly in the Nazis in contrast to their colleagues. 4. Another way of saying "Nazi Party loyalists." 5. Helmuth is counting the evenings before the expected transfer to Gestapo headquarters on Prinz-Albrecht-Strasse.

FREYA TO HELMUTH JAMES, JANUARY 3, 1945

Wednesday evening

My dear love, here the radio is playing beautiful Bach chorales, which move me but don't melt me. It's strange that in my own way, I'm doing exactly, exactly the same as you. I've written that again and again. That's why I know so well what you mean and how things are. I, too, am not tense, I, too, am cheerful, I, too, am doing well, and although my mind keeps warning me to face the facts, my inner being doesn't want to go there. I feel quite close to you, but in a matter-of-fact, natural, unagitated manner that looks to the future with confidence. Everything is quite calm and completely sheltered in you, and not as though in a matter of days my entire life will be at stake.—Early today I got the two beautiful long lovely letters. I was delighted by your description of the sick bay and read it aloud to the friends, who also enjoyed it very much. It is one of the many comic situations in a very serious matter, yet it is more than just comic. I quite liked Herr Mittelstädt from the start, by the way. It was so wonderful to catch a glimpse of you, my dear love. It was dear, but also devoid of excitement; it seemed altogether natural to me, although once I had heard that you were on the way back, I ran to the door every time I heard a key and peered through a tiny slit. I didn't have to be embarrassed in the company of the women behind me. They all have similar feelings. Then you came, all bent over and limping, my dear love. I'm not mortified by it, but it looks as though it must be very unpleasant for you. Yes, maybe it will be an advantage for you to be able to sit. Other than that, you looked the same as always. I liked your beard, too. I would have liked to go on looking at you, but the two nice old men[1] had already been so friendly.

Herr Thiele was, as always, quite friendly. I didn't say anything about postponing the trial. He's too far down in the hierarchy anyway, but I already have the permission for a face-to-face meeting in my pocket, my dear love. Isn't that wonderful? I'll come on Friday. But now it all continues. In response to a question about transportation, Thiele explained that they had no say in that matter. Lieutenant Colonel Kiesel—you surely know him—took care of that, and, better yet, Second Lieutenant Wehrstädt. Kiesel was out of town, but Wehrstädt was there. I told the girl what I wished to see happen, which is always a stupid thing to do. She pulled a card from her file and left. Then she came back and said, "You needn't worry at all, Countess, your husband will be picked up by car directly from Tegel and driven to the trial." I was skeptical and asked whether I could definitely rely on that. She affirmed this eagerly.—Peters now knows. He has come up with a different and possibly better option, which he will be calling Frau Friedrich about tonight, and tomorrow night I'll go to see her and discuss it. He's pondered the matter, and is looking to come on the 9th. Also coming on the 9th is a man who is very close to Heinrich Himmler, whom Frau Friedrich can approach. I need to hear about this. The 9th is still in time for this attempt, if it is opportune. Tomorrow I have a wonderful schedule. Listen to this: Start shortly after 6, drop off a letter with Hercher, go to Lichterfelde, make a telephone call to Kreisau. 9:45 Frau Graf, 10:45 Schellhase at Lehrter station. In between the above errands, Dr. Wickenberg. Pick up a hare for Poelchau, deliver a package to Maria [Schanda], go to see Dorothee [Poelchau]. Help with the laundry starting at 3, then drink a cup of pure coffee, go to the Trothas because Margrit [von Trotha] will be there tomorrow during the day, eat dinner there, and head to Frau Friedrich by bike, I think, because it's not far. If you have time, let your thoughts travel with me, and then everything will be unhurried and go smoothly.

Good night, my dearest. I'm yours for life and death. You know that. I love you with all my strength. I was created by God to belong to you. That is why I may accompany you on all your paths, and you on mine.

On Friday I'll come to visit you!
Yours

1. She is referring to the guards Claus and Gissel.

HELMUTH JAMES TO FREYA, JANUARY 3, 1945

Tegel, 3 Jan 45

My dear love, there will be another three letters at most, and this is one of those precious ones. How wonderful it was to see you today. I had been hoping that it would work out, and I caught sight of you when you were still quite far away. Even if that turns out to be the last look I will have had of my dearest in this life, it would still be very beautiful, as we were both buoyant and in good spirits.—It will be even nicer if you can come again, but that was already a great deal. And what treasures you brought me, my love. That was, once again, terrifically sumptuous. After I ate, I drank raspberry juice with whipped cream and then coffee with whipped cream, because the cream had to be used up.

It's already well into the evening, because I've been working like crazy. The latest unpleasant development is that Eugen [Gerstenmaier]'s lawyer told him we would each be questioned in the absence of the others, followed by a comparison, in order to convict each of us with the help of the other. So there goes my nice hope that I could provide the framework for everyone in my opening statement. The result is this: I have nothing to fear with Reisert; when it comes to Sperr, I have to hope to God that he doesn't dredge up really awful things; but it is necessary for Theo [Haubach], Steltzer, Eugen, Delp, and me to form a phalanx and not to decimate one another. This is why I wrote new secret messages for Theo and Steltzer, which I'm including in the attached material. I'll give Steltzer's to Poelchau a second time in good penmanship, in the event that he can deliver it personally. But I would ask you to think over if anything is possible with Steltzer, because he seems to me to represent the main danger. It would be a blessing if it were possible to get him the long secret message. Maybe you can shorten it, if you recall what Steltzer already knows, likewise with Theo. I'm sorry to be burdening you and the others with this business again, but now this is far more significant than before. I would also ask you to check on whether the two of them know that Maass and Reichwein are dead, and Rösch and König are gone. That, too, is important.

My love, I really have to laugh about our last pairs of letters, because we always wrote each other the exact same things. Not only did we discuss the same ideas but we even raised the same questions, and to an extent even chose the same turns of phrase. This shows how united we are.

My dear, what else should I be telling you? That I love you very much? That this will last? Yes, that is so. We married "until death do us part," but that is only because these wedding vows were made by people who were not waiting for their execution, or else they wouldn't write such claptrap. But the good Lord has something better in mind than our wedding vows; we are certain of that.—Just don't let all this trouble you. It seems to me that if you've consciously sacrificed your husband, you really ought to be immune to everything else. I just wish that the little sons may hold on to you and you on to them. May the Lord watch over you and us. J.

HELMUTH JAMES TO FREYA, JANUARY 4, 1945

Tegel, 4 Jan 45

My dear love, so this is in all likelihood, that is, in all likelihood from a human perspective, the next-to-last letter you'll be getting from me.

I'm writing that without a trace of melancholy, as if it were the most natural thing in the world. Might that be the case when I write "J." for the last time tomorrow? I'm surprised at myself, because a true Moltke ought to be at least on the verge of tears now, and that is not the case.—But now you're in Lichterfelde,[1] and you're all probably chatting away nicely, and you, my love, are thinking about your husband. It has stopped surprising me that your letter, which arrived today, once again addressed the same issues as mine. We simply have one heart and one circulatory system and are a single thought of divine creation. He shows that to us in new signs again and again, in the friendliest manner. Should my heart want to skip a few beats under the onslaught on Monday and Tuesday, then I can always think: Where is my heart? It keeps on beating very calmly, quietly, steadily, and full of faith in God in Lichterfelde, and then my own outpost, having begun to race, will grow quiet again. And that's how I will be in Plötzensee if I have to go there, and that is how it will remain. And should I return to our Father, my dear, you know that your heart will keep on beating up there, calmly and forever sheltered for you, and that it will want to soothe you if things should get too much for you.

Let's get some business out of the way first. If I could remain here, that would truly be very welcome. I wouldn't give much credence to the word of an SS second lieutenant in a matter like this. It would probably be best for the lead Reich prosecutor to be brought in as well, either Schulze or Görlich (?).[2] But to begin with that will depend on whether you've made some headway with Wickenberg (?), the doctor. If he doesn't go along with it, we'll have to rely on the word of some second lieutenant. In any case, I aim to have an appointment with him again tomorrow and I'll sing the same tune.—You'll see me tomorrow. I think I'm doing a bit better.

It is, of course, still the case that secret message transactions can be made only if things are really safe. We can't afford to make a mistake with this at the last moment.

So you're coming tomorrow, my dear love; how wonderful. I now consider that just wonderful, whereas in early December I would have been terribly worried about falling into a state of melancholy. Now

I am unreservedly happy. Today I also got a shave, so I don't look quite as wild anymore. It turns out that Thiele was quite decent about a face-to-face meeting, much better, at any rate, than Schulze.—If I only knew where this change in our attitude comes from. Might it be because we have become inured to the thought of my death? Or because now that the situation is getting serious and I may be killed in a matter of days, the flesh is revolting and won't accept the thought of it? Or because God just wants to strengthen me? I don't know, and I regard it with amazement.

My Pim, the day is over. Everything has been written, and everything has been said. Sleep well, my love, keep your sense of peace, whatever should happen, and in doing so you'll keep mine as well. May the Lord watch over you and us. J.

Another thing: Peters, about whom I was interrogated, albeit quite superficially, needs to know that he cannot mention Poelchau under any circumstances. Besides that, it is—or would be—especially useful for me if Peters could say[3] that he took part in several weekend discussions in Kreisau starting in 1927 or '28. Something along those lines.

1. At the home of Carl Dietrich von Trotha. 2. The reference is to Gerhard Görisch, but he was the senior public prosecutor; the chief Reich prosecutor was Ernst Lautz. 3. In Peters's planned conversation with Freisler.

FREYA TO HELMUTH JAMES, JANUARY 4–5, 1945

Thursday afternoon
My dear love, the laundry is done, and I've checked off all the items on my schedule, but soon I have to leave to see Carl Dietrich [von Trotha] and his wife. I'm tired now and don't want to do anything else, but today I still have to. Tomorrow it'll be calmer. Asta [Wendland] wrote a beautiful letter: starting on Monday morning she'll be staying in Kreisau: "Now we'll stand like a solid wall. On the 8th/9th I'll get to Kreisau and will stay there. I'd much rather come to Berlin to be with you and Helmuth ... Ulla [Oldenbourg] and I, we'll be

very close to you." Overall I'm not in favor of spreading the news about the trial, but I want to let Sister Ida [Hübner] know about it too, and Romai [Reichwein]. Is there anyone else you'd like to have filled in? First I met with Frau Steltzer and Frau Graf. On the 24th he[1] got your little written message by means of a cake, though not inside it but under it—it was in a paper casing made by the baker—so in a relatively careless way. The women didn't yet know how it got in there.—It occurs to me that I've yet to tell you about the unproductive talk I had with Dr. Wickenberg. I met him at Lehrter Strasse. He was neither unfriendly nor friendly; he was completely neutral and said he couldn't do anything, contending that this was simply a matter of transportation and he had no influence on that. In short, he didn't want to get involved. I figured that out from his fish-eyed glance right away, and didn't expect much. What else can I do now? I get the feeling that you're staying in Tegel. I hope that's true.

Friday morning.

Peters *can't* come until the 10th!

So, my dear, dear love, Poelchau is chewing his last bite. I embrace you with great, heartfelt tenderness. I am and will remain entirely yours. Always, your P.

1. Theodor Steltzer.

HELMUTH JAMES TO FREYA, JANUARY 5–7, 1945

Tegel, 5 Jan 45

My dear love, for a second I was sad that we wouldn't be seeing each other today, because I'm always afraid that in the end something will come up and it may not happen at all, and then, because I felt so sorry for you that you'd waited for a long time and had to leave again without having achieved anything. But aside from all that, tomorrow is of course even better, because it's even later—if it all works out. With all the changes coming at us—air raids, getting picked up by the Gestapo, etc.—something like this is always doubtful.

I was very happy to read the passage in Asta [Wendland]'s letter about how she's now staying in Kreisau and will defend the position; it's greatly reassuring to me, because it might be possible for them to take possession of Kreisau after the verdict but before it is carried out, that is, at a time that you'll still need to be in Berlin. That's how they did it with Wentzel-Teutschenthal, whose place was already a Hitler Youth camp, which is to say, a heap of rubble, while he was still living here.—But it's also possible that they won't go there at all, given the surprising fact that they have yet to do anything in that regard. They've even paid a visit to the home of Fugger, who is certainly not going to be sentenced to death. So Asta should please stay put until you're back, and actually even longer, until the matter is cleared up, because you're not able to protect it.[1]

I, too, am happy that Ulla [Oldenbourg] has been notified. I feel pretty confident, but now I notice that underneath it all I'm also feeling a bit anxious when I hear any news about postponement, being brought in, etc., though that's probably more of a nervous reflex. I'm as calm as I was before Christmas, only I'm much more confident.—Our theological dispute shrank to no more than five minutes of the thirty allotted to the free time, because we have so many concrete matters to discuss, since we unfortunately have to prepare ourselves to speak out persuasively against Steltzer if his statements really do form the basis of certain parts of the indictment. Very unpleasant. Let's hope the secret message transaction with Steltzer went well.—The theological dispute, whose precise point of contention the intelligent Delp has yet to grasp, as you will have seen from his last note, got me spontaneous support from Buchholz, who didn't hesitate to say that my opinion was the only possible one, and stuck to this view even when I told him that in my view it was in the good Lutheran tradition. He said that Gethsemane was the article of faith that was required, and salvation as such was not a permissible object of faith— that is, these are my words.—I was very pleased about that.

I'm quite happy that Frau Reisert appears to have had success at long last and extracted her husband from our case. It also works to our benefit that Fugger is now out of the way, because he's too naïve and foolish, although he's also very nice and so kind. Let's just hope that he's not brought in as a witness; that would be really bad.

I'll stop for today, my love. This letter won't go off until Sunday, and the second alarm is coming; when it's over, I want to go to bed, if I have the opportunity. May the Lord watch over you and us. J.

Tegel, 6 Jan 45

My dear, how wonderful were the three-quarters of an hour with my Pim. So dear and tender. I went back up into my cell feeling so warm, and you went to Poelchau's. My love, it would have been even better not to talk at all, but I thought I'd throw in the word Christmas, because if we had too little to talk about, he might shorten our time together. But I saw how nice your letters are, as there was not even the slightest tinge that differed from the way I'd imagined it. My love looked warm and content. It never crossed my mind—as it always had when I left Kreisau—that this might have been our final look at each other in this world, so it was not the slightest bit sad or melancholy. How different it was at the first face-to-face meeting. A whole world lies between that meeting and this one, a world of confidence and trust and, if this isn't my old friend haughtiness talking again, some humility as well, the first rudiments.

So, now the fight begins. When I came back, I waited for Hercher for an hour, and when he didn't come, I asked Gissel to call up the Trothas to say that you should alert Hercher, because I was afraid he wasn't coming. The good Gissel tried hard but couldn't get an answer at the Trothas', and I didn't want to have him called at Poelchau's. But when Gissel came back looking quite unhappy, Hercher showed up.—It's exasperating, and may complicate things quite a bit, that he hasn't read the files; I now gave him the complete set of facts concerning the Goerdeler complex, that is, that all the rumors, too, originated from the police, and that, along with Dix's letter, led him to come to the following conclusions:

a. The man who brought the charges is convinced that a death sentence will result.

b. The indictment was surely discussed in advance with Freisler, with the Gestapo, and with the minister of justice.

c. Consequently, Freisler arrives with the opinion that there will be a death sentence.

d. The explanations that I may now give concerning all the critical points alter the facts of the case sufficiently so that the court is not compelled to impose a death sentence.

e. The question as to whether Freisler can be swayed depends solely on the personal, human impression he comes away with, not on questions of evidence; if he wishes to be swayed, he'll believe me even without further evidence, to the point that he can justify his verdict; if he doesn't wish to be swayed, he won't believe anything about me so as to justify his verdict.

f. Two months ago, the facts of this case would have inevitably resulted in a death sentence; the indictment was drawn up to make it look as though I am one of the great sinners, but now they're just looking to clear the decks of the old cases, so a case involving the July 20th plot might be judged more leniently today than the same case would be judged if it were just now emerging.

g. Freisler would definitely hear me out, if for no other reason than my name. I was very pleased with Hercher once again. He knows Freisler; he knows the ploys; he may not be clever, but he's quite experienced in these trials. He also said: No dwelling on jurisprudence, which is of absolutely no importance here; no expressing viewpoints; stick to reporting the facts, but they can be spelled out down to the tiniest details. Just take whatever comes, don't shout back, don't defend yourself against insults; instead, in spite of any hollering and insults that may come your way, keep to your own presentation very calmly; even when stating opinions, couch them as facts. "Freisler is talented, ingenious, very sensitive, but not clever," was Hercher's summary assessment. In short, he said: We'll see what we can do. You see that here, too, a gradual pivoting has occurred, and that

Hercher no longer sees the inevitability of a death sentence. The declaration of guilt, he said, is not a deciding factor at all. If he's aiming for a death sentence, he has enough material; if not, he'll get around the declaration of guilt. Besides, we'll have plenty of time: he'll add on a third or fourth day; that doesn't matter.

All these flights of fancy invite the danger of diverting our attention from the goal at hand if we focus on them too much. Even so, I'm writing you so many details because the very same transformation has taken place here that we ourselves have undergone, namely that the death sentence is no longer being predicted with such an absolute appearance of certainty.

Here's something interesting, by the way: Freisler sticks closely to the indictment; he could conceivably introduce new material as well, but it's not very likely and he passes sentences only on the basis of the things that are argued in the oral trial and never on the basis of any other information.[2] All this is quite interesting, and it rounds out the picture to show that although Freisler is a fanatical and fierce political judge, he's also an eminent one.

My love, I'm happy that you felt I was standing straight. I don't notice the differences myself. Hercher has the doctor's certificate with him and would like to see Freisler grant permission for me to sit before the trial.

7 Jan 45

My dear love, our thoughts have already meshed in such a lovely way. Good morning. Of course there is absolutely nothing new. But I can go back to the very beginning again and tell you that I love you very much, that the two of us are a single idea of creation, and, when the Lord calls me to Him, you will be traveling along within me, and I remain here within you.

So off I go, well equipped, and what more could I ask for? Farewell, my very dear love, may the Lord watch over you and us. J.

1. Freya was not physically in Kreisau, and the house was owned by Helmuth and his siblings.

2. See Helmuth's letter of October 12, 1944 [Addendum to Freya's letter of October 11, 1944].

FREYA TO HELMUTH JAMES, JANUARY 6–7, 1945

Evening

My dear love, how beautiful it was today with you, and how well we parted. I hope, my beloved Jäm, you went back into your cell as happy and unsad as I went back into the world. During the time we sat there together, I felt only how steadfastly we belong together, how certain I am that it will always stay this way, and I didn't need to feel any pain in parting, even though my eyes kept skimming over you, over the most beloved thing there is for me, and I knew that I may not see all this again in this world. I knew it, yet I didn't believe it. No, let me put it another way, I thought I had to coax myself into believing it, but it didn't work. I was quite honest and didn't delude myself in the slightest, yet I could only be happy about your closeness, which is so familiar to me, so intimate, and so beloved. Once again, it seemed quite natural, but I felt that it was something tremendously precious to be able to sit so close to you. That is how it was for me! So beautiful, such an addition to our treasure. May God grant that it was not too difficult for you either, that you weren't tormented in your cell, that it wasn't too exhausting for you, that I did not once again pull you back into this splendid life we share. I hope Hercher helped you and turned your mind to your defense, your work, and your reflections, and pulled you away from sad thoughts about us. My dear love, how I love you and how glad I am to be able to love you so; what I wouldn't do to be able to preserve your life, for you and for me, yet I'm so keenly aware that we have, after all, experienced and understood so profoundly: "Thy will be done." My Jäm, my dearest, maybe this letter *is* the last one I'll ever write you, maybe, but what matters most is not letter writing, or even living together; what matters is love. Since I'm still able to write, I'm once again writing you today about my love. Whatever happens, you are the happiness of my life, you are my riches, you are my life. What would I be without you! I've grown toward you. No sooner was I grown up than you were there, and I knew I was yours. I know it now more than ever; you know it too. My love, you now have to focus everything on the path ahead of you, on the trial and on death. You mustn't think about me anymore, and you don't need to either, because my love will surround you tirelessly and irrepressibly. It will envelop and warm you when your enemies encircle you, it will go with you wherever you have to go. Never, never, never will it have an end. It has made my life rich and will keep my life rich. We will always find each other in our love, here or there. We were happy, we are happy, and we will stay happy. Together we are grateful, and together we are in good hands; we will stay together, and death cannot part us. I'm not complaining, because we have to be willing to lay our lives on the line. I approve of everything you did, from the bottom of my heart. I don't want to start making grand statements that would make it seem as though we're not as one, but since we are, this is also a part of it and it gives me courage and composure and pride. But this goes too far in pointing to your death: we ought to consider that outcome possible, but we don't have to believe in it firmly. First we need to fight, and for this fight you need my love. You have it, you have me. I will beat as your heart, and warm you and pray and hold you in my thoughts without fear, without anxiety, utterly prepared and determined to fight for us. You, too, need to stay calm and firmly anchored, safe and secure in God and united with your Pim. Then the gifts of your spirit and head and heart will come to our aid—because you are not fighting just for yourself! I could go on writing for a long, long time, but nothing else is new and all has been said between us.

—Sunday morning. Good morning, my dear love, I'm sure you wrote that to me this morning as well. I'm staying with my plan of going to Hercher early on both days and then spending the day in Lichterfelde, and will go to the friends' home in the evening after Hercher's call. That will be my schedule. My thoughts will be with you and with the good Lord, and I'll darn or sew or do anything to keep my hands busy. I won't pressure you with thoughts and wishes,

I will just be there and be led by God. He will help me stay calm and the way you need me to be. If the death sentence should come out on the second day, or whenever it comes out, I will spring into action. I will certainly not despair, I don't need to tell you that, since you know my inner workings so well—and I know yours. My beloved heart, my Jäm, my dearest.—After the face-to-face meeting, I spent a little more time with Dorothee [Poelchau], wrote to Freisler, and came to the People's Court at 1 o'clock, but no one was doing anything there by then.—I then realized, with Haus and Oxé, that the information according to which the petition for clemency was submitted to the Wehrmacht legal division was wrong. They're still sitting on it! Or it's in the wastebasket. Haus then wrote the enclosed letter right away. I wanted to have Uncle Wilhelm [von Moltke] sign. But when no one was there, I quickly signed it myself, writing "von Moltke" under his name, and the letter already left Tirpitzufer yesterday at 4:15 and today arrived on the desk of Keitel, that repulsive wimp, or his adjutant. Hewel's is with Steengracht again. The only one still en route is the one to Himmler. Haus was very nice again. "Now we have to do something for our count," he said to Frau Tharant, and then he dictated, conferring with me. What good is any sort of intelligence, if one's character isn't worth anything. Rarely do both combine in one individual. Haus is an agreeable example of that.—Blü-Blü[1] came the day before yesterday, in the evening. Might you have noticed that about me yesterday? At any rate, I'll be over it by the time of the trial, and now I'm not doing badly at all. I'm not misleading you, and you needn't worry about me. I would be incapable of misleading you now in even the tiniest of matters, not even to be considerate, because we are too in unison and you would somehow manage to realize it anyhow. No, the fortress is holding up quite well, but that is surely because of the bedrock it's standing on, and because it has such an exemplary owner! But it has always been a faithful companion, this fortress, and I know how grateful I can be for it. Few of us have one that is so secure and solid, and at times now, I have a truly detached feeling of gratitude for its constancy.—It seems to me, my love, that I've now told you everything; we're about to have breakfast here, and the peace and quiet is over for now.—Our gratitude to our friends cannot be over-stated (but that's another story), and that is also a subject that requires an explicit exchange of ideas between us, but if this should be the last letter from me that ever reaches you, a word about their love and friendship is certainly in order. What would have become of us without them, inside and out! May the good Lord protect them. She is not one bit behind him in stature, and they complement each other in exactly the same natural way that we do. They, too, belong together. I wrote our verses on a slip of paper for you. Take them along or leave them there, just as you please. You don't need to take along any material things from me, for you carry me firmly within you, just as I carry you. So this letter is neither an end nor a beginning, but merely one of the many seals on something far more beautiful and enduring, for which there are no proper words, something we possess as a precious treasure, and will never have to lose, and never *will* lose. That is why no more tears should fall onto these words, as we have reason only to be confident and joyous, grateful and happy, and to take up our human destiny as God's children together, together—that is how it will remain, both here and there. And so I say, may God watch over you, us! I am and will forever remain your P.

1. Menstruation.

HELMUTH JAMES TO FREYA, JANUARY 7, 1945

Tegel, 7 Jan 45

My dear love, how wonderful that I'm able to write to you again even though I don't know of anything left for me to write, since we've already said everything quite clearly in detail. I don't want to repeat it either, lest the repetition weaken and diminish it, like waving goodbye when a train just won't depart. So I'll simply say that it makes me happy to be able to send you another little night-and-morning greeting.

Yes, my dear, on the days of the trial, I'll look for you in Carl

Dietrich [von Trotha]'s apartment and at the friends' in the evenings. Don't do anything, not even regarding my things, because it's either too late or too early for all that; besides, you'd always run the risk of getting upset. I would arrange to have Carl Viggo [von Moltke] and/or Jowo [von Moltke] come to make sure that one of them is here the morning after the verdict; if there is no death sentence, he simply goes home again; if there is a death sentence, however, something needs to happen right away, above all to get Hercher to tell us what sorts of prospects for clemency the trial may have offered; or shall we say, how great the degree of guilt is. The target of all such efforts needs to be Himmler.

Poelchau has surely told you that I'm doing well. I pray that this remains so whatever may happen. If the Lord keeps me as I now am, nothing at all can happen to me.

Farewell, my love, good night for today. J.

HELMUTH JAMES TO FREYA, JANUARY 10, 1945

Berlin, 10 Jan 45

My dear, just think how nice it is that I have been brought back here to Tegel, that the dice, which will land in a manner that is already clearly determined, are arrested one more time in their fall, you might say, so I'm still able to write a report in peace.

Let me first jump right to the end: At about three o'clock, Schulze, who didn't make a bad impression, read out the prosecution's motions: Moltke: death and seizure of assets; Delp: ditto; Gerstenmaier: death; Reisert and Sperr: ditto; Fugger: 3 years in prison; Steltzer and Haubach: dealt with separately. Then came the defense counsel, all actually quite nice, none vicious. Then the closing statements of the accused; your husband was the only one not to participate. Eugen [Gerstenmaier] was somewhat uneasy, as I noticed in his closing statement.

Now for the course of the trial. It is, of course, forbidden to report any of this.

The trial took place in a small room that was full to bursting. Apparently a former schoolroom. After a long introduction by Freisler about the formalities—all parties bound to secrecy, ban on taking notes, etc.—Schulze read out the charges, but only the short text, which was also in the arrest warrant.[1] Then it was Delp's turn, and his two policemen stepped forward with him. The proceedings were as follows: Freisler, whom Hercher had described quite accurately: gifted, ingenious, and not clever—all three of these in the highest degree—gives an outline of the defendant's life, which is affirmed or supplemented, then come the issues of fact that interest him. He selects the details of the case that suit him, and leaves out entire sections. With Delp he started by asking how he got to know Peter [Yorck] and me, and what was discussed the first time in Berlin; then the topic of Kreisau[2] in the fall of '42 came up. Here, too, it takes this form: presentation by Freisler, into which responses, objections, perhaps new facts can be interjected; but if there's a chance that this could interrupt the flow of his argument, he grows impatient, indicates that he doesn't believe it anyway, or shouts at the person who spoke. The buildup for Kreisau was like this: First there were general discussions to lay the groundwork, then the practical case of a defeat was discussed, and finally there was a search for state administrators. The first phase might still be tolerable, although it was surprising, he argued, that all these discussions took place without a single National Socialist present but did include clergymen and all kinds of people who later participated in the July 20th plot.—The second phase, however, already constituted the blackest defeatism of the darkest kind. And the third, open preparation for high treason.—Then came the discussions in Munich. That turned out to be much more innocuous than in the indictment, but the Catholic clergy and the Jesuits got pelted with abuse: support for tyrannicide—Mariana;[3] illegitimate children; hostility to Germany, etc., etc. All this is delivered with a middling degree and level of shouting. The fact that Delp had left during the discussions that took place in his apartment was also held against him as being "typical Jesuit behavior": "Your very absence serves as your own documentation that you knew for certain that high treason was up for discussion, that you wanted to keep the tonsured little head, the sanctified holy man, out of it. He may well have gone to church during that time to pray for the plot to succeed in a way pleasing to God."—Then came Delp's visit to Stauffenberg. And finally Sperr's statement on July 21st that Stauffenberg had dropped hints about a coup. These last two points were largely glossed over. The remarkable part was that throughout the hearing, in one way or another, Freisler mentioned me in every other statement: "the Moltke Circle," "Moltke's plans," "also belongs to Moltke," etc.

The following legal principles were decreed: "The People's Court holds the view that the failure to report defeatist statements like Moltke's, statements of this kind from a man of his reputation and position, is itself an act of treason."—"Anyone who discusses highly political questions with people who are in no way competent to engage in such discussions, especially those who do not at least actively belong to the party, is already on the path to committing high treason."—"Anyone who presumes to pass any sort of judgment about a matter that is for the Führer to decide is on the path to committing high treason."– "Anyone who himself objects to acts of violence but prepares for the case that another, that is, the enemy, removes the government by force, is on the path to committing high treason, because he is then counting on the force of the enemy." And it went on and on in that vein. This allows for only one conclusion: Anyone not to Herr Freisler's liking is guilty of high treason.

Then came Sperr. He extricated himself from the Kreisau affair to an extent—somewhat at my expense. But he was reprimanded as follows: "Why didn't you report it? Don't you see how important that would have been: the Moltke circle was to some degree the inspiration for the 'Counts' circle,[4] which, in turn, made the political preparations for July 20th; since the driving force behind the July 20th plot wasn't Herr Goerdeler at all; the true motor was within these young men." All in all, Sperr was treated in a friendly manner.

Now Reisert. He was treated in a very friendly manner. He had had three meetings with me, and he was accused primarily of not having noticed by the end of the first one that I was a traitor and an arch-defeatist, and went on to have two more meetings with me. He was mainly accused of failing to notify the authorities.

Lastly, Fugger. He made a very good impression. He had been ill for some time and had now recovered, was modest, assured, didn't incriminate any of us, and spoke nice Bavarian, and I liked him more yesterday than I ever had before; not the slightest bit nervous, even though he had always been terrified here. He immediately admitted that after everything that was said to him today he saw clearly that he ought to have notified the authorities, and he was dismissed so graciously that I thought last night he would be acquitted.

By contrast, the name Moltke came up again and again in the other hearings as well. It ran through everything like a red thread, and according to the above-mentioned "legal parameters" of the People's Court, it was clear that I was going to be done away with.

The entire trial is recorded by microphone on steel tapes for the archive, so if you'd ever like to, you can have them played back to you later on. The defendant steps up to the table, along with the two policemen assigned to him, who sit down on the two chairs to the right and left; chairs were provided for Reisert and me immediately, without our asking for them. Schulze, Freisler, and rapporteur in red robes. One incident was typical: For some reason a copy of the penal code was needed because Freisler wanted to read something aloud from it. But it turned out that none could be located.

Now comes the second day. Freisler started with me. Things began in a mild tone, and quite speedily, you might even say very quickly; thank God I'm fast on my feet and I easily kept pace with Freisler, which, incidentally, we both clearly enjoyed. But if he tries that on a man who's not too quick, that man will be condemned before he realizes that Freisler has dealt with the personal data. Up to and including the discussion with Goerdeler and my position on it, everything went quite smoothly and without much ado.

Then came my objection that the police and the Abwehr had known about it, whereupon Freisler was seized with fit of rage number 1. Everything Delp had experienced up to that point was trifling by comparison. A hurricane was unleashed: He banged on the table, turned as red as his robe, and thundered, "I won't put up with that kind of talk; I won't even listen to something like that." And it went on and on in this way. Since I knew anyhow where this was heading, it was all the same to me: I gave him an icy stare, which he clearly didn't appreciate, and suddenly I couldn't help but smile. This then spread to the associate judges, sitting on Freisler's right, and to Schulze. You should have seen the look on Schulze's face. I think that if a person were to jump from the bridge over the crocodile pond at the zoo, the uproar couldn't be greater. Well, that exhausted the subject.

But then came Kreisau, and he didn't linger on the preliminaries but instead headed straight to two things: *a.* defeatism, *b.* the selection of state administrators. Both led to new fits of rage of the same quality, and when I came with the defense that all that was rooted in official business a third fit of rage ensued: "All of Adolf Hitler's agencies work on the basis of achieving victory, and the Armed Forces High Command is no different from anywhere else in that regard; I will not listen to anything of this sort, and even if this were not the case, each individual man has the duty to spread faith in victory on his own." And so on in long tirades.

Now, however, came the crux of it: "Who was there? A Jesuit priest! A Jesuit priest, of all people! A Protestant clergyman, three people who were later condemned to death for having participated in the July 20th plot! And not a single National Socialist! Not one! All I want to say to that is: Now the fig leaf is off!" "A Jesuit priest, and you discuss questions of civil disobedience with him, of all people! And you know the Jesuit provincial[5] as well! And he was also in Kreisau once! A Jesuit provincial, one of the highest officials of Germany's most dangerous enemies, he visits Count Moltke in Kreisau! And you're not ashamed of it! No German would touch a Jesuit with a ten foot pole! People who are barred from serving in the military service because of their attitude! If I know that there's a Jesuit provincial in a town, for me that's almost a reason not to go to that town at all! And the other clergyman.[6] What was he doing there? They should attend to the beyond, but leave us in peace here. And you visit bishops! What were you doing with a bishop, any bishop?

Where is your command post? Your command post is with the Führer and the National Socialist Party! That goes for you as well as for any other German, and whoever gets his orders from the guardians of the beyond, no matter how veiled these orders may be, is getting them from the enemy and will be treated accordingly!" And it went on in that vein. But delivered in a tone compared to which the earlier mad fits of rage were like the gentle rustling of a breeze.

The upshot of this hearing "against me"—because calling it "my hearing" would be ridiculous—: All of Kreisau and any conversation connected with it is preliminary planning for high treason.

Yes, of course, I have to add: After this climax, the end came in five minutes. As for the discussions in Fulda and Munich, none of that was broached at all; instead, Freisler said we could dispense with such matters, and asked, Have you anything else to say? To which I unfortunately responded after some hesitation, "No," and I was through.

Now I'll go on with my summary: If the other people whose names came up—not in the hearing, by the way, because once things were going this way, we all steered clear of naming even a single name—have not yet been arrested, perhaps it is because they are viewed as a *quantité négligeable*. But if they are arrested and have gained some sort of knowledge that goes beyond purely social conversations about these kinds of issues or that establish any connection between these issues and a possible defeat, they will have to face the death penalty. That applies mainly to Einsiedel. Carl Dietrich [von Trotha] and Peters— the whole economic component[7] didn't come up, and, for heaven's sake, there can be no mention of it—they have to stay away altogether from the following things: *a.* knowledge about Goerdeler; *b.* organized or systematic meetings; *c.* clergymen of all kinds; *d.* possibility of some part of the Reich being occupied, let alone the subject of defeat; *e.* meetings about any organizational[8] questions concerning "state administrator," "union," "map," etc.

Einsiedel has to say this: He was interested solely in the problem of a planned economy, which he defended in the face of all kinds of opposition, and he was there only in October 1942; afterward he talked to me only on occasion, in a purely social context; his trips to

Kreisau were often for the purpose of relaxation. It would be best to say that in Oct. 1942 he was also in Kreisau for two weeks of vacation, and then the others came. That has to be thought over quite carefully, because I'm afraid Maass was explicit on this point. He needs to flatly deny it all. According to the case law being applied to us, both Carl Dietrich and Einsiedel will be sentenced to death, because Carl Dietrich also knew and participated far more than Reisert. You'd better black out this paragraph quite thoroughly as soon as you've read it, because it could easily serve as evidence.

In the final analysis, this concentration on the church aspect is in accordance with the inner circumstances of the case and shows that Freisler is actually a good political judge. The enormous advantage here is that we will be killed for something that we *a.* actually did and that *b.* is worthwhile. But the idea that I would be dying as a martyr for Saint Ignatius of Loyola[9]—and that is what it amounts to in the end, because everything else was of negligible importance by comparison—is truly a joke, and I'm already trembling at the thought of Papi's paternal fury, given his anti-Catholic stance. He could endorse the rest, but this? Mami won't quite approve either.[10]

(Something else about the facts of the case just occurred to me. He asked me, "Do you understand that you are guilty?" I essentially said no, whereupon Freisler replied, "Look, if you still don't realize that, if you still need to be told so, it shows that you think differently and have thus excluded yourself from the warring national community.")

The nice part about this argument is this: We didn't want to use any force—that's established; we didn't take a single organizational step, or speak to a single man about the question of whether he would want to accept a position—that's established; the indictment reads otherwise. All we did was think—actually it was only Delp, Gersten-maier, and I; the others were regarded as hangers-on and Peter and Adam [von Trott zu Solz] as liaisons to Schulenburg, etc. And National Socialism has such a great fear of the thoughts of these three solitary men, the mere thoughts, that it wants to wipe out everything that is infected by them. How's that for a compliment. After this trial we'll be out of the Goerdeler mess, free from any practical action, we're being hanged for having thought together. Freisler is right, a thousand times right; and if we do have to die, I'm all for us dying over this issue.

I find—and now I'm coming to the practical part—that this matter, properly presented, is even a bit better than the famous Huber[11] case, because even less happened. Not even a leaflet was produced. These are just ideas without even the intention to use force. The attempts to justify our behavior that we all set forth—police know, official business, Eugen didn't understand anything, Delp always happened to be elsewhere—they have to be dropped, and Freisler rightly did so. And then one idea remains: How can Christianity be a lifeline in all this chaos? This one single idea may well claim five heads tomorrow, and later those of Steltzer and Haubach, and most likely Husen as well. But because in this trial the trio consists of Delp, Eugen, and Moltke, and the rest are involved only by way of "infection," as it includes no one who represented anything else, no one who stood for the labor movement, no one who served any worldly interest, because it has been established that I was hostile to big landowners and represented no class interests, no interests whatever of my own, not even those of my country but rather those of all mankind; because of this, Freisler unwittingly did us quite a big favor, provided that this story can be spread and used to our advantage—at home and abroad, the way I see it. This compilation of the People involved documents that it isn't plans, nor is it preparations, but rather spirit as such that is being persecuted. Long live Freisler!

It's not up to you to make use of that. Since we are to die first and foremost for St. Ignatius, his disciples ought to see to it. But you need to pass along this story to them, and it doesn't matter which of Wurm's people they bring in; Pressel is probably the best. I'll discuss that with Poelchau tomorrow. If it comes out that you received and passed along this letter, you will be killed as well. Tattenbach[12] clearly has to take that upon himself and say, if need be, that he got it from Delp with the last laundry. Do not let the original out of your hands; use only a copy, which has to be translated immediately to make it appear that it could come from Delp writing in the first person.

So, that's it for this part; the rest will come separately. J.

Clearly Konrad [von Preysing], Dietz, and Faulhaber, and probably Wienken have to be informed. But leave that to others. Matters of this nature aren't your business. If they're not totally frightened, they should be able to capitalize on our death.

1. See Appendix: Additional Documents. 2. Throughout this letter "Kreisau" refers to the three meetings the group held there in 1942 and '43 rather than the Moltke home. 3. Juan de Mariana, a seventeenth-century Spanish Jesuit who defended tyrannicide. 4. He is presumably referring to participants in the bomb plot: the counts Stauffenberg, Yorck, Schulenburg, and Schwerin among others. 5. Father Augustin Rösch. 6. Eugen Gerstenmaier. 7. None of the Kreisau Circle involved with constitutional or economic issues were arrested. 8. The Nazis were aware of the maps and leaders envisaged by the Kreisau Circle. 9. The founder of the Jesuit order in the sixteenth century. 10. Helmuth's parents had become Christian Scientists, a religious belief that stood in opposition to the Catholic Church. 11. The reference is to Kurt Huber, who was involved in writing the flyers for the Weisse Rose resistance group that were distributed by, among others, the brother and sister Hans and Sophie Scholl. All were executed for this act in 1943; see Editors' Introduction. 12. The Jesuit priest Count von Tattenbach, who kept in touch with Father Delp in Tegel.

HELMUTH JAMES TO FREYA, JANUARY 10–11, 1945

Tegel, 10 Jan 45

My dear love, I have to start by saying that the final twenty-four hours of a life are quite obviously no different from any others. I had always imagined one would experience this only as frightful, that one would say to oneself: Now the sun is setting for the last time for you, now the clock will get to 12 only twice more, now you're going to bed for the last time. That's not the way it is at all. Maybe I'm a bit giddy, for there's no denying that I'm in positively high spirits. I only beg the Lord in heaven that He would keep me like this, as it is surely easier for the flesh to die this way. How merciful the Lord has been to me! Even at the risk of sounding hysterical: I am filled only with gratitude, with no real place for anything else. He has guided me so firmly and clearly these two days: the entire room could have roared like Herr Freisler, and all the walls could have shaken, and it wouldn't have made the slightest difference to me; it truly was like Isaiah 43:2: "When thou passest through the waters, I *will be* with thee; and through the rivers, they shall not overflow thee: when thou walkest through the fire, thou shalt not be burned; neither shall the flame kindle upon thee."—Your soul, that is. When I was called up to make my closing statement, I almost felt like saying that I have only one thing to state in my defense: "And though they take our life, / Goods, honor, children, wife, / Yet is their profit small, / These things shall vanish all, / The city of God remaineth."[1] But that would have done damage to the others, so all I said was: I don't intend to say anything else, Herr President.

There is still a hard road ahead of me, and I can only pray that the Lord will go on being as gracious to me as He has been. For this evening, Eugen [Gerstenmaier] had written down for us: Matthew 14:22–33. [Marginal note: I've just seen that it was Luke 5:1–11 yesterday.] He'd had another meaning in mind; but it remains true that for me this was a day of landing a bountiful catch of fish and that tonight I'm justified in saying: "Depart from me; for I am a sinful man, O Lord." And what was that lovely thing we read yesterday, my love: "But we have this treasure in earthen vessels, that the excellency of the power may be of God, and not of us. We are troubled on every side, yet not distressed; we are perplexed, but not in despair; Persecuted, but not forsaken; cast down, but not destroyed; Always bearing about in the body the dying of the Lord Jesus, that the life also of Jesus might be made manifest in our body."[2] Thanks be, my love, above all to the Lord, thanks, my love, for your intercessions, thanks to all the others who prayed for us and for me. Your husband, your weak, cowardly, "complicated," very average husband, was allowed to experience all this. If I were now to be saved—which, by God, is neither more likely nor less likely than a week ago—the demonstration of God's presence and omnipotence was so colossal that I must say that I would have to get my bearings all over again. He can demonstrate this presence to us, quite unmistakably, when He does precisely what doesn't suit us. Anything else is nonsense.

So this is all I can say to you, my dear love: May God be as merciful to you as to me, and then even a dead husband won't matter at all. He can demonstrate His omnipotence even while you make pancakes for our sons or clean up their messes, although I hope that's a thing of the past. I probably ought to say farewell to you—but I can't; I probably ought to bewail and bemoan what you have to go through every day—but I can't; I probably ought to think of the burdens that will now fall to you—but I can't. I can tell you only one thing: If you get the feeling of absolute security, if the Lord bestows on you something you would not have without this time and its conclusion, I leave you a treasure that cannot be confiscated, one far weightier than even my life. These Romans, these pathetic creatures of Schulze and Freisler and everyone in that bunch: they wouldn't even be able to grasp how little they can take away!

I'll go on writing tomorrow, but since one never knows what will happen, I wanted this letter to touch on every topic. Of course I don't know if I'm going to be executed tomorrow. It may be that I'll be interrogated again, or beaten, or stowed away. Please keep making your presence known; maybe that will discourage them from beating me up too badly. Even though I know, after today's outcome, that God can even turn these beatings into nothing at all, even if every one of the bones in my body is broken before I'm hanged, and even if I have no fear of it at the moment, I'd still rather avoid that.—So, good night, be confident and undaunted. J.

Hercher, who is a nice man, was somewhat shocked by my good mood, which goes to show you that it couldn't be suppressed.

11 Jan 1945

My dear, I just feel like chatting with you a bit. I don't actually have anything to say. We've discussed the material consequences in detail. You will manage somehow to make your way through, and if someone else takes over Kreisau, you'll cope with that too. Just don't let anything trouble you. It really isn't worth it. I'm definitely in favor of your making sure that the Russians are informed of my death. Maybe that will enable you to stay in Kreisau. Moving about in what is left of Germany is hideous in any case. If, against all odds, the Third Reich does endure, which I cannot imagine in my wildest fantasies, you'll have to find a way to keep the poison away from the little sons. Of course I have nothing against your leaving Germany if it comes to that. Do what you think right, and don't consider yourself bound one way or another by any wish of mine. I've told you again and again: A dead man cannot rule.—But you needn't have financial worries. So long as the Deichmann house pays and so long as you maintain the Kreisau mortgage—but you must remain adamant that it was acquired with your money, partly as an inheritance from Grandmother Schnitzler, partly as a gift from Aunt Emma (Wodan)[3]—then you will always have enough to live on, and even if both don't work out, there will be enough people to help you.

I think with unadulterated joy of you and our sons, of Kreisau and all the people there; our parting doesn't seem the least bit grim at the moment. Maybe that is still to come. But at this moment it isn't a burden to me. It doesn't feel as though we're parting at all. I don't know how this can be. But there is not a hint of the feeling that came over me so powerfully after your first visit in October: no, it was probably November.[4] Now my inner voice is telling me: *a.* God can lead me back there today just as well as yesterday, and *b.* if He calls me to Him, I'll take it with me. I don't have the feeling that sometimes used to come over me: Oh, just one more time I'd like to see it all again. Still, I don't feel the least bit "otherworldly." You can see that I am happily chatting with you instead of turning to the good Lord. There is a hymn—208, 4—that says, "for he to die is ready who living clings to Thee." That is exactly the way I feel. Because I am alive today, living I must cling to Him; He wants no more of me. Is that pharisaical? I don't know. But I believe I know that I live only in His grace and forgiveness, and have nothing on my own, nor can I do anything on my own.

I'm rambling on, my love, just as things come to mind, so here is something entirely different. In the final analysis, the trial's dramatic

element was this: In the trial all concrete accusations proved untenable, so they were scrapped. Nothing remained of them. But what
triggered fear on the part of the Third Reich in putting to death five
people—in the end it will be seven people—is ultimately no more
than this: A private individual, namely your husband, is known to
have discussed things "that are the exclusive purview of the Führer"
with two clergymen of both denominations, with a Jesuit provincial,
and with several bishops, *without the intention of doing anything concrete*,
as has been established. The discussion was not about organizational
issues or the composition of the Reich—all those topics fell away in
the course of the trial, as Schulze said explicitly in his prosecutorial
statement ("differs completely from all other cases, because there was
no mention of any violence or any organization");[5] instead, issues
concerning the practical and ethical demands of Christianity were
explored. Nothing else; that is the sole reason we are being convicted.
Freisler declared to me in one of his tirades, "There is only one way
in which Christianity and we are alike: We demand the entire person!"
I don't know if people sitting near us caught all that, because it was
a kind of dialogue—a spiritual one between Freisler and me, for I
could not utter many words—in which we came to know each other
through and through. Freisler was the only one in the whole gang
who got to know me, and of the whole gang, he is the only one who
knows why he has to kill me. There was nothing about a "complicated
man" or "complicated ideas" or "ideology"; just: "The fig leaf is off."
But only for Herr Freisler. We were talking, you might say, in a
vacuum. He didn't make a single joke at my expense, as he had with
Delp and Eugen. No, he was dead serious: "Who do you take your
orders from? From the Beyond or from Adolf Hitler?" "Who commands your loyalty and your faith?" All rhetorical questions, of
course.—At any rate, Freisler is the first National Socialist to have
grasped who I am, and the good Müller is a simpleton by comparison.

My love, your very dear letter has just arrived, the first letter, my
love, in which you didn't grasp my mood and my situation.[6] No, I'm
not preoccupied in the slightest with the good Lord or with my death.
He has the inexpressible grace to come to me and preoccupy Himself

with me. Is that arrogant of me? Perhaps. But this evening He will forgive me for so much that in the end I can finally ask Him for forgiveness for this last bit of haughtiness as well, though I do hope that it's not haughty, because I'm not extolling the earthen vessel, no, I'm extolling the precious treasure that has made use of this earthen vessel, this utterly unworthy abode. No, my dear, I'm reading the very same passages of the Bible I would have read today if there had been no trial, namely: Joshua 19–21, Job 10–12, Ezekiel 34–36, Mark 13–15, and all the way through our 2nd Epistle to the Corinthians, as well as the brief passages I wrote down on that slip of paper for you. So far I've only read Joshua and our passage from Corinthians, which closes with the beautiful saying, so familiar to us from childhood: "The grace of our Lord Jesus Christ and the love of God and the fellowship of the Holy Spirit be with you all. Amen." I feel, my love, as though I've been authorized to say it to you and the little sons with absolute authority. Don't I have every right to read the 118th Psalm, which was set for this morning? Even though Eugen had it in mind for a different situation, it has become much truer than we ever would have thought possible.

This is why, my love, you'll be getting back your letter in spite of your request. I'll carry you across with me and have no need for a sign, a symbol, anything. It's not even that I was promised I wouldn't lose you; no, it's much more: I know it.

A long pause, during which Buchholz was here and I was shaved; I also drank coffee and ate cake and rolls. Now I'll go on chatting. The decisive statement in those proceedings was: "Count, the thing that Christianity and we National Socialists have in common—and this is the only thing—we demand the entirety of a person." Did he realize what he was saying? Just think about how wonderfully God prepared this, His unworthy vessel: At the very moment when there was danger of my being drawn into active preparations for a putsch—Stauffenberg came to Peter [Yorck] on the evening of the 19th[7]—I was pulled away, and thus I am, and remain, free of any connection to the use of violence. Then He planted in me the socialist leanings that free me, as an owner of a large estate, from any suspicion of representing special interests. Then He humbled me more than I've ever been humbled, which made me lose all my pride, which finally made me understand my sinfulness after thirty-eight years, which made me beg for His forgiveness, made me learn to trust in His mercy. Then He has me come here, so that I can see you standing firm and be free of thoughts of you and the little sons, i.e., free of anxious thoughts; He gives me the time and the opportunity to arrange what can be arranged, so that all earthly thoughts can fall away. Then He makes me feel the pain of parting and the dread of death and the fear of hell to their utmost depth[8] to get that over with as well. Then He endows me with faith, hope, and love, with a wealth of these things that is truly lavish. Then He has me talk and clarify things with Eugen and Delp. Then He lets Rösch and König escape, so that there aren't enough men for a Jesuit trial and at the last moment Delp is added on with us. Then He gets Haubach's and Steltzer's cases, which would have brought in unrelated issues,[9] detached from ours, and in the end, essentially puts only Eugen, Delp, and me together, and then He gives Eugen and Delp—using the hope, the human hope they have—the weakness that leads to their cases being deemed only secondary and thereby takes out the factor of religion, and then your husband, as a Protestant, is chosen to be attacked and condemned on the primary basis of his friendship with Catholics, and in this way he stands before Freisler not as a Protestant, not as the owner of a large estate, not as a nobleman, not as a Prussian, not as a German—all that is explicitly excluded in the trial, in the words of Sperr, for example: "I thought: What an astonishing Prussian"—but as a Christian and absolutely nothing else. "The fig leaf is off," says Herr Freisler. Yes, any other category has been removed—"a man who must naturally be rejected by his peers," says Schulze. What a mighty task your husband has been chosen for: all the trouble that the Lord took with him, the infinite detours, the elaborate zigzag curves, are suddenly explained in one hour on January 10, 1945. Everything takes on a previously hidden meaning after the fact. Mami and Papi, the brothers and the sister, the little sons, Kreisau and its problems, the work camps[10] and not flying flags[11] and not belonging to the party or its divisions, Curtis and the trips to England,[12] Adam [von Trott zu Solz] and Peter and

Carlo [Mierendorff]: all this has finally become comprehensible in this one hour. The Lord went to such lengths for this one hour.

And now, my love, I come to you. I haven't listed you anywhere, because you, my love, are in an entirely different place from all the others. You're not a means God used to make me who I am; it's more as though you *are* me. You are my 13th chapter of 1 Corinthians. Without this chapter, no human being is a human. Without you I would have accepted love as a gift, the way I did from Mami, for example, gratefully, happily, the way one is grateful for the sun that provides warmth. But without you, my love, I would have "had not love." It's not that I'm saying I love you; that's not right at all. It's more as though you're the part of me that I would lack on my own. It is good that I lack it; because if I had this greatest of all gifts, the way you do, my dear love, there are many things I couldn't have done, I would have found it impossible to stay so persistent, I couldn't have watched the suffering I had to see in the way I did, and much else. Only together do we add up to one person. As I wrote a few days ago in symbolic terms, we are a single idea of divine creation. That is true, literally true. This is why, my love, I am also certain that you will not lose me on this earth, not for a moment. And we were also finally able to symbolize this fact by our shared Holy Communion, which was now my final one.

I was just weeping a little, not in sadness or melancholy, not because I want to go back, no, the weeping stems from my gratitude and emotion as I encounter this proof of God's existence. It is not given to us to see Him face-to-face, but we find that we are deeply shaken when we suddenly realize that He has been moving before us throughout our lives, as a cloud by day and as a pillar of fire by night, and that He permits us to see it all at once, in the blink of an eye. Now nothing more can happen.

My love, this past week—yesterday in particular—must have rendered some of my farewell letters outdated. They'll read like yesterday's news by comparison. I'll leave it to you whether you want to send them off nevertheless, or whether you'd want to say or write anything in addition. Of course I hope that the little sons will understand this letter someday; but I know that it's a matter of grace and not of some sort of external influence.—Of course you should send my regards to everyone, even people like Oxé and Frl. Thiel and Frau Tharant. If you'd find it difficult to call them, leave it alone; it makes no difference. I'm naming them only because they are the outermost, the most extreme cases. Since God has the incredible grace to reside within me, I can take with me not only you and the little sons but all those I love and a multitude of others who are far more distant from me. You can tell them that.

One more thing: In many aspects, this letter is also an extension of the report I wrote yesterday, which is much more matter-of-fact. You need to combine them to craft a legend, but it has to be written as though Delp had told it about me. I have to stay the main character in it, not because I am or want to be but because the story would otherwise lack its center. I'm simply the vessel for which the Lord has gone to infinite lengths.

My love, my life is completed, and I can say of myself: He died in the fullness of years and full of what life had to offer. That doesn't change the fact that I would gladly go on living, that I would gladly accompany you a bit further on this earth. But then I would need a new task from God. The task for which God made me is done. If He wishes to assign me another task, we will learn about it. So do make every effort to save my life if I should survive this day. Perhaps there will be another task.

I'll stop, as there is nothing more to say, nor have I named anyone for you to greet and embrace; you know yourself who is meant in the tasks I have for you. All the sayings we love are in my heart and in your heart. But in closing, I will tell you this, by virtue of the treasure that has spoken from me and has filled this humble earthen vessel: May the grace of our Lord, Jesus Christ, and the love of God and the fellowship of the Holy Spirit be with all of you. Amen.

J.

1. Hymn 90, "Ein feste Burg," by Martin Luther, translated by Thomas Carlyle as "A Mighty Fortress Is Our God," and reprinted in George Alexander

Kohut, *A Hebrew Anthology* (Cincinnati, OH: S. Bacharach, 1913), 320. 2. 2 Corinthians 4:7–10. 3. Freya had provided a mortgage on the Kreisau estate out of funds originating from her maternal grandmother, Fanny von Schnitzler, and her aunt Emma Schroeder (née Deichmann). 4. See Helmuth's letter of November 14, 1944. 5. The prosecution was not aware that the Kreisau Circle had agreed on a structure for a new Germany in writing and hidden the documents from the Gestapo. 6. This letter from Freya, apparently written on January 9 or 10, 1945, seems to be missing. As we see from the following letter she had struggled mightily while the trial was proceeding, finally regaining her footing. 7. The date of his arrest, January 19, 1944. 8. See Helmuth's letter of December 31, 1944. 9. Issues pertaining to labor and unions. 10. See Biographical Note. 11. Because Zeumer, the overseer of the estate, attached a swastika flag to his building, the Moltkes were able to avoid displaying their own. 12. See Biographical Note.

FREYA TO HELMUTH JAMES, JANUARY 11–12, 1945

Thursday evening

My love, you're still alive: how wonderful! Schulze also told Hercher that executions are not being carried out so quickly now. I am deeply happy that I still have you with me. I also enjoyed the report and letter to the fullest at noon, even before I knew that you would still be alive in the evening. These were terribly stressful days, but at all times I was sure that you were in the sun of divine grace, and was unconcerned and so grateful that you were always in Tegel. There are many things to be grateful for—and I was, but even so, it was the most strenuous thing I've ever experienced. Slowly and deliberately, I should be parting from my closeness to you, step by step, oh God, it is terribly difficult, and even if it happens peaceably and with God, even then, even then, even then—it is very difficult to endure, in spite of all the help and all the solace and all the love and all the goodness.

Now I can fight for you once again, once again a delay that we can use to our advantage. Poelchau doesn't think that it will lead to anything, and it's stressful for you to begin anew yet again, but I'm grateful and happy that I can start over.

But now I'm tired and will sleep close by to you and go to see Carl Dietrich [von Trotha] tomorrow morning. Carl Viggo [von Moltke] is already there. Jowo [von Moltke] is coming on Saturday. I'd like to unleash Carl Viggo on Thierack. Steengracht will go to see Kaltenbrunner as soon as Kaltenbrunner gets back, and I'll try to reach out to Müller. I want to pay some visits to Schulze again as well.

I'm very happy with what you write; yes, I'm delighted that you will be dying *properly* and not for Goerdeler. It's dramatic to read! I thought, though, that your mood would be a different one, and was so pleased to discover how much unholier, how natural, how smiling it was. I'm too tired now, otherwise I'd write more about that, poor clod of earth that I am. Oh, my Jäm, today I was keenly aware of my very profound, great weakness, of my wretchedness, of my puniness. Then I gave up thinking that way and turned to the image of the iron particles moved by the magnet, and I felt fine. Shortly after that, your letter arrived. I had to spend the whole morning struggling to keep my composure and wanted *only* to be with you, wanted to, wanted to, wanted to, and couldn't, until I no longer wanted to, and then it was better. I simply couldn't just think of you, although I profoundly wished to do so. Yesterday and the day before yesterday I was quite quiet and calm, but today I was full of tears.

Now good night, my dear love! Once again, good night, good night! You're still part of this world, to which the miserable wretch that I am belongs. [Your] P. embraces you.

Good morning, I can now say, my dear love, good morning, here with me!

[The final words are illegible.]

HELMUTH JAMES TO FREYA, JANUARY 12, 1945

Tegel, 12 Jan 45

My dear, a letter once again. God's grace is so evident with both of us that it almost wouldn't come as a surprise to me if my course to

Plötzensee were to be freed of any creaturely fear or if I were to remain alive altogether. Truly, everything is possible for Him. You can hardly imagine my relief yesterday when Eugen [Gerstenmaier] got off with seven years in prison and Reisert with five. I couldn't hold myself back from turning around to look at Eugen, but I think he didn't notice because he was totally lost in thought. In addition it was, of course, a special gift for me that Kreisau is not being seized. That means that my last will and testament will be enforced, according to which Casparchen gets it and you have it as a provisional heir until he turns 25. So there can't be any family trouble.

The formal judgment gave no indication of the real debate that took place between Freisler and me. The judgment[1] didn't give even a hint of it. Needless to say, doing so would have been foolish from Freisler's standpoint. Of course it would have been even better if it had been included in the court's written decision, but that simply wasn't the case.—Eugen was sentenced to prison on the grounds that he was "a political numskull, a church bureaucrat, and far from very bright as well." "Seven years' prison" would, "it is hoped, make him reeducate his thinking" and become "a proper fellow."[2] It's good that the real debate was only between Freisler and me; otherwise Eugen would never have been able to keep on this mask. Freisler talked to me about Christianity and the church, not to Eugen, whose domain that actually is.

It grew too late for our execution the very same day because the delivery of the judgment ended at about 5:15. Hercher said to me, You're with Kaltenbrunner. Now, God willing, I'll stay alive, and I'm all set for that. But I basically assume that we, Delp and I, will be taken away today. Still, we'll find out all about that. If I'm not taken away today, you know that I'll need clothing: one shirt, one pair of pajamas, two handkerchiefs, and maybe also one pair of underpants [marginal note: also 1 pair of socks] and soap. If there should be any more serious deliberations about the issue of clemency, I could actually exchange my nice suit for a bad one and my overcoat for the blue trench coat with the camel hair lining. After all, the nice suit was only for the trial, and you can leave it in Berlin so I can put it on in case

I'm hauled in front of some bigwig. But all that applies only to the extremely unlikely case that I am not put to death today or tomorrow.

Incidentally, Reisert has been sentenced to five years for failing to report my actions, even though he didn't know, and couldn't know, that anyone else was involved, and even though it was certain that he was not questioned by me about state administrators. So this is a sign of what would await Carl Dietrich [von Trotha] and Einsiedel if they were indicted.—I am simply overjoyed about Eugen. After all, I've always taken the view that it is possible that he received a real divine promise for himself. The only thing I always disputed, with him and Delp, was that one could obtain a divine promise of this kind by sheer stubbornness. Eugen was quite upset, far more than Delp and I.

I'm in shackles again. I'm also doing much better, almost well, so I don't want to pester the nasty doctor again, but rather just stay in shackles. It's only for a few days, and if it should go on longer, well, then I'll endure that, too, although that's already far too big a word.

As long as I stay in my current condition, that is, as long as God has the ineffable grace to let me know at all times that He is looking after me, nothing bad can happen to me, absolutely nothing. That is what I have to pray and beg for.

Today we'll start the Epistle to the Galatians, my love. I have nothing more to write than the same thing again and again, my dear, my love. How many final letters have I written you already? Well, here's yet another one. But it is in God's hands whether this is actually the last, and we have every right to say:

"My times are in Thy hand."

"Deliver me from the hand of mine enemies, and from them that persecute me."

J.

---

1. See Appendix: Additional Documents. 2. Playing dumb was Gerstenmaier's strategy. It is believed that Freisler was also influenced by pressure from unknown persons to spare Gerstenmaier, who was directly implicated in the plot of July 20.

HELMUTH JAMES TO FREYA, JANUARY 12–13, 1945

Tegel, 12 Jan 45

My love, a leaden weariness came over me now at 3:30, and I'll be happy to go to bed at 6. The constant high over the course of three days has worn me out, particularly as I've been sleeping only with the help of pills for three nights because I kept drinking coffee all day long, and eating caffeine and coffee beans, so I didn't even try to sleep without pills but rather always took one when I went to bed. Now I'm yearning for a long uninterrupted night.

My poor dear, your letter of last night and this morning shows me how exhausting all this has been for you. It's much harder to look on than to be affected directly. Now, I hope, you're past that. The trial is over, and so I can calmly think about the issue of clemency and help you with it. Now I'll begin to write down everything that crosses my mind.

1. Carl Viggo [von Moltke] and Jowo [von Moltke] should see whether they can get a face-to-face meeting for me—no, with me—that does not include witnesses, in order to discuss the issue of clemency. Maybe that will be authorized for Carl Viggo in his capacity as head of the district court.

2. The fact that a seizure of assets has not been mentioned is a favorable indication, because that was proposed, and Hercher had also expected it to be a matter of course. I can't imagine that Freisler would simply have forgotten to announce that, so I consider this a certainty.—If I'm killed, my will can take effect.

3. The verdict rests on two claims: *a*. that I didn't report my discussion with Beck–Goerdeler in January '43, *b*. that I myself engaged in high treason.

4. For *a*. The verdict doesn't yield any substantial factor for the clemency process. But there is this, from the proceedings:
I have believed all along, and continue to believe, that the police and the Abwehr knew about Goerdeler, especially because my news came from them. I previously communicated that in

a written document, and I informed the Gestapo about it again. The Gestapo told Hercher in an official capacity before the beginning of the trial that it did not want its knowledge to be a subject of discussion. Consequently, during the trial I began to speak only about the knowledge on the part of the Abwehr. Freisler did not permit that to be mentioned in the trial and cut me off from using this defense. That the Abwehr did know, however, is indicated by the execution of Hansen (head of Abwehr I), which has already taken place, and the arrest of Canaris, Oster, etc., whom I saw in prison.

During the trial it was established that I stood up to Goerdeler in very harsh terms, and constantly warned all my friends not to get involved with him; no, it was more than that, not to get involved with any meetings that aimed to overthrow the government.

5. For *b.* the following was determined at the trial: After very general, basic discussions of the question of how, in the case of enemy occupation of parts of the country or of the Reich as a whole, resistance could be organized and sustained, I said that one ought to think about what kind of men might be worth considering for a task of this sort in the individual regions, and as far as I was concerned, I regarded Lukaschek as a suitable person. It has been determined beyond any doubt that I never spoke to anyone—not even Lukaschek—about whether he wanted to become a state administrator. And there was not even a single word—in the verdict there is not a hint of it—about my having had thoughts of a new central government.

6. If I paid close enough attention, there was no mention of my aiding the enemy, which in other instances is always assumed to be the case.

7. The verdict made it quite clear that I am not a reactionary in the sense that we understand the term. But "a reactionary is anyone who wants something other than the National Socialism" (Freisler at the trial).

8. Schulze's closing argument and the opinion of the court state

quite clearly: Essentially this case has nothing to do with the July 20th plot, and it was pure coincidence that they were adjoined. Indeed, Schulze said: This case differs from all the others that have some connection to the July 20th plot.

9. The tone of the opinion of the court reveals a degree of sympathy, and its final sentence, pertaining to me—"that is why he wanted to get himself into a position of power"—came out of the blue and deviated from the text as a whole.

10. The issue of defeatism was not the subject of the trial. Maybe what I had prepared for the oral trial needs to be said at the clemency proceedings. You know my statement about the war situation from the December 8th pleading.

11. All in all: this is, so to speak, a death sentence with a C-. One of the major reasons I went along with Freisler's wish to skip over my entire defense in the form of a written document—apart from what I wrote yesterday, that I didn't want to overshadow the clear line of questioning and the decision: "we both demand the entirety of a person"—was that in view of his clear determination to arrive at a death sentence, I would only have forced him to bring in additional material and provide far more compelling grounds for the verdict and thus to preclude my introducing these arguments in the clemency proceedings.

12. Under this set of circumstances we need to check on:
    a. whether I can speak to Carl Viggo so that he can bring up these things; or
    b. whether I myself should write a petition for clemency, and to whom.

That is everything I can think of in the matter of clemency. I'm too tired for anything else. It's about time for supper, and then I'll go to bed. Good night, my love, sleep well. J.

13 Jan 45

Good morning, my dear love. I slept a good long time. Since I started at 6, I lay awake for a while toward morning. That was to be expected.

But now I'm refreshed and can devote myself more tenderly to your grief than I could in the last few letters, when I was too overwhelmed with factual matters.

Yes, my love, it is sad that I'll be killed, far, far sadder for you than for me. We don't want to minimize that, and I don't want to minimize it. It is absolutely no consolation for your pain to know that for me neither death nor dying nor the pain of parting will be difficult if the Lord remains with me as He does now. Quite the opposite, in fact. If you had to tend to my anxiety and my fear as exhaustively as you have over the past few months, your grief might appear more minimal to you, whereas you can now succumb to it fully. You wrote me about your terrible Thursday, that you couldn't find me when you searched for me with all your strength, and that you weren't able to do so until you gave up the struggle. That is likely to be the right path. Once I have left this world, all your mortal qualities, all your mortal powers and abilities would not be able to work their magic to bring me back to you. They would yield no more than dreams or delusions. You'll be able to find me only in the Lord. That's where I'll be, and I'll want to beckon to you and call you and go to any lengths to have you find me there and to ensure that He holds His hand over you so that you'll find me there. But I won't be anywhere else from then on. And this will become quite clear at the time of my death, after which my ashes will be scattered to the winds:[1] No grave, no slab, no part of my mortal remains will leave a trace behind for you; instead, I'll be able to be found only with the Lord, and with Him I'll be exactly as close to you afterward as I am to you now.—And in order not just to grasp that but to know it for a certainty, we need His grace, which cannot be wrested from Him. We can only pray for Him to bestow it upon us, and He will surely bestow it upon you when heeding your prayer and mine just as He has bestowed it upon me and continues to bestow it anew every second. For it's not as though this is a possession that can be held and carried around; it has to be bestowed anew every second. In the words of Paul: "Be not highminded, but fear!",[2] namely when grace is bestowed upon us.—That has absolutely nothing to do with a clod of earth. We're all, equally, clods of earth or earthen vessels; we're all equally unworthy of His grace; we're all equally lesser beings; any differences there may be between the earthen vessels are so utterly insignificant in proportion to His grace, to the treasure He may—that is, if He wishes to—pour into these earthen vessels that they don't exist. There is no difference between the executioner, Herr Freisler, Adolf Hitler, a murderous robber, Poelchau, Eugen [Gerstenmaier], Delp, and me that could in the eyes of God provide a reason to bestow His grace on one of these and not on another.

And on that note, I'm coming to the end of this part: For you there will be no earthly solace for my death. Anything one can say to that effect doesn't seriously hold up, and ultimately comes down to this: It will be forgotten. And that's exactly what should not happen, because it needs to bear fruit.—There is also a mystical solace, which can preserve the feeling of an inner bond. I think Marion [Yorck] has that—in any case, she has a penchant for mysticism.—But that is nothing for you, my love. You can do only one thing: Keep up your humble prayers that the Lord fills you with His grace, that He, as it says in John—I think 14—comes unto you and makes his abode with you. And then, my dear, you will find me there as well. You know that I am already ceaselessly praying to the Lord today for that and I will continue to do so, and why shouldn't we believe that He will heed these prayers? It is crucial for us to believe this, and this very belief is one of the prerequisites for Him to come.

But enough of that. I, in any event, am against "composure." Grief is grief and pain is pain, and we needn't feel ashamed of feeling either of them. Composure can easily harden the heart, and for you that would be utterly impossible. You must never think that you "owe me good composure." That is of no consequence.

This may all sound very pharisaical. My love, I truly don't want to be pharisaical with you; my heart bleeds together with yours, and if I may say some things in a way that is colder, more matter-of-fact, cooler, less humane than I should, you must forgive me. I wrote you the day before yesterday that I carry chapter 13 of 1 Corinthians inside me through you, my love, through you, and not from myself. Farewell, my dear, I embrace you.

May the Lord watch over you and us.

J.

1. In August 1944, Himmler had given the order to burn the corpses of the executed and scatter their ashes on sewage fields in Berlin. 2. Romans 11:20.

FREYA TO HELMUTH JAMES, JANUARY 13, 1945

Saturday morning

My dearest, today I have to write about myself in detail again, if I can, because just as I am able to experience everything alongside you, you also have to experience it alongside me. You, my love, have stood completely in the light. Thank God things were the way they ought to be with you, my dear, very blessed and very beautiful, but I didn't help you with that, even though I wanted to so badly. All this is very difficult to describe, because it isn't clear enough to me for me to be able to describe it. I just have the distinct feeling that I didn't do it right, that the peace during those three days wasn't peace from the dear Lord, no matter how hard I tried. I spent every day, from morning to night, trying to be there with Him and for you, and all the effort we went to with all our beautiful texts, with all our precious experiences, has come to naught. People didn't notice this on the outside, nor did I notice it myself; I don't even know if Harald [Poelchau], for example, has picked up on it. But at midday on Thursday, when, in spite of it all, I was right up against my physical limits—in every way—and realized that I couldn't manage to accompany you in my thoughts all the way to your death, yet wanted to so much, again and again, your letter arrived, and I saw that I'd done it wrong; it was quite clear that my letter couldn't touch your heart, or—how should I put this—missed the mark, because I myself was off the mark. Then I grew quite small and poor, shattered and wretched, unlike any other time in my life, so small, so miserable—yet there you were, alive—what good fortune! All the activity with Carl Viggo [von Moltke] overshadowed that feeling during the day, but I was well aware of my puniness. By 5 I was here again, shattered in body and soul, and as I was lying alone on my sofa here, feeling totally exhausted, I suddenly knew the right way to go about it, and now I think I know it through and through, even though I tremble at this certainty, as you did about yours back in November,[1] and even though I don't yet dare bestir myself and am still walking carefully and as if in a new way. When I came out of my room this morning and Dorothee [Poelchau] saw me, she happily declared: Today you look altogether different again! That is true. How can I describe it. The difference between life before and life after death is truly not big, and even the step that seems so huge to us is small and so much more natural than we think. Now you're still living with me, and one day you will suddenly go on living—no longer with me but only inside me,[2] and in a different way—perhaps you will continue to live on next to us, but it is actually not so important what happens, whether you are killed or you remain alive, because what *is* important will remain, so I needn't think and wish to be there, but instead live our life, which is why *I* needn't seek to capture my closeness to you and to God from the precious books or through constant entreaties and prayers; instead, I have to live on serenely, in a self-evident, quotidian, and natural way, with my great love for you. Then He will be with me, for He has often, in fact mostly, been with me without my realizing it, but then I will also be with you, as I have always been. My love, my intercession for you is not my prayer, it's my life, my being, my existence, my belonging-to-you in life, wherever life is lived. This has now become quite apparent to me, even though my whole life and every word I have directed at you over these past few months perhaps already showed you this, and it may have been completely clear to *you*. You are quite right, the omnipotence of God is demonstrated in my case precisely when I make pancakes for the little sons, precisely then. I know exactly how much He has blessed me in everything, including the gifts that are so well suited to this life, but now He also wants me to complete myself for Him and you in this way. That is why it was wrong and pretentious and arrogant to want to seize Him for your sake by force, you had no need of that since He lets my heart beat for you anyway, and it has been beating, but whatever else I've done beyond that was nonsense—and you didn't die; instead, you are alive, still living here with me. We should no longer think about what is coming; at least I shouldn't. I feel my love and my closeness to you and when you're dead, it will stay that way. Whether you die or whether you live, which I, just like you, consider equally possible, just as before, that would be good, but in neither case does much change. During these past months I've certainly come to understand all that already. That is why I was doing so well, as all this has become so clear to us as a result of divine providence, but over these past three days I've also lived it. How should I describe that? Do you understand me well? In spite of my inept description? As I live, I live in Him and for you. That is all I need to do. I will do that in the future, for Him and for you, whether you are alive or over there. Maybe you'll be dead someday, maybe in two weeks, maybe in two years, maybe in twenty years, I now know that that doesn't make much of a difference, no, I always knew that, but I have now experienced that it isn't my task to trace this step in my thoughts but rather to be there in my life. I will do that, and that is what I am, my dear. Then it's actually not at all difficult. The enormous burden of these three days showed me that what I was doing was not right. When it's right, it is far more natural, far more tolerable, not as imposing, and this is how it will be, too, when I die. God requires of me only that I be devoted to Him, to you, and to many other people, and He will ordain all else in such a way that it is right and tolerable for me. You've seen for yourself the ease with which I've come through this year; that is how it should be, and that is how I will now also experience your death when it comes, and all that is only thanks to the kindness and help and grace He bestows on me without my having to ask for it. Along with you, I am His child, my heart is truly quite simple in that regard, and He wants to preserve me in this and possibly free me from any desire to tackle everything I have no need to tackle.—I will therefore now continue to live quietly, here and in Kreisau, day in and day out, and of course with you.—All this may strike you as nothing new, as something we both already knew quite well, but I have gained some added degree of certainty, which is why I had to report this to you as well as I could. Did you understand that, my dear! From now on no letter from me will be the last one, because I've already written all the last letters, and yet I may still be writing—just as God wills—many more letters.—So, all of that was about me, but everything that is about me is also about you!

Now a few things about the activities. Carl Viggo has now gone to see Hercher and Lautz: Hercher, in order to know more about the case, and Lautz, to discuss the prospects for clemency. Schulze was in court. I'll go to see him again. Lautz, I'm told, was very standoffish at first, but eventually he really warmed up. Carl Viggo clearly went to great lengths and invested enormous effort. He talked about you, about Mami and Daddy, about me, and fervently on your behalf. He says that Lautz was fully engaged and even convinced him to stay longer, but didn't give him much cause for hope. He told him: If some external action occurs, then something will happen immediately, but the minister of justice will do nothing of his own accord, and there's no use in paying him a visit. So essentially it comes down to Kaltenbrunner, Müller, and Himmler, as we already know. Steengracht has promised me to go see Kaltenbrunner right away once he's back, which ought to be soon. Müller won't be back here until Monday or Tuesday either. I've tried to speak to him and only ran into Huppenkothen who has now become "staff leader." But he had nothing to say, of course. I naturally assume that Müller will grant me a meeting soon, in accordance with his promise—that will then be the last thing I can do, unless you give me some other new task, my dear love.—What do you think about a face-to-face meeting? Do you want to see me? Are you inclined to meet, or would you rather not? Don't arrange it if it seems too difficult for you, but I essentially think that this, too, would be unproblematic for us if it works out technically. I think Schulze is now in charge again. Hercher was amazed by how "lackluster" Schulze's closing argument was. Might this be starting to get to him? That would speak in his favor.

I'd also like you to let me know which agronomist I should take "against" Zeumer:[3] Meier, Werkshagen, or perhaps Penke from Gütermannsdorf? I think Werkshagen isn't actually strong enough. Give this question some more careful thought, and advise me on whom I ought to talk to. That would also be a subject for the face-to-face meeting!

I'll have your arrest warrant and the notification of your death, if it comes to that, translated into Russian. That could come in handy for me at some point.

Other than that, my love, I have no worries, not even about you, no, not at all. I'm firmly convinced that God is near and with you, and even if you should have to take that last walk, it will not be as difficult as you think. I'm quite sure of that, my love. You, too, must now go on living calmly and normally, and not wait for your death. The hymn is quite right in saying that you are ready to die if you cling to Him while living. You will surely do that, so it won't be anything special if they come to get you some day. I will be with you even if I am utterly unaware of that, because I'm always with you. It is a given that I will remain as close to you as possible = here much of the time, of course. –

I'm just as happy about Reisert and Eugen [Gerstenmaier] as you. I was overjoyed.—Now Harald is coming and wants the letter. Farewell, my dearly beloved! P.

1. See Helmuth's letter of November 14, 1944. 2. This feeling remained with Freya for the next sixty-five years. When she died in January 2010, Helmuth's last letter was in her bedside table. 3. Freya needed an agricultural consultant to be an interlocutor with whom she could discuss Zeumer's agricultural decisions when she considered that necessary.

HELMUTH JAMES TO FREYA, JANUARY 13, 1945

Tegel, 13 Jan 45

My dear, yes, I understood everything very well and maybe already answered it in part this morning. That is how it is when you're not positioned correctly, and even the most beautiful sayings won't tide you over. Afterward you first feel quite insecure and timid, but when you notice that everything is back on an even keel it is that much better, and you get more humble and bold.

It's now about 3:15. I'm still shackled, but as you see, writing works quite well. Tomorrow, when another official little letter goes out to you, I want to write to the warden and see whether I can get them taken off again. If you go to see Schulze, you can see whether you're able to get me unshackled; you can say someone told you that people who are sentenced to death are shackled. There is only one rationale, and that is my sciatica, especially at night, and you have to tell him that you're quite certain that I won't kill myself.

Then, my dear, there's the permission for a face-to-face meeting. Of course I want to see you. No, no, I am absolutely not attuned to the beyond, and I have no fear whatsoever of seeing you. Just come soon, because from a human perspective, the execution can be ordered at any moment. Also, if you come soon, maybe there's a chance for a second time to work out. Yes, Schulze is probably in charge of that.

I didn't discuss the issue of clemency with Poelchau. I think that only three men are of interest: Müller, Kaltenbrunner, Himmler. While we are trying to influence them, we also need to tend to the Ministry of Justice so that they don't get miffed. I'd say that's the general approach.

The second major point, as I see it, is that Jowo [von Moltke] and Carl Viggo [von Moltke] have to act and you as little as possible, so I'm not at all sure whether your visit to Müller would be the right thing now. What Müller promised you was a consultation "when it's all over," that is, when I'm dead.

Third, I think it's right for Hercher to write to Kaltenbrunner. If he writes this sort of letter, it would have to be sent in a way that ensures that Kaltenbrunner actually reads it. I'm convinced that Müller will throw it into the wastebasket.

Overall I'd encourage all of you to do everything slowly and carefully. They won't hang me as long as they know that there are considerations of clemency afloat. Besides, you should of course get clarity on what has become of Carl Viggo's old petition. You will be able to do all that peacefully, my love. I think I am well beyond those phases in which I suddenly panic, and I hope that the Lord won't push me back in there again. Enough for today, my dear, dear love. Keep up your beating; make it strong and steady. May the Lord watch over you and us. J.

HELMUTH JAMES TO FREYA, JANUARY 14, 1945

14 Jan 45

Good morning, my dear love. Are you feeling all better again? I quickly want to read your letter through once again. Yes, my love, I understood it all well. It is nothing new, but the certainty now rests more deeply by one more rotation of the screw.[1] These rotations are just painful; that is clear. How good that I wasn't put to death on Thursday, because it would have been sad for you to have been out of step with me on the last day. Yes, my love, that was the first time in all these months that we were not totally aligned. Your letter on Saturday also had a mistake in it: You wrote that going to Plötzensee would surely not be as difficult for me as I was picturing it. At the moment—and with God's help in the future as well—I am totally past that. When I left the courtroom after the sentencing, I thought I'd be going straight to Plötzensee and was very cheerful about it, and quite lighthearted. At the moment, I think it would be a matter of indifference—that word is not the right one, but you'll understand what I mean—to me if the door were to open and I were taken away. If I think about the anxiety I used to have, especially in November, when the telephone rang in the main office and Herr Claus was summoned, I can only be filled with gratitude as I try to fathom the grace that has been granted to me.

Today, though, is a gray day. But even this gray essentially colors only the surface, and underneath it's as usual. I slept poorly; because I'm shackled, I go back to bed at 6 and then lie there for several hours and doze, hazily, by which I mean that the thoughts I'm able to come up with then are so hazy that much appears gray to me. And there's been a new change, evidently for all prisons: The outdoor walk is canceled if the temperature falls below 0° Celsius because there is no additional clothing for the prisoners to put on. Claus said that most

The courtyard of Tegel prison in 1969

of them have only a shirt and pants, and even those are often in tatters. We have to suffer under this rule too, which means, for instance, that I won't see Eugen [Gerstenmaier] again, since it won't get warmer than 0° before he goes to Brandenburg.[2] This lack of any fresh air is unpleasant. I've already been through this in Ravensbrück for a week or two, of course, but it was warm outside, so I could keep the window open all the time. I'll try to cozy up to Mittelstädt again; maybe I can continue with my light baths and thus have a little walk every day. But the thing I miss most is the daily conversation with Eugen.— Still, those are trifles, and as I said before, that gray isn't running deep, and with God's help it never will. Besides, it looks as though the sun could shine in the afternoon.

My love, the trial is over; I don't have to deal with my defense anymore, and the clemency initiatives will make demands on all of you and not on me, which means there is now room in my brain and in my time, as I can't engage with anything but the Bible and hymnal the whole day long. I may have only a short time to live, and in all human likelihood I won't survive until the end of this month, but I still want to live as though I'm to remain alive; anything else is nonsense. I'm not happy with the idea of "just reading"; instead, I'd like something to sink my teeth into, as it were. You really have to see— please—what you can get for me. I could, of course, continue with the Kant, but I'd rather like to begin learning Russian. I'm not gifted in languages, but maybe I can learn enough to be able at least to read it.

I guess you'll be going to slaughter your pig in the course of the week. Greet everyone for me and tell Ulla [Oldenbourg] to keep on working hard. Discuss everything in detail with her. My love, we will keep on going from one day to the next until we are reunited, in this world or the one beyond. J.

1. See Helmuth's letter of November 19, 1944. 2. To Brandenburg-Görden prison now that he was no longer facing execution.

HELMUTH JAMES TO FREYA, JANUARY 15, 1945

Tegel, 15 Jan 45

My dear, today is the beginning of the week that will bring you, my dear, a great deal of trouble, and surely heartache and disappointment as well, because nothing ever goes as we wish and imagine it should. I have now given more thought to the whole campaign for clemency and have the following to say:

1. The petition for clemency that went to Keitel now has to be rerouted to Himmler so that it doesn't somehow get to Hitler and is rejected by him. Maybe Haus can look into this again.

2. An offensive toward Himmler himself can work only in a roundabout way, not directly from Jowo [von Moltke] or Carl Viggo [von Moltke]. That is a question I can't assess for myself. I basically expect very little from Müller unless I'm able to soften him up a bit in regard to the case itself, which can actually happen only if he has me come to him again. Even so, your visit to him is right and important, because it cannot lead to a harsher stance. The way I see it, you can present three requests: *a.* that he might work toward a pardon for me; *b.* that he might listen to what Jowo and Carl Viggo have to say or facilitate their visiting Kaltenbrunner; *c.* that he grant me an audience. The way I see it, Jowo and Carl Viggo should visit Kaltenbrunner and not you. Basically, you're co-convicted, so to speak.

3. In my view, there is only one objective rationale for clemency, and that is the family, the many cousins for whom Kreisau is a gathering place of sorts, and several of whom were killed in the war, etc. So basically what we wrote in the letter to Himmler.

4. But there are other reasons that need to be brought in to soften the current position:
   a. what is said about me in Carl Viggo's petition for clemency;
   b. my written pleading of November 12, which I opted not to present in accordance with the wishes of the Gestapo;

c. my opposition to any inclination to stage a coup, as was established during the trial.

You can broach these three subjects, particularly *b.*, to Müller, but Carl Viggo in particular also needs to present these matters, because he can also assess the legal weight of the clemency plea dated November 12. The way I see it, he can justifiably claim that once this defense had been cut off from me for political reasons at the trial, and I complied, even though the outcome was clear to me, it would be only right and proper to take these things into account in the clemency process, particularly because, as far as he's heard, it is indisputable that my military superior in charge of these things, namely Canaris, knew about it, and I could have assumed that he would arrange for the necessary steps to be taken.

5. I imagine you discussed what needs to happen with the Ministry of Justice. If Carl Dietrich [von Trotha] is willing, he will explain it satisfactorily. In my view, they need only be informed and leave us enough time to do everything in an unhurried manner.

So, that's what I have to say about this. My dear love, the brunt of this business—by which I don't mean the main activity but the main emotional burden—falls upon you. And I can only pray that the Lord grants you a very confident, tranquil heart, which cannot be troubled by anything, even if everything categorically fails. Confident and joyful is the motto for these tasks; joyful even if I'm hanged.

I'm not balking at the prospect of going to Plötzensee; the greater danger is the passage of time up to a decision. My love, I am carrying you within me, with me, near me, next to me. You are going with me to Plötzensee, if that must come to pass, and you will be coming with me to our Father as well. I'm certain of that.

May the Lord watch over you, my love, and us. J.

FREYA TO HELMUTH JAMES, JANUARY 15, 1945

Monday morning

My dear, yes, I'm well again, and have been since Saturday morning, when I wrote you that. You're surely right that it was a rotation of the old screw, surely, but it was an important rotation. I was happy that you took this up with such love and understanding and told me all kinds of things that I had just said to myself in a similar form.

No, I wasn't asking about a face-to-face meeting because I think you're over on the other side but because I thought it could be stressful for you, yet it's true that both of those ideas are nonsensical. As for the fear of death, I didn't misunderstand you there either, as you believe. Actually, I am quite certain that this won't be difficult for you, I've always been quite sure of that, but you wrote about it as though it was the only thing that remained as a burden and I don't believe in this burden either when the moment arrives. To that extent it was not an inner but a technical misunderstanding, because you most likely weren't meaning to say that at all.

Still, my love, there are all kinds of distressing and irksome minor things to complain about: in particular the shackles, which I hate so terribly, and then the lack of time outdoors. According to Poelchau, Eugen [Gerstenmaier] could easily stay in Tegel for another three months; it doesn't go so quickly. Maybe something can also be done about the issue of taking your walks, and in any case you need to keep having lots of attacks of sciatica, even if it should be better. Discuss your schedule again with Poelchau. We wondered whether Greek wouldn't be easier and lead to more. Think it over. In addition, he should bring you a book by Lilje.[1]

I'm in the best of hands and carry you within me and keep you warm with all my strength, warm you in your state of grayness, my dear love. I am and remain your P.

1. Hanns Lilje, *Das letzte Buch der Bibel: Eine Einführung in die Offenbarung Johannes* (Berlin: Furche Verlag, 1940); it appeared in English as *The Last Book of the Bible*, translated by Olive Wyon (Philadelphia: Muhlenberg Press, 1957).

FREYA TO HELMUTH JAMES, JANUARY 15, 1945

Monday afternoon

My dear love, I love you, so, so much, and tomorrow I'm coming to visit you. That is so very wonderful!

The day was not particularly pleasant: as you've said so often, I have to live with the ups and downs of hoping and abandoning hope, and this final stage is the most taxing of all. It would be utterly unbearable if I didn't keep reminding myself from time to time that it is the good Lord we belong to, that He decides, and if He makes use of my stupidity when our endeavors go awry, that is also His will. You won't die badly if you die this way; on the whole, all is well, but it remains to be seen what His will is. So I'm still doing well now, too, which you are sure to have noticed from the very first word. First, I went to the People's Court. It suffered slight damage from the bombs, windows smashed and rubble everywhere. During the break, Schulze emerged from the session—at that time I had no idea about what I have just learned, namely that Haubach, Steltzer, Gross are up today, and then Schulze came out. He was reserved, somewhat restrained in dealing with me, but stern, matter-of-fact. He named for me the officers in charge of clemency in the Ministry of Justice who also decide, at the same time, about the "when." He said that the order to unshackle had to come from the doctor, then it would be effective right away, although only after being presented to Lautz. He gave me permission for two face-to-face meetings. I'm only getting two because I said that I now have the full responsibility for Kreisau, and I have to go right back there after a short trip home. But I assume that I may be able to get more from the Gestapo. Müller hasn't been to Prinz-Albrecht-Strasse yet; I'm told to ask again on Wednesday. Then I went to the Ministry of Justice. First I wanted to see Dr. Pippert, who was also at the trial, but of course he was with Haubach, etc. Then I went to see Franke, whom Carl Viggo [von Moltke] had already seen. He is a very unpleasant man, SS on his buttonhole, but he reports to the minister and will discuss it with him just a few days after he has the grounds for the judgment in writing, and then the minister decides, his verdict goes to the chief Reich prosecutor, and he issues the execution order. I said we needed more time, and he said we would certainly get this week, and then he would report to the minister. At first he was very uncommunicative and aggressive, but as time went on he opened up, admitting that your case had virtually nothing to do with July 20th, and he was certainly interested, too, in what the Gestapo knew. I had to tell him something beyond what he already knew from the petition for clemency in order to motivate the push for more time. Rest assured that I was cautious, but I had to say something objective. When I started saying at one point, "You will admit that..." he replied to me, "I will admit nothing of the kind, because I am not an adversary, but all of this is very important to me, and the Moltke case is certainly on our minds." All I can take away from the conversation is this: *1.* I don't think he tricked me. *2.* He was interested and has pondered the case. *3.* He had some degree of respect for me, and sent me on my way in keeping with that respect. *4.* He's not crucial to the case, but he will be discussing it with the minister. *5.* Since Carl Viggo had already been there, it wasn't wrong of me to go there alone again. *6.* Needless to say, he didn't give me any concrete hope. Afterward I went to see Eggensberger, the undersecretary Harald [Poelchau] said that Carl Viggo had to go see. I wanted to announce Carl Viggo's visit, but found out that although he is responsible for the enforcement of the sentence, it is only for the prisons, thus for Eugen [Gerstenmaier]. That's when I really noticed how nasty Herr Franke was, because Herr Eggensberger was a decent human being. He almost felt bad about not being able to do anything at all for me. I was glad to have encountered a human being again. Then I went to eat and to see Haus. There was nothing new over there, but the atmosphere was quite warm, with everyone sending their greetings and expressing real concern for you. Dr. Friede, Haus told me, knows a man who worked on your case and also attended the trial: he reported that you made a very good impression, you're essentially out of the whole Goerdeler business, but you yourself did quite a lot, and you had some sort of key role of your own! That's what Haus says. So, my love, I'm now heading to your vicinity again. Tomorrow Herr Wickenberg wants to review your situation and, I hope, once again arrange for you to be unshackled. I truly wish for you to be freed of them once more. It's horrible for me to picture you shackled in your bed. Maybe you can also have more light baths to distract you. Go ahead and make yourself look really bent over, even when I'm there.

I'm sitting and chatting with my beloved husband, with my Jäm, whom I love so much. Yesterday, when I went into the slit trench[1] at the Trothas', Carl Dietrich [von Trotha], who was still quite far away, turned his head in a way that reminded me of you for a fraction of a second. The knowledge of every little movement you make and the loving intimacy and familiarity pierced my heart with a wistful and aching feeling of joy. I hope it will continue to do so in twenty or forty years, should my senses for perceiving such things still be intact at that point. I often picture you coming through the door or toward me, you walking next to me, and often you go across the field next to me; I see your face putting up with my onslaughts. Then I'm always very happy. Oh, the flood of big and little memories.—I was blissful, really overjoyed about Eugen's and your outing to the light bath.[2] I hope that will be kept up! How very delightful. What a splendid life we have had together! How is that possible!

Yesterday, when I was talking to Kreisau, I made a point of telling Ulla [Oldenbourg] via Asta [Wendland] that she should really keep it up[3] and Asta should give her precise reports. So you can rest assured that she will stick with it. Both boys (Casparchen said he was doing "very well!!!" He sounded as if he'd added three exclamation points) said "dream about Pa" at the end, little Konrad, too, seemingly of his own accord.

Once again I'm reading your dear consoling letter,[4] which I love so much. No, there is definitely no danger of my having too much composure, but it is very unpleasant when I have to fight off my tears terribly at Steengracht's door while needing to discuss something quite concrete with him at once, and that is where the notion of composure is helpful. No, you didn't write pharisaically in the slightest; it was very affectionate and full of understanding. Yesterday afternoon I talked to Marion [Yorck] about the connection. She has what I hope to gain for myself: The knowledge that Peter [Yorck] is alive, lives on, still belongs with her, and she has the feeling that he is beckoning and calling to her, although she has quite a positive outlook on life. That is all truly so nice in her case, and it couldn't be nicer, because there is no rupture at all; things simply go on in a different manner, and she has simply discovered her consciousness of a new dimension. But all of us human beings have a facility for that! It is our task to let ourselves be found by God, to have this dependency and belonging grow and live within us. I firmly believe that! You do too, my dear love.

May God watch over you, my love. Many people are thinking of you and are praying to God for you, many love you, many are hoping for you, but I, who for this reason am happy forever, belong to you, am yours, and may God help me always to remain so. I'm sending you a tender embrace. P.

1. Deep covered trenches that served as makeshift protection from the fragments of high-explosive bombs. 2. Mittelstädt had brought Helmuth and Eugen to the light bath together, but he was then forbidden to do so. See Helmuth's letter of January 15, 1945, in Helmuth James and Freya von Moltke, *Abschiedsbriefe Gefängnis Tegel: September 1944–January 1945* (Munich: C. H. Beck, 2011), 508. 3. That is, praying for Helmuth. 4. See Helmuth's letter of January 12–13, 1945.

HELMUTH JAMES TO FREYA, JANUARY 16, 1945

16 Jan 45

My dear love, how nice it was to see you and to see that you're doing well on the whole. All this is simply far worse for you than it is for me. Just don't let it trouble you.—And you also wrote me a very beautiful letter that showed me that the shock is wearing off.

I find your conversation with Herr Franke quite remarkable. Maybe you'll be able to bore a hole in these walls after all. In any case, here's what I find: Whether or not I die, you have attained a level of negotiating skills over the past few months that will always be of great benefit to you in the times ahead. You surely see that many things are easier than one might think, if they're just approached calmly and head-on. That will give you a good firm sense of security, because if you can negotiate about your husband's life with all these enemies, you'll find some way to cope with all the other problems too.

[The letter breaks off here.]

FREYA TO HELMUTH JAMES, JANUARY 17–18, 1945

Wednesday evening

My dearest, I'm tired, but my soul is doing well. Today things were not especially encouraging, but I'm quite content and have sailed through steadily—not that I can take credit for this achievement, and you do know who provides this for us. I hope that it's that way for you, too, although in a quite different manner. My thoughts found you so, found you to be at peace, the way you were when you sat across from me yesterday. My love, being with you yesterday was especially wonderful. I had been looking forward to it with great joy, and this joy was even surpassed. It was lovely, intimate, tender, close, and natural, and not the least bit sad. I was already so glad that I was able to come with sheer joy. I could see so wonderfully how you were do-ing on the inside, it was so gratifying to feel everything that joins us together so naturally. Then it was in fact two meetings, because of the air-raid alarm, and at least we added two little kisses. Everything was quite uplifting.—Yes, I want to keep telling you about the day. The first thing I did today, before 9, was to deliver the letters. I was cold when I got up. I wasn't feeling bad inside, but I didn't wake up full of energy and ready to leap into action; it felt as though my bed was and would remain the most wonderful place of all to stay put in, I couldn't make myself start in on my daily tasks, and then I had a look at the daily Scripture readings, and I found Psalm 46:5–6, which suited me quite well and lifted my spirits.[1] I went to the People's Court with the letter to you and met up with Schulze on the stairs to the commuter train; I went into the Foreign Office and saw Dieter [von

Mirbach] and put the letter to Steengracht in his hands; I went to the Schlesischer Bahnhof and mailed the copy to Uncle Peter [von Moltke]. I went to Prinz-Albrecht-Str. and handed the letter to Himmler to the section commander. Müller still wasn't back; I was told I should ask again on Friday/Sat. Then I went to see Hercher, who assured me that he couldn't write any letter to the Gestapo, because you had been at liberty to try to defend yourself with your arguments. Evidently Lange merely said, "The police did not know anything." Not: "Moltke shouldn't defend himself this way." He would have steered clear of a statement like that, Hercher told me. He did understand quite well that a letter of this kind would facilitate things, but it wasn't true and he wouldn't be able to write it. Then he read my letter to Himmler and let out a big shout at the sentence he crossed out, claiming that it's not true! You were convicted for your own high treason; the deliberations of state administrators for territories that might be occupied, and possibly for the entire Reich, the consideration that the National Socialist government could then be gone as a result of the force of the enemy, the discussion of the unified trade union movement, the considerations about the map, that was all high treason and it says so in the verdict. If I were to leave that in, it would be considered false and achieve the opposite effect. I also discussed with him whether I could somehow convey the fact that you hadn't wanted to do anything to the Führer, but that requires too complicated an explanation, which, in my view, is completely unsuitable for Himmler. So we'll take out that sentence. I took back the letter from the Prinz-Albrecht-Str., rewrote it in Lichterfelde, gave a new version of it to Steengracht with a comment about the first letter to him as well, and went to the Schlesischer Bahnhof a second time. But that was not until the afternoon. In Lichterfelde I typed, ate, packed, and made telephone calls. I learned that Carl Viggo [von Moltke] had to go to the front at short notice, so he won't be able to come anymore. When I got back to the Prinz-Albrecht-Str., the section commander had arrived. I again had my doubts as to whether he'd been away at all. In any case, he will see me at 3 o'clock tomorrow afternoon. Tomorrow morning I'll go with Carl Dietrich [von Trotha] to see Herr Prost at the Ministry of Justice. Then I will have done pretty much every-thing I can. I don't know what else I'll be able to accomplish. I feel the inadequacy of all my steps, yet I get the sense that there is no one who could do it better. I sometimes get a fleeting image of how it would be if Jowo [von Moltke] were in and you were out, but then you wouldn't be who you are. What a wonderful advocate you would be! With Jowo the good will is definitely still there, but he does not know the facts and can act only when given instructions. I don't suffer from the responsibility because I am too firmly convinced of the certainty of divine providence, which may require that you die despite and surely not because of my poor attempts and, furthermore, because there is no one who can do it better far and wide! But my efforts certainly strike me as pitiful, and I'm anything but proud when I return here after a day like this. There you are on the inside, my love, and your pipsqueak is bumbling around on the outside, bumbling about a matter that goes to her very core and making every effort, but all's she's doing is bumbling. Still, I'm not despairing about it; I am quite secure and sheltered very close to you, and hope and pray that it can remain so, and soon the activity will also come to a halt because there will be nothing left to undertake, and then our case will take a path on which we no longer have any influence, and is surely the path that God wants for us. The whole thing is still weigh-ing heavily on Hercher's mind. He thought I should arrange to speak with Thierack, saying the outcome would also depend on him, and he had the feeling that the sentence would no longer be carried out, a different wind is blowing, or a different course is being steered. That was the way he felt, for after he had described your high treason to me so emphatically, I said it made no sense at all to do anything whatsoever. He didn't think that was the case.

This evening, while I was arranging my schedule for tomorrow, Carl Dietrich told me that Kreisau placed an order and the butcher canceled. Something about yeast was mentioned, so I actually think that those at home hadn't baked any bread for the sausage and canceled the butcher for that reason. Be that as it may, the pig has to go on living for now, and your old, real Helmuth-style question as to who will win the race, my dear, dear, good love, the pig or you, is as yet undecided. How can you even say or think something like that, Herr Hercher and the prison warden would say. In any case, I'm in no hurry to go home tomorrow afternoon. I definitely won't do it before Friday morning. I'm going to wait to find out what happens.

Thursday morning

I can write for a little while longer, and I would always like to say something, especially this: What should I do from this point on? How long can I go on sitting with you or do I need to go to Kreisau? Like you, I have to act as though you will go on living. Write to let me know what you are comfortable with and how you picture things. You know where I most like to be.

You also know that wherever I am, my life and my being are aligned with you. So if you should die without my knowledge, I am with you nonetheless.

Harald [Poelchau] is going! I'm your P.

1. Psalm 46:6: "God is in the midst of her; she shall not be moved: God shall help her, and that right early."

HELMUTH JAMES TO FREYA, JANUARY 17–18, 1945

Tegel, 17 Jan 45

My dear, there's nothing new to report about me. My thoughts are always with you on your exhausting errands and trying to keep you warm, to help you cope with the disappointments and difficulties, to stand by you. My dear love, what an undertaking for you! How will you withstand all that? This morning I was quite content, but after eating there came a wave of gray, because I had definitely counted on going with Eugen [Gerstenmaier] for irradiation, but Mittelstädt didn't come. It's totally meaningless, but it does show how important it is never to expect anything, never to wait for anything. I'm annoyed at making such a rookie mistake. It then occurred to me that you might be able to do something to ensure that Eugen stays here as long as I'm here, seeing as his presence is of course a great help to me. And if Eggensberger in the Reich Ministry of Justice is a decent human being, perhaps he can do it. But look into this only if you can do it on the side, because you'll certainly need your strength for other things. Unfortunately Claus has been ill for two weeks. That is too bad, particularly as his nice substitute is not here either today. I hope he's not ill as well, because today's team is actually not so pleasant.

But this gray mood is ebbing. It wasn't very bad, and if I'd been more careful with my discipline it needn't have happened at all. And I am writing to my dearest so as to dive quickly back into the gleaming light. If you should go to Kreisau—and that depends on whether you reach Müller today or tomorrow—bring me a new pad, because I'll be finished with this one this week; if you don't go, maybe you can get me some other paper.—My love, the radiance of your visit yesterday and of the beautiful letter are still lighting me up through and through. My dear, we belong together, so closely, so completely, that I absolutely cannot imagine your ever not finding me within you, just as I am certain that I will take you with me when I am called away. My dear, you truly don't need to worry about me. I believe that I am now so prepared to die that if God doesn't wish to subject me to any new ordeals, that walk to the gallows is no longer a major thing for me. All this is far worse for you, and you're the one who must now be cared for and warmed, not me. I've thought of one more concrete thing: When you next speak with the Reich Ministry of Justice, that is, with Herr Franke (?), you can suggest to him that he has me come in myself, since the Gestapo is simply not questioning me about these topics.—My love, I don't have anything else to

18 Jan 45

My dear, I was interrupted there when they put my handcuffs back on, and then I didn't want to keep on writing. Or maybe it was something else? Instead I wrote the letter to Zeumer and the one to Hans-Heini [Rittberg]. You'll get the duplicates along with this if I have them ready in time, and the originals will go out on Sunday. I didn't mention Penke in the letter to Hans-Heini. I thought there was enough in it already, and he ought to mend fences with you[1] before he is asked to mediate with someone like Penke. Incidentally, you won't need much advice at first, because as far as the estate is concerned, it will develop along fairly predictable lines, and you'll have to make the major decisions about remaining and going, keeping the cattle or no longer holding on to them, on your own; no one can be of much help; it's also less a question of how it should be decided than whether it will be possible to hold sway. And even Penke can't help you with that.

I'm doing well, my dear. I slept quite a bit, probably from 7 on, and didn't wake up until shortly before the alarm rang, which must have been about 5:30. My soul is safe and secure, way down deep; only the surface is ruffled from time to time, but not so much on my account, because I truly feel as though nothing could happen to me. I have only two difficulties: The first is that I have to keep cautioning myself not to waver in the belief that my life can yet be saved. I have no right to just let myself fall into this, and that's my recurrent tendency.—My second main concern, though, is my Pim. My thoughts keep flying tenderly to her, but always with the feeling: How will she fare? How will she get through that? The situation is now the opposite from the way it was before the trial: Now I have to strive to lend strength to my Pim, as well as I can; unfortunately I can't do it as well as my dear. Oh, how often I find myself thinking: Now she is going to Prinz-Albrecht-Str. and Müller isn't willing to meet with her, or is unfriendly to her, or Steengracht is not available, etc. I know, after all, how such things are; they always go worse than one thinks, with my loved one's lifeblood hanging in the balance, and she has no husband with whom she can let the gentlemen of Verona[2] flow. Oh, my love, what have I burdened you with. Just take good care of yourself. Your husband is of no interest at the moment; he's just an object, and you are far more important. Take it easy. In the interest of conserving your strength, you might do well with a short stay in Kreisau, it seems to me. But I don't mean to tell you what to do. If being in Kreisau constantly makes you feel that you're missing crucial things,

Kreisau won't be of any help to you. Oh, my love, if only I could give you better support!

My dear, dear love, I'd like to give you warmth and shelter, I'd like to offer you strength and aid; don't you worry about me at all, that is, how I'm doing on the inside. Farewell, my dear, I have nothing else to say other than that I would like to repeat the same things over and over again. I embrace you. May the Lord watch over you and us. J.

1. Rittberg was not willing to stand up for Helmuth in Freya's company; see Freya's letter of November 14, 1944. 2. An allusion, as earlier, to tears.

HELMUTH JAMES TO FREYA, JANUARY 18, 1945

Tegel, 18 Jan 45

My dear, your beautiful, peaceful letter, which I've just read, made me feel quite ashamed. I'm sitting here and trembling, and meanwhile you're moving straight ahead as though all this were nothing. Yes, yes, I know why you're able to, and it's only my common, miserable, utterly unjustifiable lack of faith. Yes, my love, it is the grace of God that enables you to do all this.

You ask about what I've been reading in the Bible: I always read three chapters from the NT two times and always try to organize my reading in such a way that I begin again with Matthew when I reach the Epistle to the Romans. In order to do so, I always wind up reading more than three chapters. Yes, when you read entire chapters, you skip over, no, overlook the same passages again and again. That is unavoidable. One reads individual verses more carefully. Only the fifteen chapters, which I have been reading daily for quite some time, have, of course, given me a very useful general overview; but for a normally active life, three chapters are probably already too much.

The question as to what and how one ought to believe and what, how, and for what one ought to pray is a terribly difficult one, and I'm not able to answer it; or rather, I answer it differently every day. The two reference points for prayer are the Lord's Prayer, which was clearly given to us in the Sermon on the Mount, and the unutterable groanings of the Spirit in Romans 8:26. Something that strikes me as well articulated and persuasive on one day sounds feeble and insubstantial on the next. Mark 11:24[1] is one particularly challenging passage, one that I will never feel up to.—Every day I also have to grapple anew to retain my faith. All of a sudden, I'm ambushed, from some ugly crevice, by the conviction that "it is all rubbish," which is dreadful, but luckily it usually lasts just a matter of minutes.

Yes, my dear, once everything has happened that can happen, you have to go back to a reasonably normal life. But let's see what the next week brings. I have the feeling that if I'm to be executed at all, it will happen soon, so maybe we can wait out the next week. You see, my dear, I'm writing this only because my reason tells me that's the way it is; but even as I'm writing, I get the feeling that I really ought not to be writing it, because it conflicts with my religious obligations. So let's wait a bit until we know about Müller and Kaltenbrunner.

May the Lord watch over you, my very dear love. Jäm.

1. Mark 11:24: "What things soever ye desire, when ye pray, believe that ye receive them, and ye shall have them."

FREYA TO HELMUTH JAMES, JANUARY 19, 1945

Friday after breakfast

My dear love, I have exactly one hour to write, then I have to catch the express train so that I can be home at 7. On Sunday night I'll come back. At 11 Carl Dietrich [von Trotha] and I went to see the dear young innocuous Ebersberg, Thierack's adjutant. It was an extremely funny situation; soon after Carl Dietrich had offered dignified words on behalf of the family, the young man said that Goerdeler was not in fact the crux of the matter; the true crux was what they technically referred to as the "Kreisau Circle." He continued with a wholehearted assertion that they noticed, again and again, that the wives would come without any inkling of what their husbands had been involved in and considered the allegations downright impossible. Sitting next to Carl Dietrich, I found it really hard not to laugh.[1] With Carl Viggo [von Moltke] the role would have been easier to play. We requested that they wait, and the young man strongly encouraged me to seek out Herr Prost himself once again, which we decided to do on the spot, without Carl Dietrich!! He also said that Thierack would be on a business trip for another ten days, and once he had let that slip, he regretted it, and said he didn't know whether the secretary of state would then not decide, which I consider out of the question. In short, the visit was funny but totally unimportant, and I was glad when I had maneuvered good old Carl Dietrich back out again. My overall impression of the Ministry of Justice is that Goerdeler's connection with you is of very minor importance compared with the perception that your own plans were *at least* as dangerous as those of Herr Goerdeler.—At 3, I was at Müller's, fortified by a cup of thick coffee at Dorothee [Poelchau]'s. I must confess that I can't provide a very detailed description of the course of the conversation. I found it increasingly unpleasant that Müller wanted to separate me from you right there (in front of him!), but he was unable to, thank God, because he eventually said they were sorry that I had been caught up in this, too—seeing as we're all Germans, after all. I was able to fend off that idea quite nicely by stating that I would be happy to be convicted along with you, because I belong to you. He immediately began by saying that one (I) wouldn't be able to do anything more for you, because you are guilty of high treason, and it was unacceptable for traitors to live while the others at the front were dying for Germany. And your sentence can't be postponed either, because they'd had bad experiences with that method in 1918.[2] He insisted that the people had emerged from the prisons and were active again. (!!!) Besides, that would be unjust—letting you live—if many others had now already been put to death for far less. An SS Reich Leader or even the Führer could do nothing to change that because in essence they had no independent will in the matter. But he said that he would of course deliver my letter to Himmler immediately and efficiently—and he's doing so. I said that they were unable to do

anything to harm me. I told them I understood that their point of
view was totally consistent, but that I knew your aims far too well
not to see that you had only the best of intentions. He asked whether
he ought to enlighten me about you or let me cling to this illusion.
He could do as he liked, I told him, seeing as neither the one nor the
other would make a dent in my certainty, because I understand them
and you, but they don't understand you. Then there was a reference
to the knowledge of what the Gestapo had known. He said you had
twisted his words around at a discussion granted for my sake and
yours, because it was unfortunately true that the Gestapo knew nothing about the July 20th plot. It was understandable that you would
clutch at any straws, but, he insisted, *that* could be explained only as
prison psychosis. I didn't try to correct everything he said, because
it would have presupposed too precise a knowledge of the details,
which I couldn't afford to let on about; I—or you—would have been
able to, because, well...for obvious reasons! The letter you wrote
afterward proved, he said, that you are essentially aware of your guilt.
(!!) He went on to claim that in the early summer he had been seriously interested in your fate; you had held an opportunity in the palm
of your hand—and missed out on it. In short, my love, this "mighty"
man has a very deep personal resentment toward you. Won't Himmler
share this feeling? Dear! They are right to resent you! It's good that
they do, because there's no compromising with them!—I found it
quite unpleasant that he was so very friendly with me personally. "If
only he had listened to you more." I didn't want to hear that kind of
talk at all. At the end came this: "If you ever have a wish or a problem,
come to us. We are not the way people say we are!" Oh, my Jäm, they
have no idea, and I felt so cheap for having made such a good impression on him! Do you understand that? It wasn't sad at all; it was
disgusting. It was altogether different with Prost. I went to see him
soon afterward, once I had managed to wrest from Frau Breslauer
the correspondence that had been given to her for safekeeping.[3] We
met in a café. Prost is a serious German official, severely injured in
the previous war, head of the district court, Franke's clerk and at the
same time the right-hand man of the minister, so probably the ap-

propriate man in the Ministry of Justice. He sat down across from me and said nothing at all, *nothing*. He said, So tell me everything you want to say in the personal arena, from your personal knowledge of your husband. There's nothing to say on a factual level, because your knowledge is no more than rudimentary. You can't know much, and I can't say anything about it. I spoke about your basic attitudes: nothing with Goerdeler, not reactionary, no professional interests, no personal interests, no coup. Then there was some back-and-forth. He said, yes, he knew every last detail of the matter. They arrived at a decision about the concrete facts after very careful and oppressive deliberation—but in arriving at this decision they also wanted to know about the personal dimension. It was far more difficult to address this issue because I couldn't read his reactions, since he remained silent. I was convinced of his profound seriousness and lack of fanaticism despite his swastika, and so I felt a strong need to speak honestly. That's why I couldn't help saying at the end: And if you had to die, you would manage that, as I would understand and manage staying alive. That's when he, too, brought himself to say: It would be good if I were not punished alongside you. I rejected that idea even more sharply and effectively than I had with Müller, and said that I belonged to you absolutely. Then he seemed to grow concerned about the upbringing of the Moltke offspring, and said I would need to believe in justice and not lose faith in Germany. Once again, I couldn't help saying: I believe that what you have always stood for will live on even without you, and it is my conviction that one way or another, it would merge with Germany's destiny; it has nothing to do with either the current form of government nor with you, and goes well beyond the personal realm. I believe in that and so I'm not the least bit afraid of internal difficulties with regard to my sons or to Germany, however things turn out with you. "I don't want to give you any false hopes, but not rob you of any either," came at the end, and a highly reverent dismissal. Perhaps, my Jäm, I said too much. I hardly think it can spoil anything, but when faced with this earnest, decent man who is guided by his own convictions, I could only react in a way that is true to us: See whether you can afford to execute that. He did understand.

I have to get going! At once! May God watch over you!

Today is the 19th.[4] I'm well aware of it! What a *rich* year!

Take a look at these Bible readings: Deuteronomy 8:18, Philippians 4:13.

I'm taking you with me and staying close to you in great, ardent, strong, unadulterated, and, God willing, unchallenged love P.

1. In fact both Carl Dietrich and Freya had been important participants in the Kreisau Circle. 2. After the revolution in Germany of 1918 there was an amnesty for political prisoners. 3. Freya trusted Helmuth's secretary Frau Breslauer implicitly and had stored this correspondence with her on an interim basis, retrieving it now to be hidden in the Kreisau beehives. 4. The anniversary of Helmuth's imprisonment.

HELMUTH JAMES TO FREYA, JANUARY 21–22, 1945

Tegel, 21 Jan 45

My dear, I'm sorry that you won't find a letter when you get back, but I had assumed that Poelchau was at the women's prison on Saturday and would come on Sunday. Well, he came yesterday and isn't coming today.—I was quite delighted to read your two letters from the 19th. I am so happy that you are being borne along so graciously through all these difficulties. I gather that both conversations, the one with Müller and the one with Prost, went well. Prost's attitude would seem to indicate that the Reich Ministry of Justice wants to preserve—or resecure—a degree of autonomy in the matter of clemency after all. Doesn't it look that way to you too? There isn't any petition for clemency on hand there. Should it prove definite that nothing can be done by way of the SS—that is, if Kaltenbrunner either refuses to see you or makes it clear in the meeting that he refuses to do anything—it couldn't hurt if the old petition for clemency, perhaps with the date changed, were now given to the Reich Ministry of Justice, that is, to Prost. No, wait, there is something that needs to be changed because the trial is over. The second suggestion is this: Shouldn't you give

Prost a brief note *a.* about the factual reasons that merit further investigation, *b.* about the personal reasons, *c.* about the family considerations. Maybe you can go to see him again and tell him this: According to what you heard from the attorney and what you saw in Drögen,[1] it is quite clear to you that I was never questioned by a man with a broad view and a judicial outlook, because there was no preliminary investigation; the detectives who questioned me—you saw them yourself for the most part, and it was quite clear that they couldn't understand me in the slightest; and ultimately the view of me was formed from their reports. Naturally you can't write that, but you'll want to say it at least once.

Of course all this is unimportant, but now that we've started collecting straws to clutch at, we'll want to stay with this line of argument right down to the end. In my opinion, the petition should be presented only in oral form: Review this case once more, have another look at the man—so far there have been nothing but Gestapo points of view—or set him aside for the time being, without a formal pardon, until the question of amnesty is examined after the end of the war.

I am very interested in the fact that when it comes to both Prost and Ebersberg, that is, the Reich Ministry of Justice, the "Kreisau Circle" is the major gravamen. I'd thought that only Freisler had discovered this so far. I get the feeling that with Müller this is not the case. Most likely Thierack and Freisler, who quite obviously discussed this in great detail, came upon it together. So it seems to me that everything that happens in the clemency case is hopeless. They have recognized that Kreisau[2] would take an ax to the very root of National Socialism, and the result would go beyond a modification of the facade, as was the case with Goerdeler. This was evident from a remark by Freisler in the trial, which went along these lines: If Stauffenberg was the driving force in the military and Goerdeler in the organizational sector, it was Moltke in the intellectual sector. When people claim that Yorck brought all this together and he ought to become secretary of state in the Reich chancellery, they're not so far off the mark. The additional penalties that were meted out are also a sign that they regard it all as highly explosive. Eugen [Gerstenmaier] was also questioned in great detail about how he met me. But Eugen is, of course, an exception; he got off so leniently as a result of pure stupidity.—The astonishing thing is that they're leaving Carl Dietrich [von Trotha], Einsiedel, and Peters alone. But they probably think that otherwise they would have to keep extending their grasp in other cases, and that getting me out of the way and liquidating those most directly involved averts the serious danger. In terms of indirect causality, that is probably the right thing to do.—I gather from Müller's remark about 1918, "they were all active again," that his confidence in victory has suffered a bit of a blow. There's really no other way of understanding the phrase. Setting aside cases without granting pardons can be justified by pointing out that amnesty is expected following a victory, and then people like that could be needed after all.

All in all, one thing is gratifying: Since I couldn't play dumb, like Eugen, it is still better for me to be done away with because of Kreisau than because of a tenth-rate role with Goerdeler.—If you should see Prost again, maybe you can tell him once more: Neither you nor I—and you've seen me—is the least bit bitter; we understand that they had to play their role, but it seems sad to us that Germans are trying to kill other Germans because they have differing opinions, particularly in a case like mine, where I always stated my differing opinion openly, and not provocatively in the least, at the proper place. Say that you know what difficult struggles of an official nature I had at the start of the war on account of that. If that attitude was unwelcome, they could at any time have used me instead in a different capacity where these fundamental questions wouldn't come up on a constant basis.

Oddly enough, the negative outcome with Müller helped me tremendously. I don't know why, but it was as though a pressure on me had subsided, and this pressure was human hope; things eased up for me once it was gone, and you might say that I no longer had to expend my energies to prop it up. Once again, the Lord is very merciful with me, actually since yesterday morning. Everything has settled back down again on the old line of preparedness to do God's will, dutifully and joyfully. But it's not entirely the old line, although I can't quite put my finger on where the difference lies.—This is the attitude I am now taking: What are Herr Müller, Herr Thierack, and the executioners before God, when all is said and done: people and instruments He may wish to use to act upon me. They don't know that, and so one can feel sorry for them, but the way I see it, all the power of a Herr Müller adds up to nothing, God willing.

I'm reading Lilje's book about the Revelation with great pleasure.[3] I don't know whether it's good, because I know too little about the Revelation, but that's why it interests me so much. The translation in particular seems to be very good. I am spending quite a lot of time thinking about what I'll actually find when I have to go to Plötzensee. And Kant and the Scripture have convinced me that I will not have to wait for the Last Judgment, but will somehow live in the kingdom of Christ without delay. I'll simply fall right out of our three categories—time, space, and causality—into a state of being that we cannot imagine precisely because we can think in only these three categories. But if time no longer exists there, the kingdom of Christ, as described in the Revelation, is already there, because everything is "now"; consequently I won't be waiting either.—The less one is able to understand this, the more one is inclined to ponder it, but for this life, the only thing that is ultimately of any consequence is that the Lord preserves my unshakable certainty that He will take me straight into His arms from the shed in Plötzensee. Nothing else will matter. I will find some way, my love, to make myself noticeable to you in the three categories.

The newspaper has just arrived.[4] So what are we going to do now, my love? I hope you do manage to come tomorrow. That will be a dreadful trip. And then you have to be back by the 26th or not at all. That is certainly a very unpleasant decision. To make matters worse, Namslau has been named in today's *Völkischer Beobachter* report about the war situation. If I'm not mistaken, that's 100 kilometers from Kreisau. The Russians have begun the attack from the south that Halder and I were expecting quite far to the north, which means that if they don't cross the Oder farther to the south, you'll be very close to the combat, and if they cut the railway line that runs via

Opole, our line will remain the only connection to the southern army. Well, maybe they'll keep turning farther south after all. I had actually expected that they would advance to the west just above the industrial zone, or that they would at least cross the Oder well above Opole. That essentially remains the likely course, because otherwise they'll get the Malapane River as well as the Neisse and the Oder, and then those will be a major obstacle. Yesterday's Wehrmacht report and everything about the situation sounds quite bleak, as the Russians have evidently now also broken through the front in the north behind the Vistula bend. What a cost to human life! All you can say is: So what does it matter if one more man is hanged. But that's not how God thinks, not how He acts; that's how Nazis try to think, and even they can't manage to do so, at least not when the life of a count is at stake. What a life, my love! May the Lord just give us the ability to cope with all this properly, that is, in the proper spirit and faith, however things continue from there.

But I've drifted away from the subject, which is: *a.* Are you coming tomorrow? *b.* If so, are you going back on the 26th? I'll be around for the first of those dates. The second is very hard to answer. You actually should be at home now. On the other hand, your presence can be very important here. The 26th is Friday. By then it ought to be clear whether you can still see Kaltenbrunner and whether you can, should, want to, etc., speak to Prost again.—Your presence is a great comfort to me, as I've already told you time and again, but when I examine the situation honestly, I conclude that you really ought to travel to Kreisau. Well, maybe everything will be decided quickly.— But in that case, we will barely be able to maintain any connection between us, because letters will take forever to get to their destinations, and if Silesia becomes an area of operations, telephoning won't be possible either, and you may have the Russians in the house before you even know if I'm dead. It's all very disagreeable. Well, we can talk about that—if you come—and we have to trust in the Lord no matter what. For you it would now be a blessing for the Russians to come soon, because they will certainly get to the Silesian border, and if they don't get through Silesia, you'll be the front line with all the delightful consequences that go along with that. Better to be occupied quickly than to have a front that goes on for months. What would Herr Müller say to that?

Incidentally, the situation makes it seem justified to use any means necessary to postpone the execution, because this offensive may be heralding the end of the war. In eight days we'll know more about that. There could just as well be a front again, of course, one that lasts for several months. In any event, as long as we don't know that it will last, we can certainly try with Herr Prost to encourage a review of individual questions—such as what the Abwehr knew.

For a change I'll get to the subject of my life here. I'd like to ask you to give me some coffee for Herr Mittelstädt: only a small bag. I don't want to give him a cigarette every time, but I want him to come to get me quite often, so I hinted that I'd be able to get him some coffee. Poelchau thinks I still have this week—but I do think it's possible that the minister will come back as early as today or tomorrow because of the situation in the east and the difficulties in traveling—and it's much more entertaining in the sick bay than it is here, where we don't get out at all and have been treated less well in every regard since Claus has been gone. In the sick bay, by contrast, it's warm, still, peaceful, it's just that Eugen can't go with me anymore, because Mittelstädt was evidently reprimanded for taking us out together. In exchange (!) I found a health-care aide there who is from Schweidnitz and whose wife is a Willmer from Oberweistritz and also lives there, a cousin, he thought, of Sister Ida [Hübner]'s. Isn't that odd. The sick-bay staff is not only defeatist, which is certainly the case, but is also counting on an insurrection and thinks everything is well prepared for it.

So, now I'm all blathered out. All I have left to report is that I'm well. My back is quite a bit better, and I have to put on quite a show just so I can keep getting my light baths. My nerves are also quite calm. Unfortunately I'm constantly monitoring myself to see whether certain things make me nervous, and that's bad. But I can't seem to stop doing it. There is a great deal of stress involved if you can be taken away at any minute between 8 a.m. and 6 p.m. to be executed, and having a situation as good as mine is cause for satisfaction. Everything is like a miracle. Normally—that is, according to the way things were done until early December—the execution would have taken place immediately, and we wouldn't have seen each other again, nor would you know anything about the trial. I could be at Prinz-Albrecht-Str., where no one can gain entrance, the people are unfriendly, the danger of interrogations always looming, there is neither exit nor sick bay nor Eugen and, most important, neither Poelchau nor Pim. The Lord is very benevolent with us, and we have to thank Him constantly.—And if I were on the outside, I would probably die now, because as someone born in 1907 I would surely have to go to the front, given the current situation, and as a poorly trained or untrained man one doesn't stand much of a chance. And for what would I die then! I think that even if I'm killed, you two, Marion [Yorck] and you, have it far better than Davy [von Moltke], because at least you're on the right side, while Davy will be haunted by the state funeral for the rest of her life.[5]

I had very tender thoughts of all of you this morning, and hoped to find that all is peaceful. Farewell, my love. May the Lord watch over you and us. J.

Addendum to the above: It strikes me that it might be better not to send a family petition for clemency to the Reich Ministry of Justice under the abovementioned conditions, but instead here too to direct our efforts from the outset at achieving a postponement of carrying out the death sentence until the question of amnesty is examined after the war is over. But think it over.

22 Jan 45

Good morning, my dear love, I fear that you're stuck somewhere on the railroad after a horrid night, with cold, overcrowded trains that are endlessly delayed. How glad I will be when I hear what is happening with you, whether you're coming, you're here, or you've stayed in Kreisau.—I had a good sleep. Yesterday I forgot to write that Rösch was arrested.[6] That poses a new danger for Poelchau[7]—I have to write you about what I need: two shirts, one towel, one pillowcase, four handkerchiefs; I also think you should give me a pair of thick socks in bad condition if you have them, because the ones you knitted last year are much too nice for the hangman's assistants; I'd better give them back to you.—As for food, I need sugar, honey; the bacon and butter will last to the end of the week. The sausage will last until Wednesday.

So, now I won't write anything more, apart from the fact that I love you very much, my love, and that is all. J.

1. That is, during Freya's visits to the Drögen police station, where the Security Service questioned Helmuth when he was incarcerated at the Ravensbrück concentration camp. 2. Helmuth is using "Kreisau" in the transposed sense of the activities of the Kreisau Circle. 3. Hanns Lilje, *Das letzte Buch der Bibel*; see Freya's letter of January 15, 1945. 4. The *Völkischer Beobachter*, the Nazi Party organ, reported the collapse of the eastern front and the Russian advance toward Kreisau. 5. Davy (Davida) von Moltke, Yorck's sister, had to suffer her husband being given a state funeral after dying while serving as the German ambassador to Spain in 1943. 6. Augustin Rösch was arrested on January 11, 1945. 7. Possible statements by Rösch could have brought to light Poelchau's involvement in the Kreisau Circle.

HELMUTH JAMES TO FREYA, JANUARY 23, 1945

23 Jan 45

My dear, I just want to write you a word or two. Where might you be, my love? Maybe you're in Berlin, or you've turned around? If you should receive this letter after my death and not be in Berlin, don't think I was sad about your not being here. The two of us have gone beyond all that, after what the past three and a half months have taught us. If you're here, that's an additional pleasure, and if we should see each other once more, it will make us very happy. Once it's clear that you can't do any more for me, you have to leave me and go home, because all sorts of things will need doing there. I wonder whether Maria [Schanda] is staying too. That would be useful. Evidently yesterday's Armed Forces High Command report used the phrase "in the area of Breslau," and the guards are reporting that women and children were being evacuated from Breslau and some had arrived in Berlin. Just fight off any panic. It would be sheer suicide to wind up in the stream of refugees. I'm quite worried that they'll slaughter the cattle. Let's hope that your pig really does die soon, otherwise it'll wind up in other people's stomachs.

I'm doing fine, my love. I'm not restless or agitated. No, not a bit. I'm ready and willing to entrust myself to God's guidance, not just forcibly but willingly and gladly, and to know that He wants the best for us, for you too, my dearest. Yesterday I was at the light bath again. I have now won over both of the trustees by giving them cigarettes, the one from Oberweistritz who gives me the light baths, and the one who serves as the health-care aide here, who is from Hirschberg and now makes sure that I get there. So I hope that this diversion will work often, as long as I'm here. Unfortunately I'll need some more cigarettes, but that's assuming I still exist next week. In the sick bay I'm getting raw rutabaga, and starting today they want to give me white bread. They assure me that they're taking it away not from the patients but from the guards!! An amazing state of affairs.—The Russian offensive has raised our popularity quite a bit: "Now even the stupidest person can see what you wanted to save us from. And for that you're getting hanged!" Words to that effect.

Farewell, my love. May the Lord watch over you and us. J.

When you arrange for the arrest warrant to be translated, I would replace "attorney" and "Berlin-Lichterfelde" with "farmer" and "Kreisau," and say that was a later correction in case someone asks you. It appears on both sides, in the preamble and in the address.

Later: My dear, how wonderful to know you are there. How very good. The guard just brought me fresh meat, whipped cream, and rolls. Otherwise nothing else to report, other than that I love you very much, my very dear heart, and that is how it will remain. J.

FREYA TO HELMUTH JAMES, JANUARY 23, 1945

Tuesday, nine thirty

My dear, here I am again, or should I say once more, because I fear that my place will now be in Kreisau again, unless you think I ought to bring the boys = flee. Wend [Wendland] would like to have Asta [Wendland] move to Mecklenburg, to the Wendlands', anyway. Where does it say: "And woe unto them that are with child, and to them that give suck!"?[1] But as your pupil (your wife, your beloved, yours), I'm for remaining. One thing I've noticed right away, my dear love, during these days of the onset of terrible turmoil: We are in such good hands with the good Lord, how little can actually happen to us, even though the pressures of hunger, cold, and long journeys are certainly not to be scoffed at. The poor, poor people! Especially the poor mothers with small children. These baby carriages, these crying, freezing children, in front of trains that can no longer let them on in Liegnitz! At the same time, though, Liegnitz was well equipped with open coke ovens on the platforms, and with good soup and milk for the children. But to come to the point: Kreisau is still quite tranquil, but the county of Schweidnitz is taking in the entire county of Oels = we're getting 350 refugees from Oels in Kreisau and twenty-five in our house. They're set to come today or yesterday. On Sunday afternoon, we cleared out the three front rooms (dining room, fireplace room, and living room), closed off the doors to the hall and the big living room, and that's where they should be coming in—but we have to have food cooked for them in the utility room, and of course a welter of minor and major problems will arise, problems that have to be solved somehow. We're also afraid that the Russians are already heading across the Oder near Opole, and then they'll quickly get to Kreisau, or this line will become a front line, and we'll have to leave after all. But these are all decisions that will have to be made from one day to the next, and we're prepared for pretty much all of that. I'm only afraid that I can't give in to our hearts but instead have to go to Kreisau, or, to put it more specifically, that my place, no matter what I do, has to be with the boys. Today's armed forces report appears to be much calmer again, and maybe it will take quite a long time; then I just may find an opportunity to travel back and forth, because I absolutely don't shy away from hardships. Yesterday my trip was actually not bad at all. It is true that the 5:28 didn't leave Kreisau until 7:28, and I was seriously worried about whether I'd get in (and the only reason I did is that the Russian girl—a pleasant and nice person who lives in Stäsche's house—pushed and shoved me from behind and didn't get inside herself), but in Keischwitz!! the man who had a corner seat near me got off, so I got a place to sit early on. I sat there, quiet and tiny, until Liegnitz, feeling reasonably warm. In Liegnitz, however, we had to wait on the platform for two hours, because the express train to Berlin ought to have been coming, but instead there were special trains with refugees who filled the platforms with their bundles and children and formed virtual villages unto themselves. Finally a short and very crowded express train arrived. Getting in seemed out of the question, but as I walked back and forth next to the crowded train, I went past the dining car and saw that only two soldiers wanted to board there, and told the last one to squeeze in a little, which he did, and suddenly I was inside. Afterward I sat up front on my bag, my backpack on my lap, and slept in some corner. If I hadn't had a headache, because I left my aspirin behind, it would have been a pleasant trip, as the ride itself was fine even though we had to get another locomotive in Arnsdorf and spent a long time at every station because the people kept squeezing together and creating new space. Shortly before Köpenick, the train stopped, and after waiting for an hour, I got out with a few soldiers, and we made our way across the tracks to the Köpenick S-Bahn station,[2] and at 11 I was here. Still, I was very tired, because I didn't exactly get to sleep much in Kreisau. On Friday I didn't get there until 12 o'clock at night, on Saturday we listened to foreign stations until late at night, and on Sunday I got to bed at 10:30, but was back out at 4:30 a.m. The boys were by far the nicest thing in Kreisau. Casparchen woke up as soon as I entered the room at 12. (None of them had been expecting me, because the phone wasn't working, but the good Maria [Schanda] woke up right away; she was the only one who'd counted on my arrival.) He was utterly happy, and even the chubby little guy opened his eyes halfway and smiled: that was quite lovely, and in the morning both got into my bed, but I had a bad headache; even so, I was delighted with my two affectionate sons. The most obvious thing I've noticed about them was that my long absence has brought them very close to each other. They are truly brothers and love each other like crazy, and because Casparchen is a baby, they also play together splendidly, racing around the dinner table together—it's now in the large living room, though it wasn't on Saturday—screeching as they go, laughing themselves to death and having a great time. On Sunday after we ate, they lay down peacefully downstairs on the sofa and wanted to sleep there together. Casparchen only because he'd eaten too much, because normally he doesn't need to nap on Sundays. When they came to me on Saturday morning, Casparchen said, in English: "Dear Mother, I love you very much!" Very nicely pronounced, learned from Maria. Little Konrad meant to say something as well, but claimed that he had cold feet. Once they were warm again, he said, with his blanket pulled over his head, "Dear Reya, you're here, we're happy tralala." That was all very sweet. Casparchen is looking quite well, and a bit heavier. He doesn't have school anymore,[3] isn't learning anything, spends a lot of time outdoors, doesn't know much about the estate, is good at cycling, and doesn't ski much, but when he does, he's utterly fearless. Little Konrad has grown somewhat thinner since Dr. Breucken said there's nothing wrong with him (apart from being overweight). That was very handy for Frau Pick! I didn't deal with the Schloss. Zeumer is doing well. He is quite upset about you. He considers it on a par with dying at the front. He wants me to let you know that he will do everything in his power for Kreisau, but I need to do quite a bit as well "in the interest of the operation," because he won't be there forever. Your letter, which I have yet to read in its definitive version, goes along with this quite well. I didn't discuss any of the essentials with him. You and the Russians were the main focus. We loaded half of the flax and we're now threshing.—Lachmann, Rehlas, and Präbelt have left for the national militia.—Brigitte [Gerstenmaier] has to leave and will take the letter with her. You see, my love, that I had very little time in Kreisau, because I—She's going. I'll come tomorrow and will write much more!

Love, love, love, my beloved Jäm; I will forever remain your P.

I carried you so securely with me. That was quite beautiful to feel.

1. Matthew 24:19. 2. With the trains unable to reach the urban center, Freya switched to the S-Bahn, part of Berlin's public transit system, on the outskirts of the city. 3. Schooling collapsed due to teachers being conscripted for military service

FREYA TO HELMUTH JAMES, JANUARY 23, 1945

Tuesday noon

My dear love, to address the Prost issue, I'll first read through your long, beautiful letter again and answer the questions as they arise there. Yes, at least the Reich Ministry of Justice is acting as though they have a say, but I don't believe it. It is difficult for them not to be able to show mercy, but I really don't think that *they* have an alternative, incl. Herr Thierack. After all, Herr Prost and Herr Franke are also there to give us a hearing; that is their so-called duty. They have a copy of the family's plea for clemency, which Prost and Franke will receive as well. Prost cut off any opportunity I had to present a factual argument and said I could know only bits and pieces, he wasn't allowed to tell me anything, so this sort of discussion was pointless. He said I should limit what I say to personal remarks. That would allow for all kinds of basic comments, of course, but it seems doubtful to me that they would be given any credence. The way I see it, your petition (arguing for deferral) is something that could make sense only to the SS Reich Leader, but not to anyone else. A halfway measure of that kind surely doesn't sit well with the judiciary, which thinks only in terms of killing or pardoning. The SS would be more likely to agree simply not to carry out the execution, but in your case, Müller is decidedly against it.—Müller is also aware of the relative significance of Kreisau, for he told me that Goerdeler was nothing but a theorist as well: you're a traitor, and such people simply have to be eliminated. I forgot to write you recently that the friendly and naïve Ebersberg said: It was only through Goerdeler that we got hold of all this; they had all kinds of lists and we got the complete set of them. But how could they have made those lists! If they hadn't, we would never have figured out all that (in other words, what they "technically refer to as the Kreisau Circle")! I have to say that on the whole, they have gained a very accurate picture of everything. So I also get the feeling that none of my (your) little arguments can bring anything into line. (I've already told Prost and Franke that you are absolutely unambitious and don't represent any interests.) In their eyes, you are and will remain a traitor; if you like, you can think of that as a loftier position, but that doesn't get you far in your pursuit of a pardon—more like the opposite. I've already told Prost something along the lines of: We're not bitter. I told him in so many words that you'll be dying for something that will definitely outlive you as an individual, which also means that I have no inner conflicts to endure, because I believe it too. I said that on the previous day we'd sat across from each other and didn't say a single word about it, but we both knew it quite clearly. That was the very highlight of our conversation, and it made an impression on Prost as well: "So then he'll die a martyr," he said *in earnest*. I found that a bit much and quickly replied, "In any event, he'll die for an ideal." But you can see that even Herr Prost was actually only speaking in terms of your death. So my Thursday came to an end with the feeling that all my endeavors and undertakings had been in vain, that there was nothing more I could do, and that I'd now have to stop doing things. My dear, dear love, the truth is that our eyes cannot catch sight of any way out from your situation, no matter where they look, nowhere do I see the tiniest spark of hope, unless the SS Reich Leader himself does something, and I consider that unlikely too. No, I don't see anything. But this past year and these past months have taught us quite palpably, and quite clearly, that this means nothing at all before God, and so we can say: You're still alive, and as long as you live, there are possibilities for you to stay alive. I'm in a state of mind that I can't characterize as hope, but I'm calmly planning where your shirts can be washed and where sausage and butter for you can come from if I need to be away, and I'm planning quite long-term without having any real reason to do so, not that I'm full of hope either, but the days from the 9th to the 11th have shown me that *I* have to live that way, continuing on, with you. How firmly I carry you in me, my love, quite, quite firmly, and with the unwavering certainty that even your death can do nothing to change that. The dear Lord has taught me this, and so have you, my love. *Your* situation, by contrast, is far more difficult, because you have to conquer a very concrete nervousness every day. This week, at any rate, Thierack *is not here yet*, and things will surely stay calm. It is easy, of course, to say from the outside what I would like to say, because you are alone with yourself the whole day long, and that is something quite different from my life. Even so I'm asking whether you can't willfully and consciously switch off any thoughts of a possible execution and just live your life in a cell, which can be quite lively, as in your case it is; whether you can't stay close to Him in life, yet not anticipate death on a daily basis. Can that be done in the cell? It would be good if you could do that. If you should then be brought in, you'll still have a lot of time, probably too much, to prepare for the actual death. At any rate, you now still have to live. Is that an impossible wish? I would very much like for you not to get caught up in this virtually unbearable tension. If it should take several more weeks, how are you supposed to endure that! Oh my Jäm, it is amazing how much is now being inflicted on everyone, and people are able to endure so much, particularly when they know that God is with them in spite of it all and knows how difficult it all is. I know, my love, how firmly I am united with you in all this. Yes, if you have to die, Marion [Yorck] and I do have it better than other wives who have lost their husbands for Hitler. I've always thought so. In this as well, my love, I know that I am quite, quite firmly united with you!

Now there's still the big question to answer: Should I go back to Kreisau? Can I stay here? Should I bring the boys here, or to Edith [Henssel]? Actually I won't be able to do the latter anymore as of Friday. The primary purpose of the restriction on trains is to stop the flow of refugees. How will you be if you don't hear anything more from us, you don't see me anymore, and you no longer have the feeling that I am very close by? An essential component of your life would cease to exist, even if it were still possible to arrange for one letter a week, which would be difficult enough. What, my Jäm, should I do? I don't want to speak of myself at all in this connection, as you are indeed the central person, you and the little sons. What lies ahead? And how will that be? If we become the front, we'll have to leave in any case. What decisions! If you were no longer alive, I'd hang on to Kreisau even more tightly than I do now. But I have the feeling that we will make up our minds within the next few days. Those back at home are anticipating that I'll remain for only a brief time and then go back home. In any case, I'll get permission for another face-to-face meeting now and see to getting something out of Steengracht.

[The letter breaks off here. Freya later added: It did not get to H.]

APPENDIX
Additional Documents

THE FOLLOWING letters are housed at the German Literature Archive in Marbach, as is the full set of the correspondence between Helmuth James and Freya von Moltke, both from the prison period and from the previous years, collected in *Letters to Freya*.

FROM FREYA VON MOLTKE'S "THE FINAL MONTHS IN KREISAU," DESCRIBING JANUARY 25, 1945[1]

On January 25, 1945, Marion Yorck and I traveled from Berlin to Kreisau. Edith [Henssel] and Henssel brought us to the train. They had the nicest sandwiches for us, and Marion had a bottle of very old Malaga. The bottle was wrapped in paper or a napkin; it looked like coffee with milk. Marion and I sat close together on a two-person bench in third class. We were traveling against the current of the refugees, so it took us exactly twenty-four hours to get to Kreisau, but in memory it was a good trip. I think we were quite jovial. In Kreisau, no one knew about Helmuth's death. I found things with Casparchen quite difficult. He was lying in my bed, where he had slept; I sat at the edge. But the feeling passed, and the next morning, when he saw that I was sad, he said, "Because of Pa? Still?!" That was truly a great source of comfort.

1. See Freya von Moltke, Michael Balfour, and Julian Frisby, *Die letzten Monate in Kreisau, Helmuth James von Moltke, Anwalt der Zukunft* (Stuttgart: Deutsche Verlags-Anstalt, 1982), 317.

FREYA TO HER MOTHER, ADA DEICHMANN,
AUGUST 24, 1945

Berlin, 24 August 45

Beloved Meki,

Yesterday I received the first news about you from Eddy Waetjen, which reached me by way of Mr. Gaevernitz. I was very, very happy to hear that you are well, indeed, quite well, and I was told that you had very nice enjoyable circumstances in Godesberg. I hope that's true. In my heart of hearts, I never feared for you and am reasonably certain that I will find you again in the foreseeable future. I had considered trying immediately to have the British or Americans take me over there with them. But it's all somewhat cumbersome and takes time, even though I think it's altogether possible in principle, yet I'm not making the attempt yet, because Silesia is so turbulent that I don't dare to leave the children and the house alone for long. I have already written to you a couple of times using various means of transport. Did you receive any of that? In any case, things haven't gone badly at all for me and the little boys during all these months.[1] We had everything we needed, and the Berghaus made it through all the storms, untouched and unplundered and unchanged. We spent a little time in the Riesengebirge,[2] during which time Marion [Yorck] and Muto Yorck looked after the house all by themselves, but then we went right back, because the Russians arrived both here and there. Nothing happened to us. Still, in the light of the gruesome pandemonium that has overtaken Silesia, I wonder how long the Berghaus can remain such an oasis, and I'm afraid that this won't work indefinitely. So I came to Berlin. That is a cumbersome process because you have to spend two days sitting in full coal cars. There is no passenger-train connection (I don't know if you can say: so far), and en route, if you're unlucky, as many are, bandits rob you of everything—hasn't happened to me yet—but you get where you're going. I'll now try to find a way to send the boys to Sister Helen in Switzerland[3] during the winter if necessary. I'm trying in two ways, both of which are good, and I'm hoping for success. I'll register for residence here, which I can do readily as Helmuth's wife, and the boys and I can then live here, if need be with Marion Yorck, where I can always be reached: Lichterfelde-West, Hortensienstrasse 50. At the same time I'm trying to get Frau Reichwein's children to Sweden, so that if the conditions become untenable, we can get the children out quickly. One can always get out, because the Poles are glad to get rid of any Germans.

I've discussed my situation with various friends here. Some take the view that I should give up Kreisau as soon as possible. Some think I should try to hold on to it until the final peace talks, because some portion of it could still stay with us. I can't really make up my mind yet to relinquish the Berghaus to the Poles voluntarily, as it is totally intact and yet so imbued with Moltke life. I'm still waiting for a better way and I think it will come to me. In any case, I have now made contact with the world from here and that was good for me. I was never alone during these months and I think it's fair to say that I'll never be truly alone again in my life, since I was able to part from Helmuth in such a beautiful manner, but I would so like to find all of you again, and you in particular, above all others. Poelchau, for instance, is also off in the west, and another man I hold in high regard is considering the idea of heading west as well. All this draws me in that direction, yet on the other hand, the Russians still interest me, and I can't quite believe that it might actually be impossible to have any real contact with them, as it appears to all of us for the present. They are wild and uncivilized, but generous, unbureaucratic, and with their power very strong people; it's just that their mentality is so utterly different from ours that they cannot be understood. Besides, their system is too familiar to us, and just as garish as ours.[4] That's the worst part. That they permit me to continue eating potatoes and bread in Kreisau without needing to go out to work in the fields—and I will certainly not do so, because I consider that wrong—is pretty astonishing, seeing as I haven't had any standing to speak of for quite some time. First it was the Poles and then the Russians that held sway there, but Herr Zeumer is still on the sidelines, and that is quite pleasant.

The atmosphere at the Berghaus is good and appealing. The six merry, carefree children, Frau Pick, and dear Liesbeth, who goes to work in the fields and whose mother, having turned up one day, eats next to nothing and does all the dirty work, Frau Reichwein brimming with energy and efficiency: that is all very pleasant. Marion and Muto were always there from time to time, and are actually the ones who are really close to me. Frau Pick was very bossy; she spoiled Konrad exceedingly and is nervous by nature, so she was often very difficult for me to put up with at a time like this, in spite of all her love and constant work; she also doesn't get along at all well with Frau Reichwein, who has the living rooms facing the front to live in for herself, but shares the household with us.

Your grandchildren are, I think, delightful little chaps. I, for one, am quite pleased with them. At the same time, I have to say that Helmuth's death hasn't changed my attitude toward them. I still have Helmuth securely close to me, so I haven't felt the need to cling to them with my love, but they are affectionate with me. You know Casparchen's dear heart. He really takes care of me and is so kind to me when I have a headache or feel unwell. He is a real friend, and the three of us make up a very nice, close-knit little club. Konrad is still peacefully introspective, but far from a serious child. He has become more and more cheerful and has now stopped disavowing his Rhenish blood, but there's quite a bit of Helmuth in him, which, of course, makes me especially happy. He is determined and acts like a young man, whereas Caspar's charm lies in his sparkling amiability and warmheartedness. He has become quite the dynamic bundle of energy and wild child. Both of them are very good-looking. Casparchen, who now proudly goes by the name Helmuth and writes that name on his notebooks, has also been getting some schooling, since we have a young, pleasant teacher living with us. She is working as an instructor in the village. At the moment the Poles have closed the school, but I hope we'll start it again, otherwise we'll continue in the Berghaus. You see, we've come through this period astonishingly, truly astonishingly well. Overall, I have experienced quite a lot of astonishing things since last year, since we last saw each other, and I have been quite uncommonly blessed. Isn't it a true miracle that I can say this after all that has happened? When everywhere I look, I see the terrible suffering people are experiencing everywhere, I feel quite reticent and humble. Is that also the case where you are, or is it just in the east? One really ought to be utterly unable to endure seeing it, but one does so anyway.

Well, Meki, I'd rather not write more than one sheet. Let's hope the letter arrives. I'm sending it off with so many warmest thoughts and wishes. My greatest wish is to see you again as soon as possible, but you'll see: it won't be much longer. Make sure you get a letter to Berlin with your British friends, and it will certainly get to me in due course. How I would enjoy seeing your dear handwriting in front of me again.

Farewell; give everyone my best regards! I embrace you tenderly and full of longing. On Wednesday I'll be going to Kreisau again.

Freya

1. See Freya von Moltke's report, in Freya von Moltke, Michael Balfour, and Julian Frisby, *Die letzten Monate in Kreisau, Helmuth James von Moltke, Anwalt der Zukunft* (Stuttgart: Deutsche Verlags-Anstalt, 1982), 317. 2. The family avoided the end of the war by temporarily fleeing to a village in the mountains just south of Kreisau. 3. Sister Helen ran a children's home in Vlims in the Engadine, to which Freya had sent her ailing sons in the winter of 1943–1944 in order to cure them. 4. Freya saw parallels between the Soviet and the National Socialist system of government.

THE INDICTMENT FOR HELMUTH JAMES VON MOLTKE, OCTOBER 11, 1944[1]
THE EXAMINING MAGISTRATE OF THE PEOPLE'S COURT O J 21/44 GRS.181/44 556

Berlin, 11 October 1944

Arrest warrant

1. Count Helmuth von Moltke of Berlin-Lichterfelde-West, former attorney, born Mar. 11, 1907
2. Dr. Theodor Haubach of Berlin-Grunewald, commercial clerk, born Sept. 15, 1896?

3. Dr. Eugen Gerstenmaier of Berlin-Dahlem, consistory councillor, born Aug. 25, 1906

4. Theodor Stelzer [*sic*] of Hamburg, former lieutenant colonel, born Dec. 17, 1885

5. Franz Sperr of Munich, colonel and envoy (ret.), born Feb. 11, 1878

6. Dr. Franz Reisert of Augsburg, former attorney, born June 28, 1889

7. Josef-Ernst Fürst Fugger von Glött of Kirchheim, Bavaria, large-scale farmer, born Oct. 26, 1895

are to be brought in for pretrial custody.

They are charged with having jointly endeavored to alter the constitution of the Reich with force and to rob the Führer of his constitutional power, and in doing so to abet hostile forces within our borders during a war against the Reich.

Crime according to §§ 80 para. 2, 81, 91b, 73, 47 of the Penal Code.

They have, within our borders, specifically von Moltke up to his arrest in January 1944, Dr. Haubach, Dr. Gerstenmaier, Stelzer, and Sperr up to the summer of 1944, Reisert and Fürst Fugger von Glött in 1943, undertaken with others to overthrow the National Socialist government, if necessary with an act of violence directed at the Führer, in order to put themselves or like-minded people into positions of power.

Pretrial detention is being imposed because there is a flight risk, as crimes that may entail a severe penalty constitute the object of the investigation.

Against this arrest warrant, legal redress of the grievance is permissible, and requires special authorization.

Signed Dr. Ehrlich, head of the district court.

1. See Ger van Roon, *Neuordnung im Widerstand: Der Kreisauer Kreis innerhalb der deutschen Widerstandsbewegung* (Munich: Oldenbourg R. Verlag GmbH, 1967), 594.

THE KREISAU CIRCLE IN THE ASSESSMENT OF THE PEOPLE'S COURT, JANUARY 9, 1945[1]
ASSESSMENT OF THE PEOPLE'S COURT, JANUARY 10, 1945

The Kreisau Circle was a group of defeatists and opponents of National Socialism that the former director of the international group in the Armed Forces High Command, War Administration Councillor (Attorney) Count Helmuth von Moltke, had been gathering around him at his Kreisau estate in Lower Silesia since approximately 1940. The group was composed of reactionary, federalist, religious, and syndicalist members. Meetings took place repeatedly in Kreisau, as well as in Berlin and Munich. The subject of the meetings was a so-called safety-net program that would be implemented if National Socialism collapsed. The program envisioned that in place of National Socialism the Christian churches of both denominations should step in as organizational institutions surviving the events. The powers of the state should not be dismantled altogether, but to a large extent transferred to twelve or so provinces organized along traditional lines, each headed by a provincial administrator. The workforce should be organized in labor unions according to syndicalist principles.

1. From the text of the trial proceedings prepared for the head of the Nazi Party chancellery, Martin Bormann, dated January 9, 1945 (Bundesarchiv NS 6/20), in Walter Wagner, *Der Volksgerichtshof im nationalsozialistischen Staat* (Stuttgart: DVA, 1974), 773.

HELMUTH JAMES VON MOLTKE IN THE ASSESSMENT OF THE PEOPLE'S COURT, JANUARY 10, 1945[1]

5. Count Helmuth von Moltke
   Thirty-seven years old, jurist (specializing in international law), war administration councillor in the international division of the Armed Forces High Command, farmer at the Kreisau estate in Lower

Silesia, related by marriage to Count York [*sic*] von Wartenburg, whose case has already been adjudicated.

In late 1942, Moltke learned about Gördeler's [*sic*] plans by way of York von Wartenburg and von der Schulenburg. He adamantly rejected them. He regarded Gördeler as a second Kerensky, whose government would inevitably be burdened with both the murder of the Führer and the stab-in-the-back myth and would therefore be of brief duration. In a meeting that took place in January 1943 at Kreisau, and in which Gördeler, Beck, Popitz, von Hassel [*sic*], Schulenburg, Jessen, and others participated, he articulated his rejection of Gördeler in strong language, which meant that the planned "bridge to the activists" failed to materialize. But instead of reporting an offense, he responded to Gördeler's "thirst for domination," that is, Gördeler's endeavor to bring people from the Kreisau Circle over to his side, only with a further activation of this circle. Consequently, despite his opposition to Gördeler, he was exactly like him in aligning himself with the camp of the enemies of the Reich from the outset. Over the course of numerous meetings, he developed his so-called safety-net program, about which I laid out the details in the telex message I sent yesterday. In the main hearing it emerged that he had obtained the map that he showed around at the meetings about the planned reorganization of the Reich, illegally (via York von Wartenburg) from the Ministry of the Interior, where it had been produced earlier in the framework of proposed structural reforms of the Reich.

A very tall, yet frail individual, he was questioned while seated on account of his health. Instead of honestly showing his colors, Moltke kept indulging in sophistry that had a supposed basis in the law or in philosophy, and even came up with the claim that on the basis of his official capacity in the Armed Forces High Command he considered himself authorized to develop his plans, that is, to prepare for the event of an enemy occupation of the Reich or of parts of the Reich "resistance movements" without involvement of the National Socialist Party and to select the appropriate people for this purpose. Freisler initially questioned Moltke in a calm manner. Eventually, however, he clearly lost patience. He barked at Moltke that he would not be made a fool of. During a brief recess, he gave Moltke's defense counsel the opportunity to make this standpoint clear to the defendant. When Freisler explained that in the view of the People's Court anyone who even considers the possibility of a German defeat is abhorrent, Moltke replied that he was not acquainted with this "judicature" of the People's Court; in his official capacity at the Armed Forces High Command he had always considered a possibility of this kind without encountering opposition from his superiors (Freisler stopped him from amplifying this point). Down to the end, Moltke tried to don a mantle of morality for his "unfathomably indecent goings-on" (Freisler). Utterly consumed by defeatism, and at the same time a peculiar scoundrel. The only depressing fact was that his name was Count Helmuth von Moltke.

1. From the text of the trial proceedings prepared for the head of the Nazi Party chancellery, Martin Bormann, dated January 10, 1945 (Bundesarchiv NS 6/20), in Walter Wagner, *Der Volksgerichtshof im nationalsozialistischen Staat* (Stuttgart: DVA, 1974), 779.

SECRET MESSAGE FROM HELMUTH JAMES TO CARL DIETRICH VON TROTHA, JANUARY 10, 1945[1]

1. Death penalty requested against:
   Moltke + seizure of assets
   Delp + seizure of assets?
   Gerstenmaier?
   Reisert?
   Sperr
   Fugger: 3 years in prison.
   Steltzer, Haubach, Gross separately.
In the opinion of the defense the court will accept these recommendations.
Sentencing tomorrow 4 p.m.
We anticipate the sentences to be carried out tomorrow evening.

2. Moltke + Delp are doing well.
   Gerstenmaier somewhat worn out.
3. Moltke not uneasy for a single moment, even during the trial, in spite of some awful shouting; not even clammy hands.
4. If possible coffee again tomorrow, fine if cold.
5. Request visit from the pastor for tomorrow.

1. The manuscript is housed at the German Literature Archive in Marbach.

THE JUDGMENT AGAINST HELMUTH JAMES ON JANUARY 11, 1945[1]

In the name of the German people!

In the criminal proceedings against

1. the former attorney, farmer, and former war administration councillor Count Helmuth von Moltke, of Berlin-Lichterfelde-West, born on March 11, 1907 in Kreisau […] incarcerated at this time on charges of treason, etc., the first bench of the court in pursuit of the indictments received from the chief Reich prosecutor on October 23 and November 9, 1944, in the main hearing on January 9, 10, and 11, 1945 […] ruled:

Count Helmuth von Moltke knew about Goerdeler's treachery. Although he did adamantly reject working with him, and he also warned his political friends about Goerdeler, he did not report what he knew.

He himself, caught up in defeatism, formed a circle that planned to seize power with non–National Socialists in the event that our Reich collapsed.

All these things have rendered him permanently dishonorable.

He is punished with death.

1. Alfred Delp, *Gesammelte Schriften, Vol. 4: Im Gefängnis* (Frankfurt am Main: Joseph Knecht, 1984), 409–12.

AFTERWORD

"But I see my hourglass running out and I'm thinking: Talk to her while you still can."

Since reading *Last Letters*, it has taken me some time to reorient myself: London, spring 2019; sunshine beyond my kitchen window, tulips in the park. I have to keep looking up to remind myself. Inside, I am still in Berlin, Lichterfelde, Kreisau, or on trains between these places. In my mind's eye, I see the People's Court waiting rooms; the Tegel prison cell with the half-boarded window, and the desk and the open Bible. Having just finished the letters yourself, you may well be experiencing this too: a feeling of connectedness, a reluctance to let go.

Despite the desperation of the months described in these letters, I find myself closing my eyes to return to them; I leaf back through the pages too—most of all, to return to Freya and to Helmuth. The intimacy they forged during his imprisonment is astonishing, precious beyond words. The picture their letters afford of those blighted times is also a rare gift to the future, to all those who wish to understand the German twentieth century.

If, like me, you have a family connection to Germany, you may also have read these letters against the backdrop of your own family's Third Reich experience. Mine could scarcely—regretfully—be more different.

My grandfather was an early adopter of the National Socialist cause; a "100-percenter," as Freya and Helmuth might have called him. At the time they began writing these letters, in the autumn of 1944, my grandfather was serving on the eastern front as a doctor with the Waffen SS. His wife, my grandmother, was from a patrician Hamburg merchant family, which—like Freya's— lost much in the hyperinflation and subsequent crash. Unlike Freya's family, however, they threw in their lot with the Nazis, believing Hitler to be the country's last and best chance against communism. Both of my grandparents found hope and purpose in the resurgent Germany of the 1930s; my Opa in his work as a GP in Hamburg's harbor district, my grandmother in her voluntary social work for the party. Their eldest daughter, my mother, was born the summer Hitler became Führer and was brought up as a National Socialist. By the time these letters were written, she was ten years old: a Third Reich child.

I thought of her often while reading; how her life was to be changed so abruptly by the capitulation, just a few weeks after Helmuth's death. Her world view, too, was to be profoundly altered: by the removal of her parents' influence (both were imprisoned), by the coming of democracy, but most of all by the fellowship with others of her generation: Germans from East and West, Dutch and French, young Europeans all, many of whom she found through the church. My grandparents were far slower to adjust, as my Opa's own, far more insular letters from his Russian captivity attest.

But I was reminded also of many other Germans as I read: the countless diarists and letter writers in Walter Kempowski's *Echolot*, Marta Hillers's record of the capitulation weeks in *A Woman in Berlin*. But perhaps key among them was Victor Klemperer: I heard echoes of his diaries in so many of the von Moltkes' experiences.

Like Helmuth, Klemperer was taken into *Schutzhaft* ("protective custody"—the Nazis were masters of the awful euphemism); he too had to go from pillar to post to seek legal assistance, navigating the terrifying vagaries of the Third Reich bureaucracy after he lost his university post in Dresden when Jews were excluded from the civil service. Like Helmuth, too, Klemperer drew strength from his marriage; indeed it came to be his only protection, his wife having been deemed "Aryan" under the Nazi race laws. But while Helmuth was to find much-needed sustenance in the honey from Freya's Kreisau bees, for Klemperer, the yearning for something sweet could only be soothed by a teaspoon of jam, filched from another resident of the "Jewish house"—the de facto ghetto—he and his wife were moved to. The jam provided the yearned-for calories, but also pointed up the indignity and deprivation he and his fellow Jewish Germans were forced to endure.

Still, while the echoes may provide an occasional counterpoint, both the Klemperers and the von Molkes faced the Nazi years with impressive resilience. Crucially, Klemperer's diary and these *Last Letters* each show the reader what such courage looks like; what it feels like too, in all its rawness. They reveal that it often involves crippling doubt; that being resolute entails fighting off irresolution, over and again. And, counterintuitive though this may seem, they also show us that hope can be as difficult to live with as despair. Or, as Helmuth would have it: "It's the old, difficult, difficult art of keeping it at the right level."

Helmuth was hanged; I knew this long before picking up these pages. And yet, and yet, as I read, I could not keep my own hopes from rising—even in the face of historical fact. As he and Freya shared news of the collapse of the eastern front, I found myself yearning with them for a stay of execution, one long enough for the Russians to reach Berlin.

Klemperer hoped and despaired to the last. Shortly after Helmuth's execution, Klemperer received notice of transportation, but Allied action saved him. The British bombed Dresden, and in the confusion of the ensuing firestorm, he and his wife fled the burning city, finding shelter in anonymity, indistinguishable from the thousands of homeless, paperless others.

For the majority of those under Nazi persecution in the end days, there was no such deliverance, of course. None for Helmuth and his Freya; none—even as late as April 1945—for so many of Helmuth's fellow Tegel prisoners, including Dietrich Bonhoeffer.

Close to my home in London is the Lutheran church where Bonhoeffer was the pastor in the 1930s. I walked there after reading these letters to pay my respects to all those imprisoned and executed for their "hope crime" of thinking beyond the Nazis. I was also, in truth, looking for some kind of solace. This spring of 2019, for all its sunshine and tulips, does not feel particularly hopeful. My country is bitterly divided over the question of whether to leave Europe; the rise of "populism" (as the current awful euphemism has it) across so many Western democracies—including Germany—has shaken me, as it has so many, jolting us out of our postwar certainties.

But at the church I think again of my mother, the Third Reich child who grew up to read Bonhoeffer, to take part in ecumenical gatherings and reconstruction works in Germany and beyond, together with young people from all across Europe who became her lifelong friends. I see echoes of the Kreisau Circle in these endeavors and connections: in the young woman she became, and in the mother who taught me to look at our family's past with clear eyes.

Helmuth and Freya were clear-eyed too. In their struggle with hope and despair, they were always grounded on the bedrock of the harshest of realities. Indeed, they found a kind of grace there: "The earth is nice and hard under our feet once again, and the pink clouds have scattered." Standing firm, they remained true to thoughts beyond their times.

The bond between them was one of ideas, a sensibility, unclouded by personal ambition, which sought connection, which believed in the human capacity to find common ground, to work together for the common good. It is a vision of the possible—at once profoundly hopeful and profoundly tangible—and I hold fast to it.

These letters are a gift indeed. Not only to those who wish to understand the Third Reich but also to any who see hope challenged in their own times.

We should listen to them while we can.

—RACHEL SEIFFERT

BIOGRAPHICAL NOTE

HELMUTH James von Moltke grew up in an unconventional household in Lower Silesia. Although he was born into one of Germany's famous families on March 11, 1907, as the third heir of Field Marshal Count Helmuth von Moltke, neither his father nor he were typical representatives of the Prussian nobility. His father suffered from a severe illness as a young man and was able to recover with the help of members of the Christian Science movement, which made him a lifelong adherent of this sect. He met his future wife, Dorothy Rose Innes, when she and her mother came to Kreisau as "paying guests." She was eighteen at the time and a South African of Scottish descent. Her father was a distinguished politician and attorney in South Africa and in time became the chief justice of the Union of South Africa, which came into being in 1910. Sir James Rose Innes was an adamant critic of Cecil Rhodes, and Dorothy came from a democratic, liberal home and raised her children in this tradition.

Helmuth did not excel as a schoolboy, but he flourished as a university student in Berlin, Breslau, and Vienna. Contacts with American journalists in Berlin and the circle around the progressive educator Eugenie Schwarzwald in Berlin and Vienna had a major impact on his thinking. In Silesia, Helmuth and his cousin Carl Dietrich von Trotha took an interest in the wretched social conditions of the coal miners in Waldenburg. With the support of Karl Ohle, the district administrator, they strove to improve the lot of the miners with a relief action. Carl Dietrich attended the university in Breslau, where he met Eugen Rosenstock-Huessy, a legal historian. The voluntary work-service camps, inspired by Rosenstock-Huessy, known as the Löwenberger Arbeitslager, brought together industrial workers, farmers, and students for discussions and collaborative work in 1927 and led to the von Moltkes meeting Rosenstock-Huessy. The young men assembled in these Arbeitslager formed the nucleus of what would later become the Kreisau Circle.

Freya von Moltke, née Deichmann, was born March 29, 1911, in Cologne as the third child of Carl Theodor and Ada Deichmann. Hers was a privileged childhood in a wealthy patrician household. Her father was senior partner of Deichmann & Company, a private bank in Cologne that had prospered in the fifty years before her birth by financing the expansion of the mighty industries of the Ruhr, which had become the backbone of the German economy. Her mother, also a native of Cologne and considerably younger than her husband, had liberal leanings similar to those of Dorothy von Moltke and ensured that her children too were brought up with an openness toward Germany's western neighbors, their cultures and languages.

The deepening depression after the stock market crash of 1929 presented substantial difficulties for both families. Kreisau, the Moltke estate, had become heavily indebted and in 1929 Helmuth—only twenty-two years old at the time—was given the difficult task of running the estate and persuading the creditors not to foreclose but to give him a chance to repay the debts. He was able to rise to this considerable challenge. He had just completed his first law degree and from this point on also oversaw the property with the help of a manager installed by the creditors. He now lived with his mother and two youngest siblings, who were still in school, in the Berghaus, into which the Moltkes had moved in 1928 from the Schloss, the manor house, which was spacious but difficult to heat.

During these years, the Deichmann family—like the Moltkes—suffered a financial crisis. The global economic crisis caused the Deichmann & Company bank to become insolvent in 1931. Freya's father was the personally liable partner and his assets were therefore seized in the insolvency. The period of prosperity came to an end for the Deichmanns as well. Their difficult straits had little discernable effect on the mothers and their children, however. Thanks to a large network of family and friends, no one suffered privation. The children all became independent in the 1930s, but the fathers did not benefit from the economic recovery. Freya's father died at the age of sixty-five, just a few days after the wedding of Helmuth und Freya. Helmuth's father had accepted a position as the German Christian Science representative and had to be in Berlin almost all the time, so his role in Kreisau was much reduced after 1929.

That summer, Helmuth and Freya met in Grundlsee, Austria. She was eighteen; he was twenty-two. As a student in Vienna, Helmuth had entered a circle of young people around the educator and social reformer Eugenie Schwarzwald. The group included artists, musicians, writers, and international journalists, among them the Austrian pianist Rudolf Serkin, the German writer Bertolt Brecht, the American journalists Dorothy Thompson and Edgar Mowrer, and the Austrian painter Oskar Kokoschka. Helmuth was invited to the Schwarzwalds' summer retreat on the Grundlsee where Freya had also come, along with her two older brothers. It was a magical summer for Freya and Helmuth. Even though it only contains Helmuth's letters without Freya's responses, *Letters to Freya*[1] conveys the emotional upheaval of this encounter, which Freya would always remember as love at first sight: "I saw him and I knew, he is the one!" In October 1931, Helmuth and Freya had a small religious wedding ceremony in the home of Freya's parents in Cologne. When Dorothy von Moltke traveled to South Africa in the winter of 1931–1932 to visit her parents, she asked her young daughter-in-law to take charge of the Kreisau household. The Kreisau estate played a central role for the extended Moltke family, and Freya took to her new tasks well. Within the family, however, there were political tensions with its more conservative members, who were critical of the liberal views of Helmuth and his young wife.

The National Socialist seizure of power spelled the end of Helmuth's plans for a career as a judge. From the outset, Helmuth and Freya rejected any notion of cooperating with the Third Reich. Until 1939 they gave no outward signs of their oppositional stance, opting instead to limit their activities to the personal sphere by warning individuals in danger—mostly Jews—about their persecutors. Even though

Helmuth did not want to work under the new rulers, he did have to earn a living; Kreisau did not bring in any money. In 1932, he and Freya relocated to Berlin, which would now become the center of his professional life. Freya was studying law, while he completed his legal traineeship and passed his assessor examination in 1934.

In that same year, Helmuth and Freya began a series of visits abroad. Twice—in 1934 and 1937—they spent extended periods with his grandparents in South Africa. Helmuth realized that by specializing in private international law, he had a way of justifying frequent trips abroad and contacts with people outside the Nazi sphere of influence. He therefore opted to gain accreditation as a lawyer in England. He began studying at one of the four British Inns of Court, the Honourable Society of the Inner Temple in London, and met the qualifications to become a barrister in 1938. He joined a law firm in Berlin and built a list of clients—many of them Jewish—who sought to save themselves and their assets as they left Germany. During this time, Freya was able to complete her doctorate in law without receiving any other legal degree.

In 1935, Dorothy von Moltke died suddenly at the age of fifty-one. She had been the focal point of the family in the Berghaus. Freya stepped in to fill the big gap left by Dorothy's death. She now essentially relocated to Kreisau, which meant that she and Helmuth were often separated. A lively correspondence ensued. Helmuth's letters to Freya have been housed at the German Literature Archive in Marbach since 2009. They constitute a valuable personal and historical archive. In addition to those in the present collection, many of the letters Helmuth wrote in 1939 and the following years were published in *Briefe an Freya*[2] (*Letters to Freya*) and *Im Land der Gottlosen*.[3] In spite of Helmuth's misgivings about bringing children into the world in such trying political times, their first son, Helmuth Caspar, was born in November 1937, and they had a second son, Konrad, in 1941.

When World War II began in September 1939, Helmuth was conscripted as a war administration councillor and, as an expert in international law, entered the foreign division of the Armed Forces

High Command. In this position he could attempt to mitigate some of the excesses of the regime. Particularly in issues pertaining to the treatment of prisoners of war and hostage-taking, he constantly endeavored to hold National Socialist legal interpretations to the standards of international law. He used his official trips abroad to contact opponents of the Nazis.

In his private life, Helmuth, along with Freya, moved from a general opposition to the regime to active resistance when the war began. Early on, he had learned the value of rigorous, focused work. Four years of strenuous efforts ensued, aimed at drawing up the outlines of plans for a new Germany after what Helmuth regarded as the inevitable loss of the war. Working with Peter Graf Yorck von Wartenburg, who shared his vision, Helmuth developed a common basis for a broader discussion. At the same time he called on the friends he knew from the Löwenberger Arbeitslager, and little by little they expanded the circle with trustworthy people of highly diverse backgrounds and points of view: socialists, large landowners, unionists, capitalists, and Social Democrats, as well as Catholic and Protestant Christians and church representatives. In numerous small groups, most of them in Berlin, and at three large gatherings at the Kreisau estate, they discussed a fundamental restructuring of Germany after the end of National Socialism. They focused on the future democratic organization of government and society; issues of law, the economy, and education; and the integration of Germany into the community of European states. The approaches and transcripts that emerged from these meetings, the "Kreisau plans," were not discovered by the National Socialists in their written form even after the assassination attempt on Hitler on July 20, 1944, although these meetings, even without documentation, provided enough facts for the prosecution of the participants.

But they were not just making plans. Helmuth and some of his friends were also determined to inform the Allies about the existence of the various resistance groups so that they would abandon demands for unconditional capitulation and work together with the resistance in Germany. However, their calls went unheeded.

In January 1944, Helmuth was arrested because he had warned an acquaintance, Otto Carl Kiep, about a Gestapo informer. After a brief incarceration at the Prinz-Albrecht-Strasse Gestapo prison in Berlin, Helmuth was transferred, as a prisoner in protective custody, to the prison building adjacent to the Ravensbrück concentration camp. Following the discovery by the Gestapo of his connection to the men involved in the July 20, 1944 assassination plot, his prison conditions became harsher. On September 28, he was brought to Berlin for incarceration in the Tegel prison. Thanks to the help of the prison chaplain, Harald Poelchau, he was able to carry on a secret correspondence with Freya over the course of almost four months. On January 11, 1945, he was sentenced and was executed on January 23.

At first Freya and her sons stayed in Kreisau, along with Rosemarie Reichwein (also a widow) and her four children. When the Soviet troops approached, they temporarily fled to the Riesengebirge, but soon came back and lived at the estate, which was under Polish-Russian occupation until the fall of 1945. Lionel Curtis, a British friend, was able to arrange for emissaries of the British embassy to evacuate Freya and her sons from Silesia in October 1945 and bring them to Berlin.

After spending time in Switzerland, Freya and her children moved to Cape Town, South Africa, in 1947. Helmuth's grandparents had died, but earlier friendships were still intact, so Caspar and Konrad could grow up in peace there. Freya found a job as a social worker at an organization for disabled children. By 1956, however, she'd had enough of the injustice of the apartheid laws in South Africa and returned to Germany. She and Annedore Leber co-authored a history book about the Weimar Republic and the Third Reich for secondary schools, and began transcribing Helmuth's letters, which were later edited by Beate Ruhm von Oppen for an edition that spanned August 22, 1939, to January 18, 1944.

In 1956, Freya crossed paths with Eugen Rosenstock-Huessy, whom she had met briefly in Berlin before he emigrated to America in 1933. The two fell in love and after the death of Rosenstock-Huessy's wife in 1960, Freya moved to Vermont, where they spent the remaining thirteen years of his life together, and where Freya would continue to live until her death in 2010. Rosenstock-Huessy had been a legal historian, sociologist, and philosopher who had taught at several universities and written many books. There were visitors of all kinds at his home, and they were now joined by Freya's friends and family. As she had in Kreisau, Freya ran a large convivial household. After Rosenstock-Huessy's death, she was kept busy into her old age disseminating his work and keeping Helmuth's legacy alive.

As of 1945, Kreisau was behind the Iron Curtain. From early on, Freya had considered a return of the Moltkes as owners both impossible and undesirable. She and Helmuth had always assumed that ceding the estate to Poland was part of the price that had to be paid for the crimes of the National Socialists. But in the 1960s, Freya began to entertain the idea that Kreisau could once again play a role in fostering the relationship between Poland and Germany, and in 1989, with the help of Polish and East German citizens' initiatives, a "New Kreisau" to promote German–Polish and European understanding began to take shape. On November 12, 1989, three days after the Berlin Wall fell, a reconciliation mass, initiated by the heads of both governments, was held in Kreisau. Freya vigorously supported transforming Kreisau (now called Krzyżowa) into the Foundation for Mutual Understanding in Europe.

Freya faced the unexpected death of her son Konrad on May 19, 2005, in Vermont; she herself died at the age of ninety-eight on January 1, 2010. Memorial stones in Kreisau and at the cemetery in Norwich, Vermont, bear the names of Freya and Helmuth.

1. Helmuth James von Moltke, *Letters to Freya, 1939–1945*, edited and translated by Beate Ruhm von Oppen (New York: Knopf, 1990). 2. Helmuth James von Moltke, *Briefe an Freya, 1939–1945*, edited by Beate Ruhm von Oppen (Munich: C. H. Beck, 1988). 3. Helmuth James von Moltke, *Im Land der Gottlosen: Tagebuch und Briefe aus der Haft 1944/45*, edited by Günter Brakelmann (Munich: C. H. Beck, 2009).

FURTHER READING

Michael Balfour and Julian Frisby. *Helmuth James von Moltke: A Leader Against Hitler*. London: Macmillan, 1972.

Ian Kershaw. *The End: The Defiance and Destruction of Hitler's Germany, 1944–45*. London: Penguin, 2012.

Klemens von Klemperer. *German Resistance Against Hitler: The Search for Allies Abroad, 1938–1945*. Oxford: Clarendon Press, 1992.

Annedore Leber. *Conscience in Revolt: Sixty-Four Stories of Resistance in Germany, 1933–1945*. Boulder, CO: Westview Press, 1994.

Dorothee von Meding. *Courageous Hearts: Women and the Anti-Hitler Plot of 1944*. Providence, RI: Berghahn, 1997.

Freya von Moltke. *Memories of Kreisau and the German Resistance*. Lincoln, NE: University of Nebraska Press, 2003.

Helmuth James von Moltke. *Letters to Freya: 1939–1945*. Edited by Beate Ruhm von Oppen. New York: Knopf, 1990.

Ger van Roon. *German Resistance to Hitler: Count von Moltke and the Kreisau Circle*. London: Van Nostrand Reinhold, 1971.

Antje Starost and Hans Helmut Grotjahn. *Love in the Time of Resistance: Freya*. 87 mins. Antje Starost Filmproduktion, www.starostfilm.de

Dorothy Thompson. *Listen, Hans*. Boston, MA: Houghton Mifflin, 1942.

Krystyna Węgrzyńska-Kimbley and Anna Cichón. *Towards a New Europe: How the "Krzyzowa" Foundation for European Understanding Originated*. Wroclav: The Society of Krzyzowa's Friends, 2002.

ANNOTATED INDEX OF NAMES

The annotated index does not include the names of children (other than Helmuth James and Freya's), estate employees, and persons appearing solely in the footnotes. Following German style the "von" is ignored, so the von Moltkes are listed under "Moltke, von" etc.

THE KREISAU CIRCLE

Persons involved in the detailed discussions were organized in concentric circles on a need-to-know basis. Besides Helmuth James and Freya von Moltke, the following individuals mentioned in these letters were members:

Ernst von Brosig
Alfred Delp, S.J.
Horst von Einsiedel
Eugen Gerstenmaier
Hans Bernd von Haeften
Theodor Haubach
Paulus van Husen
Lothar König, S.J.
Julius Leber
Hans Lukaschek
Carlo Mierendorff
Hans Peters
Harald Poelchau

Adolf Reichwein
Augustin Rösch, S.J.
Theodor Steltzer
Carl Dietrich von Trotha
Margarete von Trotha
Adam von Trott zu Solz
Eduard Waetjen
Irene Gräfin Yorck von Wartenburg
Marion Gräfin Yorck von Wartenburg
Peter Graf Yorck von Wartenburg

Aunt Leno: *See* Hülsen, Leonore von

Bamler, Rudolf (1896–1972): Lieutenant general; chief of staff for the German army in Norway (1942–1943)

Bausch, Viktor T.: "Vikki" (1898–1983): Brought Theodor Haubach into his company, Felix Schoeller & Bausch, in 1938 after his release from a concentration camp

Beck, Ludwig (1880–1944): Resigned as the chief of the general staff of the army in 1938 because of Hitler's plans for war; head of the military, nationalist, conservative resistance along with Carl Friedrich Goerdeler; after the failed assassination attempt of July 20, 1944, forced to commit suicide that same night

Bergmann, Hugo: Public defender at the People's Court

Bertram, Adolf Johannes (1859–1945): Cardinal; archbishop of Breslau; chairman of the Fulda Bishops' Conference, which pursued a policy of appeasement and accommodation toward the National Socialist system

Bismarck-Schönhausen, Gottfried Graf von (1901–1949): Chairman of the regional council for Stettin in 1938 in Potsdam; in 1943 SS-Oberführer; incarcerated in a concentration camp on suspicion of participating in the assassination attempt of July 20, 1944; acquitted on October 23, 1944

Bonhoeffer, Dietrich (1906–1945): Theologian; confidant of Hans Oster and Hans von Dohnanyi (of the international bureau of the Abwehr in the Armed Forces High Command); with Helmuth

James in April 1942 on an official trip to Scandinavia; incarcerated April 1943; executed in Flossenbürg concentration camp on April 9, 1945

Bormann, Martin (1900–1945): Head of the Nazi Party chancellery; as of 1943 "secretary of the Führer"

Borsig, Ernst von (1906–1945): Owner of the Gross Behnitz estate at which several Kreisau Circle meetings about agricultural policies took place

Breslauer, Katharina: Trusted secretary in Helmuth James's law office

Buchholz, Peter (1888–1963): As of 1943 Catholic prison chaplain in Plötzensee; largely in agreement with his Protestant colleague Harald Poelchau, with whom he also tended to the inmates in Tegel prison

Bürkner, Leopold (1894–1975): Navy captain; chief of staff in the international bureau of the Abwehr in the Armed Forces High Command from September 1, 1939 to June 30, 1944; supervisor of Helmuth James

Canaris, Wilhelm (1887–1945): As of March 1938 head of the international bureau of the Abwehr of the Armed Forces High Command; dismissed in 1944; arrested after July 20, 1944; executed in Flossenbürg concentration camp on April 9, 1945

Carl Bernd: *See* Moltke, Carl Bernhard von

Casparchen: *See* Moltke, Helmuth Caspar von

Claus: Head guard at Tegel prison who was kind to Helmuth James

Curtis, Lionel (1872–1955): British official and author; co-editor of *The Round Table*, a foreign-policy quarterly; founder of the Royal Institute of International Affairs; member of Milner's Kindergarten in South Africa; friend of the Rose Innes family; mentor and correspondent of Helmuth James

Daddy: *See* Rose Innes, Sir James

Davy: *See* Moltke, Davida von

Deichmann, Ada: "Mütterchen Deichmann" (née von Schnitzler; 1886–1975): Freya's mother

Deichmann, Carl (1906–1985): Freya's brother; Helmuth James's contact with the Dutch resistance

co-wrote the first English history of Helmuth James and the Kreisau Circle after the war

Fritzi: *See* Schulenburg, Fritz-Dietlof Graf von der

Fugger von Glött, Joseph-Ernst Fürst (1895–1981): In the monarchist resistance in Bavaria; sentenced to three years in prison in trial with Helmuth James; his cell was on the same corridor as that of Helmuth James in Tegel prison

Gaevernitz, Gero (né Gero von Schulze-Gaevernitz): Emigrated to the United States; worked in Allen W. Dulles's intelligence operation; recipient of US Presidential Medal of Freedom

Gentz, Werner: Criminal lawyer; circuit judge during the Nazi years; in the Ministry of Justice until 1933; helped Poelchau get his position in Tegel prison

Gerstenmaier, Brigitte (née von Schmidt): Wife of Eugen Gerstenmaier

Gerstenmaier, Eugen (1906–1986): Colleague of Bishop Theophil Wurm in the Protestant foreign church office; member of the Kreisau Circle; arrested on July 20, 1944; incarcerated with Helmuth James and Alfred Delp in Tegel prison; sentenced by the People's Court to seven years in prison; president of the German Bundestag from 1954 to 1969

Gissel: Head guard in Tegel prison

Goerdeler, Carl Friedrich (1884–1945): Jurist and politician; mayor of Leipzig before 1933; head of the conservative military and civilian resistance; executed along with Alfred Delp and Johannes Popitz on February 2, 1945

Gollwitzer, Helmut (1908–1993): Theologian of the Protestant Confessing Church; pastor in Berlin-Dahlem; friend of Harald Poelchau

Görisch, Gerhard: Senior public prosecutor; lead prosecutor in trial of Carl Friedrich Goerdeler, Wilhelm Leuschner, Josef Wirmer, Ulrich von Hassell at the People's Court on September 8, 1944

Graf, Frau: Tended to Theodor Steltzer in the Lehrter Strasse Gestapo prison

Granny: *See* Rose Innes, Lady Jessie

Gross, Nikolaus (1898–1945): Miner; secretary in the trade association of Christian mine workers; editor of the newspaper *Westdeutsche Arbeiterzeitung*; knew Alfred Delp; contacts with Carl Friedrich Goerdeler and Jakob Kaiser; in the prison at Ravensbrück concentration camp with Helmuth James; executed on January 23, 1945, along with Helmuth James

Haeften, Hans Bernd von (1905–1944): Student of law; exchange student in England; worked in the Foreign Office beginning in 1933 without joining the Nazi Party; along with Adam von Trott zu Solz, a representative of the resistance in the Foreign Office; member of the Kreisau Circle; executed on August 15, 1944; his youngest daughter, Ulrike, married Freya and Helmuth James's son Konrad

Halder, Franz (1884–1972): As of 1938, colonel general of the general staff of the army; dismissed by Hitler in September 1942; arrested after the assassination attempt of July 20, 1944, and incarcerated in the Ravensbrück cell block with his wife, Gertrud; liberated by American troops in Südtirol

Hansen, Georg Alexander (1904–1944): Colonel; served under Wilhelm Canaris, head of the military Abwehr; arrested in connection with the July 20, 1944, assassination attempt and executed on September 8, 1944

Hapig, Marianne (1894–1973): Social worker; stayed in contact with Alfred Delp at Tegel prison

Hassell, Ulrich von (1881–1944): Senior diplomat in the diplomatic service; retired from his post by order of Joachim von Ribbentrop, foreign minister of the Reich; in 1938, was part of the resistance group around Carl Friedrich Goerdeler, Ludwig Beck, and Johannes Popitz; sentenced to death by the People's Court and executed on September 8, 1944

Haubach, Theodor (1896–1945): Writer; editor of a Social Democratic newspaper; leading member of Reichsbanner Schwarz-Rot-Gold, which campaigned for Weimar democracy; press officer with minister of the interior Carl Severing and with police commissioner Albert Grzezinski in Berlin; after 1934 spent two years in the Esterwegen concentration camp; member of the Kreisau Circle; executed on January 23, 1945, along with Helmuth James

Haus: Captain; loyal colleague of Helmuth James in the international law group in the international bureau of the Abwehr in the Armed Forces High Command

Henssel, Edith: Friend of the Moltke and Deichmann families; married to Karl Heinz Henssel

Henssel, Karl Heinz (born 1917): Bookseller and later publisher; friend of the Moltkes by way of his wife, Edith

Hercher, Wolfgang: Berlin attorney, public defender of Helmuth James

Hermes, Andreas (1878–1964): Reichstag delegate for the Catholic Center Party as of 1939; connections with Wilhelm Leuschner, Josef Wirmer, and Carl Friedrich Goerdeler; arrested after July 20, 1944, assassination attempt and sentenced to death January 1, 1945; with Helmuth James in the prison at the Ravensbrück concentration camp; execution delayed; survived the war

Hewel, Walther (1904–1945): Early Nazi supporter; participant in the 1923 Hitler putsch; fellow inmate of Hitler in Landsberg in 1920s; during the war, liaison between Foreign Affairs and the Reich chancellery; close to Hitler; committed suicide on May 2, 1945

Himmler, Heinrich (1900–1945): From 1929, Reichsführer-SS and top Nazi; attempted secret negotiations with the Western powers near the end of the war; in April 1945, Hitler dismissed him from all his positions; in May 1945 committed suicide while in British custody

Huber, Kurt (1893–1943): Musicologist and psychologist; member of the Weisse Rose resistance group; executed on July 13, 1943

Hübner, Ida: "Sister Ida": District nurse; in Kreisau from 1907 until the end of the war in 1945; in charge of health care and nursery school; very close relationship with the Moltkes

Hülsen, Leonore von: "Aunt Leno" (1875–1961): The wife of Karl von Hülsen (1859–1903); sister of Helmuth James's father; her son, Hans Carl von Hülsen, and his wife, Editha, died when a plane crashed into their house in November 1943, after which their children (Ignes, Editha, Renate, Hans-Viggo, and Matthias) stayed with their grandmother in the Kreisau Schloss

Huppenkothen, Walter (1907–1979): SS-Standartenführer; leader of Task Force I in Poland; as of July 1941 section commander in the Gestapo; member of the Special Commission Regarding July 20; interrogated Helmuth James in Drögen

Husen, Paulus van (1891–1971): Centrist politician; district administrator in Silesia; in contact with Hans Lukaschek; at the Supreme Administrative Court in Berlin starting in 1934, then cavalry captain with the Armed Forces High Command; member of the Kreisau Circle; arrested in August 1944; sentenced by the People's Court to three years imprisonment in April 1945; liberated on April 25, 1945, when the Soviet troops invaded

Jessen, Jens Peter (1895–1944): Political scientist and economist; participated in the July 20, 1944, assassination plot; executed on November 30, 1944, in Plötzensee

Jowo: *See* Moltke, Joachim Wolfgang von

Kaltenbrunner, Ernst (1903–1946): SS-Obergruppenführer; general in the police and the Waffen-SS; as of January 1943 head of the Reich Main Security Office and the Gestapo

Keitel, Wilhelm (1882–1946): Chief of the Armed Forces High Command; promoted to field marshal in 1940; sentenced by Allies to death at Nuremberg and executed

Kempinski, Hans: Jewish owner of Hotel Kempinski in Berlin; advised by Helmuth James in questions of emigration

Kiep, Otto Carl (1886–1944): In the diplomatic service; from 1939 to 1944 liaison between the Foreign Office and the international bureau of the Abwehr in the Armed Forces High Command; arrested as a member of the Solf Circle in January 1944; with Helmuth James in the Ravensbrück concentration camp; executed on August 26, 1944

Kleinert, Frau: Lived in the neighboring village of Gräditz; her brother was a priest

Kleist, Ewald-Heinrich von (1922–2013): Son of Ewald von Kleist-Schmenzin (1890–1945); participant in the assassination plot of

July 20, 1944; with Helmuth James in the Ravensbrück concentration camp; released from Tegel prison in December 1944

König, Lothar (1906–1946): Jesuit from Munich; member of the Kreisau Circle; went into hiding after July 20, 1944

Krebs: Superintendent of the Schweidnitz church district; in charge of the Gräditz district, to which Kreisau belonged

Kurth: Director of Building I in Tegel prison

Langbehn, Carl Julius (1901–1944): Attorney in Berlin; conveyed conversations between Johannes Popitz and Heinrich Himmler in 1943; with Helmuth James in Ravensbrück; executed on October 12, 1944

Lange, Herbert (1909–1945): SS-Sturmbannführer and Gestapo detective, at the beginning in 1942; head of the Special Commission Regarding July 20, which was relocated to Drögen

Lautz, Ernst (1887–1979): As of 1939 chief Reich prosecutor at the People's Court for the trial of Helmuth James

Leber, Julius (1891–1944): Social Democratic member of the Reichstag beginning in 1924; imprisoned from 1933 to 1937, then worked as a coal merchant in Berlin; member of the Kreisau Circle; arrested after meetings with communists; interrogated along with Theodor Haubach and Helmuth James in Drögen; sentenced and executed on October 20, 1944

Leuschner, Wilhelm (1890–1944): Trade unionist and Social Democrat; initially member of the Kreisau Circle; contact with the Goerdeler–Beck Circle; sentenced and executed on September 8, 1944

Lilje, Hanns (1899–1977): As of 1927 secretary-general of the German Student Christian Movement in Berlin; contact with resistance members who attended his services, including Helmuth James; imprisoned and tried after July 20, 1944

Lukaschek, Frau: Wife of Hans Lukaschek

Lukaschek, Hans (1885–1960): Member of the Catholic Center Party; district administrator and governor in Silesia; attorney in Breslau as of 1933; member of the Kreisau Circle; acquitted by the People's Court; released from Gestapo custody on April 22, 1945

Maack: Attorney who worked for the Moltkes in Schweidnitz

Maass, Hermann (1897–1944): Social Democrat; 1924 general manager of the Reich Committee of German Youth Associations but was dismissed in 1933; co-worker and business partner of Wilhelm Leuschner; in the union resistance; initially a member of the Kreisau Circle; executed on October 20, 1944

Mami: *See* Moltke, Dorothy Gräfin von

Margrit: *See* Trotha, Margarete von

Maschke, Walter (1891–1980): Unionist and Social Democrat with connections to Wilhelm Leuschner and Hermann Maass; sentenced to two years in prison on January 19, 1945

Mierendorff, Carlo (1897–1943): Journalist and Social Democratic Party politician; from 1933 to 1938 in various concentration camps; member of the Kreisau Circle; died during an air strike on Leipzig on December 4, 1943

Milner, Alfred Viscount (1854–1925): British politician; high commissioner for Southern Africa; war cabinet member in World War I, then colonial secretary; patron of the talented young politicians whom Helmuth James met in England: Lionel Curtis, Philipp Kerr (later Lord Lothian) et al., who gathered to produce the periodical *The Round Table*

Mirbach, Dietrich von: "Dieter" (1907–1977): Relative of Helmuth James, worked with Baron Gustav Adolf Steengracht von Moyland in the Foreign Office

Mittelstädt: Tegel prison guard who worked in the sick bay; critical of the Nazis

Moltke, Anne Marie Gräfin von: "Pension Annie" (née Altenberg, 1902–1952): Second wife of Helmuth James's father; asserted her right to Kreisau and an inheritance

Moltke, Carl Bernhard von: "Carl Bernd" (1913–1941): Brother of Helmuth James; killed in action on December 30, 1941, in Greece

Moltke, Carl Viggo von (1897–1990): Uncle of Helmuth James; district court president; important source of aid in legal matters and in formulating the petition for clemency; contacts with Roland Freisler

Moltke, Davida von: "Davy" (née Gräfin Yorck von Wartenburg,

1900–1989): Sister of Peter Graf Yorck von Wartenburg and Irene Gräfin Yorck von Wartenburg; married to Ambassador Hans-Adolf von Moltke

Moltke, Dorothy Gräfin von: "Mami" (née Rose Innes, 1884–1935): Wife of Helmuth Graf von Moltke and mother of Helmuth James

Moltke, Erika von: Distant relative who had contact with Heinrich Himmler

Moltke, Hans-Adolf von (1884–1943): Relative of Helmuth James; joined foreign service in 1913; senior diplomat and German ambassador in Poland (1931–1939) and in Spain (1943); received a state funeral in Breslau in 1943 following his sudden death

Moltke, Helmuth Graf von: "Papi" (1876–1939): Father of Helmuth James

Moltke, Helmuth Caspar von: "Casparchen" (b. 1937): Eldest son of Freya and Helmuth James

Moltke, Joachim Peter von: "Uncle Peter" (1880–1963): Uncle of Helmuth James

Moltke, Joachim Wolfgang von: "Jowo" (1909–2002): Brother of Helmuth James

Moltke, Johannes Helmuth von (1916–2006): Distant relative; served with distinction

Moltke, Konrad von (1941–2005): Youngest son of Freya and Helmuth James

Moltke, Wilhelm von (1881–1949): Son of Helmuth von Moltke, chief of the German general staff (1848–1916)

Moltke, Wilhelm Viggo von: "Willo" (1911–1987): Brother of Helmuth James; in the United States during World War II; served in US Army

Müller, Heinrich (1900–?): As of 1939, Gestapo chief with the rank of general; missing since 1945; the boss of Adolf Eichmann; a participant in the Wannsee Conference of January 1942 that ordered the Holocaust

Muto: See Yorck von Wartenburg, Irene Gräfin

Mütterchen: See Deichmann, Ada

Nan: See van Heerden, Anna Petronella

Neuhaus, Karl: SS-Sturmbannführer at the Gestapo branch on Meinekestrasse; head of the department of churches in the Gestapo; in charge of interrogating the members of the Kreisau Circle

Oldenbourg, Ulla (née Schultz, 1876–1953): Christian Scientist and friend of Helmuth James's parents

Oster, Hans (1887–1945): In 1938 participated in preparing a military putsch; chief of staff in the international bureau of the Abwehr in the Armed Forces High Command; arrested after July 20, 1944, and executed on April 9, 1945, at the Flossenbürg concentration camp

Oxé, Werner: Colonel; immediate superior of Helmuth James in the international law group of the Abwehr

Papi: *See* Moltke, Helmuth Graf von

Pension Annie: *See* Moltke, Anne Marie Gräfin von

Peters, Hans (1896–1966): Catholic administrative lawyer; officer in an air force command during World War II; member of the Kreisau Circle; drafted documents on self-governance, higher education, church and state, and other issues

Pfuel, Curt-Christoph von: Colleague of Helmuth James in the working group on international law at the international bureau of the Abwehr of the Armed Forces High Command

Pick, Frau: Housekeeper for Helmuth James, first in Berlin, later in the Berghaus

Pieper: Attorney in the Reich Ministry of Justice

Pippert, Hans: Clerk in the Ministry of Justice; after 1945 senior public prosecutor in Dortmund

Planck, Erwin (1893–1945): Son of Max Planck; opponent of Nazis; worked with Goerdeler group; arrested after July 20, 1944, and sentenced to death; executed on January 23, 1945, along with Helmuth James

Poelchau, Dorothee (1902–1977): Wife of Harald Poelchau

Poelchau, Harald (1903–1972): From 1933 to 1945 prison chaplain in Tegel; member of the Kreisau Circle and active resistance figure; hid Jewish and other endangered persons; enabled Helmuth James and Freya to conduct their secret correspondence

Popitz, Johannes (1884–1945): Administrative lawyer, state secretary, and Reich finance minister; contacts with the civilian and military resistance movements; executed on February 2, 1945

Power, Eileen Edna Le Poer (1889–1940) Economic historian; professor at the London School of Economics; specialist in medieval economic history

Pressel, Wilhelm (1895–1986): Member of the High Consistory in Stuttgart; liaison between Bishop Theophil Wurm, Eugen Gerstenmaier, and Helmuth James

Preysing, Konrad Graf von (1880–1950): As of 1935, Catholic bishop of Berlin; critic of the National Socialist system and the stance of the Catholic bishops' conference under the leadership of Adolf Cardinal Bertram; important Catholic interlocutor of Helmuth James

Prost: District court director in the Reich Ministry of Justice; clerk for Dr. Franke; right-hand man of the Reich minister of justice

Rehrl, Franz (1890–1947): Politician in Austria's Christian Social Party; governor of Salzburg until 1938; contact with Helmuth James by way of Augustin Rösch; was envisioned as a political delegate for the Salzburg military district; incarcerated in the Lehrter Strasse Gestapo prison until the end of the war

Reichwein, Adolf (1898–1944): Professor of history and civics in Halle/Saale; dismissed in 1933; teacher at a rural school in Tiefensee, outside of Berlin; educator at the Berlin Museum for German Ethnology; Social Democratic member of the Kreisau Circle; arrested after meeting with the communists Anton Saefkow and Bernhard Bästlein in June 1944; executed on October 20, 1944, along with Julius Leber and Hermann Maass

Reichwein, Rosemarie: "Romai" (née Pallat, 1904–2002): Married Adolf Reichwein in 1933; mother of Renate, Roland, Katrin, and Sabine Reichwein; living in Kreisau from 1943

Reisert, Franz (1889–1965): Attorney in Augsburg; contact with the circle around Franz Sperr and with Helmuth James by way of Augustin Rösch and Alfred Delp; sentenced to five years in prison

Reisert, Frau: Wife of Franz Reisert; in contact with Freya in Berlin

Scholl, Hans (1918–1943): Active member of the Weisse Rose student resistance movement in Munich

Scholl, Sophie (1921–1943): Active member of the Weisse Rose student resistance movement in Munich

Scholz-Babisch, Friedrich (1890–1944): Cavalry captain; Silesian farmer; in the circle of Claus Schenk Graf von Stauffenberg; executed on October 13, 1944

Schulenburg, Fritz-Dietlof Graf von der: "Fritzi" (1902–1944): At first a confirmed National Socialist, then outspoken opponent of Hitler; contacts with the military and civil resistance movement; interlocutor of Helmuth James; arrested on July 20, 1944, in the Bendlerblock building complex and executed on August 10, 1944

Schulze, Kurt: District court director; served as the deputy of the chief Reich prosecutor at the trial of Helmuth James

Schwarzwald, Eugenie (née Nussbaum, 1872–1940): Austrian educator and social reformer; met Freya and Helmuth James in 1929 at Seeblick, her summer villa on the Austrian Grundlsee

Schwerin von Schwanenfeld, Ulrich Wilhelm Graf (1902–1944): Estate owner; in close contact with Peter Graf Yorck von Wartenburg and the international bureau of the Abwehr in the Armed Forces High Command; arrested on July 20, 1944, in the Bendlerblock; briefly incarcerated in the Ravensbrück cell block; executed on August 21, 1944

Sister Ida: *See* Hübner, Ida

Solf, Johanna (1887–1954): Wife of Wilhelm Solf, state secretary in the foreign office who died in 1936; invited women and men critical of the system to the Solf Circle, a "tea party" for discussions that were leaked to the Gestapo; arrested but survived

Sperr, Franz (1878–1945): Jurist; until 1934 Bavarian envoy to the Reich; enabled through the Munich Jesuits to stay in contact with Helmuth James; sentenced to death on January 10, 1945; executed on January 23, 1945, along with Helmuth James

Stauffenberg, Claus Schenk Graf von (1907–1944): Main figure in the assassination-minded military resistance movement along with

of Carl Dietrich von Trotha; aunt of Helmuth James; lived in Kreisau Schloss

Trott zu Solz, Adam von (1909–1944): Rhodes scholar at Oxford University; contacts with leading British politicians; as of 1939 close contact with Helmuth James and active member of the Kreisau Circle; in June 1940 began working in the Foreign Office; numerous trips abroad in the interest of resistance work; arrested on July 25, 1944; executed on August 26, 1944

Trott zu Solz, Clarita von (née Tiefenbacher, 1917–2013): Wife of Adam von Trott zu Solz; after July 20, 1944, briefly in Moabit prison with other wives

Truchsess, Dietrich Baron von: "Dietz" (1900–1980): Incarcerated in Tegel prison

Truchsess, Hedwig von: Wife of Dietrich Baron von Truchsess

Uncle Peter: *See* Moltke, Joachim Peter von

van Heerden, Anna Petronella: "Nan" (1887–1975): First female Afrikaner to become a physician in South Africa; friend of the Rose Innes and Moltke families

Waetjen, Eduard: "Eddy" (1907–1994): Attorney and colleague of Helmuth James; during the war in the Abwehr; member of the Kreisau Circle; mostly in Switzerland; contacts with the American secret service; interlocutor and adept informant for Helmuth James

Wedemeyer, Maria von (1924–1977): Fiancée of Dietrich Bonhoeffer

Weismann, Arno: Public defender at the People's Court

Wendland, Asta Maria (née von Moltke, 1915–1993): Sister of Helmuth James; married to Wend Wendland, later to Karl Heinz Henssel; present at Kreisau meetings of the Kreisau Circle

Wendland, Wend (1912–1979): Husband of Helmuth James's sister, Asta

Wentzel-Teutschenthal, Carl (1875–1944): Farmer; in contact with Carl Friedrich Goerdeler; executed on December 20, 1944

Wickenberg, Dr.: Medical health officer in the Tegel and Lehrter Strasse prisons

Wienken, Heinrich (1883–1961): Auxiliary bishop; head of the commissioner's office of the Fulda Bishops' Conference in Berlin

Wild, Frau: "Frau Pastor": Wife of Hermann Wild, the deceased pastor in Gräditz

Willo: *See* Moltke, Wilhelm Viggo von

Wirmer, Josef (1901–1944): Attorney in Berlin; in contact with the unionists Max Habermann, Jakob Kaiser, Wilhelm Leuschner, and Carl Friedrich Goerdeler; incarcerated in August 1944 in the Ravensbrück cell block; executed on September 8, 1944

Wurm, Theophil (1868–1953): Regional bishop of Württemberg; in close contact with the members of the Kreisau Circle

Yorck von Wartenburg, Irene Gräfin: "Muto" (1913–1950): Sister of Peter Graf Yorck von Wartenburg; physician; participant in all three Kreisau gatherings of the Kreisau Circle

Yorck von Wartenburg, Marion Gräfin (née Winter, 1904–2007): Doctorate in law; wife of Peter Graf Yorck von Wartenburg; hostess to many meetings of the Kreisau Circle and later to meetings with Claus Graf von Stauffenberg; jailed briefly after July 20, 1944

Yorck von Wartenburg, Peter Graf (1904–1944): Public-service lawyer; as of January 1940 correspondence between him and Helmuth James grew into the Kreisau Circle; related to Claus Graf von Stauffenberg, whom he joined in assassination attempt; arrested on July 20, 1944, on Bendlerstrasse; executed on August 8, 1944

Zeumer, Adolf: Overseer of the estate in Kreisau since 1929; in constant contact with Helmuth James by way of Freya and through correspondence

IMAGE CREDITS

THE FOLLOWING images appear here by permission of their respective rights holders. Best efforts have been made to ascertain the copyright of the drawing of Helmuth James by M. Schneefuß and the aerial view of the New Kreisau / Krzyzowa. All other images are from the collection of the von Moltke family.

Page 13: Tegel Prison: View from a cell in 1944 (bpk Bildagentur / Art Resource, NY)

Page 52: Harald and Dorothee Poelchau, 1927 (Harald Poelchau)

Page 99: Letter from Helmuth to Freya, November 10, 1944 (DLA Marbach)

Page 103: Letter from Freya to Helmuth, November 11, 1944 (DLA Marbach)

Pages 158–159: Helmuth's sketches of his prison cell (DLA Marbach)

Page 165: Tegel Prison: Cell Block C in 1969 (bpk Bildagentur /Erika Groth-Schmachtenberger / Art Resource, NY)

Page 225: Helmuth's sketch of his Christmas table (DLA Marbach)

Page 240: Drawing of Helmuth James by M. Schneefuß, 1930 (© unknown)

Page 244: Harald Poelchau, 1949 (ullstein bild / dpa)

Pages 245–247: Helmuth at the People's Court and Helmuth conferring with his attorney (bpk Bildagentur / Heinrich Hoffmann / Art Resource, NY)

Page 250: Aerial view of the New Kreisau / Krzyzowa (© unknown) and the Berghaus today in the New Kreisau / Krzyzowa (Krzyzowa Foundationi)

Page 310: The courtyard of Tegel prison in 1969 (bpk Bildagentur /Erika Groth-Schmachtenberger / Art Resource, NY)

CONTRIBUTORS

SHELLEY FRISCH, who holds a PhD in German literature from Princeton University, taught at Columbia University and Haverford College, before turning to translation full-time. Her translations from the German, which include biographies of Friedrich Nietzsche, Albert Einstein, Leonardo da Vinci, Marlene Dietrich, Leni Riefenstahl, and Franz Kafka, have been awarded numerous translation prizes. She lives in Princeton, New Jersey.

HELMUTH CASPAR VON MOLTKE is the oldest son of Freya and Helmuth James von Moltke. He grew up in South Africa after 1945, read law at Oxford University, and was called to the bar in England. Working for a German industrial company, he had a thirty-year career in five countries, terminating in the United States. Since retiring he has pursued the success of the Kreisau Foundation for Mutual Understanding in Europe, heading not-for-profit organizations in Germany and the United States. He lives in Vermont and Montreal.

DOROTHEA VON MOLTKE, who received her BA from Yale University and PhD from Columbia University, is a co-owner of Labyrinth Books, in Princeton, New Jersey, for which she also organizes and hosts a popular speakers series. She is the granddaughter of Freya and Helmuth von Moltke.

JOHANNES VON MOLTKE is Professor of German Studies and Film, Television, and Media at the University of Michigan, and the president of the German Studies Association. He has published widely in English and German on German film, theory, and cultural history. He is the grandson of Freya and Helmuth von Moltke.

RACHEL SEIFFERT has published four novels—*A Boy in Winter*, *The Dark Room*, *Afterwards*, and *The Walk Home*—and a collection of short stories, *Field Study*. Her novels have been short-listed for the Booker Prize and long-listed three times for the Women's Prize for Fiction. In 2011, she received the E. M. Forster Award from the American Academy of Arts and Letters and, in 2018, the Association of Jewish Libraries Honor Book Award.